The Origins of Mexican Catholicism

History, Languages, and Cultures of the
Spanish and Portuguese Worlds

*This interdisciplinary series promotes scholarship
in studies on Iberian cultures and contacts from the premodern
and early modern periods.*

SERIES EDITOR

Sabine MacCormack, Theodore M. Hesburgh Professor of Arts and Letters,
Departments of Classics and History, University of Notre Dame

SERIES BOARD

J. N. Hillgarth, emeritus, Pontifical Institute of Mediaeval Studies
Peggy K. Liss, Independent Scholar
David Nirenberg, Johns Hopkins University
Adeline Rucquoi, École des Hautes Études en Sciences Sociales

TITLES IN THE SERIES

The ORIGINS of

MEXICAN CATHOLICISM

———

Nahua Rituals and Christian Sacraments
in Sixteenth-Century Mexico

Osvaldo F. Pardo

THE UNIVERSITY OF MICHIGAN PRESS
Ann Arbor

First paperback edition 2006
Copyright © by the University of Michigan 2004
All rights reserved
Published in the United States of America by
The University of Michigan Press
Manufactured in the United States of America
⊛ Printed on acid-free paper

2009   2008   2007   2006   5   4   3   2

A CIP catalog record for this book is available from the British Library.

Library of Congress Cataloging-in-Publication Data

Pardo, Osvaldo F., 1963–
    The origins of Mexican Catholicism : Nahua rituals and Christian
sacraments in sixteenth-century Mexico / Osvaldo F. Pardo.
        p.   cm. — (History, languages, and cultures of the Spanish and
Portuguese worlds)
    Includes bibliographical references and index.
    ISBN 0-472-11361-5 (hardcover : alk. paper)
    1. Nahuas—Religion.   2. Nahuas—Rites and ceremonies.
3. Nahuas—Missions.   4. Catholic Church—Mexico—History—16th
century.   I. Title.   II. Series.
F1221.N3P37   2004
282'72'08997452—dc22   2004006185

ISBN 0-472-03184-8 (pbk. : alk. paper)
ISBN 978-0-472-03178-3 (pbk. : alk. paper)

To Osvaldo Pardo,
in memoriam

Acknowledgments

This book owes a great deal to Professor Rolena Adorno, who guided me through its earliest versions and has proved a source of constant support throughout the years. From Professor Sabina MacCormack I have tried to learn how to read and pose questions as a historian. No one should ever be subjected to read as many versions of a manuscript as she has done with mine. Sabina's good humor, demanding intellectual discipline, and unfailing generosity helped bring this project to its overdue conclusion. Frances Karttunen introduced me to the Nahuatl language in the summer of 1989 in Austin, Texas; later I benefitted from her comments and suggestions on chapter 4. Norman Fiering, director of the John Carter Brown Library, made me feel at home during my stay in Providence in the summer of 1994 as a Paul W. McQuillen Fellow. David Weisberg, with characteristic enthusiasm, always made himself available to read and discuss several drafts. Ruth Hill and my colleagues Benjamin Liu and Jacqueline Loss made invaluable editorial suggestions. David Harms translated chapters 2, 3, and 4, forgave my sloppiness, and patiently put up with last minute additions and changes. Jesús Bustamante García and Mónica Quijada welcomed me in Spain and made for vibrant conversation. The completion of the manuscript was possible thanks to a grant from the Research Foundation of the University of Connecticut and the support of Professor David Herzberger, who in fall 2001 released me from my teaching obligations.

Special thanks to James Amelang, Walden Browne, Sergio Chejfec, Leo Cotlar, Jay Cummings and the Cummings clan, Parizad Dejbord, Melissa D'Inverno, Margaret Higonnet, Betina Kaplan, Natalie Marshall, Alejandro Mejías López, Graciela Montaldo, Michael Moore, Gabriela Nouzeilles, Victoria Pineda, Marcelo Prizmic-Kuzmica, Laurietz Seda, and Angel Rivera.

A shorter version of chapter 4 appeared in *Latin American Colonial Review* 5, no. 1 (June 1996).

Contents

Figures

xii | *Figures*

The Origins of Mexican Catholicism

Introduction

The origins of Mexican Catholicism are indelibly linked to the Spanish military victory over the Mexicas and their allies that brought about the fall of Tenochtitlan in 1521. The association of warfare with the expansion of Christianity was, needless to say, not new. Since its beginnings, Christianity had resorted to war imagery to convey a message that addressed both the individual's inner battle with temptation and the church's struggle against its enemies. The portals of Romanesque cathedrals offered images of young female warriors representing Faith in battle against Idolatry. The literary source for this allegorical combat was the *Psychomachia*, a Latin poem composed in the fourth century by the Spanish-born Christian poet Prudentius. The poet merited the scholarly attention of the Spanish humanist Antonio de Nebrija, who in 1512 published an annotated edition of his works in an effort to rescue his fellow countryman from oblivion.[1] Gothic art abandoned the motif of battle scenes, preferring instead to portray the everlasting triumph of Faith in the figure of a young woman sitting calmly above the vanquished vices.[2]

The military conquest of Mexico was quickly translated as the triumph of Catholicism over the Mexican gods or, in more sophisticated fashion, over a fundamentally misguided brand of religion. The destruction of the Mexican sacred images recorded by Cortés lent some credibility to this view. As a shorthand for the Christianization of the Mexican Indians that the Spanish Crown envisioned, the simile proved appealing. In the seventeenth century the Augustinian chronicler Juan de Grijalva spoke of a spiritual conquest to characterize the religious task that accompanied the military subjugation of the Mexican population and that should ideally supersede it.

As the fall of Tenochtitlan receded in time, Spanish friars grew somehow more ambivalent about associating their own enterprise with the affairs of war past and present. Religious writers reacted differently when they came to assess the impact of the military actions by Cortés and his men on the directions taken by the conversion process. In contrast, those Spanish soldiers who participated in the conquest of Mexico and benefitted from it were far less hesitant in perceiving their military victory in religious terms. Regarding the friars working in Mexico, one could say that very soon they found themselves caught between the ideals expressed in the traditional images of Christianity at war with its enemies and the far more concrete and problematic legacy of Spanish domination.

The close identification of Cortés's military actions with the triumph of Catholicism expressed in a dramatic and economic way the religious goal that the Spanish Crown would see achieved only over a very long period of time and with a relative shortage of the kind of heroic deeds and defining moments that are the stock of military narratives.

This book focuses on the role played by ritual in that slow process of bringing Christianity to the Nahuas of Central Mexico in the sixteenth century. During this crucial period that witnessed the radical transformation of Nahua religion, Spanish missionaries reflected on the nature of Christian and Nahua rituals and, in doing so, found themselves wrestling with old questions on religion, the individual, and society in an entirely new setting. This is a study of how ritual—both as an object of inquiry for the missionaries and as a cross-cultural process—was instrumental in the shaping of Mexican Catholicism in colonial times.

The Mendicant friars who arrived in Mexico between 1524 and 1533 were the product of the reformation of Spanish monasteries undertaken by Cardinal Francisco Ximénez de Cisneros following the designs of the Catholic monarchs.[3] In 1524 a group of twelve Franciscans landed in Veracruz led by Fr. Martín de Valencia. Martín de Valencia had been a disciple of Fr. Juan de Guadalupe, a Franciscan friar who had succeeded in establishing monasteries that adhered to the strictest observance of St. Francis's rule.[4] In 1518 Martín de Valencia was elected as the first provincial of the reformed Franciscan province of San Gabriel in Extremadura, from where he would soon recruit friars for the Mexican enterprise. According to Fr. Toribio de Benavente–a member of the original group better known to the Nahuas as Motolinía—Martín de Valencia had received in a vision the revelation of his mission: to help bring infidels to Christianity in preparation for the last age of the world.[5] For Motolinía, the Mexican mission gave meaning and reality to that revelation. Apocalyptic expectations of this nature, which Fr. Martín de Valencia shared with a small number of Franciscans—including Motolinía–had been a distinctive feature of a particular strand of Franciscan thought and spirituality that had found its inspiration in the exegetical works of the twelfth-century monk Joachim of Fiore and whose adherents were known as Spirituals.[6] On Mexican soil, such expectations, duly modified to account for the impact of Spanish secular institutions on the Indian population, decimated by devastating epidemics, would leave their mark on Franciscan interpretations of historical developments in the colonies.[7]

Three years later, the first contingent of Dominican friars arrived from Española led by Fr. Tomás Ortíz. In its beginnings the Dominican mission in New Spain was faced with the death of several members, a misfortune that led to an initial period of inactivity regarding any direct involvement with the conversion of the Indians. Upon the early departure of Fr. Tomás Ortíz to Spain, the Dominican mission fell into the hands of Fr. Domingo de Betanzos, an Observant friar from the monastery of San Esteban in Salamanca. A controversial figure both within and without the order for his strict adherence to observance and an ambivalent attitude toward the Indians, Betanzos would, however, define the order's profile in New Spain for years to come.[8] A small number of Augustinians arrived in Veracruz in 1533; most of them had been recruited in Salamanca, and their vicar was Francisco de la Cruz.[9] With few exceptions, the writers whose works I have examined for this study belonged to these three religious orders.

The arrival of the Dominican and Augustinian friars soon altered the face of the evangelization in New Spain, which hitherto had been almost exclusively in Franciscan hands. Rifts among religious orders did not take long to occur, especially between Franciscans and Dominicans, religious groups that shared a long and sometimes colorful history of rivalry. The grounds for disagreement were numerous and diverse. Soon, territory and jurisdiction over the native population for evangelization and pastoral care became a point of contention that escalated as the number of friars from each order kept growing.[10] On few but important occasions their conflicts reflected the confrontations of political factions fighting for power that was taking place in the secular world, leading the orders to take an active stand in civil affairs. One such occasion was the crisis triggered by the actions of the first *audien-*

cia (court and governing body under the jurisdiction of the viceroy) presided over by Nuño de Guzmán and the rival political faction led by Hernán Cortés. During this conflict, which ended with the arrest of Nuño de Guzmán in January 1537, the Franciscans stood in strong opposition to the members of the first audiencia.[11] At the core of this much-publicized affair that polarized the small Spanish population of Mexico lay a deep fracture between those who, like the Franciscans, aligned themselves with Cortés and those, including the Dominicans, against him. This split of opinions around the figure of the Spanish captain lasted well beyond the particular circumstances that found Cortés and Guzmán in opposing camps. Franciscan and Dominican chronicles succeeded in keeping it alive; in them the figure of Cortés became a powerful if equivocal symbol of the Spanish presence in Mexican lands: as either an inspired crusader with a sacred mission or an agent of destruction.

Aside from the individual traits that historically distinguished each order from the other, we can say that a hope for a change in the practice and spirit of Christianity was very much in these friars' minds. And change, if not precisely in the terms they had originally envisioned it, was exactly what the missionaries would bring about in the new territories. Together with their expectations of transforming and breaking away from what they deemed as the undesirable turn that Christianity had taken in Europe, both inside and outside the church, these friars also brought with them a readiness to challenge accepted models of authority, secular as well as ecclesiastical. Their own desire for reforming Christianity went hand in hand with an acute if diverse sense of experiencing and conceptualizing what was new in the Mexican environment. The debates among friars revolved around how to deal with the novelty of converting millions of Indians whose main cultural beliefs and practices would take time to identify and apprehend. This preoccupation itself was far from new, having accompanied the expansion of Christianity in Western Europe. Change, the ability to deal with unexpected situations, as well as a taste for the local had been part and parcel of church history. Some friars found in the novelty of the unknown a reminder of the old, as when they thought of themselves reliving the times of the primitive church; for others, an extreme enthusiasm for the new entailed possibly dangerous departures from church teaching. Whatever the terms in which the Mexican missionaries assimilated the new, the awareness that Christian tradition offered a wide repertoire from which to select, choose, and borrow was as much an essential part of their mental make up as the so-called "trade-store model" that has been invoked to describe it.[12] The friars' firm beliefs in an institutional claim to universality and the portability of Christian teachings do not suffice to explain the complexity of missionary thinking as it is revealed to us in religious literature and documents. Such beliefs may define a general attitude but do not tell us much about specific ways of thinking and decision making. Mexican religious sources show missionaries, more as agents than mentalities, who responded according to their own beliefs or the group's to the everyday challenges posed by an alien culture by seeking solutions in the less than uniform tradition available to them.

A fair amount has been written about the influence of Erasmus—whether direct or filtered through the lenses of Spanish authors sympathetic to his call for a return to the values of the primitive church—on the intellectual makeup of religious men in Mexico, and especially on its first archbishop, Fr. Juan de Zumárraga. Years ago John Elliott remarked that, with very few exceptions, sixteenth-century European writers largely ignored the importance that European contact with the Amerindians might have on their own moral and political reflections.[13] Elliott's assertion can safely be applied to Erasmus. Regarding the new territories and their inhabitants, the humanist found little to put into writing. The impact that the discovery of the new continent had on European geographical knowledge of the times had little bearing on Erasmus's philological endeavors. This can be gathered from Erasmus's edition—the first to appear in the Greek language—of Ptolemy's *Geography* in 1533. Prefaced by a letter in which references to America are absent, the edition did not include maps.[14] Erasmus's correspondence with contemporary cartographers proves, on the other hand, that he was familiar with current developments in mapmaking. As to the conversion of the Amerindians taking place overseas, he was equally circumspect. This is not entirely surprising given Erasmus's abhorrence of any form of coercion associated with religious endeavors and the intensely private character of Christian spirituality he championed. In terms of practical pointers on how to go about converting peoples to Christianity and setting up missions, though, Erasmus had not much to offer, except to express his conviction, shared in other religious circles, that it should be achieved by peaceful means, even in the case of the Turks. By way of illustration I point to the distance that separates Erasmus's comments on the parable of the banquet in Luke 14 from Jeróni-mo de Mendieta's interpretation decades later. Erasmus's distaste for prophecies and apocalyptic fervor is well-known; this may explain why in his *Paraphrasis on Luke* he did not pause to ponder in any detail the meaning of the household lord's call to compel attendance to his ban-quet (Luke 14:23).[15] On the other hand, the Franciscan chronicler Mendieta, following a long tradition of apocalyptic readings of the pas-sage, found in it a source of authority to validate Spain's mission to bring about the conversion of the Indians by instilling in them fear and respect for their ministers.[16]

Closely related to this, there stands the often repeated assertion that the religious orders shared Erasmus's impulse to restore the ideals of the primitive church through the conversion of the Mexican Indians. While such characterization seems at first accurate, it is only so in a rather gen-eral sense because it obscures the fact that there did not exist a consen-sus among the friars as to what precisely those ideals consisted of. At their most fanciful, the religious chroniclers did not hesitate to affirm that early on the spirit of the primitive church had found new roots in Mexico. They reported on massive conversions achieved in record time, as well as on the vigorous religious devotion that followed them. The Franciscans also stressed how quickly the Indians followed their exam-ple by embracing wholeheartedly a life of poverty and humility. In con-trast, the archbishop Zumárraga referred to the primitive church to bet-ter convey the idea of the kind of harmony existing between friars and the religious authorities of Mexico—something far from the truth for Mexico and the early church.[17] A closer reading of the sources shows that by "primitive church" different writers meant different things; still, the pervasive invocation of the primitive church as a model by writers from across religious orders indicates that such a contested notion was assumed to have, at least at a superficial, rhetorical level, a particular and immediate persuasive force capable of eliciting positive associations with lofty and legitimate spiritual purposes. The church at the time of the apostles (whom the friars strove to imitate) became both a model along whose lines the evangelization of the Mexican Indians was to pro-ceed and a source of authority for the evangelization program. Regard-ing views on the primitive church, in chapter 1 I call attention to the opposing claims made by Franciscans and Dominicans on how the bap-tism of adult Indians should be carried out. In relation to this rather explosive issue that polarized the Mendicants, divergent opinions were put forth regarding the precise contours of the baptismal ceremony in the primitive church. At the core of the debate lay the issue of ritual integrity and, along with it, the limits between ritual and ritual formalism. Thus, in a context seemingly far removed from Europe, we encounter a discussion that, in essence, reflected similar debates confronting the European church and the reformed factions.

Inextricably associated with the desire to bring back to life the ideals of the primitive church was the impulse to restore through the conversion of the Mexicans a simplicity of devotion, long identified with the spirit of early Christianity. Evidence that the friars believed they had succeeded in this fashion comes to us in pages where they depicted an elusive golden age before the orders faced the direct challenge of the secular clergy. The obstacles that soon put to the test the friars' initial optimism about the progress of Christianity among the indigenous peoples did not result in a generally shared feeling of frustration, although such a feeling did exist. Paradoxically, the limits that Nahua culture imposed upon the conversion enterprise facilitated the acceptance of simple forms of Christianity, which some religious minds found satisfying, even when the particular brand of Catholicism that was taking root may not have matched the missionaries' original ideals of simplicity. This is precisely what comes across in the writings of Fr. Juan Bautista, a Franciscan expert in the Nahuatl language equipped, like few were, with a deep understanding of the barriers that kept Indians from a full participation in the Christian religion. When at the end of the sixteenth century Juan Bautista reflected on existing opinions regarding whether a penitent should receive the confessor's absolution when lacking adequate knowledge of Christian doctrine, he sided with those theologians who sought to alleviate the burden of those looking for the remission of their sins. The penitents should not be expected to know the articles of faith and the Ten Commandments in the same order in which they were presented in the *cartillas,* the printed leaflets for religious instruction. Moreover, when it came to the Ten Commandments, it was enough for the penitent to know that everything expressed in them could be summed up as follows: "Do unto others as you would have them do unto you, and do not do unto them as you would not have them do unto you."[18] Simplicity has come full circle. Similarly, a few decades later, the Augustinian chronicler Juan de Grijalva, praising the simplicity of the Indians' confessions, declared that, regarding salvation, it was better to experience contrition than to know its definition.[19] To a great extent, there is the sense that at one point or another friars and parish priests alike thought that they—and Christianity—could very well live with less than perfect Christians, showing, if not whole satisfaction, at least a good deal of toleration, maybe more than they were willing or allowed to concede openly.

Although it did not take long for alphabetic literacy to spread among the Nahuas, no personal account either in Spanish or any of the native languages spoken in Central Mexico has surfaced that would provide us with a glimpse of how a Nahua individual might have experienced the first contact and subsequent conversion to Christianity.[20] So far, testimonies of the Nahuas' reaction to Christianity have been confined to those extreme cases involving a handful of individuals who, after having accepted Christianity, turned against it and subsequently faced charges as *dogmatizadores* (proselytizers) under the inquisitorial authority of the archbishop Zumárraga.[21] On the other hand, despite the fact that Nahua wills, due to their formulaic nature, do not allow much room for elaborate personal narratives, they have nonetheless allowed historians to gain information on the personal devotional preferences of the Nahuas who complied with the church's expectations for a good Christian.[22]

Whether we imagine it either as a sudden turn of heart or a slow process of inner transformation assisted by instruction and an increasing exposure to the ritualized routine that soon came to preside over the interactions between Nahuas and friars, the conversion proceedings that culminated with the baptismal ritual of the Mexican Indians remain, for the most part, elusive.

Both within and without the boundaries of academic disciplines, religious conversion remains a charged term, and maybe rightly so; it turns into an even more uncomfortable notion if we are dealing with cultures brought under colonial domination. Moral responses aside, we tend to ascribe to conversion distinctive features whether we consider it as a collective or individual phenomenon. To a great extent we still cling to a concept of conversion as an experience of such intimate nature as to resist translation. This idea of conversion seems as hard to shake off as the literary tradition that gave it shape, that keeps it alive, and to which we are heirs. This may explain in part why conceiving of religious conversion in absolute terms is common—in a more immediate context, one could argue that the last two decades have witnessed the emergence of a culture of conversion in the United States where the mechanisms of personal and social rehabilitation or reentrance have blurred any clear boundaries between secular and religious. In the particular case of the evangelization of Mexico and other Spanish colonies we have witnessed periodical declarations that conversion—"real" conversion, that is—may have never taken place. The church itself has allowed more shades in evaluating its own activities, and not simply because of its built-in optimism based on the monopoly of truth and its ultimate triumph but rather as a matter of its very particular sense of historical consciousness and adaptation.[23] In abandoning any attempt to answer whether Christianity triumphed in Mexico or not, I share with other scholars a reluctance to accept the limiting perspective and inevitable reductionism implicit in such a question.[24]

In the introduction of Christian rituals among the Nahuas, especially the sacraments, more than colonial coercion was at work. We can better understand this important religious transformation by studying the cognitive and communicative dimensions of ritual as addressed by the missionaries themselves. My close examination of Nahua rituals side by side with contemporary Christian theology reveals that a hitherto neglected relationship emerges, one that helps account for the transformation of missionary thought and practice, as well as the conditions under which the Nahuas reconfigured their own spiritual and cultural autonomy.

The impact that knowledge of Nahua rituals had on missionary thinking and practice helps explain, first, the complex negotiations that took place in the process of making the sacraments available to the Indians and, second, the ways in which the friars took cognizance of Nahua rituals. Both of these features raise the central issue of the book: What did rituals—both Christian and Nahua—tell the friars about human action and social order?

Religious chronicles produced within Franciscan quarters recorded in minute detail the numerical growth and geographical expansion of Christianity since the arrival of the first brothers in Mexican territories. The Indians baptized by the friars were counted in the thousands and in some estimates in the millions, but these latter figures are debatable.[25] In these chronicles as well as in official documents, Mexico's Christian beginnings soon became identified with the successful conversion of the Indians carried out by this order. Such historical precedence, which the Franciscans in Mexico saw as their major source of authority in religious matters, also found expression in the narrative form chosen by the order's historians. Accounts of the teaching of Christian doctrine and the introduction of the different sacraments occupy an important place in these chronicles and provide them with a clear and simple narrative structure. A case in point is the second book of Motolinía's *Historia de los indios de Nueva España,* which opens with the first baptisms administered by the Franciscans and then proceeds to deal with penance and marriage. Later chroniclers such as Jerónimo de Mendieta and Juan de Torquemada took up the use of the sacraments as an ordering principle in their historical narratives. Other writers who set out to write the history of their respective orders did not feel compelled to follow the example of the Franciscan chroniclers. If we turn to the first major history written by the Dominicans, Agustín Dávila Padilla's *Historia de la fundación y discurso de la Provincia de Santiago de México* (1596), we are on very different ground. Whereas the Franciscan historians had built their narratives on teaching and bestowing the sacraments, the Dominican historian Dávila Padilla organized his history as a series of discreet biographies of varying lengths arranged in chronological order. This method of composition had already been explored by his predecessors Andrés de Moguer and Pedro de Córdoba, but Dávila Padilla perfected it. More complex in style than its Franciscan counterparts, and displaying a careful design in its overall composition—which goes hand in hand with the praise that the author lavished on the Dominican preachers for their rhetorical skills—Dávila Padilla's work found its historiographical model in Plutarch's *Lives.* Plutarch was not an obvious choice for a religious historian, as can be gathered from Dávila Padilla's concern that his use of the Greek historian could be mistakenly perceived as a departure from the conventions of ecclesiastical history. Even so, the author saw his borrowing from Plutarch as a way to broaden and enrich the writing of sacred history, not as the slavish subordination of this history to a pagan literary form.[26]

In collecting information about the ancient religion of their new charges, the Spanish friars were often struck by what they saw as similarities between certain Nahua rites and the Christian sacraments. Few religious writers employed, as did the Dominican Fr. Diego Durán, for instance, the term "sacrament" to refer to native rituals.[27] In general, a more cautious approach prevailed where this kind of usage was avoided. The friars were inclined to think that the sacramental system could only be found and made sense of within the boundaries of Christian religion. For religious matters such linguistic reservations were of great consequence, and more so when it came to translating Christian notions into Nahuatl or other indigenous languages. The Dominican historian Fr. Antonio de Remesal informs us that early on Franciscans and Dominicans alike had debated whether to translate the term God with a native word designating a local divinity.[28] Similar misgivings were voiced by the Franciscan Fr. Bernardino de Sahagún regarding the rendering of the concept of devil into Nahuatl.[29] The *Vocabulario en lengua castellana y mexicana,* composed by the Franciscan lexicographer Alonso de Molina, lacks an entry for *sacramento* (sacrament); in his doctrinal writings Molina would stick to the Spanish word.[30] In general, Spaniards would refer to native rituals as *ceremonias* or *ritos* and sometimes employ the more inclusive *costumbre.*[31] In fact, the last two words appear closely associated, as attested in Alfonso de Palencia's vocabulary from 1490 and Sebastián de Covarrubias's work in 1611.[32] As for *rituales,* both in Latin and Spanish, it still retained the meaning of "ancient books" on how to conduct ceremonials.[33] At the same time, "ceremonies," "rites," and the words "customs" had developed their own separate meanings in the context of Christian liturgy, a field of no immediate concern for the humanist Alfonso de Palencia, author of the *Universal vocabulario en latín y en romance.*[34]

Europeans accounted for these perceived similarities by asserting that Amerindian religions offered nothing but a distorted and sometimes inverted image of the Christian sacraments, a phenomenon attributed to the influence of the devil. This idea, popularized in Europe as part of the church's fight against popular practices and, more aggressively, against witchcraft, did not always appeal to those missionaries in Mexico who developed a familiarity with Nahua culture as well as a strong commitment to understanding its workings for teaching purposes. Most of those who held that the devil had created and introduced his own brand of sacraments among the Indians were eager to find an explanation for the apparent resemblance between rituals. At a practical level such a view would prove unproductive—its corollary being the eradication of all suspicious practices—dooming beforehand any attempt to inquire into the meaning and function of particular native rituals. As I show in the second chapter, the Franciscan Alonso de Molina took the opposite path, first identifying how Nahua young men became warriors in the past and the social values attached to such a state, in order to explain the sacrament of

confirmation. The sacramental system and the history of its development, as they were known to them, was the closest thing the missionaries had to a heuristic theory of ritual. Their understanding of ritual
as a form of social action and instrument of discipline enabled them to
describe, interpret, and eventually alter the ritual and social life of the
Nahuas.

The impact of the Mexican experience upon the friars, as Europeans
and Christians, played a crucial role in the evolution of missionary
thought. The friars' explanation of the sacraments to the Nahuas was
shaped by the interface of their theological background and their
increasing knowledge of Nahua culture and its rituals. Knowledge of
the ancient Nahua rituals became instrumental for the friars' teaching
of Christian doctrine. The Nahuas' older traditions shaped the doctrinal instruction itself, which carried within it images and assessments of
the Nahua culture and of its projected transformation under Spanish
rule. As the missionary literature of the times makes apparent, Nahua
culture became the unavoidable frame of reference within which Christianity had to be explained. This book addresses two salient features of
the evangelization process: the theological traditions that informed the
friars' enterprise and the impact that everyday interaction between missionaries and Nahuas had upon the latter.

One of the features through which Christianity came to distinguish
itself from other philosophical schools with which it shared similar
assumptions concerning moral life was that Christianity not only
offered a reason to believe and to act in a determined manner but it
also provided the necessary means to satisfy its demands and requirements, that is, the necessary channels to receive grace.[35] Hence the fundamental place occupied by the sacraments in the Christian economy
of salvation.

Seven sacraments seem to have been recognized by the time that
Peter Lombard was preparing a systematic exposition on them in his
Liber Sententiarum in the twelfth century.[36] The sacramental system
consisting of seven sacraments would finally be recognized officially by
the Council of Florence in the fifteenth century. Peter Lombard put the
sacraments in the following order: baptism, confirmation, Eucharist,
penance, extreme unction, holy orders, and marriage.[37] Following the
same sequence, Thomas Aquinas, in the thirteenth century, justified the
relationship among the seven sacraments arranged in that order by
drawing a parallel between spiritual life and the human biological cycle,

paying special attention to the ideas of development and perfection in both domains. Aquinas conceived of two ways of approaching the process of perfection in the life of a Christian, one centered on the development of the individual and the other on the relationship of the individual with the community.[38]

From the perspective of the individual, perfection is achieved through a natural process that begins with birth (generation) and continues with growth, through which the individual reaches full development; however, this process is possible only when there exists nutrition to sustain the person. Generation would correspond to baptism, through which one is born to Christian life; growth and fortification, to the sacrament of confirmation; and finally, nutrition, to the Eucharist. But individuals are also exposed to external influences that threaten their physical and spiritual health and development, so just as there are cures for physical illnesses, penance exists on the spiritual plane to eliminate sins. Extreme unction coincides with the end of the individual's earthly existence.

The analogy of the sacraments with key stages of human biological and social development persisted in doctrinal treatises and catechisms in sixteenth-century Spain. Thus, Fr. Luis de Granada compared baptism, confirmation, and communion to the generative, augmentative (which helps growth), and nutritive virtues, respectively.[39] Although the seven sacraments cannot be easily ordered in a temporal sequence—Eucharist and holy orders, for example, pose some problems—it is certain that baptism, confirmation, matrimony, and extreme unction show a clear correspondence to significant stages of human life, covering both the biological and social domains.[40] In the second chapter I analyze the conclusions that Mexican friars drew from such comparison as applied to the sacrament of confirmation.

The well-known altarpiece of Rogier van der Weyden, painted for Jean Chevrot, bishop of Tournai, is an excellent example of European sacramental iconography (fig. 1).[41] The administration of the sacraments is represented in the interior of a gothic church, beginning with the baptism of a newborn infant in the left panel and ending with extreme unction in the right panel. The primacy of the Eucharist is underscored by the figure of Christ on the cross that dominates the central panel, which corresponds to the central nave of the church and stands here for the altar. The administration of the Eucharist is not represented, but its content is: the real presence of the body of Christ. At the same time the scene of the crucifixion in the central position makes clear the ultimate source of the power of all the sacraments. Similar arrangements of the sacraments around a centrally positioned crucifixion—also within the framework of a gothic church—were seen again in later altar paintings (fig. 2).[42] In México, a fresco finished in 1577 in the Augustinian convent of Los Santos Reyes, Metztitlán, depicts the tree of life with a crucified Christ at its center surrounded by the sacraments (fig. 3).[43]

As the cornerstone of salvation, the sacraments defined a central interaction of Christians and their god, one that ritual action helped illuminate. At their core, the sacraments had a human matrix: they dealt with human events that went beyond the narrow confines of theology: birth, maturity, marriage, and death. The cycles of human life were thereby invested with culturally specific meanings. In dealing with obstacles to the administration of the sacraments, the ministers became aware of the limitations that Nahua rituals and beliefs imposed on their own Christian practices and assumptions, and this caused them to reexamine the meaning of the sacraments in light of an alien culture. Their reflections, recorded in treatises on native customs, official documents, and religious chronicles, grappled with the meaning of events in the human life cycle as revealed in Aztec rituals. For Spanish missionaries ritual was not only a focus of evangelical concern but also a window that opened onto the social world of the Nahuas: their notions of self, of emotions, and of social and cosmic order. These reflections in turn impinged on their understanding of Christian culture.

The friars' daily contact with indigenous culture brought to the fore certain tensions that had long remained unsolved within sacramental theology, for example, the coexistence of different opinions regarding the exact role of the priest and the penitent in the sacrament of penance. This crucial aspect has been largely overlooked, and yet it allows us to evaluate the variety of approaches to the conversion of the Mexican Indians. Such omission springs from the misguided and still rather pervasive view of Christian theology as a uniform and monolithic system. As a consequence, the doctrinal and theological literature produced in Mexico has, to a great extent, been neglected as a documentary source.

Although this is a book about the administration of the sacraments in Mexico, it has not been primarily conceived as a comprehensive account or synthesis of the existing—and considerable—literature on the subject. Rather, I have privileged the administration of the sacraments over other aspects of the evangelization because, as a well-defined area of missionary activity, it offers a unique vantage point for understanding how the friars conceived the uses and functions of ritual in society, relying both on the teachings of sacramental theology and their own knowledge of Nahua ritual life. The chapters that make up the book deal with the sacraments of baptism, confirmation, confession, and the Eucharist, constituting what can be loosely called a model of Christian initiation, although I am aware that some authors may have reservations regarding the use of such a term. Marriage has not been included mainly because the problems faced by the friars in administering this sacrament and the discussions that ensued were conducted, as could be expected, within the framework of canon law, while theological issues remained marginal.[44]

The perspective that I bring to the study of the contact between Nahuas and European friars is a partial one. I have chosen to focus on how the missionaries reflected on their own tradition as they went about administering the sacraments to the Mexican Indians at the same time that they strove to gain a more complete understanding of their culture. In this sense, this is a study of Christianity in context. This choice was dictated in part by the missionary sources themselves as I was searching for cues on how the Nahuas responded to Christianity, my original subject of research. What emerged from my reading was a picture of the missionary mind at once richer and more nuanced and revelatory in its contradictions than I had learned to expect. This appreciation, however, did not lessen the overall ideological direction of the sources; if anything, it made it more intriguing. In their capacity as specialized agents of Christianity, friars and priests alike shared a common body of knowledge both technical and speculative, yet their opinions and perceptions regarding the conversion of the Mexican Indians were far from conveying a unified view. This diversity did not escape the attention of the participants themselves who found plenty of occasions to defend their views on conversion and different Indian groups or build consensus over contested issues. Nevertheless, the friars were not primarily interested in reflecting on the general framework that allowed them to formulate their opinions and defend their validity. If we are to account for the formation of missionary experience and ultimately the particular brand of Christianity that took hold in Mexico, it seems necessary to understand first the particular nature of the friars' conceptual tools that helped them make sense of Nahua culture and formulate a course of action to bring the Indians to Christianity. That an account on the interactions between Spaniards and Nahuas could do without an inquiry into the ways in which the intellectual background of the friars were tested in the Mexican context seemed, until recently, taken for granted by historians interested in contact history. Historical research on religious figures, from the most salient to the lesser known, as well as on missionary methodology and ecclesiastical policy in Mexico, has been the province of historians with religious affiliation. Their contribution, especially in filling up the gaps of the historical record with new documentary evidence, can hardly be underestimated. However, these scholars have sometimes found it difficult to extricate themselves from the debates that often broke among their respective religious orders during the sixteenth century. In what reads at times like a justification of the viewpoints of fellow brothers from the past, this body of scholarship has in general underplayed the impact that indigenous cultures had on missionary thinking. Whatever the particular reasons for this absence, the reluctance to focus on this important aspect of the conversion process cannot without distortion be attributed to a certain inadequacy of the church to account for the transformation of its teachings throughout history and the coexistence of diverse lines of thought. However it was not until recently that historians outside the church have started to fully acknowledge this dynamic dimension of Catholicism in Mexico.

The adaptability of the Catholic Church to new historical and cultural contexts has become by now almost a commonplace. Only rarely has this commonplace been subjected to scrutiny by historians studying the conversion of the Mexican Indians; these historians have either largely ignored its implications or approached it with suspicion, as if acknowledging the awareness that the church has historically shown of its need and capacity to adapt might somewhat inhibit further inquiry on how this process has taken place and under which conditions. On the other hand, historians affiliated with the Catholic Church have taken the adaptability of the missionaries as a matter of course, often limiting themselves to pointing to historical antecedents, thus certifying the legitimacy of particular missionary approaches to conversion. The vision of the church as a resourceful institution whose reproduction has been frequently attributed to its capacity to take hold across cultures by adaptation has resulted in a curious distribution of roles for colonial actors: missionaries "adapt," while the Indians "respond." Adaptation seems a mitigated form of change, along lines somewhat preconceived, as if the missionaries' doctrinal arsenal were enough to take care of contingencies and obstacles prior to their real occurrence. When natives are said to respond, it is the undeniable and at times brutal asymmetry that governed the exchanges between Mexican Indians and Spaniards that is brought to the fore—and also the idea that their response is seemingly less scripted or less easily understood by recourse to a set of religious, social, or cognitive frameworks of their respective cultures.

Fortunately the division of labor that I have sketched has started to look more and more untenable, as historians and anthropologists have come to realize that the theological background of the Spanish missionaries and their interpretation of church traditions was also an integral part of contact history, but not necessarily for the same reasons that religious historians have advanced. When discussing missionary approaches to the conversion of the Mexican Indians, the latter have, for the most part, distinguished two main trends: one that sought not to leave anything to chance and emphasized the thorough preparation of the Indians on each step in their process of becoming a Christian, and another that allowed for a somewhat more flexible integration in the first stages of Christianization. Both approaches are thought as having their own legitimacy within church practice and rest on historical antecedents. This apparent flexibility, however, comes to us as defined beforehand, but what is more important, it does not account for how and why they came to dominate in a particular context.

Since the inception of their discipline, anthropologists have occupied themselves with the study of ritual; the Christian sacraments, however, have not warranted the kind of scrutiny mostly reserved for ritual life in non-Western societies.[45] The fact that the sacraments have come to be inextricably associated with a long history of theological interpretations may have acted as a deterrent for further examination from an anthropological perspective. Such oversight is unfortunate since there is much to be learned about Christianity by studying how theologians conceptualized these particular rituals and the analytical tools they employed to do so. Sacramental theology amounts to a special kind of theory of ritual, one in which anthropologists would be surprised to discover that Christian theologians had to tackle issues similar to their own such as the relationship between knowledge and ritual action, the connection between meaning and context, and the role of emotions, to name just a few. While I have not undertaken research along these lines, I briefly touch upon some of these issues when relevant to my discussion of the Mexican case.

Recent research on the Christianization of New Spain can be read as a series of responses to the pioneering work of Robert Ricard, *The Spiritual Conquest of Mexico,* published in 1933. Adopting the point of view of the first Spanish friars in charge of the conversion, Ricard's narrative gives an account of the complex activity that made possible, in a short period of time, the consolidation and development of the Mexican church as an institution. Ricard's account tells us about a victory, the evidence of which, given the strong presence of the church in Mexico today, can hardly be disputed. There is, however, an aspect of this history that is worrisome: Ricard's confidence in the declarations of success made by the very parties involved in the conversion of the Mexican Indians.[46]

The perspective brought by Ricard rests on the notion that the Nahua and Christian religion each possessed definite and identifiable boundaries or, rather, that such demarcation is in a certain sense methodologically necessary. The result is a static portrait in which the diverse and problematic dimensions of the colonial experience for both the Mexican Indians and Spaniards are absent.

The confluence of the emerging field of ethnohistory and social history brought about a significant shift in the study of Latin American colonial societies and the study of religious contact and evangelization in Mexico. Scholarly works based on newly discovered documentary sources in Spanish and Nahuatl have helped redefine our vision of the spiritual conquest by showing that the relationship between Spanish priests and Mexican Indians was characterized by daily negotiations and accommodations.[47] These studies, however, have shown little interest in grasping the intellectual infrastructure that made possible the exchange between friars and Indians.[48] This limitation has prevented us from considering the evangelization of Mexico as a dynamic process with a logic of its own; our understanding of the religious colonial experience has remained subordinated to explanations of Spanish colonialism conceived for areas other than religion.[49] The present study addresses some of these historiographical issues.

My account, fragmented and partial as it is, is intended to recover a small portion of the particular dynamics of Spanish Christian culture in the sixteenth century. There is no better example than the friars working among the Mexican Indians to help us understand how one unassailable conviction was put to the test daily—that being European and Christian formed one unbreakable equation. The Mexican experience showed the Spanish missionaries the fragility of that identification. If, as Europeans, their contact with the Nahuas affected their own sense of cultural identity, as religious men, the conversion enterprise made apparent the inherently problematic nature of their assumptions. In the process of translating, interpreting, and reinterpreting, the friars discovered that the power of the religious tradition to which they belonged did not rest exclusively in the alleged power of its dogmatic truths but rather in its capacity to embrace and make intelligible an extraordinary diversity of human actions. Christianity forever marked Moctezuma's descendants, but their own culture in turn did not cease to modify the ways in which the missionaries came to conceive and experience their double condition as pilgrims in spirit and geography.

CHAPTER I

Conversion and Baptism in Sixteenth-Century Mexico

The Meanings of Baptism

The controversy over the baptism of adults that pitted Dominicans and Augustinians against Franciscans is a well-known episode in the early history of the Mexican church, and one that can still stir up old feelings in religious quarters. Since the first systematic account by Robert Ricard, newly found documentation has shed significant light on the negotiations undertaken by the orders to have their respective views officially sanctioned, as well as on the friars and officials involved in them on both sides of the Atlantic.[1] This conflict is worth revisiting for what it can still teach us about the problems that would absorb the friars' minds years after its apparent resolution: the role of Christian ritual in a cross-cultural context, the search for working notions of conversion, and the delicate boundaries between coercion and free will.

Diego Muñoz Camargo, born around 1529 to a Spanish conqueror and an Indian noblewoman, spent most of his adult life in Tlaxcala, his native city where he became an influential figure of its small society.[2] A successful landowner raised and educated in a Spanish milieu, Muñoz Camargo belonged to that first generation of privileged mestizos for whom it was possible to participate actively in the public life of the colonies by holding administrative offices. A speaker of both Nahuatl and Spanish, he was an official interpreter for the city, a post that took him to Spain accompanying a delegation of Tlaxcalan Indian leaders in the 1580s.[3] He also worked as an officer of the *alcaldía* (mayorality) of Tlaxcala and was later appointed land administrator. It was while occupied in his administrative duties that Muñoz Camargo had the opportunity to reacquaint himself with the history of the people on his mother's side as he consulted the genealogies of local lords in search of information on lands and titles. This historical information dating back to preconquest times was put to use in the reports of varied length that Muñoz Camargo authored as part of his administrative duties while in office.[4] Luckily, the possibility of transforming his historical findings on the Tlaxcalan past into an independent and coherent narrative was not lost on him. In 1592, just a few years before his death, he finished the *Historia de Tlaxcala,* a historical narrative of the province and the city that he lived in. This work, derived in great measure from the documentation produced during his years in office, comprises the history of the province from its foundation to 1585, the year when Alvaro Manrique de Zúñiga became the seventh viceroy of New Spain.

Halfway through the *Historia de Tlaxcala,* Diego de Muñoz Camargo recorded in detail a momentous meeting between Hernán Cortés and the four ruling lords of the city. The circumstances that led Cortés to Tlaxcala after his successful entrance and brief stay in Tenochtitlan were not cause for celebration. Having been unable to contain the assault launched by Mexica warriors that followed the massacre of Indian noblemen during the Toxcatl festival, the Spanish captain and his soldiers had been forced out of Tenochtitlan to find refuge among their first allies, the Tlaxcalans.

The Tlaxcalan historian underscored the significance of the meeting between the temporarily defeated Cortés and his hosts by framing it as a sequence of solemn speeches that reflect the special weight of the occasion as well as the social stature of the speakers. At this meeting, the four lords, relying on the friendship with the Spaniards that had been sealed with the participation of Tlaxcalan warriors in the expedition to Tenochtitlan, urged Cortés to open his heart and reveal to them the true motive of his presence and his plans for the future. Cortés complied, informing them that his mission in Mexican lands was to bring his hosts and their people a new and true religion that would forever replace the false idols that kept them enslaved. He also gave a second reason, stating that the Spaniards were ready to help the Tlaxcalans to exact vengeance over their oppressors from Tenochtitlan. Cortés concluded with a double request to the lords: to give up all their idols and sacrifices as a requisite to embrace Christianity before submitting to baptism and to join him in a definitive attack against their long-standing foes. His call for the destruction of the idols was prefaced by a general explanation of Christianity and the importance of baptism by water as a means of cleansing sins and breaking free from the devil's hold. Only through baptism, explained Cortés, could the lords earn the name of true Christians.[5]

At this point in the narrative an element of suspense is introduced. The rulers went out to inform the population about the foreigner's petition and listened as their aggrieved subjects expressed fear of the irreparable consequences that the abandoning of the traditional gods might bring upon the city.[6] For a reader acquainted with the Christian polemics against the pagans, the nature of the Tlaxcalans' fear will surely strike a familiar note.[7] In spite of the reluctance on the part of some Tlaxcalans, their lords had already made up their minds, and back in the presence of Cortés, they agreed to see their idols destroyed and be the first to submit to the ritual required by the Christian visitors. The lords also accepted placing themselves under the leadership of the Spaniards. The priest Juan Díaz carried out the public ceremony of baptism during which the city rulers were given Christian names. Hernán Cortés and Pedro de Alvarado themselves are said to have served as godfathers (fig. 4).[8]

Writing in the beginning of the seventeenth century, the Franciscan chronicler Juan de Torquemada relied heavily on Muñoz Camargo's history and included an abridged version of this episode in his monumental *Monarquía indiana* (1615). Torquemada declared Tlaxcala the very first place the Mexican Indians had been administered the Christian sacraments.[9] In this, as well as in other matters concerning the spread of Christianity in New Spain, his authority loomed large: the eighteenth-century edition of the Mexican church councils ordered by the archbishop Lorenzana repeated Torquemada's assertion regarding the beginnings of baptism in Mexico.[10]

As is often the case with the recording of historical turning points, the events in which Muñoz Camargo took so much pride belong to legend, in this case, one that began taking shape in the second half of the sixteenth century and to which the chronicler lent a thorough literary treatment.[11] Contrary to his view of Cortés as an agent of conversion to Christianity—an image already spread through the Franciscan writings with which Muñoz Camargo was thoroughly familiar—historical evidence indicates that at the time the events referred to allegedly took place, a concerted effort to impose Christianity was not in the conquerors' minds. It has been reasonably assumed that at such a crucial point for the future success of the Spanish forces, as well as for their present survival, any urgent attempt to bring the Tlaxcalans to Christianity must have surely been overridden by strategic and military considerations.[12]

The legend, however, tries to reconcile the fundamental difficulties associated with religious conversion in a seamlessly harmonious fashion. It keeps the possibility of conflict to a minimum, underplaying the negative consequences that might accompany a rejection of the Spaniards' demands. Moreover, when a discordant note does arise, it stems from peripheral and unidentified characters, rather than from the main actors at the center of the drama. Cortés's speech exalting the moral superiority of Christianity and its ready availability through the sacrament of baptism deliberately leaves out any element that might suggest coercion. This is precisely why the lords' change of heart is left to take place during the time elapsed between the petition of the Spaniards and the return of the lords to their quarters once they had consulted with their subjects. The story tells us that the momentous decision came about because the lords themselves had enough time to reflect on what was being offered them, aided only by the persuasive force of reason advanced by the Spaniards, and not at all due to coercion.

Legends such as this possess the odd quality of giving historical turning points an air of inevitability; they forge a middle ground that betrays the distance between two widely divergent worlds as well as the real possibility of an order able to encompass them both, promised by the Christian message. The story of the four lords could accommodate this vision because Tlaxcala's Christian beginnings, tentative as they might have been in reality, had not been marred by the twists of fate that befell Moctezuma and the Spaniards in their first attempt to gain control of Tenochtitlan.

In this regard, it is instructive to contrast Muñoz Camargo's presentation with the baptism of one of Moctezuma's sons, which took place soon after the Franciscans arrived in Mexico City. The event was witnessed and later recorded by Fr. Toribio de Benavente, better known as Motolinía, one of the first twelve Franciscan friars to land in Mexico.[13] A son of Moctezuma had requested to be baptized, and being unable to leave his home because he was ill, a group of friars went to assist him. The sick nobleman was carried on a chair outside his house where, in the midst of the ceremony, an extraordinary event took place. At the precise moment the friar uttered the formula of exorcism, both the chair and the Indian started to shake violently as if a demon were struggling to leave his body.[14] It appears that baptism, after all, may not have been entirely devoid of political meaning. Whereas Cortés and his men had fought Moctezuma and his people, the Tlaxcalans had been his willing allies. No wonder then that Moctezuma's son had to be freed of a demon before being baptized. There is thus more than a surface meaning to this story. For the story, in spite of its brevity, is rich in symbolic details suggesting that something other than merely the baptism of an individual from a tenaciously heathen lineage was at stake. This is why Motolinía did not stop with the account of the baptism but reinforced its veracity by reminding his readers that the church of San Hipólito was now located where the house of Moctezuma's son used to stand. The man's removal from the domestic space that was considered polluted—by the demons, by the disease—and therefore unsuitable for ritual purposes, besides responding to the baptismal ceremonial protocol, nicely contributes to a kind of double narrative where the baptism of an individual and the creation of sacred space converge.[15]

Given the widespread reports by Spaniards on the ubiquitous presence of demons in Mexican lands until Christianity gradually pushed them away, one would have expected friars to have taken special measures against demonic forces. This, however, was not the case, if we are to judge by the scarce references to exorcism in historical and religious sources. In this regard, the advice concerning exorcism found in a manual by the Dominican Martín de León published in 1614 appears to be an exception.[16] Martín de León showed a similar confidence in the power of blessings for fields and vineyards, as well as the use of religious formulas against hail and locusts.

The baptismal ceremonies recounted by Muñoz Camargo and Motolinía offer a sharp contrast that springs from each author's choice to emphasize one particular ritual step over others. In the first case, the Tlaxcalan lords' acceptance of Christianity reads as a public ceremony that marks the beginning of a political and military alliance entered into by the Tlaxcalans of their own accord. Motolinía's anecdote by contrast focuses on the power of exorcism, a reminder that baptism is also an effective weapon in the spiritual struggle against demons.[17]

Muñoz Camargo's story, evocative of many similar episodes in the spread of Christianity in medieval Western Europe, carries an all too clear meaning when it makes the baptism of the Tlaxcalan lords coincide with their submission to aliens whose military and spiritual force was greater than their own. In turn, and with the inevitable paradox that is part and parcel of the colonial protocol, this subordination is accompanied by the implicit promise that as Christians the Mexicans would enjoy a religious status equal to that of the Spaniards.

Baptism was called to play a significant role in the complex reality that grew out of the first contacts between Europeans and Mexicans, as well as in the interpretations of that reality that were soon put into writing, because its ritual, packed with rich, powerful, yet malleable symbolism, was able to effect manifold transformations at both the individual and social levels.[18]

Beyond their most obvious religious meaning, the Christian names adopted by the baptized conferred upon them a new social identity that set them apart from their nonbaptized brethren with whom they often lived under one roof.[19] Moreover, baptism was also instrumental in the forging of new social ties among families and individuals through the institution of *compadrazgo,* or spiritual kinship.[20] Regarding the Nahuas' sense of past, the annalistic historical traditions kept alive in postconquest times started to record the baptisms of local lords and other important town members as significant events for the community at large (fig. 5).[21] From a legal standpoint, baptism established an entirely new set of binding legal responsibilities for both the Spaniards and their new subjects. As the religious history of colonial Mexico shows us, it fell upon the friars of the Mendicant orders and a handful of Spanish officials to remind the Spanish Crown of its duty to live up to its new obligations.

Sixteenth-century religious and secular writers who occupied themselves with the Spanish colonization understood too well that the religious and legal meanings attached to baptism might be opened to contest. This awareness helps explain, for instance, the significance that they assigned in their writings to questions such as whether Moctezuma had actually undergone baptism by the time of his death, the circumstances of which were under dispute.[22] Historical works produced in and about Mexico offer us a glimpse of how baptism can assume a wide array of meanings depending on the role it is called to play within different kinds of narratives.

The overall meaning of baptism results from a sequence of well-defined ritual stages culminating with the official admission of an individual to the church community. From the exorcism by the priest, the anointing of the candidate, the blessing of the water, the participation of parents and godparents to the actual baptism, each ritual step carries its own meaning. From the standpoint of sacramental theology, the act of exorcism was not, strictly speaking, considered an essential part of the sacrament, yet exorcism was a ritual step intimately linked to the ceremony, one that enjoyed a special place in the popular imagination.[23] Moctezuma's son did indeed receive baptism; it was, however, the act of exorcism and its efficacy in casting off the demons closely associated with Moctezuma's lineage that takes center stage in Motolinía's story. By contrast, in Muñoz Camargo's story, exorcism does not merit mention: the power of the new religion is conveyed through Cortés's doctrinal explanation that serves as the preceding and necessary stage for the actual ritual of baptism.

The Debate about Baptism and the Language of Ritual

Most disagreements among the orders revolved around questions of missionary methods and strategies. It can be said that in discussing conversion-related matters, the friars also found a way to channel less noble emotions and motives—long held rivalries with other orders, personal resentments, the desire to gain more influence—into an acceptable language. This was the language of sacramental theology, a well-circumscribed branch of theological inquiry and teaching that concerned itself with the systematic explanation of how the sacraments work. Whereas a contemporary observer might have found it nearly impossible to discern an underlying unity among competing opinions regarding the workings of the sacraments, sacramental theology had developed a recognizable set of notions that provided a basic conceptual framework for the discussion of sacramental matters. As an illustration, let us return to the episodes found in the works of Muñoz Camargo and Motolinía. For the twelfth-century theologian Peter Lombard, whose *Sententiae* were still taught in sixteenth-century universities, both exorcism and catechism had to be considered, strictly speaking, sacramentals, by which he meant that they did not play an essential role in the sacrament.[24] As defined by Peter Lombard and later theologians, the sacrament of baptism consisted of the combination of an element, water, and the form, the word.[25] All the other features usually found in the ritual had the function of enhancing the solemnity of the ceremony.[26] For Aquinas water was the matter of the sacrament (*propria materia*); the priest's words indicating the act of baptism proper with the invocation of the trinity corresponded to the sacrament's form (*forma*).[27] The basic distinction between materia and forma was crucial in Aquinas's explanation of how the sacraments operate to channel grace and soon found a permanent place in sacramental theology. His formulation was more than an intellectual construct borrowed from Aristotle and had a direct import on how the priest was to conduct baptisms for the sacrament to work its efficacy on the recipient. This is why the first archbishop of Mexico, Fr. Juan de Zumárraga (1528–48), seeking to ensure the proper administration of the sacraments, expected that all the friars who were to work in Mexico be thoroughly familiar with the forma and materia of each sacrament.[28]

While from a purely theoretical perspective the distinction between essential and nonessential ritual elements and actions was to find wide acceptance among several generations of theologians, it had, in practice, the potential to become a source of strong disagreements, as indeed occurred in the first decades of evangelization in Mexico. The Mexican case was not unique in having provided an occasion for disagreement over the administration of this sacrament since the evolution of baptism had in no small measure been shaped by the practical discussions that accompanied the conversion of European pagans, as during Charlemagne's campaigns of conversion of the Saxons and Avars—a historical reference not lost to the Mexican missionaries gathered in 1539 to advance a solution.[29] Centuries of liturgical usage had smoothed out past conflicts and tensions that arose in the course of preparation for baptism, as well as baptism itself. Although the established ritual reveals none of these earliest issues and uncertainties about, for instance, the nature and duration of prebaptismal instruction, and the conditions upon which the ceremony could be abridged, these were exactly the issues that came to dominate the thoughts and actions of the first missionaries in Mexico.

We owe to Motolinía the first full-fledged account of the dispute. The fact that subsequent Franciscan chroniclers felt the need to retell this episode, while writers such as the Dominican Dávila Padilla chose to ignore it altogether, suggests that the Franciscans came to regard this early conflict as a turning point in their search for self-definition, a necessary narrative block in the history of the Franciscans in New Spain, which also meant the history of Mexican Christianity.

The signs of trouble started soon after the arrival of the Dominicans and Augustinians in Mexico, when there arose different opinions among the friars on when and how the sacrament of baptism should be administered to the Indians. These disagreements had the immediate negative effect of disrupting what, for Motolinía, was the uniformity that had prevailed in the administration of the sacrament from the time of its successful reception among the Indians under Franciscan guidance.[30]

Early on, the first Franciscans had agreed on baptizing twice a week, on Sunday mornings and Thursday afternoons.[31] But, what did the ceremony of baptism as practiced by the Franciscans precisely consist of? Motolinía described it as follows:

> At the time of baptism, they placed together all those who were to be baptized, putting the children in front, and they all performed the baptismal ritual, and on a few the ceremony of the cross, with the breathing [*insufflatio*], salt, saliva, and the white cloth. Then they baptized each child in holy water, and this order has always been followed for as long as I have known.[32]

In describing the procedure followed by his brothers and enumerating all its different ritual stages, Motolinía skillfully invited the reader both to contemplate the complexity of the ceremony and to imagine the daunting task of performing it on each individual.[33] Significantly, he chose to focus almost exclusively on the baptism of children. As for the baptism of adults, Motolinía only briefly commented that they were all instructed and examined before receiving the sacrament.

Upon their arrival the Franciscans acted quickly to remove Nahua children in noble households from their unbaptized parents in order to instruct and baptize them.[34] Understandably, the *caciques* (local lords) did not always welcome this measure and were reluctant to see their sons and daughters taken away by strangers. In some instances they were forced to hide their offsprings from the friars.[35] The practice was not new within the church, having been sanctioned by the Fourth Council of Toledo (633) in an attempt to bring about the conversion of children from Jewish households.[36] Following ecclesiastical law regarding the baptized children of Jews, the Franciscan theologian Juan Focher recommended that they be separated from their parents.[37]

From the Franciscan point of view, the main dividing issue was about ritual performance. Motolinía's efforts are indeed directed to assure his reader that the disagreements boiled down to questions of procedure and formalism. According to him religious parties were split between those favoring the strict observance of ritual formalities—those inclined to "guardar ceremonias"—and the Franciscans who by way of accommodating themselves to the new missionary situation sought to simplify the ritual by preserving the essentials of the sacrament. Later Franciscan historians held to this interpretation.[38] In Mexico, distinctions between essential and nonessential components of the sacrament that had been worked out during centuries past in the sacramental theology that was taught in European universities now offered theoretical grounds for modifying the ritual. These same theoretical grounds, accordingly, became instruments to quickly characterize the two positions of Franciscans and their opponents. Surprisingly, Motolinía did not explicitly acknowledge that profound ideological differences regarding the formation of new Christians could be derived from the two approaches. For him, the urgent need to put the Mexican Indians under the safeguard of Christianity granted by baptism took precedence over any formal requirement expected in normal circumstances. In exceptional situations the church allowed a simplified baptismal ceremony. Because of the overwhelming number of Indians who were to be baptized, the Mexican situation, as the Franciscans would argue, could not be farther away from what in church tradition might be judged as normal. This is why the friars defended their actions by appealing to the same notion of *necesidad,* or necessity, that the church had used to define when and how the baptismal ceremony could be simplified.[39]

While Motolinía took the disagreements over baptism as a direct challenge to Franciscan authority on matters of evangelization, the archbishop Fr. Juan de Zumárraga, seeking to arrive at a practical and expedient solution, showed a more nuanced perspective. Zumárraga was himself a Franciscan, but his ecclesiastical responsibilities as archbishop extended both to Spaniards and Indians alike. His writings show that conciliation was for him an obligation by virtue of his office. Keenly aware of the challenges facing the young Mexican church, Zumárraga thought it was imperative to reach a consensus regarding missionary methods for two reasons. First there were the conceivably disastrous political consequences that could come as a result of a much publicized division among religious groups. Zumárraga was conscious of this danger and sought to prevent unfavorable outside opinions about the animosity among the orders by explaining their differences as normal and legitimate expressions of divergent viewpoints. A second and more strictly religious motive lay in Zumárraga's concern with the possibility that the Mexican Indians might be led to confusion if they noticed any divergence in ceremony, an occurrence that could jeopardize their conversion.[40] Writing on this very same subject in the seventeenth century, the Augustinian Juan de Grijalva invoked a similar reason, which he expressed in more precise terms. The Augustinian took for a fact that the Mexican Indians, unfamiliar as they were with the scholastic distinctions between what was to be considered essential and what was to be considered ceremonial in a sacrament, were troubled by the disparities they observed in baptismal practices.[41] These observations introduce an external criterion in support of ritual uniformity, as well as the assumption that Mexican Indians might perceive a Christian ritual led less by the understanding of its meaning than by its visual manifestation. Mexican Indians were good observers, or so the friars surmised upon reflecting on the striking attention to visual composition and details that the Nahuas displayed in their highly choreographed ceremonies.[42] As I discuss later, the perception that the Nahuas were heavily invested in ritual clued the friars into a feature of the native culture that could greatly work to their advantage—but could also create uncertainties.

Those who feared that the lack of ritual uniformity could adversely affect the Indians' disposition toward Christianity also knew that the Nahuas could still rely on the more familiar rituals through which they had traditionally taken care of newborn babies. Just as Christian baptism was required to be performed with water, so the Nahuas made the ablution of the newborn, together with the act of naming, a central feature of their birth rituals.[43] Instead of the priest's baptismal formula, selected participants or the midwife addressed the child and the mother with orations.[44] For the missionaries who with a certain sense of wonder recorded the proceedings in detail, the words, actions and elements that made up the ritual had a familiar ring. Yet this familiarity needed to be explained, and religious writers felt free to propose their own interpretations.[45]

Before the First Mexican Church Council was held in 1555, all matters pertaining to the evangelization of the Indians as well as the administration of the Mexican church were formally discussed in meetings presided over by religious authorities. It was in these *juntas eclesiásticas*–as these meetings are commonly known—where, among sometimes wildly discordant voices, recommendations and decisions regarding missionary methods and policy were made.[46] At the request of the newly arrived viceroy Antonio de Mendoza, an ecclesiastical meeting took place in the second half of 1536 in Mexico City with the goal of attending, among other matters, to the escalating conflict over baptism.[47] The bishops of Mexico, Santo Domingo, and Tlaxcala, present at the meeting, produced a document containing five points that should be observed in the baptism of adults. All the Indians to be baptized were required to have been previously instructed and exorcised. Regarding the *insufflatio* and the use of salt, candles, and cloak, they were to be restricted to a group of only four Indians of both sexes. While this recommendation corresponds to Motolinía's account of Franciscan practice, the bishops' attempt to reach a compromise led them to include that the Indians be apprised that these particular ritual steps were meant to add to the solemnity of the sacrament and not its essence.[48] This recommendation is striking in that it calls for the explanation of a rather specialized distinction drawn from sacramental theology to the very participants in the ritual. Such information was most commonly expected from priests and rarely made it into Christian doctrines for the instruction of the populace. Manuals for the instruction of prospective and recent converts that were printed in Mexico omitted this distinction.

As to the rest of the ritual, it was expected that the Mexican Indians would be anointed with the baptismal chrism and oil individually. Two contentious issues were left unresolved at the meeting: the times of the year when baptism should be made available—entirely absent from the document—and a precise definition of what constituted a case of necessity. As to the latter, it was up to the minister to determine, based on his judgment, when a situation could fall under this category. The measures emanating from this junta did not succeed in bringing the dispute to an end.

The discussions from 1536 were taken up the following year in another ecclesiastical meeting called in preparation for the upcoming general church council that was to take place in Mantua.[49] Zumárraga's plans to attend the council were not met with the approval of the viceroy Antonio de Mendoza, who instead instructed the archbishop to select and send two *procuradores,* or proxies.[50] The Augustinian Pedro de Oseguera and the Franciscan Cristobal de Almazán were appointed to represent the Mexican church at the council.[51] In an instruction drafted in 1537 for these friars, Zumárraga wrote that the solution for the conflict on baptism was more likely to emerge thanks to the intervention and counsel of an overseas authority than from an agreement reached by the parties directly involved.[52] Meanwhile his brothers in the order, disinclined to recognize the Mexican religious authorities, entertained a similar hope and claimed that they were under the direct authority of the pope.[53] In a letter from the same year briefing the Council of the Indies on the instructions carried by his envoys, Zumárraga wrote of the polarization between the orders around the baptism of adults and urged a solution without altogether hiding his sympathies for the methods defended by his Franciscan brothers:

> I send to this high Council the persuasive opinion of the Franciscans on the ceremonies of baptism, which they gave to me at the chapter that they held at the beginning of the year. And the other Dominican and Augustinian friars hold and defend the contrary opinion that the ceremonies ordered by the church should not be omitted, except in the case of death or under the threat of death.[54]

Tradition and Innovation: The Role of the Letrados

Motolinía's presentation was informed by the desire to defend his order against accusations of wrongdoing in the crucial years that followed the introduction of Christianity in the new territories. He argued that the baptism of an unprecedented number of Indians by only a handful of friars had made necessary the modification of the ritual for the sake of expediency. In so doing, the friars were still complying with established tradition; the changes in ritual, he added, had been introduced after serious reflection on both past church practices and the situation at hand and were not the product of improvisation or caprice.

The Franciscan approach to baptism dated back to the beginnings of the order's activities in Mexico and, as Motolinía reminded his readers, had been laid out by Juan de Tecto in strict accordance to instructions received from ecclesiastical authorities in Spain and church doctrine.[55] Regarding this Juan de Tecto, who had been professor of theology at the University of Paris and confessor to Charles V, Motolinía declared in praise, "no haber pasado a estas partes letrado más fundado ("no man with more solid erudition in legal matters has yet arrived in these lands").["56] Juan de Tecto had arrived in Mexico some months before Motolinía and the original contingent of twelve friars and was accompanied by two other brothers in religion: Pedro de Gante and Juan de Aora, all of them natives of the Low Countries.[57]

The highlighting of Juan de Tecto's academic credentials as proof of his authority on religious matters stands in stark contrast to Motolinía's portrait of the first group of twelve Spanish Franciscans as the inspired and strong-willed group of friars who had successfully brought back to life the order's ideals of simplicity. These ideals allowed little room for scholastic thought and the abstract preoccupations of theology such as represented by Juan de Tecto.[58] The Franciscan chronicler Fr. Jerónimo de Mendieta, less inclined to dismiss the importance of study within the order, would decades later try to balance Motolinía's stance by recognizing the intellectual training and accomplishments of his brothers:

> These overzealous guardians of the law (who thought themselves to be *letrados*) brought much uneasiness and disorder to those who had first come and had with their sweat planted this vineyard of the Lord; who although out of humility and self-deprecation enjoyed being taken for simple and uneducated, all had an education, some in canon law, others in sacred theology.[59]

Motolinía's low regard for the *letrados* is nowhere better expressed than in the chapters about baptism, where they are represented either as too deeply steeped in vanity and personal pride to apply themselves to the pastoral care of the Indians or as simply ignorant.[60] In a telling passage he recalled having heard of only one case of baptism by aspersion—sprinkling with holy water—and it had been carried out by a letrado who, ironically, would later join ranks against the Franciscans.[61] What makes this aside revealing is that up to this point in his account the practice of baptism by aspersion had passed unmentioned, although it had been openly discussed in the 1536 meeting. While the anecdote seeks to deride a letrado, it obliquely responds to the accusations and rumors that the Franciscans had baptized with an *aspergillum*, the ritual implement to sprinkle the faithful during Mass.[62] In short, the Franciscans stood accused of breaking asunder the personal bond between priest and catechumen that was articulated by the baptismal ritual and then of depriving the ritual of its visual and social efficacy. This is an important point to which I return later.

Motolinía's dislike for theologians and jurists was more than a matter of personal preference; it went to the heart of the Observant movement, which, in its effort to restore the original meaning of the Franciscan rule, regarded speculative theology more as a deterrent than a fruitful way to fashion a Christian life after Christ. The world of the letrados as the Franciscans conceived of it could not easily be reconciled with Motolinía's expectations regarding the role of his order in Mexico. It was to the formalism of the letrados that Motolinía and some of his peers opposed their own version of the primitive church as the only viable model for the conversion of the Mexicans. The primitive church offered a historical point of reference that helped the Franciscans to articulate their own desire for spiritual renewal and the concomitant critique of ecclesiastical and civil authority that came with this aspiration.[63]

This view of the letrados, however, was far from being shared in other religious quarters. As a result of the friction among religious groups, for a Franciscan like Zumárraga, it soon became apparent that in order for the evangelization to succeed it required an intellectual infrastructure that the spiritual zeal and efforts of the friars could not simply replace. In considering the important role that the letrados could be called upon to play in solving questions arising from the conversion of the Mexican Indians, the archbishop Zumárraga requested in February 1537 that at least twelve friars well trained in doctrinal matters be sent to Mexico.[64] Despite this suggestion, Zumárraga still found himself torn between the authority of church tradition and the opinion of the seasoned members of his order.[65]

While Zumárraga considered the concerns raised by the other orders as legitimate and deserving of thorough consideration by a body of local experts, Motolinía saw this course of action as an intrusion that ultimately impinged upon the authority bestowed by the pope on the Franciscans working in Mexico. Nonetheless, both Motolinía and Zumárraga did agree that the task at hand, despite the much-sought similarities with the primitive church, opened uncharted territory for the ministers. Motolinía skillfully construed this novel situation as a challenge to the competence of the letrados, both on practical and spiritual grounds, and championed an approach that did away with a reliance on legalistic antecedents found in books. In place of law and learning, the friars would convert the multitude of Indians based on a distinct brand of knowledge comprising vernacular languages and local customs, which were both readily accessible to them through direct contact with the Indians.[66]

Central to the Franciscan self-image promoted from Motolinía's pages stood the idea that neither the learning of the letrados nor scholastic speculation could ever aspire to harvest the fruit of a life led according to the order's ideals of poverty and simplicity. This particular standpoint, which had come to separate the Franciscans from the Dominicans in Europe, played itself out with renewed vigor in Mexico. In telling contrast to this attitude, Fr. Juan de Córdova recorded with particular care in his account of Dominican beginnings in the new land the intellectual background and skills of his brothers.[67] By the time we arrive at Dávila Padilla's massive Dominican chronicle published in 1596, both learning and intellectual achievement—features that were at the core of the order—have been successfully reinscribed as an integral part of the Dominican order's life in Mexico.

Toward a Solution

The escalation of the dispute made it necessary to consult with authorities in Spain who, in turn, appealed to the pope to settle the matter. The pope's response came in June 1537 with the issue of the bull *Altitudo divini consilii*. Two years later, three Mexican bishops, Zumárraga, Vasco de Quiroga (for Michoacán), and Juan de Zárate (for Oaxaca), met in the city of Mexico to evaluate and discuss the papal document.[68]

The bull before the Mexican religious authorities did not accept an outright abridgement of the baptismal ceremony of the kind defended by the Franciscans. It rather asked that in the future all the Indians would approach baptism after having received instruction and undergone exorcism, allowing for the administration of salt, saliva, and candle and to be done on a few individuals wearing the baptismal cloak in representation of the whole group. Each person would be anointed with chrism and oil.[69] Rather than taking for granted the view that nonessential ritual steps could be easily dismissed as of no consequence, it made a case for the preservation of ritual solemnity, based on the need to highlight for the Mexican Indians the differences between Christian baptism and their traditional ceremonies of ablution.[70] Here we find a justification for ritual integrity based not on traditional arguments to defend church usage but rather on the awareness that an alien culture might view Christian rituals through its own cultural practices and reach different conclusions about the meanings of these rituals.

Adopting the guiding principles of the bull, and supporting the position held by Vasco de Quiroga, bishop of Michoacán—and a letrado himself—the junta restricted the times when the baptism of adults could be administered to Easter and Pentecost, except in cases of extreme necessity, which also allowed for the abbreviation of the ritual to its essential elements.[71] Whereas regarding the notion of extreme necessity the junta chose to adhere strictly to the canons, the papal bull left room for ambiguity by allowing the priest to use his discretion to decide on unspecified difficult cases. With some irony, Motolinía would comment that this lack of precision left the doors open for continuing disagreements.[72]

In order to ensure the desired uniformity as well as the friars' compliance with the newly adopted principles, the bishops also agreed on the need of a manual for the proper guidance of ministers of the sacraments. As part of this initiative the friar Juan Focher, theologian and canonist, was asked in 1544 to compose a treatise on adult baptism. Focher complied, although his manual, like most of his writings, never saw the light in print. Nevertheless, together with his treatise on marriage, it served as the basis for the *Itinerarium catholicum* published by the Franciscan Diego Valadés in 1574.[73] The notion of baptism in Focher's manual, which closely follows the teachings of canon law, in its view of what constitutes a true catechumenate, clearly differs from Motolinía's. Notwithstanding the differences, Focher defended the Franciscan practice of baptizing adults at any given time of the year as being well established within church tradition. According to his interpretation it was the solemnity reserved for baptisms celebrated at Easter and Pentecost—which he called "solemn baptism"—that could not be transferable to baptismal ceremonies taking place at any other time during the year.[74] By tying a particular baptismal ceremony to a specific holiday, Focher sought to prove that there existed no reason why a simplified form of baptism should not be available at any time. Focher's manual clearly dramatizes the conflict of someone caught between his sympathies for his fellow Franciscans and the weight of his own legal mindset. It is significant, however, that the intellectual production of this Franciscan letrado only circulated in manuscript at a time when influential members of the order were vocally rejecting the legal tradition of the church as an inadequate instrument for dealing with Mexican reality.

Most unhappy with the bishops' decision, the Franciscans ceased to baptize adults only to resume doing so a few months later in accordance with their past practice. Motolinía's *Historia de los indios de Nueva España* vividly illustrates the tensions that accompanied the initial years of religious activities in the Central Valley. About the particular issue of baptism, which our chronicler was especially keen on reporting, there arose diverging attitudes concerning the reconciliation of tradition and novelty, of the autonomy bestowed upon the friars by papal authority and the respect for episcopal authority. It is therefore not entirely surprising that the conflict that Motolinía felt compelled to delve into does not reach any kind of clear-cut narrative resolution. A deep gulf expands between the bishops' will and the determination of the Franciscans, and we are left with the friars' act of disobedience, a gesture that neatly fits in the overall ideological design of the *Historia de los indios*.

Ultimately, Motolinía's message conveys the idea that, at least for his order, no real changes had taken effect after the 1539 meeting. When in the seventeenth century the Augustinian Juan de Grijalva revisited the historical beginnings of his order's activities in Mexico, he could not but acknowledge the impact of the early debate while taking pains to pinpoint how his own brothers had first gone about baptizing the Mexicans. Significantly, he noted that his source for the period in question—the writings of his fellow Augustinian Martín de Coruña—lacked sufficient information, even though it did mention that early baptisms had been carried out with all the required solemnity.[75] On the frequency of baptisms, Grijalva stated that the first friars had decided in favor of four times a year, not without having given serious consideration to ancient usage that prescribed only two.[76] Reporting on the debate, in which the Augustinians aligned themselves with the Dominicans—a fact that Grijalva chose to omit—he was forced to explain how his order had first proceeded in the baptism of the Mexican Indians. His account is, at best, tentative but nonetheless revealing in his hinting at a certain continuity in baptismal practices before and after the 1539 ecclesiastical meeting, which had by then become a historical watershed for the Spanish friars. In retrospect the distinctions seemed less harsh, at least for certain authors. In a letter dating from 1562 addressed to his superior Fr. Francisco Bustamante, Mendieta greatly underplayed the early quarrels among religious orders over the sacraments. Such caution came at a time when the religious orders forged a common front against the Crown's designs to curtail their influence in favor of the secular clergy. Mendieta wrote:

> That there may be once differences over the administration of doctrine and the sacraments between the bishops and the friars or among the friars themselves should neither frighten nor scandalize anyone, for such differences are nothing new even among very perfect servants of God nor are they founded in malice, but rather in all sincerity of conscience, because great men and saintly prelates of the Church had disagreements among themselves, motivated in each case by holy zeal.[77]

Baptism and Coercion: The Mudejars of Valencia

As we have seen, Motolinía interpreted the dispute on the baptism of adults as having revolved around the dichotomy between a strict adherence to the formal aspects of the ritual and a less rigid approach that found its justification in the need to expedite the conversion of countless Indians. Contemporary scholars who have contributed invaluable documentation on this controversy have cast it in similar terms, sometimes going to great lengths to show how the Franciscans were acting within the limits of accepted ecclesiastical practice.[78] It is worth noting that in Motolinía's cursory treatment of the bull the pope's judgment regarding the abridged baptisms performed by the Franciscans until that time goes unmentioned.[79] The papal document in fact upheld those baptisms, deeming them valid. This outcome was not unexpected, given that church authorities rarely pronounced baptisms invalid, opting instead for recommending measures that would ensure that the baptized would remain within the new faith. In recognizing the validity of those baptisms a new set of difficulties were thus averted; the Franciscans did not see their past labor put entirely into question, and more importantly, the Mexican Indians who had been baptized by the friars had their Christian status confirmed.[80]

Motolinía's silence surrounding the papal validation of the baptisms performed by the Franciscans merits a short examination. His account seems to be haunted not only by recent events in Spain, but also by earlier episodes of religious conversion in which the cultural distance between missionaries and prospective converts made the formulation of consistent missionary methodologies quite simply useless.

In sixteenth-century Spain concerns regarding the validity of baptisms surfaced in the context of the Crown's changing policies to bring about the conversion of the Muslim population. Initiatives urging gradual conversion fostered by instruction were often cut short by political measures that left the Muslims facing a choice between embracing Catholicism and leaving the territories within a set time limit. Even though conversions that took place under the impending threat of expulsion could legally be described as falling short of having been involuntary acts, the specter of forced conversions would long hover over the Crown's decisions.[81] But while baptism was thought to be the fundamental step toward religious unity, it also signaled, on the practical side of things, the beginning of new difficulties. The possibility that Muslims who had been baptized en masse might, due to a lack of proper religious instruction, not have been familiar with the basics of Christian tenets, the meaning of the baptismal ritual as well as the obligations attached to it, proved, at least to some sectors of the governing elite, especially troubling. Motolinía's mention of prebaptismal instruction for adults as a requisite for the reception of the sacrament in the early days of conversion can be read as aiming to dispel preexisting doubts about the willingness of the Indians to be baptized. There were good reasons for such doubts.

Between 1519 and 1522 the kingdom of Valencia was shaken by an antiseigneurial rebellion initiated by artisans of the Valencian guilds, or *germanías,* who would soon have the enthusiastic support of large numbers of farmers and peasants. The revolt of the *agermanats* against the nobility and the royal authority of the new king Charles I was also a violent response to a deepening economic crisis—a dwindling of the agrarian production, inflation, higher rents—made more acute by the threat posed by foreign competition, especially from Italy, to local manufacturers of textiles.[82]

The Muslim population of Valencia had remained untouched by the campaigns of forced conversions witnessed in Castile at that time.[83] Placed under the protection of the nobility, these Valencian Mudejars had been able to preserve their religious autonomy in exchange for payment of rents considerably higher than the ones exacted from their Christian counterparts. In the summer of 1521, however, as the revolt was reaching its peak, the Mudejars became targets of violence at the hands of the armed rebels. In addition to property damage, the consecration of mosques into churches, and killings, the outbreak of anti-Muslim violence came to include forced baptisms. Both the baptisms and the slaughter of six hundred Mudejars appear to have been carried out by the followers of Vincent Peris, one of the most important military leaders of the uprising.[84] Some sought baptism out of fear for their lives; others were hastily baptized in large groups, in some instances, probably, by laymen.

By the time the revolt was crushed as a result of the successful campaign of Diego Hurtado de Mendoza, count of Mélito,[85] hundreds of Mudejars had been brought to the Catholic faith under some kind of coercion or other, often in baptismal ceremonies that dispensed with the observation of the ritual formalities prescribed by the church. Among the irregularities that seem to have plagued the proceedings, besides the lack of appropriate religious instruction, the sources point to the absence of chrism, the use of nonconsecrated water, as well as baptisms by aspersion, administered with brooms, branches, and the aspergillum that the Franciscans came to be accused of using in Mexico years later.[86]

The outcome of such events left authorities facing new difficulties since an important number of those Mudejars baptized in the midst of the upheaval had returned to practicing the Muslim religion as the conflict died out. They did so after having been reassured by their lords that the state of affairs prior to the revolt would soon be restored and, with it, the autonomy of religion and customs that they had once enjoyed. Those Mudejars who reverted to their former religion were now legally subject to sanctions, a course of action that the Spanish authorities were not too ready to embrace because of legal and, most importantly, political reasons. Given the unusual and confusing circumstances surrounding the baptisms, as well as the adverse reaction on the part of the Valencian lords that the Crown could certainly face, any immediate action against the alleged backsliders had to wait until a consultation with a body of experts took place.

In February 1524 Charles I issued a call for a meeting with theologians and jurists with a view to designing and implementing adequate measures to deal with the delicate situation posed by the Mudejars. Cardinal Alonso de Manrique, archbishop of Seville and the recently appointed inquisitor general, took a special interest in the affair. It presented him with an opportunity to formulate a policy that could later be applied to similar cases.[87] In 1535, this same Cardinal Manrique would appoint the archbishop Fr. Juan de Zumárraga general inquisitor in Mexico.[88] The Inquisition of Valencia, headed by the *licenciado* Churruca, received instructions from the general inquisitor and the king to inquire as to how and when the Mudejars affected had been baptized, together with a recommendation to show leniency toward them. In 1525 the ensuing report was discussed at the Franciscan monastery in Madrid, where the king himself and the presidents of the royal councils had gathered, including Fr. García de Loaysa, representing the Council of the Indies.[89] Among those attending the meeting was the Franciscan Antonio de Guevara, preacher to the king, who would soon after be sent to Valencia on a mission to impart religious instruction and further the conversions of the Muslims.[90]

As to the controversial conversions, the opinion resulting from the discussions yielded no surprises: the baptisms were to be considered valid, which meant that for all legal purposes the Mudejars baptized during the uprising were Christians. Despite the reassuring words of the Valencian nobility to its Muslim vassals, the rebellion of the *agermanats* marked the end of their fragile alliance and sealed the fate of the Mudejars. A desperate attempt at regaining their previous social status took the form of armed revolts in Espadán and Benaguacil, which were put down between February and March 1526.[91]

The events in Valencia are but one more example of the capacity of ritual to open up new meanings in changing contexts. There seems to lurk in ritual the potential to put into question too narrow notions of context that historians have frequently attempted to grapple with as well as escape from. Franz Kafka's humorous parable of the jaguars casually drinking from ceremonial pitchers to see their action later synchronized with, and incorporated into, the ritual is an example that comes to mind.[92]

The Valencian case also suggests that because ritual actions and meanings can be modified and changed, in the process, certain concepts of social action, such as violence, and distinctions, such as sacred and secular, legitimate and illegitimate, are also transformed. Regarding the baptisms under discussion, the boundaries blend between physical aggression and the ritual actions anchored in the particular symbolic syntax of the sacrament. Thus, from a common ground in which the Mudejars' familiarity with the Christian ritual converges with the rebels' cognizance of this fact, baptism assumes all the features of an act of violence. To grasp at a conceptual level the implications of what I have sketched, we could start by revising the category of ritual violence that has hitherto proved helpful in understanding the unspoken rules governing the interactions and clashes among religious groups.[93]

We have seen how in both Valencia and Mexico, albeit with different intensity, the issue of ritual integrity was raised by way of casting doubt on the legitimacy of conversion. In Mexico, these concerns were voiced by religious groups; in Valencia we encounter the protest of the Muslims themselves and of few religious dissident voices. Concerning the Mudejars, the question of ritual integrity was subordinated but inextricably linked to the difficulty posed by allegations of conversions exacted by force, charges that lent the case enough weight to merit examination before authorities and theologians. That this consultation did take place, regardless of the fact that, as Charles Lea pointed out long ago, the king himself had simultaneously cleared the Inquisition to handle the alleged backsliders, remains significant.[94]

Force is nowhere to be found mentioned in the Mexican case; in its stead, there are intimations that because of lack of thorough instruction, compounded by hurried and altered baptismal ceremonies, the full assent of the baptized Indians may have been compromised. These are the charges that the Franciscan historians felt pressed to address: Motolinía in oblique fashion, Mendieta and Torquemada, head on.

Torquemada's treatment of the baptismal controversy is particularly instructive. Often dismissed for his liberal use of historical sources, Torquemada is nonetheless a very useful writer if we are willing to see his work for what he intended it to be: a careful attempt to tie up the loose ends that he found in the historical writings of his predecessors. Especially invested in offering a unified and polished worldview of the Franciscans in Mexico, Torquemada did so by supplying arguments based on a wide array of authorities. This feature betrays a very different approach to the record of the past and to the new reality of the Franciscans in Mexico. Early accusations about the Franciscans baptizing by aspersion having already been denied by Motolinía, Torquemada went a step further to show that the practice itself had a place in church history starting with the primitive church and reaching to the conversion of the Muslims in Granada.[95]

Searching for possible historical antecedents to the missionary enterprise in Mexico, scholars have turned their attention to the methods implemented by the Spaniards in the conversion of the Morisco population of Granada.[96] The appropriateness of such focus remains fully justified given the special attention paid in Franciscan sources from Mexico to the conversion of the Moriscos.[97] Because of its unique trajectory and development, the particular chapter in the history of the Valencian Mudejars that took place in the years immediately before the Franciscans' departure for Mexico can hardly be said to offer any lesson in matters of conversion methodology. The importance of these episodes in our present context lies elsewhere. For although the circumstances were extraordinary, the baptism of the Mudejars of Valencia did raise issues that had a direct bearing on the practical and legal dimensions of religious conversion. The most central of these was the extent to which rapid or forced conversion was enforceable, and the same issue also arose in Mexico. The questions that authorities in the Peninsula, more or less disingenuously, set out to tackle find their echo in the Mexican accounts of the baptismal controversy.

The Question of Baptismal Instruction

Despite its image of simplicity associated with the powerful symbolism of water, the early baptism of the Mexican Indians proved anything but a simple endeavor. While the 1539 meeting had sought to settle the dispute over how and when baptisms were to be performed, there had remained all along disagreements on the kind of instruction that adult Indians should receive before being accepted for baptism.[98] To a certain extent, diversity of opinion on this issue seemed unavoidable, since the recurring preoccupation over the scope and depth of doctrinal knowledge expected from a recent convert before baptism had accompanied the development of Christianity from its beginnings. The evolution of this sacrament had been intimately linked to the answers this question elicited at several points in the history of the church.

In 1539 the Dominican theologian Francisco de Vitoria, who held the Prime Chair of Theology at Salamanca, was asked by the king to produce an opinion based on the information concerning the instruction and conversion of the Mexican Indians presented by the Augustinian Fr. Juan de Oseguera to the Council of the Indies.[99] By that time the situation of the American colonies was indeed very much present in Vitoria's mind; in that same year Vitoria offered his views on the rights of the Spanish Crown to the new territories in two lectures at the university.[100] A similar royal request was issued in 1541; this time the pressure on the Crown to demand proper religious instruction of all those to be baptized stemmed from the vocal Dominican Fr. Bartolomé de Las Casas.[101] The future bishop of Chiapas had been in Mexico during the years that saw the controversy about baptism unfold. It is assumed that Motolinía's animosity toward Las Casas might date back to this period.[102]

The opinion sought by the king was finally issued on July 1, 1541, carrying the signatures of Vitoria, Domingo de Soto, and other theologians.[103] In essence, the document views prebaptismal instruction as the cornerstone that would ensure the new converts a full participation in a Christian life. In Vitoria's case, this view was entirely consistent with his position regarding the forcible conversion of unbelievers expounded in his lectures on Aquinas's *Secunda Secundae* in the years 1534–35, which had direct bearing on the situation of the Muslims in the Peninsula and the Amerindians. In commenting on Aquinas's text, Vitoria delved into the relationship between ignorance of the Christian doctrine and coercion in order to highlight that the baptism of uninstructed unbelievers should be considered a formal kind of coercion since it may be potentially harmful for the right development of a true Christian.[104]

As to the duration of the instruction, it was left unspecified, and not by accident, since the notion of instruction advanced by the theologians of Salamanca departed in significant ways from the rather restricted concept of religious instruction implied in the second royal request. The opinion stressed that the instruction of the Indians was to encompass both doctrinal matters and Christian customs as taught by the Gospels: "Those heathen barbarians should not be baptized without having previously received proper instruction, not only in matters concerning faith, but also in Christian mores."[105] An unspecified number of native customs, qualified as perverse and vicious, were declared to be incompatible with a Christian life and therefore needed to be uprooted by means of instruction.[106] Christian baptism, then, finds its true meaning only when seen as a thorough individual transformation achieved by doctrinal as well as moral instruction.

By redefining the notion of prebaptismal instruction that they had been handed, Vitoria and his colleagues restored baptism to the preeminent place that it had enjoyed in the beginnings of Christianity. For it was in the primitive church where the theologians of Salamanca found the all-encompassing and dynamic notion of Christian initiation that they proposed for the American Indians. At its core lay the acknowl-edgment of the intimate connection between baptism and the sacrament of the Eucharist.[107] According to this perspective, then, once instruction had done its job, there was no room to postulate or demand a moral and spiritual distinction between those individuals ready to receive bap-tism and those prepared for communion. Nevertheless, while from an individual perspective this instruction would grant, ideally, an equal access to both sacraments, baptism and the Eucharist were not on equal standing. Baptism took place once; communion, on the other hand, was expected to occupy a central role through the life of a Christian, both acknowledging and rewarding the moral and spiritual commitment of its recipient.

The opinion drafted by the theologians of Salamanca amounted to an entire reelaboration of the question posed by the Crown; it amounted, in fact, to a proposal outlining the basic principles that should guide the evangelization of the new royal subjects. Instead of approaching the problem from a purely practical viewpoint, the opin-ion made religious conversion, conceived as a process in its own right, the center of all possible discussion on Christian initiation and the role of the sacraments. The First Mexican Church Council that took place in Mexico City in 1555 ordered that no adult, Indian or black, should be baptized without previous doctrinal instruction.[108]

The initial discussions about adult baptism evolved, almost by necessity, into the formulation of two distinct approaches to the evan-gelization of the Mexican Indians. By the time the bishops first dealt with the need for uniformity in baptism in 1536, the lines had been drawn; however, these two main conceptions did not find their more articulate expression simultaneously, nor did they develop exclusively in response to each other. The opinion signed by Vitoria and his associ-ates echoed the spirit of Las Casas's comprehensive vision of conversion found in *De unico modo vocationis,* a treatise conceived and written in 1534 that had considerable influence on the discussion about baptism.[109] There, Las Casas provided the Dominicans with a set of principles that in theory, if not in practice, became a central feature of their ideological outlook and self-definition. To give an example, we can turn to Dávila Padilla's history where the Dominican makes a point of presenting the conversion of the Mexican Indians as having proceeded along these lines.[110]

As for the Franciscans, the most salient features of their program started to be heard and articulated with increasing poignancy when the Crown unveiled its plans to have parish priests gradually replace the friars in the pastoral care of the Indian population. In reaction to the Crown's design the Franciscans joined ranks with the other religious orders, forging a common front to oppose it. The image of diverse religious orders working together on a common agenda, sharing the same assessment of the orders' accomplishments and objectives found in the official documents, owes much to this particular move. In 1557 the orders jointly issued a document opposing the collection of tithes from Mexican Indians, the proceeds of which would be destined to support new parish priests. By this time, the friars felt comfortable enough to assure the Crown that there was no real need for new ministers to baptize children, tend to marriages, and celebrate Mass, with the exception of a shortage for the administration of confession.[111] With this declaration the friars were openly acknowledging that regarding the areas under their direct control the initial stage of the spiritual conquest could be said to be over, as indicated by a shift from the baptism of adults to that of children.

There emerged in the writings of Fr. Jerónimo de Mendieta a picture of the Franciscan missionary experience that became the basis of his argument against entrusting the spiritual care of the Mexican Indians to the secular clergy.[112] Mendieta's concerns embraced both the future conversion of the remaining non-Christian Indians, as well as the pastoral care of those who had already turned to Christianity under the friars' guidance. This latter group, Mendieta argued, required a kind of supervision that the friars, as the only group thoroughly acquainted with the habits and particular weaknesses of the new converts, could provide. A preoccupation with ensuring the success of the conversion by means of an open-ended tutelage of the converts seems now to have displaced any questions left concerning the passage of the Mexican Indians to the new faith. By depicting the new converts as feeble in matters of faith, Mendieta was then able to propose a solution to this problem by presenting a model of authority that required the reimagining of the relationship among Indians, ministers, and secular institutions. With regard to their moral development as individuals, adult Mexican Indians were compared with ten- or twelve-year-old children in need of sustained discipline and oversight.[113] In essence, such characterization was far from new since, early on, the friars had expressed their belief that the Mexican Indians appeared only to be capable of acting under threats of punishment, as children were.[114] It was later, however, when the future of the orders' hegemony could no longer be taken for granted, that the image of childlike Indians would become a fundamental assumption for the elaboration of the Franciscan agenda. According to this line of thought, the friars' authority over the Indians was to resemble the authority of a father over his offspring, which included the parental right to impart punishments to correct offenses and improper behavior.[115] This view had serious institutional implications, the most obvious of which was the impingement of the ecclesiastical sphere on matters of secular justice. Franciscans such as Mendieta, with their aversion to the rank of letrados, did not hesitate to cast doubt over the effectiveness and validity of the Spanish legal system for Indian affairs.[116]

Each of the two viewpoints briefly sketched here assign widely different significance to the role of Christian initiation in the promotion of a new generation of adult Indian converts. The papal bull *Altitudo divini consilii,* which reflected in part the Dominican and Augustinian positions and was finally endorsed by the bishops in Mexico, upheld the traditional practice of baptism of adults by refusing to accept an abridged ceremony as the norm. While the Franciscans were ready to dismiss this move as an unnecessary subjection to mere ritual formalism, the words of the theologians of Salamanca helped dispel this charge by advocating an informed participation of the individual in baptism, made possible by proper instruction. By explicitly stating that the articles of faith were but one element in the education of the convert, an education also intended to affect native customs, the theologians' document recognized and warned against the possibility of reducing religious instruction to its formal and ritualistic elements, to a mere transfer of doctrinal formulae.

It would be tempting to capture in a generalization each religious order's attitude toward ritual as a tool for conversion. It is to some extent safe to say that for the early Franciscans, and some of their followers, ritual formalism was a burden from which ritual itself had to be purged. Ritual formalism built a separation between Indians and friars that conspired against the Franciscan idea of authority and tutelage based on an interpersonal experience unmediated by the constraints of secular law and authority. The more in-depth elaboration of Christian initiation found in the works of Vitoria and his fellow theologians acknowledges the dangers of ritual formalism but at the same time fights these dangers by placing ritual—and not ritual authority—in a direct and intimate connection to the initiate. In this sense ritual is seen as an integral part of individual experience, and one in which the Mexican Indians could partake. This particular way of conceptualizing the relationship between convert and ritual appears to be absent in the Franciscan accounts.

CHAPTER TWO

The Uses of a Sacrament

Confirmation and Spiritual Maturity

The Spiritual Age of the Christian Nahuas

Around 1537, Friar Toribio de Benavente, better known as Motolinía, pointed out that in a ten-year span Indian converts to Christianity had experienced an extraordinary spiritual growth. Motolinía cited as proof of this remarkable fact the Indians' adoption of practices of inner devotion and their own statements indicating that their faith kept growing stronger.[1] The Franciscan illustrated his assertion by reporting the case of three or four young men who resolved in 1527 to prepare themselves for the priesthood. Shortly afterwards, however, they changed their minds, having realized that they were not quite ready for religious life. By 1537, when Motolinía was writing, the young men were married and living as good Christians.[2]

In contrast to the spiritual condition of the Indians in 1527, Motolinía considered that in only ten years their Christian sentiment had progressed to such an extent that it was inevitable that some Mexicans would soon be entering the priesthood. Reflecting on their failure, the young men later declared to Motolinía that in those early days they were not sufficiently prepared for pursuing the priesthood: "And since their [Christian] sentiment now is different from that of back then, they say that then they were like children."[3] Those words placed in the mouths of the four young men closely follow the recommendations of Paul concerning the careful and gradual manner in which doctrinal content should be presented to those recently initiated in Christian doctrine.[4] The Indians who had failed in their religious vocation had not first taken in the "soft food" that was appropriate to their condition as children in the faith. Nonetheless, the purpose of Motolinía's anecdote was not to point to a failure but, instead, to illustrate the spiritual transformation of the Nahuas under the direction of the Franciscans. The young men, after all, had been converted into good Christians.

Motolinía's observation coincides with others that underscore the rapid spiritual growth of the converts, testimony of which can be found both in their adoption of elaborate and systematic forms of devotion and their regular participation in the Christian sacraments. At the same time, the story of the young men conscious of their own spiritual development serves as evidence in favor of allowing indigenous people into the priesthood, a proposal that was vigorously resisted both inside and outside of the church and which, in the end, failed.[5]

By the end of the sixteenth century and in the same Franciscan order, the idea of creating an indigenous clergy had been abandoned. The arguments against accepting the Indians into the priesthood were laid out by Fr. Jerónimo de Mendieta, who wrote that, even if the friars were to discount their well-founded fear that the Indians would fall back into their old superstitions, there remained another important reason to oppose their becoming priests: "the majority of the Indians are of a strange nature, different from that of other nations (although I do not know if some of the Greeks share this same quality), which is that they are not good for leading and ruling but rather for being led and ruled."[6]

Mendieta based his opposition to allowing Indians into the priesthood on the belief that they could not develop into autonomous individuals able to exercise authority.[7] This particular belief, widely held by the Spaniards, had by then become a commonplace intended to rationalize the form of government embodied by the Aztec state and the prominent role of the ruling elite in society. Mendieta resorted to this same idea in order to explain how the Indians under Spanish domination had been left without models for conduct and discipline, responsibilities fulfilled earlier by the indigenous nobility.[8] It should be noted that the reasoning advanced by Mendieta could otherwise have been used to defend the opposite idea, if his goal had been to emphasize another fundamental quality of a member of the priesthood: the ability to adhere to the vow of obedience so important within the hierarchical structure of the religious orders.

In spite of the indisputable ideological similarities between Motolinía and Mendieta—and the special attraction that Mendieta felt for the ideals that had inspired the initial years of evangelization in Mexico—the manner and context in which the two writers approached the question of spiritual growth of the Nahuas differ significantly. From

[handwritten marginalia: Motolinía – sustained spiritual evolution; Mendieta – "forever subject + disciples"]

the point of view of Motolinía's history, the success of the evangelization efforts could be measured by considering the sustained spiritual
evolution of the converted Nahuas. From Mendieta's perspective, however, the Indians, even though they had become Christians, were destined to be "forever subjects and disciples."[9] Whereas during the first
stage of evangelization it appeared reasonable and even desirable to
conceive of the possibility of a Christian spiritual development among
the Indians that would acknowledge a certain degree of spiritual autonomy, by the end of the sixteenth century, individual control had given
way to individual subordination to priestly authority.

Motolinía's enthusiasm for promoting the Nahuas to the priesthood
appeared justified by his particular vision of the early church, in which
the priesthood was open to recent converts. Mendieta's position, however, directly attacks the appropriateness of such a model, given the
unique situation in Mexico, where the danger of the Indians' regressing
to their old customs had not yet been eliminated.[10] The example of spiritual maturity presented by Motolinía is the culmination of his vision of
the successful transformation of the Indians' behavior within Christian
norms, a change made apparent by the role that the sacraments now
played in their lives. The ecclesiastical meeting of 1539 reflected that relationship between the sacraments and the optimism surrounding the
course of the conversion of the Nahuas in its proposal to admit literate
Indians and mestizos into the minor orders. Accepting as a given that the
Indians had been successfully converted into Christians, the bishops concluded that "they are entitled to the sacraments, since they are accepted
into baptism, which is no less important than the priesthood."[11]

The version of conversion that Motolinía recorded in his history of
the Franciscans was not necessarily accepted by other friars of the day.
In 1556, Fr. Alonso de Montúfar, then archbishop of Mexico City, gave
the Council of the Indies a far different account of the evangelization
and the fruits of that labor. Montúfar's caustic criticism of the process
was designed in part to demonstrate the impossibility of merely embracing the methods and ideals of the early church as a model for converting the Mexican Indians, a practice that was supported most vocally by
the Franciscans. As often happens with documents of this kind, Montúfar's criticism of the Franciscans goes far beyond questions of missionary methods. In this instance, the criticism is nothing less than a defense
of his ecclesiastical authority as archbishop, which was under attack by
the Franciscans, who opposed the payment of tithes by the Indians.

Montúfar wrote to the council that most Nahuas died without ever having confessed their sins to a priest, thus having experienced only one of the sacraments, baptism.[12] According to Montúfar, the Indians' infrequent participation in the sacraments was directly due to the deficient doctrinal preparation they had received. The words of Mexico City's second archbishop are pointed: "Lacking all this, a new theology is needed in order to say and believe that some of the adults will be saved."[13] While Zumárraga had recognized the novelty of the Mexican situation and had quickly seen the necessity of relying on the opinion of letrados in order to undertake the complex task of converting the Nahuas, Montúfar resisted innovations and changes in missionary policies based on the alleged uniqueness of the reality at hand. Only an entirely new theology could accommodate the kind of Christianity that was taking hold among the Nahuas.

Regardless of the varied opinions that were issuing from religious and secular quarters about the results of evangelization in New Spain, it is certain that the presence of the regular clergy during the first years of evangelization and the decisive expansion of the secular clergy during the second half of the sixteenth century resulted in a sizable number of Indians considered to be Christians. Indeed, they were considered *good* Christians, whose souls deserved the pastoral care of the church.

What kind of Christian was the fruit of evangelization in Mexico during the first decades? Although the answers to that question varied widely, the view that triumphed by the last quarter of the sixteenth century, which the Third Mexican Church Council sanctioned in 1585, held the Indian to be a neophyte in the faith who could not possibly move beyond that state and who was, therefore, in need of constant guidance.[14] Thus, a parallel to the political subjugation of the Indians appeared in the spiritual realm, where the church could not imagine that in the foreseeable future the converted Indians could reach a state of spiritual maturity.

Even though hyperbole led Motolinía to suggest that the converted Indians had come almost naturally to incorporate into their spiritual life European monastic practices, one cannot overlook the decisive role of the Franciscans in promoting among the Indians their own ideas and expectations about spiritual development through a continuous labor of instruction. As already noted, instruction in the new faith was an important question in the heated debate that culminated in the recommendation made by the ecclesiastical meeting of 1539 to adopt a manual for instruction to ensure the uniformity of doctrinal teaching among the Nahuas. At an important series of meetings in 1546, bishops in Mexico considered in greater depth the question of religious instruction of the Indians and decided to have catechisms written and published.[15] The bishops identified two classes of converted Indians whose respective knowledge of Christian doctrine determined their instructional needs: the novices and the proficient. To meet the differing needs, they ordered two catechisms, one basic and the other more extensive and detailed.[16] In spite of their efforts to produce catechisms in indigenous languages, the friars often found that their expectations that the Nahuas would gain knowledge of Christian doctrine were hard to meet. Throughout the sixteenth century, there was concern about the strength of the faith of the new converts and the kind of knowledge of doctrine to be expected of them. In their chronicles and other documents, the religious clearly show that evaluating the spiritual maturity of the Indians under their care was no mean feat. Only through the reconciliation of a diversity of experiences, expectations, and opinions could a consensus on that question be reached.

Mexican missionaries often found themselves reflecting on the results of their activities among the Indians and evaluating their spiritual condition. What was the spiritual state of the Indians several years after their conversion to the Catholic faith? What were the characteristics of a perfect Christian within this new context? These are some of the questions that appear regularly in the sources. Both religious and secular officials wondered about the kind of Christianity that the Amerindians could and ought to embrace. The future society and culture that missionaries envisaged for their new flock depended on that difficult issue. While we possess excellent studies that provide a picture of the linguistic and cultural changes, we have no similar picture of the intellectual infrastructure that accompanied those changes.

We should therefore consider the problem of the spiritual maturity of the Indians by examining the place of the sacrament of confirmation— the anointing of the forehead with oil and the laying on of hands by a bishop in New Spain. From the perspective of sacramental theology, the meaning of confirmation is directly related to the growth and spiritual maturity of Christians. Through documents and catechisms, one can trace the increasing importance that confirmation acquired in the thought and practice of the religious. It is in a sermon by Fr. Alonso de Molina, overlooked by scholars, where the call to confirm converted

Indians can be read as a response to and a resolution of the question concerning the spiritual maturity of the Indians. Alonso de Molina offered us an eloquent example that serves as a starting point for our consideration of how some religious confronted the problem of determining the spiritual improvement of the Indians after fifty years of church activity in Mexico.

Confirmation as Sacrament

As seen in the introduction, Aquinas developed a scheme of correspondences between the seven sacraments and the human life cycle. In his model, confirmation appears identified with the growth and strengthening of the individual. If through baptism one is born into Christian life, the sacrament of confirmation helps spiritual growth by strengthening faith and by increasing the grace received in baptism, thus contributing to the perfection of the Christian.[17] Although confirmation, unlike baptism, is not indispensable for salvation, it is indispensable to achieve another goal: perfection.[18]

Of course, an explanation of spiritual growth and the sacraments through a comparison to human biological and social development will fail to account for those particular features of Christian spiritual life that do not have a neat correspondence in the natural or social world. The autonomous character of the soul and the spiritual world, both of which exist outside of linear time, marks them as radically different from the physical and social worlds of human beings. Thus, the development of spiritual maturity may not necessarily follow the physical development of the individual, a discrepancy that, according to Aquinas, may allow a child ("in puerile aetate homo") to be spiritually mature.[19] In addition, we should remember that there is no specific age for one to be received into the church and to participate in the power of grace. The system that fixes the sacraments in chronological order, that distributes them throughout the year, and that also specifies the age at which the faithful may receive them serves as a reminder of the obligations of Christians. Those obligations, translated into action, constitute a model of Christian conduct that starts at birth.

This is not the place to review in detail the different conceptions of the spiritual ages of man and their relationship with the various representations of physical ages.[20] However, the tensions that result from associating too closely the stages of spiritual development with those of physical development, while at the same time affirming the irreducible character of spiritual life with respect to physical life, have important consequences. One of them became apparent in the disagreements over the age at which a Christian should receive the sacrament of confirmation.

At the time of the church fathers, the sacrament known today as confirmation was not an independent ritual but rather, along with baptism, a part of the rite of initiation into Christian life.[21] The authority of the bishop for laying on of hands was supported by the practice of the apostles, recorded in the Acts of the Apostles (19:6 and 8:17). Because the growth of the church made it difficult for bishops to be present to perform their part of the initiation rite, there were often long lapses of time between baptism and the acts reserved for the bishops. Consequently, on a number of occasions, priests took responsibility for that part of the ritual.[22] In addition to the problems arising from the absence of a bishop, the rite was met with indifference among the people since it certainly could not compete as symbolic drama with the first half of the initiation rite, baptism.[23] Such circumstances contributed to the progressive disintegration of the early rite and the emergence of the sacrament of confirmation with an identity of its own. The term "confirmation," which, referring to a ritual action distinct from baptism, did not come into use until the fifth century, combined in its meaning the ideas of fortification and perfection of the spirit.[24] It was at this time, and especially after the practice of infant baptism had become the norm, that confirmation spread throughout Europe, maintaining significant local variations with respect to the appropriate age of the confirmands.

In England during the thirteenth century, we find differing opinions about the age at which confirmation should be administered. Some held that baptized infants should be confirmed within their first year of life. Others recommended confirmation when children were three years old. Still others, favored the age of five.[25] In Spain, the catechism of Pedro de Cuéllar (1325) emphasizes the unity of baptism and confirmation, distributing the seven gifts of the Holy Ghost among the different steps that include both rites.[26] On the one hand, this catechism presents baptism and confirmation as components of the original initiation rite ("one should not be left without the other"); on the other, it recognizes in confirmation some characteristics unique to it. Thus, a baptized individual should be confirmed "in order to be stronger and better armed against devils,"²⁷ and in this way the confirmand becomes a part of the army of Christ, a theme to which we return shortly. With respect to the age of the confirmands, the metaphor of the Christian soldier appears to justify the opinion that "they do not send little children into battle against enemies until they are older and stronger: thus we speak of the baptized."²⁸

For Pedro de Cuéllar, one should not fail to receive the sacrament of confirmation, but if one were not confirmed until the age of seven (the age of reason), Cuéllar saw no problem since the delay could not be attributed to negligence on the part of the Christian. While the comparison with the soldier suggests that this sacrament is not completely necessary for baptized infants, this catechism, nonetheless, stresses the desirability of administrating it to children under seven years of age.²⁹

As the sixteenth century progressed, the idea of confirming children who had reached the age of reason was becoming more and more widespread in Europe (fig. 6):³⁰ the *Catecismo Romano,* for example, recommends it.³¹ Sixteenth-century Spanish synodal legislation shows the coexistence of both trends regarding confirmation.³² The synod of Plascencia of 1589 explicitly prohibited the confirmation of children under ten years of age.³³

The controversial archbishop of Toledo, Bartolomé Carranza de Miranda, acknowledged the differing opinions concerning the appropriate age of candidates for confirmation in his *Comentarios sobre el catecismo christiano* (Antwerp, 1558).³⁴ According to Carranza, in the early church, Christians who had reached the age of discretion presented themselves before the bishops first to be examined in the catechism and then to be confirmed.³⁵ Carranza also made reference to the reformer Jean Gerson, who believed that children should be confirmed before they reached the age of reason. Carranza, in contrast, supported the practice that he said had prevailed in the early church:

> It always seemed to me that children were to wait until the age of discretion and follow the oldest tradition of the church, that they be instructed in the religion that they had professed in baptism and, afterwards, examined and confirmed when they were at least 12 or 15 years old.³⁶

For Carranza, that age range was very important, for within the human life cycle it corresponded to the beginning of the war "against the world, the devil, and the flesh." Once again, it is the image of the Christian soldier that determines the opinion about the appropriate age for confirmation. This image is further validated by Carranza's references to sexual development and the entrance of the individual into the social world. We also find in Carranza's work a particular interest in the examination of confirmation candidates in doctrinal matters as a necessary step to gain access to the sacrament, an interest that we have already seen expressed by Aquinas, whom Carranza followed closely. According to Carranza, faith strengthened by confirmation helps the Christian to proclaim his faith outwardly, and for that reason, he needs an adequate knowledge of doctrine.[37]

Carranza's opinion was shared by his less controversial Dominican brother Fr. Luis de Granada, who in his *Compendio y explicación de la doctrina cristiana* (Lisbon, 1559) wrote,

> Now it is the custom to confirm infants in the arms of their mothers; it would seem more appropriate to wait until they reached the age of discretion so that they might remember and even know Christian doctrine; that practice was the custom in times of old. And when they had sufficient understanding, they were taken to the bishop, and there they made a confession of faith and Catholic obedience; and with this they released their godparents of the duty that they had promised to their godchildren.[38]

Both Carranza and Fr. Luis de Granada assigned great importance to the knowledge of Christian doctrine, which they saw as a crucial component of the sacrament of confirmation. In infant baptism, this component was absent, so godparents had to be present to take the responsibility of answering on behalf of the infant. In its reduction of the sacramental character of confirmation, the Reformation was to emphasize precisely doctrinal instruction as the means to consolidate knowledge of youngsters in matters of faith, thus transforming the ritual into a univocal expression of the individual's entrance into social puberty.[39]

Up to this point I have briefly outlined an aspect of the problem of spiritual maturity, focusing on a sacrament whose significance is explicitly linked to the idea of spiritual growth. Next I analyze the relation between confirmation and spiritual maturity in the context of evangelization in sixteenth-century New Spain and look first at the administration of the sacrament among the indigenous population and then at the place confirmation held in some Mexican catechisms.

Confirmation in Mexico

According to Mendieta's history, in the first years of evangelization and before the arrival of the first bishop, confirmation had been administered in New Spain by a single individual, the Franciscan Motolinía.[40] Motolinía's authority to administer a sacrament usually reserved to bishops issued from a papal privilege granted by Leon X in 1525. The papal document allowed the friars, in the absence of bishops, to administer all the sacraments, including confirmation and holy orders.[41] The Council of Trent (1545–63) firmly established the need for episcopal authority to administer confirmation.[42]

An engraving in Fr. Diego Valadés's *Rhetorica christiana* (Perugia, 1579) illustrates the activities of the first Franciscans in New Spain (fig. 7). It depicts religious instruction and the administration of baptism, marriage, and confession in the new sacred space of Indian churches designed by the Mendicant orders.[43] The engraving does not show Motolinía confirming the Indians, as he is described doing in Mendieta's account. Nonetheless, confirmation does appear in another engraving by the Tlaxcalan friar (fig. 8). Here the ecclesiastical hierarchy is represented in the form of a tree; each branch corresponds to a specific office and its responsibilities; the bishop is seen administering the sacraments reserved to him: holy orders and confirmation. In this case the confirmed person is a young man.

Two bishops who happened to belong to the Franciscan order received special attention in Mendieta's *Historia eclesiástica indiana*: Fr. Juan de Zumárraga, first archbishop of Mexico, and Fr. Martín de Hojacastro, second bishop of Tlaxcala (1546–58). Mendieta reported that the two bishops confirmed numerous Indians during their visits to the towns in their respective bishoprics.[44] For Mendieta, the bishops' dedication to their duties was exemplary, with both men having gone so far as to neglect their own health in order to fulfill the exhausting task of making episcopal visits. In Zumárraga's last letter to the king, written May 30, 1548, just days before the archbishop's death, he described his activities:

[I]t is true that there was a 40-day period during which, with the help of the friars, I began to confirm the Indians of this city, and making sure that they should not receive confirmation more than once, they numbered over 400,000 souls who received the oil and were confirmed. They showed so much fervor that they waited in the monastery for three or more days to receive it, and even then it seemed like they had only begun to arrive; others will attribute my death to my ministering to so many, but I consider it life.[45]

Zumárraga's testimony is corroborated by a pictographic document from Tepechpan in the Valley of Mexico (fig. 9). The drawing shows the figure of the bishop sitting in front of a kneeling Indian wearing a cloth wrapped around his forehead.[46]

Among the numerous difficulties encountered by the friars in the administration of baptism and confirmation was the lack of the elements essential for the two rites. In a letter of November 30, 1537, dealing with the preparations for the General Council of Mantua, the bishops of Mexico, Oaxaca, and Guatemala expressed to Spanish authorities their concern over the scarcity of oil and chrism from Spain. They also commented on the difficulty in following the ceremonies prescribed by the church to consecrate holy oils every year on Holy Thursday.[47] Traditionally, the ceremony of consecration mandated the presence of numerous ministers, a requirement that was difficult to meet in the bishoprics far from Mexico City, which had only a few ministers. The cost of the elements only added to the bishops' challenge.

Chrism was indispensable for baptism and confirmation ("it fortifies the virtue of the soul, and it is just and proper that all should enjoy it"[48]) as well as for the ordination of presbyters and the consecration of bishops. In their letter, the bishops requested papal authorization to use balsam produced in Mexico "since it is a natural liquid distilled from trees, marvelous and very effective for illnesses and injuries."[49] A similar request to the emperor on November 1, 1555, as a result of the First Mexican Church Council, makes reference to the scarcity of balsam from Spain and, once again, cites economic factors, such as the elevated price of the Spanish product and the wonderful effects of its local counterpart, as valid enough reasons to allow the use of the Mexican equivalent.[50]

The *hoitziloxitl* tree, from which the balsam mentioned by the bishops is extracted, came to be known as "balsam of the Indies" because of its association with the "balsam of Syria," from which the substance used in baptism and confirmation came (fig. 10).[51] The opinion of the bishops is a good indicator of how rapidly the Spaniards had become familiar with Nahua pharmacopoeia. In 1562 Pope Pius IV granted to the bishops the right to consecrate balsam of the Indies, allowing the ceremony to be carried out with however many ministers were available.[52]

In 1541 the first bishop of Tlaxcala, the Dominican Fr. Julián Garcés, described in a letter to Charles V how he routinely administered the sacraments:

> I perform baptisms three days a week and then I confirm those whom I baptize, *quoniam episcopus nunquam baptizat nisi confirmat.* Each week I baptize 320 or 330, never fewer than 300 and always more. Where so many are born and incomparably fewer die, imagine how many people there were![53]

The letter seems to indicate that baptism and confirmation were performed together, thus reflecting the practice of the early church. Concerning age, Garcés did not explicitly mention whether he was baptizing and confirming adults or children, but his last comment about children suggests that he may have also confirmed infants. Later I discuss how Archbishop Zumárraga also recommended the confirmation of small children.

Juan López de Zárate, who became the first bishop of Oaxaca in 1535, wrote to Prince Philip (later King Philip II of Spain) about the terrible situation regarding the administration of the sacraments in his bishopric. Among the reasons for the lamentable state of Christianity in the region, the bishop mentioned the vast size of his jurisdiction, the perpetual shortage of friars, and the widespread poverty of the indigenous population; poverty, in particular, made it extremely difficult to carry out episcopal visits, which were costly. Commenting on the burden those limitations placed upon his episcopal tasks, López de Zárate wrote,

> And although I myself perform baptisms and have baptized and confirmed an infinite number of persons, I cannot do all that is required for such sacraments, because rather than spending the time that I should in each town, I must go hurriedly from place to place, for the people are poor and cannot afford to feed me.[54]

The bishop's characterization of the effects of poverty on the population is puzzling, for immediately after writing that the economic conditions of the towns prevented the Indians from feeding him and his entourage, he added about these very same Indians under his authority that "they are as dedicated to acquiring and saving as those who have more: and now it is not like in the past, when they used to offer food and presents."[55] In spite of these difficulties, compounded by the lack of means to sustain his retinue, López de Zárate explained that he tried to make a yearly visit to every place that he could.

We should remember that a certain amount of money was required to carry out episcopal visits, although it was common for the faithful to provide food, as the bishop revealed. Nevertheless, in its twenty-fourth session the Council of Trent ordered that visits be conducted without imposing any cost on the town visited.[56] One bishop who tried to become the kind of exemplary shepherd envisioned by the Council of Trent was Pedro Moya de Contreras, third archbishop of Mexico. Moya de Contreras conducted his first episcopal visit in the summer of 1576 and others in 1579 and 1583, but we do not know exactly how many he carried out during his tenure.[57] In a letter from 1579, written soon after his visit to the Huasteca, the archbishop told Philip II about the great number of baptisms and confirmations that had been administered in that region, which had not been visited until then due to the advanced age of his predecessors.[58]

It is important to consider another factor that had an unfavorable effect on the administration of confirmation to the indigenous population. In addition to the normal difficulties in organizing the regular episcopal visits, we must also keep in mind the periods during which the bishop's position remained unfilled. The archbishopric of Mexico, for example, was vacant for six years between the death of Zumárraga in 1548 and the consecration of the second archbishop, Fr. Alonso de Montúfar. In 1554, it was again vacant between Montúfar and his successor, Pedro Moya de Contreras. The other bishoprics experienced vacancies of similar lengths throughout the sixteenth century. In the bishopric of Tlaxcala, Fr. Martín de Hojacastro became bishop four years after the death of his predecessor, Fr. Julián Garcés, and five years passed between the death of Hojacastro and the arrival of the third bishop, Fernando de Villagómez. This troubling situation did not pass unnoticed by the friars, as Fr. Francisco de Toral showed in his letter of May 25, 1558, to the Council of the Indies. In that year, New Spain had only two bishops, Antonio de Montúfar in Mexico and Vasco de Quiroga in Michoacán, neither of whom enjoyed Toral's support. In his letter, Toral urged the council to resolve the situation "because there is no one within 300 leagues who can consecrate an altar or a chalice and no one who can confirm an Indian."[59]

A survey of the catechisms published in Mexico and Spain during the sixteenth century shows that, with few exceptions, the treatment of confirmation was concise. We begin with *Doctrina breve,* published by Juan Cromberger in Mexico in 1544 through the initiative of Juan de Zumárraga. In this catechism, confirmation is defined as "a ratification and confirmation of baptism" ("una ratificación y confirmación del bautismo"). Through this sacrament, the baptized individual ratified personally the faith that his godparents had held in trust during baptism. For this ratification the confirmed individuals should be older than seven (that is, the age of reason) and should have certain knowledge of Christian doctrine. Nonetheless, immediately after considering the age of the confirmands, Zumárraga recommended that small children be confirmed because they ran the risk of dying before reaching the age of reason: "it is more certain and approved that they be confirmed in childhood so that they not remain imperfect Christians and, lacking the grace of this sacrament, not have less grace, one modicum of which is worth more than all the riches of this world."[60]

Zumárraga's inclination to confirm children who had not reached the age of reason reflects a practice that was quite common in Spain— Fr. Luis de Granada remarked about the custom of confirming children in the arms of their mothers. Zumárraga's support for confirming small children was based on the importance of acquiring sacramental grace and its effect on the Christian's path toward perfection. He put less importance on the declaration and ratification of the faith, which required a knowledge of doctrine.

In the *Doctrina cristiana,* which Zumárraga published in 1546, the references to confirmation are few. The paragraph that introduces the section on the sacraments reads as follows:

> I should like us to move on to the doctrine of the sacraments, but these things require contemplation. We shall now tell in a few words the manner to be followed in confession and in communion and in hearing mass. The rest [of the sacraments] will wait for another day, as a matter that is longer, not so necessary, and not so much a part of everyday life.[61]

Limiting itself to offering only the means that were absolutely necessary for salvation, this catechism includes no information concerning
confirmation. The reasons for this omission require some explanation.
The *Doctrina cristiana* is nearly a faithful recasting of the *Suma de doctrina cristiana,* written by the Spanish Erasmist Constantino Ponce de la
Fuente and published in Seville in 1543.[62] While the *Suma* was written in
the form of a dialogue, the version published by Zumárraga is entirely
expository. The words in the preceding quote follow almost exactly
those of Dr. Ponce de la Fuente. The prologue to the *Suma,* which out-
lines the topics to be covered in the work, mentions only two sacraments: penance and communion. There are also a few observations concerning how best to benefit from hearing Mass.[63] Ponce de la Fuente
focused exclusively on those sacraments that were absolutely indispensable to gain salvation and whose authority could be corroborated by
the tradition of the early church;[64] therein lies Zumárraga's attraction
to this treatise in particular. Both the first archbishop of Mexico and
Ponce de la Fuente shared a similar enthusiasm for Erasmus's reenvi-
sioning of Christian life and, in particular, for his call to spiritual renovation through a return to the values and forms of devotion of the early
church. For Zumárraga, the evangelization of the Indians offered a
unique opportunity to realize the ideas of renovation expressed by
Erasmus and partially shared by the reform movement within the religious orders in Spain.[65]

What unites the sacraments selected for consideration in the *Suma*
and in the *Doctrina cristiana* of 1546 is the fact that they are precisely
those of which the faithful could and, according to the recommendation
of the church, should partake on a regular basis: penance and communion. Through regular participation in confession and communion, the
faithful could strengthen the bond between them and the church. It was
believed that frequent participation in those sacraments would lead to
the formation of a habit and, thus, to the eventual realization of a full
Christian moral life. From this perspective, then, confirmation could
not aspire to the position held by those sacraments that could play a
decisive role in the formation and development of Christian habits. As
some scholars point out, the omission of confirmation in the *Suma* may
simply reflect the lesser importance of confirmation in comparison with
the other sacraments on which the pastoral efforts in Spain were princi-
pally concentrated.[66] Nonetheless, we should not forget that, by the
time of the publication of the *Suma,* the system of seven sacraments was
already well established, yet there is no mention of it in Dr. Constan-

tino's treatise. This fact is significant, especially if we consider the catechisms and cartillas published before the *Suma*. Although different in their genesis and development as well as in their absence of elaborate doctrinal explanations, the earlier works tend to present the sacraments so that the faithful will memorize them, along with the articles of faith, the works of mercy, vices, and virtues, the five senses, and the most common prayers.[67]

The two *doctrinas* by Zumárraga mentioned thus far (he composed more than two) differ markedly. While the *Doctrina breve* presents a systematic development of Christian doctrine (articles of faith, sacraments, the ten commandments, mortal sins, and so forth) and includes a detailed description of the different forms of idolatry, the *Doctrina muy cristiana y provechosa*, taken from Ponze de la Fuente's *Suma*, lacks this systematic and all-encompassing dimension and shows greater interest in Christian conduct and the kind of devotion the true believer should aspire to develop. One can very well consider the *Doctrina breve* as a text to be used by the faithful as well as a guidebook for priests, while the work of 1546 presents a well-defined type of Christian religiosity anchored in the individual.[68]

In Mexico, Erasmus's opinion concerning confirmation was embraced by the controversial and picturesque Franciscan friar Alonso Cabello, who was persecuted by the Mexican Inquisition because of his heterodox ideas and behavior. He is said to have declared that Christians should be confirmed when they reached adulthood, but according to a ritual that differed from the traditional one.[69]

The *Doctrina cristiana breve* (1546), translated by the Franciscan Fr. Alonso de Molina and reprinted in 1571, pays scarce attention to confirmation.[70] The sacrament appears only in a list together with the others,[71] which is not surprising given that this work was intended to provide only a succinct exposition of Christian doctrine. Franciscan sources tell us about the obligations of the *tequitlatos* (town officers in charge of assessing tribute) regarding religious activities. In the event of an episcopal visit, they were to recruit Indians who had not been confirmed so that they might receive that sacrament.[72] The *Doctrina cristiana* (1544) by the Dominican Fr. Pedro de Córdoba differed from the other catechisms published in Mexico up to then by offering a succinct historical narration that included the fall of Adam and the role of Christ in the redemption of humankind. In explaining the sacraments, Pedro de Córdoba devoted to confirmation a brief paragraph in which he highlighted the strengthening of faith that the Christian experienced upon receiving the sacrament: "it is given so that the Christian will be stronger and firmer in the faith."[73]

In the *Doctrina cristiana en lengua española y mexicana* (1548), written by the Dominicans, the doctrinal content is developed through forty sermons, one of which explains that the function of confirmation is to give spiritual strength (*teoiotica techicaualiztli*) and that only the bishops may administer it.[74] This sermon exhorts the faithful to receive the sacrament and to make sure that their children receive it as well. Although there is no mention of the age of the confirmed, the catechism advises that Christians be confirmed only after they have gone through confession. Since Christians must reach the age of reason before they can confess their sins, one can infer that the confirmand should be at least seven years old. In addition to penance and fasting as conditions to receive confirmation, the believers are advised that, after receiving confirmation, they should refrain from washing the place on their heads where the bishop anointed them, leaving in place the cloth that had been tied around their heads.[75]

We end this brief survey with *Doctrina christiana con una exposición breve* (1622), by the Jesuit Jerónimo de Ripalda. This catechism was published in Spain much later than those mentioned up to this point. However, it enjoyed wide distribution in the Americas; indeed, Ripalda's work replaced the catechism that had been planned by the Third Mexican Church Council.[76] In Ripalda's *Doctrina christiana,* the effect of confirmation is directly related to baptism, for it is defined as "a spiritual increase of the being that baptism gave us." This increase manifests itself in the form of a strengthening "with which we confess the Christian faith,"[77] a notion that we already found in Aquinas.

Father Alonso de Molina and His Nahua Soldiers of Christ

We now turn to the *Confessionario mayor en la lengua mexicana y castellana* (Antonio de Espinosa, 1569), by the Franciscan Fr. Alonso de Molina. In the section on sins caused by sloth, Molina did something that has no equivalent in any of the doctrinal texts discussed up to this point nor in those produced in Spain: he devoted considerable space to the sacrament of confirmation. The lines concerning confirmation have all the characteristics of a sermon destined to exhort the Nahuas to receive the sacrament. The inclusion of this sermon in a section titled "Questions Concerning Sloth" is not completely surprising since, although confirmation was not absolutely necessary for salvation, not having received it because of negligence was, as the *Doctrina* of the Dominicans pointed out, a sin.[78] Thirty years after the publication of the *Confessionario mayor,* Juan Bautista in his *Confessionario en lengua mexicana y castellana* (1599) included in his section on the sin of sloth a question addressed to penitents inquiring if they had failed to be confirmed due to idleness.[79] The same connection between sloth and confirmation is found as well in the *Catecismo Romano,* where the limited dissemination of the sacrament of confirmation among believers is attributed to the general negligence of the population.[80]

In addition to exhorting the faithful to participate in the sacrament, Molina described in detail the obligations of the confirmands and paused to praise the effects of the episcopal anointing on the Christian soul.[81] Even though Molina used the Spanish name of the sacrament in his Nahuatl version, the verbs related to the sacramental action and their effects convey, in the Nahuatl text, the idea of spiritual strengthening. In his *Vocabulario,* Molina translated "confirmation" into Nahuatl as *teoyotica temachiotiliztli* as well as *teoyotica techicaualiztli,* the same form we find in the doctrines of the Dominicans and the Franciscans (the latter of which was written by Molina as well) and in the later *Doctrina christiana muy cumplida* (1575), by the Augustinian Juan de la Anunciación.[82] The first form, *teoyotica temachiotiliztli,* refers to the idea of being set apart, signaled, or marked, an action that occurs in confirmation when the bishop uses the chrism to make the mark of the cross upon the forehead of the confirmand.[83] The second form given by Molina, *teoyotica techicaualiztli,* corresponds to the idea of strengthening. According to Molina's *Vocabulario, chicaua* conveys the idea of growing: "man or beast becoming old" ("hacerse viejo el hombre o la bestia"). Thus, one of the forms chosen emphasizes the outward act of the bishop, while the other is focused on the effect on the recipient. Modern ethnography shows that *chicahualiztli* is related to the complex concept of *tonalli,* which designates a vital force associated with heat thought to play a crucial role in the determination of human individuality.[84]

Like the Dominicans' *Doctrina,* Molina advised that one must confess before being confirmed; however, there is no explicit mention of the age of the confirmands. We may again infer that Molina had in mind those persons who, because of their age, would already be under the obligation to confess to a priest.[85]

According to Aquinas, confirmation strengthens the Christians' faith to such an extent that even in the most adverse situations, including persecution, Christians will not fail to declare their belief publicly. Through confirmation, what was expressed inwardly in the act of baptism can be declared outwardly with one's voice, just as the apostles did after the Paraclete.[86] According to Aquinas, the declaration of faith related to confirmation is more complete than in baptism.[87] I discuss later in what way this distinction allowed Molina to privilege confirmation over baptism as well as why such praise for the sacrament emerged toward the year 1569.

One of the most salient features of Molina's illustration is his elaboration of the idea that the confirmed individuals become, by virtue of the grace bestowed upon them, soldiers of Christ. The origin of such a comparison stems from the important homily of Pentecost by Faustus de Riez from about the year 460, which came to be included in the *False Decretals* before becoming an authorized text. In this homily we read, "In baptism we are reborn to life; after baptism, we are confirmed to the fight. In baptism, we are cleansed; after baptism, we are strengthened."[88] Molina did not fail to recall the words in Job 7, "the life of man on earth is a battle" ("Que es batalla la vida del hombre en la tierra") to build the image of a Christian soldier in constant battle with God's enemies. The Franciscan was clearly aware of the significant echoes that the statement in Job would have among the Nahuas, who themselves had come to live the truth of that assertion since warfare was the ideological foundation upon which the social order of the Aztec state rested. Molina's task of translating Christian teaching from one culture to another was not new. In the ninth century, during the sometimes brutal campaign of conversion and conquest launched by Charlemagne against the Saxons, a monk wrote the *Heliand,* an epic poem in which the Christian gospel was presented with characteristics that were easily recognizable for the warrior society of the Saxons.[89]

Aquinas explained the significance of making the sign of the cross on the foreheads of the confirmed and the accompanying words uttered by the bishop ("consigno te signo crucis") as the induction of soldiers into the military. The bishop here would have the role similar to that of the captain.[90] The sign of induction into the army of Christ together with its strengthening effect makes the confirmed into soldiers who are thus equipped with the vigor necessary to defend their faith; strength and spiritual maturity go hand in hand (fig. 11).

Molina points out time and time again that the confirmand receives from the bishop "the insignia and the arms for war,"[91] a phrase rendered in Nahuatl as *yntlauiztli iyaotlatquitl. Tlahuiztli,* in Molina's *Vocabulario,* means "armas e insignias," arms and insignia, and *tlatquitl,* "vestidos," garments, with *yaotlatquitl* meaning "vestimenta de guerra," clothing of war. The term "tlahuiztli," which always refers to the world of the Aztec warriors, is an article of clothing that covers the arms and legs as well as the hairstyle and shield for the warrior.[92] The tlahuiztli could take different forms that indicated the different levels of the military hierarchy; military ranks were distinguished through the design of the tlahuiztli (in the form of a coyote or a jaguar) in combination with particular types of insignia highly codified hairstyles and cuts (fig. 12).[93] Within Nahua society, the tlahuiztli carried special meanings: it was an article of male clothing worn by warriors and warrior priests and, in essence, a sign of prestige. As a symbol of prestige, the tlahuiztli was a visible sign, an indicator of the hierarchical level that the warrior had achieved as a result of his successful waging of war. That success was based not only on the number of prisoners that he had taken but also on the quality of those prisoners, for they, too, were ranked according to the ethnic group to which they belonged and to the differing degrees of ability and ferociousness associated with each of these groups. That classification varied in accordance with the different historical circumstances that produced war situations with surrounding tribes.[94] Warriors as well as priests who returned from the battlefield with prisoners received the tlahuiztli as recognition for their courage (fig. 13).

Molina tried to demonstrate that confirmation is a sacrament of utmost importance, and by exploiting the possibilities offered by the traditional image of the Christian soldier, he constructed his exhortation by appealing precisely to the dignity and prestige of the warrior within the old Nahua society. What was often, but not always, read in the Christian tradition in terms of a spiritual battle acquires in Molina's text a strong referential value easily recognizable to the Nahuas, who in 1569 could, without doubt, still remember or had some knowledge of the role and status that warriors held in the past. That past existed in colonial Mexico not only in local histories handed down through oral tradition but also, transformed, in public and religious functions. The

Códice de Tlatelolco captures vividly the ceremonies marking the beginning of the construction of the Cathedral of Mexico in the year 5 *tochtli* (5 rabbit), or 1562. In the scene, three Nahua warriors, with their eagle and tiger garments, dance before the second viceroy, Antonio de Velazco, Archbishop Montúfar, and the caciques of Tenochtitlan, Tlacopan, and Texcoco (fig. 14).[95]

Molina used the figure of David, warrior and king, to illustrate the strength that could be obtained from God. Thus, after referring to the origin of confirmation by recalling the classic example of Pentecost, he added an example from Psalms, in which David asks for strength of spirit.[96] Psalm 17 met Molina's goal perfectly because of its proliferation of references to David's battles against his enemies and to the role of God as the provider of strength, who made David's arms as strong "as a metal bow" (*tepuztlauitolli*).[97]

When the Christian receives confirmation, Molina pointed out, "at the same time God our Lord makes him his knight and special soldier." The key word in Nahuatl is *tlaçopillo*, the possessive form of *tlazohpilli*, which means "legitimate son" according to the *Vocabulario*. *Tlazohpilli* designated one of the ranks of the hereditary nobility in Aztec society within the group of the *pipiltin*, made up of the sons of the lords and noblemen, *tlatohqueh* and *teteuctin*.[98]

Molina offered the terrestrial counterpart of the soldier and knight of Christ when he compared the spiritual status acquired through confirmation with the emblems that identified a soldier of the emperor as a knight or *caballero*, a word left untranslated in the Nahuatl version. In this way, the character that confirmation imprints upon the believer appears translated in terms of the Spanish imperial hierarchy; the insignia of the knights express their "nobility and greatness."[99] Once again, Molina used other terms associated with the Mexican ruling class when he referred to the new status of the confirmed by calling them "*Emperador ca pipiltin ca tlatoque.*"[100]

The explanation of confirmation through a language that evokes one of the sanctioned ways to advance one's social status in the Nahua world appears again when Molina explained the role of the bishop in the administration of the sacrament. Just as emperors conferred knighthood on and armed their subjects, bishops were the only ones who could arm and knight the soldiers of Christ. Here, the figure of the bishop is juxtaposed to that of the governing lords: *tlatoque obispome.*[101]

Conscious of the echoes that his elaborate use of imagery rooted in the Aztec military world could find within his Indian audience, Molina attempted to frame it in the Spanish world. Through confirmation, the Christian becomes a soldier upon receiving the tlahuiztli, the symbol of the warrior with honors within Nahua society, which identifies him— and here is Molina's transformation—as a soldier knight of the Spanish emperor. What is essential for the persuasive force of his argument is the homology that he established between the state of perfection of the confirmed person and the rise of social status anchored in a reality that had ceased to exist. Regarding the socially sanctioned means through which the *macehuales,* or commoners, were allowed to gain social prestige within Nahua society in the past, the Dominican Fr. Diego Durán noted

> that the humble man, who excelled in arms and had accomplished some exceptional deed, having returned to court at the end of the war, was presented to the lord, who, praising his deed, would order him to trim the hair above his ears and would give him a quilted cuirass, covered with skin of a tiger or a stag, white, buff colored, extending no further than the waist, and an elegant and wide *braguero* that completely covered his thighs. They would give him a white shield with five tufts of feathers.[102]

We know that the insignia that awaited the fortunate *macehual* who had stood out on the battlefield reflected not only the prestige he had gained as a warrior but also his humble social origin.[103]

The breaking down of the early rite of Christian initiation, which resulted in two different sacraments—baptism and confirmation—was followed by long-debated questions among theologians (indeed, until a short time ago): What was the special grace received in confirmation? Through what action of the bishop—the laying on of hands or the anointing—was it conferred? How was this grace different from the grace acquired in baptism?[104] As already mentioned, in Spain Pedro de Cuéllar had assigned the gifts of the Holy Spirit to the different steps of the initiation ceremony, which included baptism and confirmation. In the sixteenth century, Carranza explained in his *Comentarios sobre el catecismo christiano* that "it is a characteristic of this sacrament to give the gifts of the Holy Ghost."[105] His contemporary, Fr. Luis de Granada, commented that through confirmation "we are infused with grace and an increase of all the gifts of the Holy Spirit."[106]

Motivated by these questions, some theologians were led to ask which sacraments were the most important. In his *Sententiae,* Peter Lombard briefly considered this matter without reaching a conclusive opinion, which is not surprising, given the specific functions of each of the sacraments. However, it is instructive to consider how Peter Lombard tried to formulate ways to reach possible answers. Lombard proposed two perspectives to deal with the question. On one hand, if one were to consider those sacraments administered by the highest ranks of the ecclesiastical hierarchy to be the most important, then confirmation would certainly be included among them. On the other hand, if one were to consider the virtue conferred by each sacrament, the virtue of confirmation would be greater than that of baptism, as Rabanus Maurus had suggested. Nonetheless, Peter Lombard recognized that the latter solution presented certain problems since confirmation lacked the power to wash away sins, which corresponded to baptism.[107]

Molina did not sidestep the question, but his treatment should be read in rhetorical terms. The Franciscan's praise of confirmation culminated in a new development in which he explored the relation of confirmation with baptism. If baptism confers grace, confirmation, Molina proposed, confers a greater amount of grace, through which the confirmed Christian achieves some perfection.[108] Molina assured readers that those who have been confirmed "will have much honor there in Paradise and glory of Heaven, and those who have not received it will not be so renowned and honored," just as knights are more esteemed than the "macehuales and humble people."[109]

The class distinctions of the Nahua world prior to the Conquest, which included a hierarchy of moral values that corresponded to each group, with the noblemen at the top, is still in effect in the celestial sphere. For there, too, those who were confirmed stand out from the others. To the sign that the confirmed received as a visible mark identifying them in paradise, Molina added other distinctions: the confirmed will wear two crowns of gold on their heads, while the baptized will wear only one.[110] It is appropriate to recall that for warriors who fell on the battlefield and for captives who were sacrificed there was reserved, according to Mexican traditions, a special place where the sun lived (*Tonatiuhichan*).[111] We can read here an equivalent mark of distinction, expressed this time in a similar shared place, the Christian paradise.

The power of Molina's sermon does not rest exclusively on the complex task of transposition that operates on the image of the *miles Christi* but also on the ideological aspects evoked in that construction. We are not simply presented an elaborate translation of that image but rather the incorporation of the ideological world from which that new image was constructed and upon which its intelligibility depends. Molina described a ritual and, in addition, evoked a kind of society that provides the key to deciphering it. But that society is, at the same time, an image of the Christian community etched upon the warrior society of the Mexicas.

Aquinas had classified confirmation among the sacraments geared fundamentally toward the salvation of the individual, as opposed to those others, such as marriage and holy orders, which dealt with individuals in their relation to society. Although Aquinas included confirmation in the first group, it may very well also be included in the latter since the confirmed individuals were conceived as being Christian soldiers ready to openly defend their faith when under attack. In practice, the connection between confirmation and society was underscored by the administration of the sacrament to youngsters, making, as Carranza noted, their entrance into the social world. In the case of Molina's sermon, the meaning of confirmation is not confined to the spiritual development of the individual; its effect is projected throughout all of society. In spite of Molina's care to frame his sermon within the world of the Spanish hierarchy, he could not, however, fail to invoke the ancient order of Nahua social values, the very order that was being dismantled before him as he wrote.

In Molina's sermon there is a clear consciousness of the delicate negotiation upon which the persuasive force of the text rests, as can be gathered from his instructions of how the confirmand should prepare to receive the sacrament. Molina advised "that you bring a candle and a strip of white cloth that is not dirty."[112] In the Nahuatl version, "venda de lienzo blanco," strip of white cloth, is expressed as "mo paño iztac," "tu paño blanco," your white woolen cloth. The *Vocabulario* offers two citations for "strip": "strip of linen" (*tlaxochtli*) and "a strip of something very luxurious and embroidered with which they tied the crowns or miters to [the heads of] the lords or to the high priests of the idols" (*tzonquachtli*). It is fitting that one should wonder about the reason behind Molina's lexical selection. One possible explanation is that he was trying to avoid any type of association between the strip of cloth the confirmand was to wear for seven days and the various kinds of

cloth with adornments and feathers that senior officials and priests cus-
tomarily wore in the past.[113]

The complex process of translating the sacrament of confirmation
into the context of Nahua culture is not without paradoxes. While
throughout the *Confessionario mayor* we find a condemnation of the
idea of honor as a privilege linked to restricted social groups, Molina,
nonetheless, resorted to that same concept in the case of confirmation—
but to transform it into a purely spiritual notion.

Molina's argument is built on his understanding of the social structure of the Aztec world. As if to bring an end to the seemingly unavoidable dissolution of the old social order that would very soon erode the
hegemony of the Nahua nobility, Molina forged a continuity between
the moral worlds of both the Spanish and the Mexican elites. Toward
1569 the world of values and prestige represented by the Mexican warriors no longer existed except in the memory of the Indians and, in
particular, in the memory of those surviving members of the elite who
were still claiming their old privileges through legal channels.[114] Since
the beginning of the colonization of Mexico, the friars and a small
fraction of colonial functionaries frequently expressed their admira-
tion for the early success of the Nahuas in forging a political community with strict boundaries between social groups.[115] With the exception of certain traits that these early observers associated with
tyrannical forms of government, this almost extinct community could
easily have been taken as a model of human governance. Opinions of
this kind were not without motivation since the friars often praised the
old social order of the Mexican Indians to denounce as pernicious the
current transformation of the colonial social map, which had opened
for Spaniards new opportunities for social mobility. Friars such as
Durán tried to exorcize the uncomfortable erosion of boundaries
between social classes that he was witnessing by clinging to an ideal-
ized version of Nahua society not yet touched by the Spaniards.[116] The
same phenomenon noted and resented by Durán was taking place in
the Peninsula, as well.[117]

We still need to analyze the question of the age of the confirmands.
Molina did not address this issue explicitly. However, it would not be a
stretch to infer the ideal age of the confirmands by considering in particular the numerous references to the military world of the Nahuas.
From the comparison of confirmation with the induction of a warrior

into the military there can be derived a significant detail: it would be very difficult to imagine a female assuming those functions or even reading or hearing the sermon.[118]

This apparent exclusion, inherent in the metaphor of the Christian soldier and perpetuated in Catholic tradition, had been noticed by Boniface, another missionary, centuries before.[119] The world invoked by Molina is a world of men in which the taking up of arms and insignia marked a decisive step in the social life of the young male warrior, who had gone through intensive and specialized training.[120] Information on the ways the Nahuas conceptualized the different periods of human life is, regretfully, heterogeneous and scant;[121] nonetheless, we are able to explore briefly why the moment when the future Nahua warrior took up arms for the first time became invested with such immense symbolic power and how this event was reelaborated by Molina.

The sons of the macehuales received their instruction in the *telpochcalli* (house of youths), dedicated to the god Tezcatlipoca. The youths who entered this institution, to which their parents had promised them shortly after their births,[122] were responsible for various tasks, such as sweeping the temple and collecting wood to feed the fire that burned there, in addition to being trained in matters of warfare.[123] Before going to war as a soldier, the youth went out on the battlefield as a squire. Having completed this phase and fully prepared to fight in war, the soldier went into battle, and if he demonstrated skill in capturing enemy soldiers, he became a *telpochtlato* (commander of youths). The sons of noble families received their instruction in an institution reserved mainly for members of their class, the *calmecac*. According to Sahagún, the young noblemen entered the *calmecac* when they were between ten and thirteen years of age. They were introduced to weapons when they were fifteen and were ready to fight in war when they were about twenty.[124] This stage in the formation of young men thus completed an important cycle that had begun with birth. In the case of the macehuales, the parents usually pledged that their newborn son would be sent to be raised in the calmecac to serve later in the temples or in the telpochcalli to become a warrior. I should add that the Nahua words associated with the education and training of youths as recorded in the *Florentine Codex* highlight both growth and strength, two ideas that in Christian sources were associated with the effects of confirmation.[125] Regarding newborn sons, Mendieta dared to give a spiritual interpretation to the old Nahua custom of placing an arrow and a shield in the hands of the baby immediately after he was ritually bathed. Underlining the similarities with baptism, Mendieta saw in the ceremony a preparation for the battles of the soul and even considered the possibility of including it in the traditional baptismal rite.[126] In the seventeenth century Hernando Ruíz de Alarcón, a priest strongly influenced by European demonology and engaged in a personal crusade against idolatry, wrote that the beginning of the life cycle of Nahua males was propitiated by an agreement between the parents of the new-born and the devil. This agreement was later corroborated by the male upon reaching puberty. Ruíz de Alarcón's interpretation was based on an analogy with the sacraments of baptism and confirmation.[127]

Regarding ages, the information gathered by Motolinía differs from the data gathered by Sahagún. According to Motolinía, the sons of noblemen were sent to the calmecac when they were about five years old.[128] Referring in general to both the nobility and the macehuales, Motolinía wrote that Nahua males entered their respective educational institutions when they were *muchachos,* or children. Fr. Diego Durán recorded that once the youths had completed their instruction in their respective institutions, they moved on to another house, the *tlamacaz-calli.* "This word," Durán explained, "is composed of *tlamacaz,* which means 'perfect man,' and of *calli,* which means 'house.' And that is how they called the house of young men at the perfect age of youth."[129] Durán also reported on the cycle of the ages of the Nahua male, in which we can find echoes of the well-known European system of the four ages of man.[130] A drawing from the Lord Kingsborough collection shows, by contrast, a tripartite model. In this case, the ages of man are represented as the ascent and descent of a mountain. At the summit we find a young warrior, who illustrates the period between age twenty and forty (fig. 15).

Around the age of fifteen, as Sahagún reported, young men received arms and began to acquire a practical knowledge of war by accompanying warriors onto the battlefield.[131] We may infer that the age of the confirmand implicit in Molina may very well coincide with the age at which the Mexica male took up arms. This interpretation seems plausible since we have already seen that several Spanish theologians recommended the confirmation of youths beyond the age of reason by relying on the image of the Christian soldier, which excluded infants.[132]

Taking into account what we have seen regarding confirmation in Mexico and its treatment in the catechetical literature of the time,

Molina's sermon stands out for both its rhetorical complexity and its exhaustive approach to a sacrament that was generally regarded as secondary. Why did Molina assign to this sacrament such importance for the Indian converts and those who had been born into the Catholic faith? We know that the administration of the sacraments led to a considerable number of controversies in Mexico, from the discussions concerning baptism to those about the administration of the Eucharist.[133] The importance of the sacraments was ceaselessly preached by the friars among the indigenous population. The Indians were expected to memorize the sacramental system as it was presented in cartillas and catechisms; friars and priests called on them to participate regularly in the sacraments because these rituals were the indispensable means of salvation for a Christian.[134] Despite all the efforts, the administration of the sacraments remained far from uniform, with a great number of Indians who were neither baptized nor confirmed, as attested by numerous sources. Concerning the differences between baptism (an absolutely necessary sacrament), confirmation, and the Eucharist, Juan Focher observed in his *Itinerarium,* (1574), that

> Confirmation and the Eucharist are necessary indeed for men because they provide spiritual strength and nourishment. Without them, if actual contempt be absent, a man can still be saved, as it has been seen in the case of the Indians, the vast majority of whom have received neither.[135]

Since confirmation required the presence of a bishop, there were few opportunities for Christians to receive it, particularly in remote areas of Mexico or Spain. Protestant theologians launched a powerful attack on the integrity of the sacramental system by questioning whether some sacraments had, in fact, been divinely instituted. The result was a drastic reduction in the number of rituals that the Protestants were willing to accept as sacraments. Although Protestant criticism concentrated mainly on penance, the other sacraments did not remain untouched. Several attacks from reformers were directed at unmasking the superstitious dimension behind the sacraments.[136] Reformers also tried to undermine the power of the priests, which was seen as an extension of the superstitions underlying Catholic sacramental rituals. In doing so, such theologians questioned the value of an ecclesiastical hierarchy and the reason for its existence. Martin Luther attacked the sacramental character of confirmation by showing that it had not been instituted by Jesus Christ.[137] He humorously speculated that once the task of administrating the sacraments was divided among the clergy, confirmation gave bishops something to do.[138] For Luther, confirmation was nothing more than just another ceremony in the church; it was not a sacrament.

With the Reformation, the catechetical aspect of confirmation gained special strength to the detriment of its sacramental side, a feature that also took on great importance for Catholic theologians such as Fr. Luis de Granada and Bartolomé de Carranza. As we have already seen, these two men advocated the administration of confirmation to young people rather than to infants to ensure that the confirmands had sufficient knowledge of Christian doctrine. The catechetical dimension of confirmation complemented the sacramental effect of the reception of grace (an aspect denied by the reformers) at a moment in life in which the young Christian began to confront a new set of temptations, among them the temptation of the flesh. The Council of Trent defended the integrity of the sacramental system against the assault of the reformers and, in the case of confirmation, explicitly condemned those who denied the need of episcopal authority to administer it.[139]

At the time that Molina was writing his *Confessionario mayor,* mostly infants were being baptized. The sacrament of confirmation requires that the spiritual strength it provides—in the form of an increase in grace upon that already attained in baptism—be accompanied by an outward declaration of faith on the part of the confirmand. That declaration presupposes an adequate preparation in the Christian doctrine. Hence, the attention to a sacrament that could be seen as an important instrument to secure an entire generation of Christians with firm beliefs at a time when the lukewarm convictions of the native Christian converts were a serious concern among the religious. Knowledge of Christian doctrine and, in particular, the theme of explicit faith appear frequently in the context of evangelization in Mexico and in other parts of America. Opinions on the kind of knowledge that a Christian should have were based on the different judgments that the friars had formed about the cognitive faculties of the Indians, as well as on personal criteria of spiritual maturity. The sacrament of confirmation, from that perspective, can be seen as an instrument through which the deficiencies of catechism could, ideally, be remedied.

The question of explicit faith is linked to that of the spiritual development of the Mexican Indians. This is why around 1569, the year in which the *Confessionario mayor* was published, the preoccupation over the spiritual maturity of the Mexican Indians can be read as well as a broader concern over the results of more than four decades of mission-ary activity. In this sense, the question about the spiritual development of the Mexicans becomes inseparable from the question about the maturity of the church as an institution and the regularization of its functions after a period dominated by the religious orders. From this point of view, Molina's exhortation to the population to embrace the sacrament of confirmation was also an attempt to secure the continuity of the sacramental system, the unity of which had been upset by the evangelical practices during the first years of religious activity.

In explaining confirmation to the Nahuas, Molina did not limit him-self to merely describing the actions and meanings associated with the sacrament; toward the end of his sermon, we have before us the image of a society that was no longer present, no longer actual. Molina under-stood the old and, now, unrecoverable order, and through the ritual of confirmation, he found a way to provide symbolic continuity to that order by recasting it in the guise of a Christian community.

CHAPTER THREE

Politics of Salvation

Penance and Contrition among the Nahuas

Subjugation or Salvation?

For Spaniards living in the sixteenth century, the familiar image of a penitent on his knees beside a priest would surely remind them of their annual obligation and the sense of tranquility that this obligation promised. Obligation along with the promise of salvation defined the special relationship between Christians and their God.[1] To make sure that such a notion took hold among the Mexican Indians was one of the friars' principal tasks (fig. 16).

The manuals for confessors produced in Mexico have generally been examined with the intent of illustrating how Spanish colonial domination sought to extend its influence over the Indians beyond the legal and economic spheres by trying to transform the everyday behavior of its new subjects. Indisputable as this observation may be, it is not free of certain reductionism since such readings more often than not fail to do justice to the richness of this literature by overlooking the debates that shaped the administration of penance among the Indians.

In recent years, the study of confession in colonial Mexico has attracted the interest of scholars seeking to better understand under which conditions the communication between friars and Indians took place. Their research has often focused on the problems posed by the translation of Christian concepts into indigenous languages, that is, on the scope and boundaries of Christian teaching in a cross-cultural context. This perspective tries to correct and overcome the deficiencies perceived in standard historical accounts that very often reproduce viewpoints similar to those found in sixteenth-century sources, such as the boundless optimism that informs certain religious historiography.

But why, among the multiple practices introduced by religious orders—preaching, instruction, Mass, and so forth—has confession emerged as a focal point to understand a process that reached well beyond the occasional encounter of confessors and Indian penitents? Confession has come to be regarded as a privileged site that allowed the Mexican friars to further their knowledge about indigenous beliefs and customs and to modify them in their attempt to impose a new model of moral subject on the Indian population; a moral subject rooted in the notions of conscience and individuality. Confession is thus taken in its dual aspect: as an apparatus of control and as a mechanism to acquire knowledge.[2] It was in the light of this cognitive aspect—inseparable from a particular will to truth—whose influence is thought to reach beyond the strict boundaries of the sacramental ritual that scholars have suggested a filiation between Sahagún's ethnographic work and the practice of confession.[3]

These works have helped us see the distance that separated Spanish Christian culture from Nahua culture at the particular moment of confession, a moment at which different notions of the individual and his or her relationship with society and the supernatural coexisted.[4] These studies share the notion that confession was a privileged mechanism of individual and social control, the object of which was the subjugation and transformation of Indian subjects. Confession is thus conceived as a cipher condensing both the general attitude of the friars toward Christianized Indians and the overall spirit of domination that characterized the Spanish colonial enterprise. Such a view has guided a reading of Mexican manuals for confessors that is narrowly focused on those aspects that best lend themselves to be taken as proof of the immutability and resilience of the friars' categories of thought and classification. Whereas such interpretations—sometimes overtly dependent on the most simplified theses of contemporary theorists—shed light on the more general features of this literature, they, nonetheless, remain partial.[5] The same historical sources offer us sufficient evidence that the ministers' desire and will to convert the indigenous peoples did not exempt them from reflecting upon the traditions of thought in which they had been educated. A careful consideration of the religious literature produced in Mexico in the light of European theological thought about the sacrament of penance allows us to tease out the layers of thought and action that informed the contact between Nahuas and the friars.

Although the disagreement in New Spain over the administration of the sacrament of penance was heated, it did not reach the level of virulence that baptism inspired. The opposing opinions on the quality of the Indians' confessions voiced at the time reveal not only the existence of different expectations among confessors but also the complexity of the sacrament itself. Such complexity became more and more apparent to the friars once they started to confess larger and more diverse groups of Indians. The avatars of the sacrament of penance in New Spain show us the distance that separated scholastic speculation and practice as well as the efforts of the friars to overcome it.

In the course of Christian instruction, the Mexican Indians were repeatedly told that in order to fully enjoy the benefits of penance, they had to prepare themselves before approaching the sacrifice. Theologians and ecclesiastical authorities showed similar concern about the preparation of confessors, who were expected to be properly trained to hear confessions and to be thoroughly familiar with the most authoritative books on cases of conscience. In 1565, for instance, the Second Mexican Church Council ordered all priests to have *summae* for confessors either in Latin or Spanish and recommended some authors.[6] In addition, priests were expected to have an adequate knowledge of indigenous languages and native culture to be able to detect any surviving traces of practices and beliefs incompatible with the new religion.

The Dominican Fr. Diego Durán, bemoaning the existence of unskilled confessors, warned emphatically about the importance of and need for effective confessions, which could be achieved only by competent priests and friars who knew both the language of the Indians and their ancient religious practices, which still coexisted alongside Christian rituals.[7] Doubting the thoroughness and validity of a great number of Indian confessions, Durán pointed out that the deficiencies in the administration of the sacrament compromised its integrity from the start: "[w]hence I believe many sacrileges derive from formless confessions, which lack the parts that the sacrament requires, which are sorrow, repentance, the purpose of sinning no more and satisfaction, and a truthful declaration of all sins."[8] Durán was referring here to the three parts that had traditionally been thought to make up the sacrament: contrition, auricular confession, and satisfaction.[9] Whereas much has been made of the confessor's authority over penitents (a point that remains indisputable), his crucial role in ensuring that the sacrament is carried out appropriately and efficiently has not received equal attention. Durán brought home the point that a poorly prepared confessor endangered the ritual process and ran the risk of bringing sin upon himself.

Private confession in Europe came about as the result of a series of changes and compromises prompted in part by theological discussions about the role of each of the sacrament's three parts (contrition, confession, satisfaction) and its specific contribution to the overall sacramental effect. A review of the principal phases of medieval thought about penance will help us understand more fully the way in which the Mexican friars conceived the administration of this sacrament in light of their own interactions with the Nahuas and the theological traditions with which they were familiar. This approach will also allow us to trace the emergence of tensions surrounding the role of the three parts of the sacrament, as a result of the obstacles encountered among the Mexican Indians by confessors in their daily experience. A particularly revealing instance was the clash of opinions concerning contrition.

The objective of this chapter is to examine the place that contrition occupied in the accounts of the Mexican friars concerning the Christianization of the Nahuas, as well as in the religious literature on confession. The importance that the friars came to attach to this notion can be seen as well in their interpretation of preconquest rituals of purification, in which they sometimes discerned likely correspondences with the sacraments of the church.

Contrition and Priestly Authority in European Theological Thought

The debate among theologians from different philosophical traditions over the meaning and role of contrition in the absolution of sins constitutes an essential chapter in the development of the sacrament of penance. The discussions from the beginnings of scholasticism in the thirteenth century to the decisive moment of confrontation and dialogue at the Council of Trent contributed to the formulation of the doctrinal foundations of the sacrament as we know it today.[10]

Public penance seems to have been the normal practice sanctioned by the church in Europe until the sixth century, when private confession as practiced in Ireland and England started to spread onto the continent with the introduction of *libri poenitentiales* (handbook of penance) from the islands.[11] Public penance neither entirely nor suddenly disappeared, however; although by the eighth century it had fallen into general disuse, it survived in some regions until the thirteenth century.[12] The new form of penance, born in Irish and English monasteries, radically transformed the penitential practices in the European church, offering the faithful a means of reconciliation—and a promise of salvation—closer to their own capabilities and more in tune with the reality of their everyday lives. The novelty of the penitential books consisted in their providing confessors with precise information on the works of satisfaction that they should impose on penitents according to the sins committed. Their introduction onto the continent affected the traditional institution of penance in three fundamental ways. First, the new form of penance was private, while the old canonical penance, reserved for serious sins, was public. Second, the new form, based on a "tariff," could be repeated, while canonical penance could be administered only once during a person's life. Third, the works of satisfaction imposed under the new system were much less severe than those demanded by canonical penance.[13]

The consolidation of private confession opened a new series of questions related to the way the justification of the penitents took place. While in the old penitential practice the effectiveness of reconciliation was intimately linked to the works of satisfaction imposed upon the penitent, the relaxation of those penalties and the new focus on private confession forced theologians to reimagine the sacramental operation in light of the sacrament's new configuration.

The change in the relationship among the parts that formed penance together with a new theological definition of the concept of sacrament required a satisfactory explanation of how these three components related to each other to give unity to the sacrament.[14] The crucial issue for theologians was to determine which roles the contributions of the penitent and the confessor played in the removal of sins and the infusion of grace worked by the sacrament. When the church accepted as valid the deathbed reconciliations of penitents unable to carry out works of satisfaction, it acknowledged that one component of the sacrament was not entirely indispensable. This step led then to a closer consideration of the role of contrition in the process of salvation. Regarding the reconciliation of the dying, in the tenth century some theologians affirmed the superiority of contrition over satisfaction. However, it was in the doctrinal developments that took place in the twelfth century where contrition emerged as the essential element of penance.

With the increasing devaluation of the role of satisfaction, it was now left to theologians to sort out the precise relationship between contrition and the absolution of sins.[15]

Contrition had traditionally been defined as the profound, sincere sorrow of sinners for their sins. As theologians elaborated doctrines about the remission of sins, they wondered what might happen if the penitent's sorrow were less than adequate or perfect. The notion of attrition, which would play a fundamental role in the sacramental theology of Duns Scotus and would leave its mark on the conceptualization of penance in post-Tridentine theology, was born out of the consideration of such a possibility.[16]

In early theological explanations, what distinguished contrition from attrition was a matter of degrees in the intensity of the penitent's sorrow. Later, scholastic theologians worked out a general explanation of the sacraments as a particular set of rituals that, when performed, resulted in the infusion of grace on the penitent. Thereafter, the presence of grace itself became the key element to distinguish contrition from any other form of sorrow experienced by the penitent. This is how attrition came to be conceptualized as repentance and sorrow not informed by grace and, consequently, thought to be insufficient for the remission of sins. This is basically the doctrine found in Aquinas.[17]

But the search for alternative and more satisfactory explanations continued. Among these was the attempt to differentiate contrition from attrition by considering the variety of motives behind the penitent's repentance. Thus, in addition to taking into account the intervention of grace, the Dominican Durandus de St. Pourçan, in opposition to Aquinas, specified that the operating motive behind contrition should always be the love of God, while the sinner's fear of punishment—a mere expression of self-love—characterized attrition.[18]

Before Aquinas, Peter Lombard laid out in book 4 of the *Sententiae* a systematic exposition on the sacramental system, an account that would become an authoritative source for later theologians. According to the *Sententiae,* penance consisted of three parts: "compunctio cordis, confessio oris, satisfactio operis."[19] These tripartite divisions became part of the standard definition of penance that found its way into catechisms, cartillas, and doctrines throughout Europe and the Americas. The compunction of the heart, which corresponds to contrition,[20] has a privileged place in Peter Lombard's theory of penance, which makes it the key element in the forgiveness of the penitent's sins. Although, as we

shall see, Mexican friars were thoroughly familiar with the crucial doctrinal developments concerning penance that followed Peter Lombard's
formulations, the *Sententiae* continued to hold a prominent place in
their readings.

For Lombard, penance was a virtue that allowed the penitent to
experience profound grief for the sins committed, with the purpose of
sinning no more.[21] Contrition was then defined as a particular kind of
sorrow located in the soul of the penitent, a specific state that, through
the work of God, led to the remission of sins. Although Lombard discerned three components in the sacrament, contrition, together with the
penitent's intention to confess, was considered by him to be the determining factor in the reconciliation of sinners.[22] In Lombard's doctrine,
contrite penitents did not need to confess their sins to a priest to be
absolved; it was enough for them to address their confessions directly to
God in order to be reconciled. If contrition played a pivotal role in the
remission of sins, as shown in the case of inner confession, what was the
exact function in this process of the priest and priestly authority represented by the keys? Although the forgiveness of sins could only be the
work of God, it was also true that priests had received through divine
authority the power to loosen and bind the sins of the faithful. The
priest's authority to absolve sins or to deny absolution, according to
Lombard's explanation, manifested itself in two different ways: first,
while only God could bring about the remission of sins, the priest's
function was to show that the penitent's sins had been forgiven.[23] Thus,
the priest holds a declarative function in the process of absolution,
which, in a way, has already taken place. In addition, Lombard saw the
advantages of confessing to a priest because, by openly acknowledging
their sins, the penitents were very likely to experience the benefits of
both humility and shame.[24] Whereas the presence of the priest is seen as
necessary,[25] this presence becomes overshadowed by a ritual action carried out almost entirely by the penitents. In Lombard's formulation, the
boundaries between penance as virtue and as sacrament are hard to
draw.

Peter Lombard's doctrine left open a series of questions that later
theologians would try to answer. His treatment of contrition is a case in
point. Even though contrition was thought by Lombard to be an essential component of the sacrament, its particular nature remained elusive.
Such a conceptual flaw was not without practical consequences, for
how could anyone affirm with any certainty whether contrition had

taken place? In addition, the emphasis placed on the penitent's contrition—that is, on penance conceived mainly as virtue without being clearly integrated into the dynamics of the sacrament—resulted in the devaluation of the priest's authority in the process of reconciliation. The absence of an adequate account of how the three parts of penance related to each other threatened to dissolve the sacrament's unity. Aquinas and Duns Scotus proposed their own solutions to the problems that Lombard left unresolved; these solutions should be considered in light of a decisive event in the history of the sacrament of penance. In 1215 the Fourth Lateran Council imposed the yearly obligation of confession on all Christians of both sexes who had reached the age of discretion.[26] The implementation of this measure, which recognized the parish priest as the authority on matters concerning the salvation of his parishioners, was, without doubt, an important factor in the subsequent modification of Lombard's views on the confessor's role in the absolution of sins.

Aquinas introduced a decisive change in his search for an explanation of the efficacy of the sacrament that would adequately account for the contributions of both the penitent and the confessor, the subjectivity of the former and the objective authority of the latter. Although to some extent Aquinas's formulation remained indebted to Lombard's, particularly his view on contrition, it also represented a significant attempt to assign the confessor—as listener and authority—a more active role in the reconciliation of the penitents. Without confessor, the sacrament was incomplete.

As with all the sacraments, in the case of penance Aquinas identified matter and form;[27] the penitent's actions—sorrow and repentance, most notably—corresponded to the former, and the confessor's uttering of the words of absolution, to the latter.[28] By resorting to these Aristotelian categories, Aquinas tried to show the relation of necessary dependence between the contribution of the penitent and that of the confessor. The words uttered by the priest, just as the formulae used in the sacraments of baptism and the Eucharist, have now become instrumental for the remission of sins.[29]

By distinguishing in penance a matter and a form, Aquinas recast the confessor's participation as an integral part of the sacrament without which there was no sacrament efficacy. Although this formulation departed from Peter Lombard's notion of sacramental efficacy as *ex opere operantis,* or by the action of the penitent, contrition continued to hold a prominent place in Aquinas's explanation of the absolution of sins.

It is appropriate to mention briefly an important development in Aquinas's attempt to define the efficacy of penance in terms of the entire rite and not just in the act of contrition. Aquinas noted that in confession the penitent's act could vary in terms of perfection. How could one determine, then, these particular degrees of perfection? According to Aquinas, there are two ways of looking at the act of penance. We can consider it an habit infused by God, albeit one that generally requires some kind of participation of the penitent. Penance can also be understood as a human act through which Christians cooperate with God. Such act may stem from different sources such as god, faith, or servile fear (*motus timoris servilis*), among others. This particular fear causes sinners to reject their errors in anticipation of divine punishment, and stands in contrast to filial fear (*motus timoris filialis*), which springs from the penitent's free choice to repent and reform. Although imperfect, filial fear prepares the penitent to experience contrition.[30] Contrition has its origin in charity and filial fear, while attrition, a less perfect act of sorrow, originates in servile fear and an act of selfish love not informed by charity.[31] Although Aquinas recognized the place that attrition, or imperfect contrition, has in the preparation of penitents toward the reception of justifying grace, that grace is possible only if true contrition takes place. In the case of penitents who received the sacrament believing themselves to be contrite when in reality they were only attrite, Aquinas appeared to accept the possibility of justification through the workings of the keys. However, and despite this particular observation, it would be inaccurate to infer from Aquinas that the sacrament itself could transform attrition into contrition by supplying whatever quality was lacking in the penitents' sorrow.[32] For Aquinas, contrition is shaped by grace, while grace is not present in attrition.[33]

Working within a philosophical tradition very different from Aquinas's, the Franciscan theologian Duns Scotus developed in the fourteenth century a theory of penance that was at variance with the Dominican's. Duns Scotus radically reduced the role of contrition in the process of reconciliation; for him, the confessor's act of absolution alone determined the effectiveness of the rite of penance.[34] In this way the doctrine of Duns Scotus tried to resolve the conceptual problems posed by Aquinas's ambiguous solution. In practical terms, Duns Scotus's formulation sought to eliminate the inevitable obstacles that stemmed from the improbable task of verifying the penitent's contrition. Even though Duns Scotus recognized that contrition was a possible path to justification, he also realized that it was not the easiest and surest path, given the difficulty both in achieving perfect contrition and being certain about it. For sinners, the sacrament, the efficacy of which was guaranteed by the power of the priest, remained the surest and most effective way to be reconciled. As long as penitents did not pose any obstacles, they could receive absolution whether they were contrite or attrite. While for Aquinas contrition and attrition were two perfectly distinguishable phenomena, for Duns Scotus they formed part of a continuum since attrition was transformed into contrition once the priest allowed sacramental grace to be instilled in the ritual.[35] The sacrament of penance was the best and safest way available to penitents seeking the remission of their sins because, as Duns Scotus put it, the efficacy of the sacrament—as well as of all the others—had been assured by God himself through a pact.[36] In contrast to Aquinas, Duns Scotus viewed contrition as a disposition and not as an integral part of the sacrament since it lacked a visible sign.[37] The sacrament's efficacy no longer depended on the penitents' contrition; rather, it came about *ex opere operato,* allowing attrite penitents to have their sins removed upon receiving the confessor's absolution.

I now turn briefly to the legacy of Aquinas's thought on penance among sixteenth-century Spanish theologians. Although Aquinas's position on penance could in part be called contritionist,[38] we have seen how it also left room for another kind of explanation when it acknowledged that penitents without contrition—but who sincerely believed themselves to be contrite—could be absolved upon receiving the sacrament. This admission led later theologians and historians to see in Aquinas the intimations of an attritionist position. Spanish theologians such as Francisco de Vitoria, Melchor Cano, and Domingo de Soto came to accept, albeit with some modifications, this explanation.[39] For these three theologians, attrition was repentance motivated by selfish fear. Nonetheless, for Melchor Cano, any kind of sorrow was sufficient to achieve the forgiveness of sins through the sacrament.[40]

The three doctrines that I have quickly sketched coexisted in different guises during the sixteenth century, but they also confronted each other formally at Trent during the sessions dedicated to answering the reformers' attacks against the sacrament of penance. At the end of this chapter, we return to Duns Scotus and the impact that the Tridentine

decrees had on the ways the friars thought about contrition in New
Spain.

Nahua Rites of Purification and Contrition

The study of the Mexican indigenous cultures had its origin in the evangelization enterprise launched by the religious orders. The Franciscans
took a leading role among them, carrying out linguistic and ethnographic research that with time achieved a high degree of systematiza-
tion.[41] Startled by a seemingly endless variety of alien religious practices, the friars soon started to compile and organize a vast body of
information on the Indians' religious life that would eventually help
them eradicate or neutralize those cultural elements at odds with Christianity and European mores. As the friars familiarized themselves with
local practices and beliefs, some were quick to detect striking similarities between Mexican ceremonies and the sacraments of the church,
such as baptism, communion, and penance. These perceived similarities
in the rituals of the two religions opened up for the friars a new area of
reflection, both speculative and practical, on religious matters.[42]

The resemblance between indigenous religious practices and the
Christian sacraments invited some friars to speculate about the origins
of such correspondences. Others, however, warned that such an exercise needed to be accompanied by a healthy dose of suspicion since
demonology already offered an acceptable explanation of these correspondences. This tradition taught the friars to take those religious ceremonies that closely resembled Christian rituals as nothing more than a
distortion or parody of the sacraments wrought by the devil with the
intention of spreading confusion among the Indians—and among ill-
informed friars who could be hastily led to assert the equivalence of two
disparate rituals.[43]

Another response to the question of origins altogether avoided the
attribution of similarities to the work of the devil, seeking instead an
explanation based on simple human motivations. Alonso de Molina's
sermon on the meaning of confirmation, discussed in chapter 2, best
illustrates this approach. As already stated, Molina rewrote an ancient
Mexican social institution in Christian terms to make confirmation
both intelligible and appealing to an indigenous audience.

Based on information about a Mexican rite of purification, in which the Indians were allowed to confess serious moral faults once in a lifetime, the Franciscan Bernardino de Sahagún concluded that the Nahuas had grasped the principle behind this ritual by natural reason, a reason present in all people: "There is no little basis to argue that these Indians of New Spain held themselves obliged to confess once during their lifetime, and this *in lumine natural,* without once having heard of Christianity."[44] I should also mention another friar, the Dominican Fr. Diego Durán, who, with many qualifications, suggested the hypothesis of an evangelization that preceded the arrival of the Spaniards; however, the original teachings of those early efforts had been altered and irrevocably transformed with the passing of the generations.[45]

Among the variety of indigenous rituals described by the missionaries, few seem to have received as much attention as those that resembled the sacrament of penance. The friars' speculation on the ultimate origin of the apparent correspondences between Nahua and Christian rituals cannot be quickly dismissed as a minor intellectual distraction far removed from the practical goals of conversion, for the missionaries kept in mind the similarities in ritual practices when closely monitoring the behavior of Indian penitents during confession. Friars familiar with the ancient rites of purification interpreted the confession of the Nahuas based on two different ways of conceiving the continuity between rituals past and present. In addition, just as the friars had perceived similarities between the two rituals, so could the Indians perceive them according to their own perspective and particular designs. Some friars deemed it necessary to proceed with caution, fearing that the Indians might continue their ancient practice in the new rite without a true understanding of the sacrament's meaning and scope. Others, in turn, thought that Christian penance could be easily recognized and accepted by the Indians as a more perfect version of their old ritual.

Contrition, confession, satisfaction: these three elements formed in the minds of the friars a basic guide to describe and explain the ancient rites of purification as well as the possible correspondences between them and Christian penance. Those concepts offered missionaries a way to observe and classify the actions of the indigenous rituals; in the process, they also projected their own values and expectations onto them. A brief examination of the role played by the notions of contrition and confession in the missionaries' ethnographic accounts helps illustrate this point.

According to the testimony of Motolinía, the administration of penance in New Spain began in the city of Texcoco in 1526, only two years after the first contingent consisting of twelve Franciscans entered the city of Tenochtitlan.[46] In order to introduce penance among the Nahuas, the friars first had to instruct them in the meaning of the sacrament and the proper way to receive it. Notwithstanding the practical difficulties posed by this preliminary but essential task, Motolinía did not hesitate to affirm that the Mexicans started to partake in the sacrament very quickly and enthusiastically. Soon the Franciscans saw both their expectations and capacity to respond to the increasing demands of the recent converts surpassed. According to Motolinía, it was not unusual to see Indians traveling several leagues from their villages in search of confessors and, in more than one instance, with a frequency that exceeded the yearly obligation to confess stipulated by the church.[47] Such early enthusiasm for confession on the part of the Indians was also recorded by the Augustinians.[48]

Motolinía's account, which, as in the rest of his work, highlights the fundamental part played by his fellow Franciscans in attracting the Mexicans to the new faith, would be dutifully repeated by later Franciscan writers. Motolinía did not provide any precise details on how those early confessions were carried out, although he did indicate that they lacked the perfection of those that came soon afterwards. According to Motolinía, the integrity of the sacrament, around which much of the debate concerning baptism had revolved, had been at no time compromised because each of its three parts had been adequately observed.

The Nahuas' successful reception of the sacrament was best conveyed through a description of their readiness to repent and offer a thorough account of their sins to confessors. The abundance of tears spilled by Nahua penitents confirmed for the Franciscans the sincerity of a deeply felt repentance. Moreover, having mastered the difficult art of self-examination, some penitents approached confession "with intimate tears from the heart."[49] Thanks to the work of a group of devoted widows dedicated to the spiritual care of the sick, many of the infirm came to confession "contrite and satisfied" ("contritos y satisfechos").[50] As an example of the Nahuas' devotion toward the sacrament, Motolinía reported the case of a handful of individuals who, having been baptized, sought the sacrament to confess all their sins because "they are not sure whether they received baptism with as much contrition and preparation as necessary."[51] While the friars who later were responsible for confession openly acknowledged the difficulty of attesting with any certainty whether the Indians were properly prepared, Motolinía's penitents approached the sacrament manifesting the kind of sorrow that was most perfect to attain forgiveness of their sins. According to Motolinía, the Nahuas' preparation for penance was one more example of the Nahuas' adoption of systematic forms of contemplation of monastic origins:

> Many of these natives have their ordinary devotions, but what is more, once or twice each day they have a special time to give themselves over to mental prayer, and they have their exercises distributed for each day; one day they think about their sins and make an effort to feel intense sorrow because of them.[52]

The projection of monastic contemplative practices onto the Nahuas, which, in Motolinía's case, sprang from the author's commitment to the reformed branch of his order, was not limited to the field of religious historiography. It suffices to recall the publication of Jean Gerson's *Tripartito* (1544) and Zumárraga's *Regla cristiana breve* (1547), treatises that promoted practices of this kind.[53] In 1536, the bishop of Oaxaca, Fr. Julián Garcés, wrote his well-known Latin letter to Paul III, presented to him in Rome by the Dominican Bernardino de Minaya.[54] In the letter, Garcés offered numerous examples that illustrate the successful reception of Christian teaching among the Nahuas and praised the natural disposition of the Indians to easily grasp the tenets of the new religion. Significantly, the majority of the examples document the active participation of the Mexican Indians in the sacrament of penance, thus not only showing the missionaries' success in instructing the Nahuas but also the latter's inclination to fulfill their Christian obligations. As in Motolinía's case, these confessions also met the requirements of the church perfectly: the Indians repeated their confessions if they happened to have forgotten to declare some sin previously, they went as far as confessing sins produced by *memoria deleitosa* (*delectatio morosa*), and they were capable of experiencing great sorrow for their sins, which they expressed through copious tears.[55]

Decades later the Franciscan Fr. Jerónimo de Mendieta would attribute the success of the sacrament of confession among the Nahuas to the continuity that the Indians themselves had perceived between their ancient rites of purification and the new ritual brought and explained to them by the friars. Following Las Casas very closely, Mendieta described an ancient form of penance as follows:

In some provinces of this New Spain, the Indians had, in their gentil-
ity, a kind of vocal confession, and this they did two times a year to
their gods, with each one seeking solitude in a corner of his house, or
in the temple, or they would go into the bush, or to the fountains,
each one to the place where they felt the greatest devotion, and there
they showed signs of the greatest contrition, some with many tears,
others by clasping their hands as does one who is very afflicted, or
twisting and weaving their fingers together, and contorting their
faces, confessing their transgressions and sins.[56]

Mendieta also found that moral faults could be communicated "to
doctors or to soothsayers" ("a los médicos o a los sortílegos")[57] who
had the authority to assign appropriate corrective acts, which generally
entailed a prohibition against eating certain foods and abstinence from
sex.[58] These doctors were also able to determine the causes of physical
pain and diseases by examining the severity of the transgressions committed by an individual. According to Mendieta, in the cases of grave
illnesses, these experts encouraged the patients to confess their crimes.[59]
Four characteristics of penance stand out in the first ritual: some form
of vocal confession directed to the gods, its frequency, the absence of
priestly intervention, and contrition, which is treated in greater detail.
The lexical selection is significant: Mendieta chose to point out the contribution of the penitent by using the word "contrition" rather than a
similar term not associated with the language of sacramental theology,
thus indicating, according to Aquinas, the highest kind of sorrow
informed by grace. In this case the distance between the Nahua ritual of
purification and Christian penance is minimal. While the first variety of
Nahua penance does not seem to differ from the forms of forgiveness
found in the Old Testament, the second kind, which includes the presence of priests, is closer to established sacramental practice.[60] The contrition of the Indians is corroborated through gestures, and its intensity
revealed in the simultaneous occurrence of these gestures: the proliferation of tears and the distortion of the face. For Mendieta, the meaning
of these manifestations is unequivocal; their sincerity, unquestionable.

Mendieta's information on the previous existence of an indigenous
vocal confession accompanied by an intense act of contrition is directly
related to the way in which, following Motolinía, he reported on the
administration of the sacrament to the Nahuas. According to the chronicler, the Indians approached penance "con muchas lágrimas y dolor"
("with many tears and sorrow").[61] We must bear in mind that *dolor,*

both in Latin and Spanish, refers to physical as well as emotional suffering. Another Franciscan author, Fr. Diego Valadés, wrote about his experience hearing the Indians' confessions in similar terms. Valadés bore witness to the Indians' devotion to the sacrament, which they expressed through a profusion of tears. Moreover, Valadés characterized the contrition experienced by Indian penitents as "contritio maxima."[62] Regarding this observation, it is important to point out that Valadés chose to include at the end of his *Rhetorica christiana* a compendium of Peter Lombard's *Sententiae*. In the section on penance, Valadés summarized Lombard's idea that as long as penitents had not ignored the sacrament, they could receive absolution for their sins through sincere contrition in their hearts and without the need to confess their sins vocally, that is, without the presence of a priest. In fact, Valadés made no reference to the function of the priest, thus ignoring the doctrine of the keys that was, as the doctrine sanctioned at the Council of Trent.[63] Even though it could be argued that Valadés was merely summarizing Lombard's doctrine, the omission is, in itself, significant. Why? During the sixteenth century, Peter Lombard's *Sententiae* was gradually replaced as a textbook in Spanish universities. Despite this change in status as an authoritative work, the *Sententiae* continued finding new readers in Mexico, particularly among the missionaries. A document containing a list of banned books seized around 1573 by order of the Mexican Inquisition mentions the existence of several copies of the *Sententiae* in the convent of Xochimilco and the need to amend the section about penance so that "the Master, in the section concerning the Sacraments, seemingly believing in part what he says, may turn to the doctrine of Saint Peter."[64]

Sahagún offered a detailed description of the practice of confession among the Nahuas that took place in a ritual in honor of the goddess Tlazolteotl.[65] This ceremony was known as *neyolmelahualiztli,* literally the act of straightening or reforming one's heart.[66] Tlazolteotl, a goddess belonging to a group of terrestrial deities,[67] was associated with sexual excess in two complementary ways: as a promoter of sexual excess among human beings and as the agent of purification of transgressions of this kind. The penitents had to confess before a priest who acted as an intermediary for the goddess, to whom through a propitious prayer he communicated the penitents' intention to be purified. The priest also had to judge whether the penitents had the appropriate disposition, namely a feeling of sadness accompanied by tears.[68] According

to Sahagún's version, this ritual required that the penitents declare their
sins vocally. Once the confession was completed, the priest directed the
penitents to fulfill a series of purificatory acts such as fasting and blood-
letting during the festivities dedicated to the goddess.[69] Individuals were
allowed to benefit from this ritual only once in their lifetime, which
explains why, according to Sahagún, most Nahuas submitted to it when
they had reached an advanced age. The individuals who were thus
purified no longer faced the punishment to which, without purification,
they would have been subject because of their transgressions.[70] Sahagún
used this last feature to explain the contemporary behavior of Indians
who, with certain frequency, requested confession and did penance in
the monasteries in order to escape civil punishment for crimes they had
committed.[71] This interpretation locates the origin of the particular
behavior of the converted Nahuas regarding secular justice in a practice
of the past and underscores the persistence of ancient modes of behavior and beliefs and their capacity to adapt to new contexts.[72] Interestingly, this interpretation overlooks the possible influence of the friars
themselves on the Indians' peculiar attitude toward secular justice. The
omission becomes significant if we consider the repeated complaints
launched early on by authorities about the friars, especially the Franciscans, who, they claimed, were usurping the jurisdiction of secular justice on a regular basis.[73] As it happened, the authorities were not simply
exaggerating. A number of Franciscan friars were convinced that in
order to ensure the complete evangelization of the Nahuas they should
not be under the jurisdiction of secular justice but rather be under the
direct supervision of their friars. Mendieta was a forceful proponent of
doing away with the principles and cumbersome procedures of the
Spanish legal system when dealing with the Nahuas.

Nahua customs and laws from the past were not completely irrelevant in the new colonial context. In the sixteenth century the Spanish
Crown was inclined to recognize the legitimacy of indigenous customs
and legal procedures as long as they did not violate natural law; nevertheless, the gradual imposition of the Spanish legal system became an
inevitable reality in the evolution of the new colonial society.[74] It is
worth considering whether in this example Sahagún was not covertly
lobbying for the recognition of religious legal jurisdiction over the Indians and against the intervention of secular justice.[75]

I have already mentioned how Mendieta partially interpreted the
adoption of Christian penance by the Nahuas as the result of an alleged

continuity with ancient penitential practices and rituals. Other writers chose to differ. Among them we find the Dominican Fr. Diego Durán, who, ever suspicious when it came to assessing the ritual life of the Christianized Nahuas, offered a different picture of both the confessions of the Indians and their old penitential rites. Durán was especially aware that Christian confession offered the priest a privileged space for the detection and correction of habits, customs, and beliefs rooted in the old religion. For Durán, the alleged similarities between Nahua and Christian penance had given other friars—the Franciscans, in particular—a false and dangerous sense of confidence that led them to take the confessions of the Indians at face value.

Mendieta had held to the idea that Nahuas used to confess their sins with true contrition in the past. Durán, when describing a Nahua ritual, made reference to a kind of sorrow experienced by the penitents that he judged incompatible with the type of contrition that could grant a Christian penitent absolution. According to Durán, during the festival of Toxcatl, dedicated to the god Tezcatlipoca and held every four years, the Nahuas could count on the forgiveness of their faults and crimes. Those transgressions were of a serious nature, such as theft, fornication, and adultery. The ritual did not include a vocal confession with specifics about the nature of the crimes, but it did require that the penitents show signs of repentance: "And thus each of those days they did not ask for anything except that their crimes not be made known, shedding many tears with extraordinary confusion and repentance, offering quantities of incense to appease that god."[76] Those seeking forgiveness for their crimes ingested earth, prayed, and moaned "like people who regretted their sins" ("como gente que se dolía de sus pecados"). Whereas the ritual allowed its participants to openly acknowledge their guilt for having committed punishable crimes by displaying signs of regret, it did not, however, demand from them a vocal declaration of their moral lapses. This ritual taught Durán to proceed with caution when judging the actions and disposition of Nahua penitents and to quash the temptation to hastily accept the Indians' demonstrations as tokens of true contrition. The participants' display of repentance required by the old ritual, warned Durán, could not be equated with the Christian notion of contrition. To move beyond the deceiving surface of gestures and external signs, Durán proposed taking a close look at the possible motivations behind the penitential acts of the ancient Nahuas. Durán was not willing to question the sincerity of the penitents' sorrow of old; however, it was necessary to discern the causes of that sorrow. Durán's improbable endeavor amounted to scrutinizing the penitents' motives, a difficult task not unknown to European confessors, but unlike his European counterparts, Durán attempted to scrutinize the past. For him, the sorrow that the Indians expressed as they submitted to the ancient rite most likely could not have originated in the fear of eternal condemnation—a notion unknown to them—but rather in a fear of an earthly nature: the corporal punishment that was the penalty imposed for certain transgressions and crimes.[77] Here the distance between the dispositions required of the ancient Nahuas for the forgiveness of faults and the dispositions required of the Christian penitent becomes clear.

In Durán's work, contrition is understood by considering the motives of the penitents' sorrow, and fear of eternal condemnation is thought to be a legitimate disposition for the reception of the sacrament. This opinion, widespread in the sixteenth century, would be echoed in the definition of contrition approved by the Council of Trent, which also explained attrition based on the motives that caused it. It is worth pointing out that the notion of contrition, traditionally understood as sorrow, did not always satisfy the theologians' demands for a definition that would leave no doubts about the essential function that the penitent's will played in the process of reconciliation. That was the opinion of Cardinal Tommasso Di Vio, or Cajetan, who was widely read by Spanish theologians. Cajetan defined contrition as *displicentia,* (displeasure) explicitly rejecting its identification with sorrow.[78]

Durán was a friar and not a theologian, so it would be imprudent to characterize his position on the place of contrition in the sacrament of penance on the basis of isolated observations. If he insisted on restricting the use of the notion of contrition to a Christian context, it was more to prevent a quick—and tentative—identification with forms of religious behavior that were not Christian than to express a clear position regarding the process of reconciliation. That Durán was in no way making a statement about this process becomes apparent if we consider one of his comments deploring the lack of adequate preparation of Nahua penitents. According to Durán, without the assistance of confessors, the Mexican Indians would continue to approach the sacrament without even showing signs of attrition.[79]

Harsh judgments such as Durán's were not uncommon. But despite his severity toward both penitents and unskilled confessors, he never expressed an opinion against administering penance to the Indians.

Nevertheless, similar concerns about Indian confessions seem to have led other friars and priests to cast doubt about the advisability of continuing doing so.[80] Moreover, there were also friars in Mexico who, influenced by the ideals of religious reform, thought that the Indians, given that they were so new to the faith, should be exempted from the obligation to confess.[81]

I would like to go back to Motolinía to consider the role he assigned to fear in regard to confession. While Motolinía declared he had seen the maximum kind of sorrow in the new converts, his vignettes on the confession of the Nahuas made a point of showing that fear of punishment was a common motivation among penitents. Two of these anecdotes tell of two Indians who, while sick, had a vision of heaven and hell that prompted them to seek confession to save their souls. Anecdotes such as these may very well reflect the type of rhetoric that informed Franciscan teachings on the theme of salvation among the Indian population. Another story concerned a convalescent young man named Juan who stood out for assisting the friars by keeping records of births and baptisms. The youth also had a vision in which two black visitors took him on a tour to observe the suffering of the damned. Overcome with fear when confronted with this vision, Juan invoked the Virgin and bore witness of his conduct as a good Christian.[82] In 1537 another youth, Benito, from Cholula, shared a similar vision soon after falling ill and a few days after having confessed. Visibly weakened by the illness, he confessed again and had the opportunity to report his vision to Motolinía: "After having confessed and resting a bit, he told me that his spirit had been taken to hell, where from sheer terror he had suffered much torment; and as he told me, he trembled from the fear that had remained in him."[83] In addition to the clear intention of illustrating the Franciscans' success in indoctrinating the Nahuas, the two narratives make fear of eternal punishment crucial for confession, an experience likely to linger in the individual, as in Benito's case.

If Durán's interpretation served as a call for confessors to exercise prudence in the administration of the sacraments and in the evaluation of their fruits, it also posed a new problem by laying bare the tensions between contending doctrines within sacramental theology and the concrete experience of the missionaries, for whom theological formulations could be both a guide and an obstacle. When Durán described the ceremony dedicated to the goddess Xochiquetzal, which offered an opportunity to obtain forgiveness for transgressions, he pointed out

two ways to achieve this goal. Slight transgressions, which the Dominican identified with venial sins, were forgiven through a purifying bath
ordered by a priest.[84] More serious transgressions, which Durán did not
hesitate to call mortal sins, required an external manifestation of guilt
of a general character and was accompanied by offerings, a practice
that reminded one friar of similar offerings in the Old Testament.[85]
Durán rejected the opinions of those who ascribed to the Indians a kind
of vocal confession that required a detailed account of particular sins
and their circumstances. For him, the Nahuas' reticence to make private
confessions of their sins had its roots in the absence of vocal confession
among the Nahua rituals of the past.[86]

Contrition and Attrition: Duns Scotus
and the Tridentine Solution in Mexico

Throughout this chapter we have seen the weight that contrition had
both for the description of the ancient indigenous practices of
purification as well as in the friars' opinions on the Indians' participation in Christian penance. The conclusions reached by the missionaries
were shaped by their respective degrees of confidence in the Nahuas'
ability or willingness to assimilate Christian teaching and, in particular,
by a variety of expectations about the contribution that the penitents
were to bring to the sacrament. The sources that I have so far examined
show that the missionaries tried hard to make sense of their observations of Indian behavior during confession by relying on their own historical reconstruction of indigenous penitential rites. An examination of
sixteenth-century religious chronicles does not provide us with a solid
enough ground to determine the opinions that writers such as
Motolinía or Mendieta may have favored regarding the role of the penitent in the process of absolution. These authors reveled in describing
confessions in which the penitents were filled with perfect contrition.
But when Mendieta referred to these confessions, he made clear that
they belonged to the past, to the early years of evangelization to which
Motolinía could refer more comfortably than he could to the present.

Beyond the disputable veracity of such reports, to carefully observe
the Nahuas' behavior in confession was but one aspect of a pastoral
activity that, with the gradual expansion of the secular clergy, came
soon to require the training and supervision of new confessors. The

manuals for confessors produced in Mexico during the second half of the sixteenth century are evidence of a growing need to improve the preparation of confessors.

As already noted, Fr. Diego Durán attributed the deficiencies in the confessions of the Nahuas less to an inadequate disposition on their part than to the confessors' ignorance of indigenous languages and traditions. These shortcomings—which Durán's work, in part, aimed to remedy—were to blame for the impatience and irritability displayed by ill-prepared confessors before their penitents, who, as a result, often became distrustful of the sacrament.[87]

The administration of penance posed numerous obstacles for the missionaries, some of them very concrete, such as the linguistic barrier between confessors and penitents. Equally significant, although of a different order, were the difficulties in achieving uniformity when administering the sacrament due to the friars' lack of agreement on how much Indian penitents should contribute.

Regarding the fate of sixteenth-century theological opinions about the place of contrition in the reconciliation process, we need to consider the impact of the Tridentine decrees on the evangelization of Mexico. The sacraments of penance and extreme unction were considered in session fourteen of the council, held in 1551.

The Catholic Church set out to respond to the attacks against the sacramental system launched by Luther and other reformers. In the case of penance, the church had to revisit its own stand on the role of attrition in the forgiveness of sins.[88] Luther's opinion that the act of repentance motivated by fear of eternal damnation made the penitent a hypocrite had already been condemned in the bull *Exsurge Domine* on June 15, 1520. Luther's attack on penance put into question the authority of the confessor and his role as mediator in the reconciliation of believers.[89] The Council of Trent faced the difficult task of formulating a set of basic principles that made clear the doctrinal boundaries that separated the church from the reformers. Much of this difficulty stemmed from the existence within the church of different doctrinal opinions about how the absolution of sins took place through the sacrament. This diversity exposed a lack of agreement on a sacrament of capital importance and made penance an easy target for reformers.

The decrees on penance resulting from the Tridentine sessions were the product of negotiations and compromises among different schools of theological thought. Although Trent did create in part a space for the exchange of theological viewpoints, the council's main objective was not to arrive at a consensus on theological matters but rather to clarify those doctrinal questions that had come under criticism by the reformers. The council did not completely clear up doctrinal disagreements, leaving open the possibility for further theological discussions on doctrinal points whose elucidation was of no immediate consequence. The vagueness and ambiguities that later interpreters found in the council's chapters and canons were the direct result of such an attitude. Penance did not escape this fate.

The council considered contrition, confession, and satisfaction to be the parts that gave integrity to the sacrament. These parts also happened to coincide with the acts of the penitent, the sacrament's *quasi materia*.[90] This dual characterization shows that the council held to the traditional distinction of three integral parts, while it departed from Aquinas by adopting the term "quasi materia." As to the sacrament's form, the theologians followed Aquinas, who had determined that it corresponded to the priest's words of absolution. The council made clear that the efficacy of the sacrament resided in the formula of absolution pronounced by the confessor.[91] Contrition was defined as follows: "animi dolor, ac detestatio est de peccato commisso, cum proposito non peccandi de caetero."[92] The council also declared that contrition, if perfect and accompanied by the intention of confessing,[93] produced the remission of sins even before the penitent received the sacrament.[94] In this case, the text made clear that the remission of sins should not be understood as the product of contrition alone, even perfect, but rather as taking place because of the penitent's intention to confess. Nevertheless, Trent sought to secure the power of the keys and the judicial function of the priests by condemning in canon IX the line of thought represented by Peter Lombard, who had viewed the confessor's role as merely declarative.[95]

Despite the questions about contrition that were left open, there is little doubt about the importance that the Council of Trent assigned to the intervention of the priest and the power of the keys. In doing so, the theologians at Trent were trying to sort out questions about the place of attrition in the economy of the sacrament. Attrition, or imperfect contrition, whether caused by detestation of sins or fear of hell, was declared to be sufficient for the sinner to be reconciled after receiving the priest's absolution, as long as the penitent had resolved to sin no more and seek salvation. Although attrition was of imperfect nature, the council held that it was a form of divine assistance to help the sinner find forgiveness through the sacrament.[96]

Mexican missionaries were certainly divided when it came to evaluating the performance and disposition of Indian penitents. Durán's doubts were, by no means, an exception among confessors, if we believe the testimony of religious writers who took it upon themselves to offer guidelines for the confessors of Indians. In the hands of these writers, the Tridentine position regarding attrition furnished a useful way to assuage the confessors' anxiety and dissatisfaction over the Indians' alleged lack of true contrition. The Jesuit Joseph de Acosta, whose work reflected the Spanish missionary experience in Peru, saw the perspective adopted by the Council of Trent as especially appropriate for the pastoral care of American Indians, who, because of their undeveloped faith and the inferiority of their senses, might find it difficult to achieve perfect contrition.[97] Thus, the imperfect contrition that the Indians were only capable of obtaining was enough to allow them to participate in and benefit from the sacrament.[98]

In Mexico, the intervention of the Franciscan Fr. Juan Bautista, in his *Advertencias para los confessores de los naturales* (1600), stands out.[99] A staunch defender of administering confession to the Indians, Bautista offered responses to and advice about the most frequently heard complaints and concerns among fellow confessors. One such concern was that the Indians appeared to approach the sacrament "without sorrow nor repentance of their sins."[100] Bautista's answer to this issue came not from the Tridentine text but from another Franciscan, the theologian Duns Scotus. Just as Acosta had welcomed the position of Trent as tailor-made for the Indians, Bautista found Duns Scotus's doctrine perfectly suitable for them since, in his words, "many do not have perfect knowledge of the requirements to receive the sacraments; because they are generally people of limited intellect, they do not achieve the level of quality that contrition should have."[101] Bautista, following Duns Scotus closely, indicated that, although a certain kind of sorrow was necessary, the imperfect disposition of the penitents was no obstacle whatsoever to their receiving the sacrament, the effect of which was ensured through divine compact regardless of the sinners' disposition.[102] In adopting Duns Scotus's formulation, which, as we have seen, did not triumph at Trent, Fr. Juan Bautista went somewhat beyond Acosta by eliminating in part a source of problems for both ministers and Indians. It is interesting to note the distance between these two solutions resulting from the consideration of a single problem. Both were inspired by the same desire to make sure that the Indians had access to a means of salvation, such as confession, and to give comfort to the confessor's conscience.

By examining some of the issues raised by the Mexican friars about the behavior of their penitents, I have isolated and analyzed one particular aspect of a complex ritual transaction. Now it is time to return to the complaints of the ministers to whom Acosta and Bautista offered their advice and examine the nature of their doubts about how to verify the contrition of the Indians. With this goal in mind, we consider the specific demands placed on the penitents as well as the objective obstacles that kept Indians and confessors apart. This is the subject of the following chapter.

CHAPTER FOUR

The Mute and the Barbarian

Verbal and Nonverbal Communication in the Confession of the Nahuas

Confession and the Limits of Communication between Friars and Indians

European religious art after the Council of Trent (1545–63) offers numerous examples of paintings depicting the spectacular repentance of a sinner. In the tradition of Christian art prior to Trent, the representation of sorrow had found its most dramatic expression in the image of the *mater dolorosa*. The multiple paintings dealing with the repentance of Mary Magdalene and St. Peter produced after Trent introduced the representation of a different kind of sorrow, a sorrow that was no longer associated with the passion of Jesus Christ but focused rather on the penitent's grief for having sinned. The works of Titian and El Greco on these themes are poignant examples of a new relationship between gestures and emotion that dominates the representation (figs. 17, 18, and 19).[1] In addition to his paintings of Mary Magdalene in penance, which closely follow Titian's model,[2] El Greco created over the course of thirty years several paintings of the repentance of St. Peter, thus introducing a motif that the art of the Counter Reformation would spread throughout Europe.[3] In the first of the series, dating from about 1585,[4] the crying apostle raises his eyes to heaven while clasping his fingers over his chest (fig. 20). In later versions, his face shows a more pronounced distortion, and the keys granted by Christ hang from his arm (fig. 21).[5] El Greco combined in one image two distinct moments in the life of the apostle, one before and one after the resurrection: his repentance for having denied Jesus three times and the episode in which he received from Jesus the keys that came later to symbolize the authority of priests to loosen and bind sins.[6] St. Peter's tears had been viewed in the Christian tradition as a dramatic example of true contrition and penance, penance conceived as virtue. The inclusion of the keys in an already eloquent image served as a post-Tridentine reminder of the absolute necessity of priestly authority in the remission of sins; the keys highlighted the sacramental nature of penance by affirming its divine institution, which the reformers had put into question.[7] The presence of the keys invites us to consider the meaning of the paintings in light of the defense of priestly power to absolve the penitent, a question that was settled for once and for all in the Council of Trent. The artistic challenge behind these paintings seems to rest less on the adequate representation of a doctrinal proposition than on the successful depiction of a sorrow of such an intensity that it could only be measured by recalling Peter's denial of Jesus. The raised eyes, the outline of the distorted face, the clasped hands, and, in particular, the tears are part of the grammar that expresses the perfect repentance of St. Peter; they are also the external signs of an internal drama that confessors had to verify, decipher, and, in some cases, induce in the penitent.

I discuss here a fundamental yet hitherto little explored aspect of the administration of confession to the Nahuas in light of the issues raised by these paintings. These confessions presented a rather specialized kind of communicative situation in which the physical proximity of friars and Indians was often contradicted by the distance between their respective conceptual worlds. Nevertheless, verbal communication was only one dimension of a communicative situation that exceeded the realm of spoken language, just as auricular confession was traditionally considered only one part of the sacrament of penance. Whether through questions or an examination of external signs, the confessor needed to recover and verify a crucial event taking place within the penitent: contrition. In this chapter we explore the function of nonverbal language within Nahua confessions and the role assigned by the friars to human emotions in new cultural contexts. I first look at the ways in which the linguistic barrier between confessors and Indians affected the administration of penance. By doing so, we can bring into focus this other more elusive mode of communication based on gestures.

Confession, Translation, and Linguistic Diversity

According to Motolinía's testimony, the sacrament of penance was first administered in New Spain in 1526, attracting within a short time many converts who, to the friars' surprise, presented themselves thoroughly prepared to receive it. Furthermore, communication between friars and Indians seems not to have posed any problem.

As a way of illustrating how well acquainted with the sacrament the Mexicans had become, Motolinía told the story of a group of schooled Indians who went to confess carrying with them a piece of paper on which they had carefully written down their sins and attending circumstances.[8] For Motolinía, these personal records were undeniable proof that the penitents had truly grasped the purpose of self-examination prior to confession, as taught by the friars. Motolinía's reference to the Nahuas' use of alphabetic writing points less to the idea of writing as an instrument of communication than as an organizing principle and cognitive tool.[9] While some Indians used the Latin alphabet to write down their sins, others, at Motolinía's request, used figures to communicate with their confessors. Let's examine the circumstance that prompted Motolinía to use this method.

> [T]here were so many who came to confess that I could not give them the care that I would have liked to, and I said to them: "I will confess only those who have brought their sins written down or drawn in figures." This is something that they know and understand, because this was their way of writing.[10]

Oddly absent from Motolinía's explanation is any reference to the need for a more effective form of communication. Rather, in underscoring the disproportionately high number of Indians to the number of available priests, Motolinía's request seems to have been exclusively motivated to expedite the proceedings. By asking the Indians to present themselves at confession after having examined their conscience and taken down their sins, the confessor could administer the sacrament without spending too much time questioning the penitent. In these examples, Motolinía took for granted the effective communication between penitents and confessors; writing was viewed as a simple means to facilitate the administration of the sacrament and as evidence that the penitent's self-examination indeed had taken place. However, the specter of a failure in communication looms large in these accounts, an impression reinforced by the surprising, and revealing, turn of phrase Motolinía chose to assure his readers that the Indians had no difficulty understanding his request: "*And my request did not fall into deaf ears,* because soon so many began to bring their sins written down that I could not make use of them" [emphasis added].[11] The Indians happened to understand him too well.

As his account makes clear neither the written word nor the drawings can replace confession. By the time Motolinía was writing, there existed different opinions about the validity of written confessions within the church. Whether written confessions might be considered valid was a question that theologians and legal experts had addressed when considering special circumstances such as the geographical separation of the confessor from the penitent.[12] The small treatise *De vera et falsa poenitentia,* attributed until the fifteenth century to St. Augustine, declared that auricular confession and the physical presence of the penitent were absolutely necessary.[13] For Aquinas, auricular confession of sins was obligatory[14] since it not only was a virtue but also an integral part of the sacrament.[15] Nonetheless, Aquinas admitted the possibility of accepting confessions made in writing or by gestures (a situation to which we return shortly) when the penitent was unable to speak or did not share a common language with the confessor.[16] Lea inferred from a decree from the Council of Strasbourg in 1435 that the practice of written confession was not all that infrequent. In the sixteenth century, Spanish theologians such as Domingo de Soto and Martin de Azpilcueta considered the practice to be valid, but similar opinions were later condemned in 1602 by Clement VIII.[17]

Now let's return to Motolinía. The absence of barriers in the communication between Spaniards and Indians is even more significant in his account of the celebration of Easter in Tehuacan in 1540:

> I saw something very noteworthy, and it is that among those who came to hear the divine offices of Holy Week and to celebrate Easter were Indians and nobles from 40 provinces and towns, and some of them from 50 and 60 leagues; and they were not compelled or called, and among them there were 12 different nations and 12 different languages.[18]

On this occasion, the friars celebrated Mass, baptized, confessed, and married Indians. Even though—or maybe because—a point was made about the linguistic diversity among the participants, the manner in which the communication with the friars took place was left unmentioned. In those places where verbal communication was truly impossible, the fervor of the Indians seemed to have sufficed, as demonstrated by fifteen mutes wishing to be baptized by the Franciscans: "these mutes made many gestures, placing their hands [together], shrugging their shoulders, and raising their eyes to heaven, making known the will and desire with which they came to receive baptism."[19]

Grounding their authority on their rapidly acquired knowledge of indigenous languages, the friars did not hide their profound reservations toward parish priests whom they derided for lacking the adequate preparation to work among the Indians. Testimonies by priests working among the Mexican Indians in 1569 give us a somewhat more adjusted vision of the daily reality of the conversion enterprise. The collection known as *Descripción del Arzobispado de México* contains reports supplied by priests at the request of the second archbishop of Mexico, Alonso de Montúfar. In writing the reports, the authors organized the information following a standard questionnaire designed by the licenciado Juan de Ovando, who was appointed *Visitador del Consejo de Indias* (Inspector of the Council of Indians) in 1569. The information thus collected was to be sent to Spain to serve as the basis for future reforms in the colonies.[20]

The chapters outlined in Ovando's instruction cover a wide range of information such as the jurisdictions of the archdiocese, the names of *cabecera* and *sujetos*, the number of clerics assigned to each area, the population of each town and isolated settlement (both those that paid tribute and those that did not), the names and languages of the different ethnic groups, as well as the number and distribution of hermitages, churches, and hospitals. Ovando's accompanying document betrays a clear concern about the suitability of priests and members of the Mexican ecclesiastical hierarchy. It cites, for example, the common practice of appointing unqualified candidates to the ecclesiastical chapter (*prebendados*).[21] Just as Zumárraga had done decades earlier, so Ovando stressed once again the need for letrados in high positions; among the capitulars, for example, the number of letrados amounted to three.[22] This dissatisfaction with the low qualifications of religious officials, and the questionable ways in which the appointments were usually made, also extended to the priests working in rural areas. This explains why Spanish authorities were interested in requesting information about the priests such as their place of birth, knowledge of indigenous languages, place of ordination, and how they carried out their daily religious activities.

The reports share the conviction that the Mexican Indians had, for

the most part, come to accept Christianity; they also agree that conversion was an ongoing process that required daily efforts, adjustments,
and negotiations. They raise two important questions: What kind of
Christianity was taking hold in Mexico around 1570? What were the
expectations that the priests could deem fulfilled when affirming that
the new religion had been embraced by the Indians?[23] Most informants
concurred that the best way to secure the proper spiritual care of their
charges was to gather them into settlements. Such an arrangement
would make visits less cumbersome and would ensure greater control
over the behavior of the Indians.

Among other concerns, the reports mention the almost perpetual
shortage of religious ministers, the effort that went into making regular
trips to towns located far from the priest's residence—often through
rough terrain—and the ubiquitous linguistic diversity. An examination
of this phenomenon helps to understand the conditions under which the
communication between confessor and Indian took place.

Before the arrival of Cortés, Tenochtitlan, Texcoco, and Cholula
had expanded their power over a wide expanse of territory, establishing tributary relationships with newly dominated peoples. The Nahuatl language had accompanied that expansion, soon becoming a lingua
franca that was widely spoken as a second language.[24] In addition to
providing Indians with religious instruction, the Crown made the
encomenderos responsible for the gradual hispanization of the indigenous population, a desire that proved difficult to realize.[25] Religious
orders were far better equipped to implement their own program since,
from their arrival in Mexico, they made the study of native languages
the indispensable step in the evangelization of the indigenous peoples.
On a smaller scale, schools such as the Colegio de Santa Cruz de
Tlatelolco, founded by the Franciscans in 1536, provided the sons of
the lords with a higher education that also included the study of
Latin.[26]

In a letter to Charles V from 1550, the Franciscan Fr. Rodrigo de la
Cruz affirmed that it was impossible to teach Spanish to the Indians and
that those Indians who did not speak Nahuatl should learn it.[27] His
statement should be considered bearing in mind that the Franciscans
had been frequently accused by the other religious orders, and in particular by the secular clergy, of trying to continually expand their control over new geographic areas and Indian groups. The dispute between
the orders and the secular clergy should not obscure, however, the fact

that the Franciscans, like no other order, had by that time several years of missionary experience and linguistic training.

In the same year that Friar Rodrigo wrote his letter, Charles V issued a decree whereby he declared Spanish to be the most appropriate instrument to carry out the religious instruction of the Indians and encouraged the adoption of Spanish customs.[28] However, the friars decided to ignore the official initiative.[29] In 1565, Philip II, reversing the previous policy, ordered the teaching of religion in the Indian languages, thereby recognizing the advice of the friars.[30] The use of the Nahuatl language, already widespread prior to the conquest, became even more prevalent as a direct result of both the linguistic policy implemented by the missionaries[31] and the dramatic decline of the population.[32] Philip III did not modify the policy on languages adopted by his predecessor.[33]

The *Descripción* shows that the language most widely spoken by the Indians was Mexican,[34] followed by Otomí. In addition to these two, the reports mention other languages spoken within the limits of the archbishopric, such as Chontal,[35] Tuztec, Matlatzinca, Mazatec, Tlatzihuizteca, Tlacotepehua,[36] Mazahua, Izcuca, Yope, Tarascan, and Texome.

The geographic concentration of languages varied widely, from areas with an overwhelming majority of Nahuatl speakers to others, such as Acamalutla in the province of Acapulco del Mar del Sur, where four languages were spoken: Tlatzihuizteca, Tuztec, Yope, and Tlacotepehua.[37] Knowledge of native languages also varied greatly among priests. Some priests did not speak Nahuatl or had only a rudimentary knowledge of it.[38] Other priests, such as Francisco Aguilar of Xiquipilco, spoke both Nahuatl and Otomí.[39] In 1575, when the third archbishop of Mexico, Francisco Moya de Contreras, began to implement the Ordenanza del Patronazgo (Ordinance of Patronage) (1574), knowledge of indigenous languages became a requirement for those who aspired to hold positions in rural parishes.[40]

In the majority of cases, the language used both for confession and instruction was Nahuatl. Joan Martínez, working in Tepecuacuilco, an area where five languages were regularly spoken, thought that in order to facilitate and make the work of priests more effective the Indians should be asked to adopt the use of Nahuatl. Martínez declared: "I am giving this order so that everyone learns the Mexican language in order to be confessed [in that language] from this point forward."[41]

The reports show two distinctive moments in the process of Christianization: the teaching of the basic tenets of the new religion and a more advanced stage in which the linguistic barrier more dramatically heightened the flaws in communication between friars and Indians, most obviously in the administration of confession. A good portion of the priests' efforts went into making the Indians memorize the basics of Christian doctrine as set out in the cartillas, whether in Nahuatl, Otomí, or Latin.[42] Often religious instruction was in the hands of a bilingual Indian chosen by the priest.

From a linguistic point of view, confession presented priests with rather particular difficulties since it required a more thorough and active understanding of the native language. In some instances when the priest was not familiar with the language spoken in the area, confession was administered through the use of an interpreter. Alonso Pacho listened to confessions in this fashion. In the archbishopric of Mexico, Nahuatl was the most commonly used language in confessions, and there were very few ministers who spoke an Indian language other than Mexican. Fernando Gómez of Atitalaquia, an area with a majority of Otomí Indians, noted that prior to his arrival there had never been in the area a priest who spoke this language; as a consequence, Gómez found that the Otomís were "very lacking in doctrine."[43] The problem posed by the absence of priests familiar with the Otomí language was compounded by the frequency with which they moved from place to place.[44] Hipólito Farfán blamed these brief stays on the character of the Otomí Indians, who, unhappy with the priests, ended up expelling them. In spite of this observation about the character of the Otomís, Farfán suggested that the successful Christianization of the group could be achieved by awarding benefices and granting positions in perpetuity.[45] Joan de Cabrera of Mizquihuala shared Farfán's perspective, confident that such an arrangement would encourage priests to learn languages.[46]

The informants ranked ethnic groups according to their demonstrated capacity or willingness to accept Christianity. In this regard, the Otomís fared rather poorly, whereas the Nahuas ranked on top. The Otomís' well-known resistance to be resettled, and the priests' difficulty learning their language, had greatly contributed to this widespread perception. Juan de Sigura from Xalatlaco commented that in matters related "to our holy Catholic faith, the Mexican Indians are the most instructed because they are the most intelligent."[47] Francisco Román from Tepozotlan conceded that, although he kept a record of the Nahuas who had confessed, he found it almost impossible to create a similar census for the Otomí population under his responsibility since they were "very dispersed throughout the hills, mountains, and cliffs, and the houses are very far from each other and not in towns." While the Mexicans confessed twice yearly, the Otomís confessed only once.[48] According to the *Descripción*, the groups who did not speak Nahuatl were the most likely to be left out of the administration of penance.

The population of Zumpango was largely Otomí. However, Pedro Infante never kept a record of these individuals, having limited himself to confess Nahuatl speakers and a few Otomí Indians who happened to speak this language.[49] It was not unusual for the Otomís to be bilingual. Hierónimo de Villanueva, for example, reported on the Indians of Heuypuchtlan under his supervision: "All the natives are Otomís and Nahuas; all the Otomís understand the Nahuatl language, and most of them speak it."[50] The distinction between those who only understood Nahuatl and those who spoke it suggests two different ways in which Indians related to Christianity: either through the passive reception of religious doctrine or through direct participation in the sacraments.

On occasion, in order to administer confession, priests unfamiliar with the languages made agreements with members of the religious orders. Such was the case of Alonso Martínez de Zayas from Teutenango and Matlacinco, where Nahuatl and Matlacinga were spoken. He listened to confessions in Nahuatl and let the Franciscans take care of those who spoke Matlacinga.[51] Meanwhile Martínez de Zayas was learning Matlatzinca and hoped to confess penitents in that language in the future. Despite these efforts, a portion of the population had never confessed. According to him, two causes had contributed to the present situation: the frequent epidemics that made it difficult for a single priest to administer the sacraments to all those who requested them[52] and, more troubling, the deceit of the Indians who avoided confession "excusing themselves saying that they do not understand the Mexican language."[53]

Some informants made brief observations about the causes of bilingualism in the towns under their supervision. Writing about Yohuala, where the population mainly spoke Nahuatl and Chontal, Alonso de Maldonado observed that "[h]alf of the people of these isolated settlements are probably Chontal, and all of them have little or great understanding of the Mexican language, which is sufficient for confession, because they come and go to the markets [*tianguez*] in area towns to sell their produce and they understand and trade with the Mexicans."[54] For

Maldonado, the bilingualism of the Chontal speakers was the result of their trading activities in the *tianguiz*. Joan Martínez of Tepecuacuilco, where five languages were spoken, noted that most of the individuals also spoke Nahuatl "because in their tianguez they deal in it more than in their native [languages]."[55]

The process of bilingualism prior to and after the conquest is well documented. Yet one might ask how the confessor came to determine when an individual was fit to confess in a language that happened to be the mother tongue of neither the confessor nor the penitent. As we have seen, Maldonado indicated that all of the Chontal speakers "have little or great understanding of the Mexican language"; this range of abilities did not, however, keep him from affirming that confession was indeed possible under such linguistic circumstances.

Maldonado did not tell us much about the proficiency of the Chontal speakers in Nahuatl, except that it greatly varied from individual to individual. Trading can be fairly well described in general terms as a highly ritualized form of interaction in which the participants know and abide by a set of rules and conventions. Trade in Mexico, where the tianguiz was a market as well as a ritual space, was no exception. It may not be unreasonable to assume that an advanced proficiency in Nahuatl was probably not an essential condition to successfully participate in a commercial transaction at the tianguiz. But what about confession? It is possible that the Indians might have identified the Christian activities carried out in Nahuatl—catechism, ceremonies, and confession—with transactions not unlike those in the marketplace. For both kinds of activities and interactions took place outside the linguistic—and often geographic—boundaries of their respective communities.

Regarding bilingualism, the *Descripción* also contains other interesting references. As A. Fernández reported, in Mayanala there were two main language groups. Most of the people spoke Mexican, except for fifty Indians on an outlying settlement who spoke Tuztec. Among them, "the men [on the settlement] also speak Mexican, and the women do not," so the females confessed through interpreters.[56] Hernández Negrete of Zalzapoltla, an area of great linguistic variety, observed a similar phenomenon. Although the Indians there spoke Yope and Nahuatl, they all confessed in Nahuatl, except for six women.[57] In the town of Citaltomaqua and its outlying settlements, Hernández Negrete noted again that "there are women who do not understand the Mexican language, although the rest do."[58] Even though more evidence is needed to conclude that these observations reflect a larger linguisitc reality, the references to nonbilingual women are intriguing. As James Lockhart noted, the extent of women's participation in the markets remains difficult to assess.[59] The same could be said about the relation between exchange and bilingualism.

According to testimonies from the regular clergy, Archbishop Montúfar seems to have approved the use of interpreters for Indian confessions. Franciscans, Dominicans, and Augustinians, who had been consistently critical of Montúfar's policies, did not welcome the archbishop's decision. In a document sent to Philip II, the friars opposed the use of interpreters, arguing that their orders had enough confessors proficient in indigenous languages who were ready to administer the sacrament to the Indians.[60] In 1583 Fr. Juan Salmerón informed Philip II that interpreters were commonly used in towns across Oaxaca and Tlaxcala to teach Christian doctrine and to confess the Indians.[61] In cases of necessity, for example, when a sick Indian requested confession but the parish priest or friar happened not to speak the language, the Second Mexican Church Council (1565) requested that confessors inform the individual about the benefits of confessing through a discrete and reliable interpreter, although the church did not consider this alternative an obligation. The Third Council (1585) adhered to the same solution.[62]

The Jesuit Joseph de Acosta offered an opinion equally adverse to the presence of interpreters during confession. Although he conceded with reservations that interpreters could be employed in the teaching of Christian doctrine,[63] Acosta believed that the use of interpreters in confession that the church had authorized for exceptional cases should by no means become the norm when confessing Indians.[64] Acosta was well aware that the number of missionaries and priests truly skilled in indigenous languages was relatively small. This situation led him to believe that if the confessor knew the penitent's language just enough as to understand this person's most serious sins and offer advice, the prudence of the priest made up for his lack of linguistic knowledge.[65] The Franciscan chronicler Jerónimo de Mendieta agreed with Acosta: only the priest's desire and efforts to learn the Indians' languages could help overcome linguistic obstacles in an age when the missionaries could no longer expect to receive the gift of tongues.[66]

Whereas the friars' accounts of Indian confessions appear inevitably colored by their pride in their linguistic abilities, the reports that make up the *Descripción* offer a more accurate picture of the relationship between confessors and Indian penitents. The information provided by the priests working in the archbishopric of Mexico allows us to analyze confession as a particular brand of communicative interaction. This perspective may help correct the rather restricted view that holds that confession was the spiritual equivalent of the economic exploitation of the Indians. The will to control the penitent clearly expressed by the manuals for confessors printed in Mexico was not substantially different from the one that gave rise to their European counterparts. Such a narrow focus, however, has led scholars to overlook the conditions that shaped the administration of confession in Mexico. Too much confidence put into a rather abstract notion of subjection that comes too close to resembling an autonomous force that operates endlessly regardless of its context has unfortunately precluded a more careful analysis of the interactions between confessors and Indians. If viewed exclusively as a mechanism of control, confession ends up transforming both penitent and confessor into passive figures. Sources indicate that this was not the case. Indian penitents, for example, seem to have feigned ignorance of the confessor's language in order to avoid confession. Confessors, on their part, revisited theological and ecclesiastical legal traditions in search of solutions to the most pressing problems posed by the the administration of penance.

Despite plenty of evidence to the contrary, the assumption that religious literature may only occasionally be used as a reliable source for historical reconstruction has not entirely disappeared. Such mistrust may explain in part why the conceptual theological framework that informed both the religious and ethnographic works written in Mexico has not received all the attention that they deserve. It is rather difficult to understand how the Mexican experience transformed missionary thought without understanding first the different intellectual traditions that made up this complex theological framework. By not doing so, we run the risk of viewing the process of Christianization as the blind imposition of a model that left no room for options and doubts.

Although knowledge of indigenous languages was crucial to the administration of penance, the penitent's vocal confession was but one component of the entire ritual. As we have seen in the previous chapter, the penitent also had to make another kind of contribution: sorrow and sincere repentance for the sins committed. It was up to the confessor to determine the quality and sincerity of the penitent's sorrow. Under normal circumstances, the confessor could make that determination by examining the penitent through questions; the existence of a linguistic barrier, however, forced the confessor to consider other elements in order to assess the sincerity of the penitent. In this case, bodily gestures added a new dimension to the communication between confessors and Indians. We explore next the function of nonverbal communication in the confession of the Mexican Indians.

Contrition Explained to the Faithful

In the theological debates about contrition and its place in the process of justification, the problem of the psychological states of the penitent resurfaced time and again.[67] In Aquinas the question regarding the psychological process that accompanies the sacramental operation is a direct result of the unresolved tension between the work of grace, on the one hand, and the act of contrition, on the other. The act of contrition, originating in the penitent's will, lends support to a psychological process that both comprises and transforms the nature of the penitent's act. From this perspective, it was necessary for the theologian to define the specific characteristics of the act of contrition to distinguish it from any other kind of act and psychological state. If a theologically satisfactory explanation of the sacramental operation required a precise definition of contrition, from a practical but no less important viewpoint involving the penitent, such definition was equally necessary. Otherwise, how could penitents recognize that they were contrite?[68]

There is also the issue of the language that informs the theological treatment of contrition and, in particular, the effort of the theologians to conceptualize contrition as a state separate from the domain of human emotions. A clear example of this conceptual distinction is found in Aquinas's definition of penance as a virtue. For Aquinas, repentance implies sadness and sorrow, but these two concepts can be understood from two different points of view. They can be viewed as passions, that is, as movements of the soul that originate in its appetitive part; in this sense they are emotions and are not related to virtue.

Penance, however, has its origin in the will and, as such, requires the active participation and intellectual consideration of the penitent. Thus, sadness and sorrow should be viewed as virtues.[69] A similar distinction, with an implicit warning against identifying contrition with a passion, is also found in the *Catecismo Romano*.[70]

Following Aquinas's distinction between a sorrow based on emotion and one based on the intellect, the Dominican Bartolomé de Ledesma in his *De septem novae legis sacramentis summarium* (1566) explained contrition by proposing as a model another emotion as a cause of sorrow: "Strictly speaking, contrition should be understood as abhorrence of or a deep dislike for sin from which *dolor* and sadness come and are felt in the lower appetitive power. Contrition is called *dolor* as a result of its effect."[71] We certainly do not know how much Mexican confessors thought about these detailed theological dissections of human actions and emotions when listening to an Indian penitent. Nevertheless we do know that the path that led from theological treatises to manuals for confessors and popular religious works intended for the preparation of the penitents is one of progressive conceptual simplification.[72] In this latter type of literature, human emotions and their visible signs became the main point of reference to discuss so elusive a concept as contrition.[73] As the paintings by El Greco so eloquently show, contrition, when rendered intelligible and visible through the language of human emotions and gestures, brought the penitent closer to the sacrament and the confessor.

The section on penance in *Doctrina breve* (1544) defines Zumárraga's contrition as follows: "Contrition is named thus because it means affliction and sorrow experienced or achieved by intervention of the will. Because it is necessary that all the powers of the soul, which are memory, understanding, and will, and the external senses with all the body be sorrowful and have contrition for the offense perpetrated against God."[74] This definition seeks to capture the distinct character of the sorrow (dolor) that constitutes the necessary disposition of the penitent by referring to other doctrinal points contained in the same work (such as the senses and the powers of the soul). Not only did penitents have to grasp what contrition was, they were also expected to experience and recognize it, which was not an easy task. This is why Zumárraga included a suggestion for those who had trouble experiencing or assessing this particular state: "And if the sinner should not be able to feel so much sorrow, it should cause him sorrow and affliction because he cannot feel sufficient regret."[75]

Although the *Doctrina breve* declares that all three parts of the sacrament must be observed, contrition is given a prominent role. The section on penance begins with an interesting comparison of baptism with confession: "baptism is done in water through the virtue of the holy spirit [a]nd this sacrament [penance], through the grace of God, in water of contrition and weeping of compunction, which is the water of tears."[76] This comparison highlights for didactic purposes the similarity of the matter in both sacraments. The scholastic distinction between matter and form did not present great difficulties in the case of baptism since the matter is the water and the form, the words of the priest. Confession, however, lacks a material object that acts as a sign, so the matter/form distinction is not perfect and left room for different interpretations.[77] The comparison is based on the affinity between the waters of baptism and the external signs of contrition, tears. In this regard, we should recall the example of St. Peter's repentance and the tradition of commentaries that exalted the power of tears in the absolution of sins.[78]

In the *Doctrina cristiana* (1546), which faithfully follows the *Suma* of Constantino, Zumárraga approaches confession by focusing on the steps that the penitent should follow in order to gain full conscience of the sins committed. Whereas the *Doctrina breve* encourages troubled penitents to experience sorrow by considering their own limitations to become contrite, the *Doctrina cristiana* tells the penitents that their sorrow has taken place aided by divine intervention.[79]

Although Zumárraga professed a strong enthusiasm for Erasmus, as evidenced by the influence of the *Enchiridion* and the *Paraclesis* on the *Doctrina breve*[80] and by his use of Ponce de la Fuente's *Suma*, Erasmus's elusive position on the sacrament of confession finds no echo in the doctrinal works he wrote or compiled. Ponce de la Fuente's treatment of baptism, confession, and the Eucharist, in particular, do not seem to have owed much to Erasmus's formulations.[81] Erasmus had questioned the divine origin of the institution of penance as well as the need for auricular confession. For him, true contrition on the part of the penitent and a confession directed to God alone were all that was required for the absolution of sins; in this regard, his opinion puts him close to the contritionists.[82] We should also remember that Zumárraga was also in charge of the publication of the *Tripartito* by Jean Gerson, the second section of which is dedicated entirely to confession.[83]

The sermon about confession in the *Doctrina cristiana* of the Dominicans (1548) characterizes contrition as a distinctive brand of sadness that is accompanied by external signs, especially tears. To distinguish this kind of sadness from an earthly emotion, the authors explained that its intensity was even greater than the sadness usually experienced for the loss of loved ones.[84] Penitents were thus discouraged from identifying contrition with a simple and all too familiar human emotion; the tears expected from them were but the external sign of their own process of self-examination.

A different approach to contrition is found in the *Doctrina en lengua mexicana* by the Franciscans, translated by Fr. Alonso de Molina. In this work, the concept of contrition is expressed through a diphrastic construction: *neyoltequipacholiztli-neelleltiliztli*.[85] Molina's *Vocabulario* records the verb *yoltequipachoa* as "tener pesar de lo que hizo," and the noun *neelleltiliztli*, "arrepentimiento, pesar de lo que hizo." *Yoltequipachoa* contains the form *yol-*, which corresponds to *yo:lli*, "heart," and is derived from the verb *yo:l(i)*, "to live, resuscitate, revive." In Nahua culture, the heart was associated with vital energy, understanding, and will.[86] *Neelleltiliztli*, in turn, contains the root of *e:lli*, "liver," which implies vitality and also encompasses the field of intense but not necessarily pleasant emotions.[87] The construction *neyoltequipacholiztli neelleltiliztli* is revealing because it covers both the intellectual and the emotive aspects of the process of repentance. It is in the heart, identified in the Western tradition with the site of emotions, where European descriptions and illustrations located the act of contrition (figs. 22 and 23). In these examples, the representation of the act seems to have taken precedence over the representation of its external manifestations, which may have left room for ambiguities.

In Molina's *Confessionario mayor* (1569), preceding a discussion on how to discern sins through an act combining memory and reflection, we find the following characterization of contrition and its origin: "and from these two things [it is advisable to know], from the knowledge of sin and the fear of God, contrition and repentance of sins have their beginning and proceed."[88] Just as in *Doctrina en lengua mexicana,* Molina expressed the idea of contrition through a diphrastic construction; instead of *neelleltiliztli,* we find *timoyolcocohua,* whose meaning in the *Vocabulario* is "to have sorrow or repentance in the heart."[89] In opting for *yol-*, Molina chose to emphasize volition, thus avoiding any reference to the realm of emotions invoked by *el-*. The mention of "the fear of God" (*ynteo ymacaxiliztli*) as one of the sources of contrition is explained more clearly in the following pages, where Molina discussed the legitimate motives that should lead the penitent to seek confession; the phrase should be interpreted in its positive meaning of brotherly love. Molina rejected all those feelings born out of the fear of hell since the penitent should solely be moved by the love of God.[90] This qualification is based on the traditional distinction between contrition (*dolor perfectus*) and attrition (*dolor imperfectus*) that we find in, for example, Bartolomé de Ledesma's treatise on the sacraments. Ledesma explained that "Attrition stems from a servile fear of punishment. But contrition stems from filial fear, and it is an act of virtue because it is brought out by the virtue of love."[91]

Molina advised in his *Confessionario mayor* that the declaration of sins be accompanied by external signs of contrition, such as tears, reminding us of their power to help bring about the remission of sins.[92] Although Molina's advice about tears refers to sacramental confession, his reference to sinners whose tears gained them absolution through direct divine intervention conveys the idea that contrition alone without the intervention of the priest remains a possibility for the penitent. Tears were important, and the priest was well advised to start confession by asking the penitent the following question: "Do your sins make you cry?" The question was intended to help the priest assess the penitent's disposition.

The feelings and emotional states that are so important in Molina's discussion of confession reappear in his *Vocabulario*. Although the first section does not include an entry for "contrición," the word does appear in the second section in the explanation of *yolchichipatilia*, "to feel grief or regret, or to have contrition." Regarding Nahuatl equivalents for "affliction," the *Vocabulario* divides them into two groups according to whether they refer to physical or mental and emotional affliction. The latter kind is expressed as *yollo chichinaquiliztli*, "to have grief in the heart," and *yoltoneuiliztli*, which also is used as a synonym of contrition in the *Confessionario mayor*. Equally abundant are entries related to repentance, which are similar to those describing the feelings of affliction of the heart. A quick comparison of the entries in Molina's *Vocabulario* and Antonio de Nebrija's *Vocabulario de romance en latín* for words related to sorrow shows that the Franciscan had a special interest in knowing how the Nahuas expressed different states of physical pain and emotional distress.

Contrition and the Language of Gestures

Although repentance and sorrow for sins was a phenomenon that took place within the penitent and could only be known with certainty by God, it was the confessor's duty to verify the penitent's state of contrition during the ritual of penance. To that end, the confessor could trust the words of the penitent (in some cases by asking questions) and also evaluate external signs. Both theological and popular religious works touched frequently on the external signs of contrition. For Albert the Great, Aquinas's teacher, contrition, in essence, consisted of the act of repentance born out of the penitent's will, an act that had, in addition, external manifestations and signs that were merely incidental.[93] Aquinas advanced the opinion that the priest should not grant absolution if he was not sure that he had detected signs of contrition in the penitent.[94] Now, what did those signs consist of? A set of mnemonic verses in wide circulation throughout the Middle Ages and quoted by Aquinas enumerated sixteen necessary conditions for penance to be complete; one of them was that penance should be "lachrimabilis."[95] A Spanish treatise, the *Arte para bien confesar* (1500?) repeated those conditions. Confession should be, among other things, "tearful,"

> because (according to Chrysostom) the sinner should have great sorrow and be tearful if he can for the sin that he committed, intending never to repeat [it]. And this condition is the most necessary and accomplishes more than all others through which we draw closer to God and give satisfaction to God; as long as we cry with the intention of confessing, we are in grace.[96]

Another work of the same genre, the *Confessional,* by Alonso de Madrigal declares that the tears that accompany contrition lend it greater power in the remission of sins.[97] The idea that contrition with tears (e.g., St. Peter and Mary Magdalene) was somewhat more perfect and desirable was widely accepted and was supported by a long tradition within Christian thought.[98] In the Christian tradition, the ability to produce tears in the process of repentance received a double treatment: it was thought that some individuals could experience this state because they had a special gift; most, however, reached that state through due diligence. The latter view was inextricably linked to the techniques and exercises of contemplation originated in monasteries; hence Cassian's interest in elaborating a classification of tears. He categorized tears according to their respective causes. Thus he discerned weeping originating in the sincere remorse for sins ("qui peccatorum spina cor nostrum compungente profertur"), tears produced through the contemplation of eternal good ("qui de contemplatione aeternorum boborum et desiderio futurae illius claritatis exoritur"), and finally those resulting from the fear of eternal punishment for the sins committed ("de metu gehennae et terribilis illius iudicii recordatione procedunt").[99] Cassian's classification can be found later integrated into a complex system of meditation in Catherine of Siena's *Dialogue,* which was widely read in sixteenth-century Spain.[100] Based on the motives that moved the Christian, Catherine of Siena identified five kinds of tears representing five different stages of the soul. At the bottom of the hierarchy lay the tears caused by the fear of condemnation; at the top, those caused by love of God and fellow human beings.[101] She wrote that it was possible for an observer to discern the species of tears since the eyes were the only organ capable of transmitting the true state of the heart.[102] This commonplace was frequently repeated in physiognomic treatises, including those written by Erasmus and Juan Luis Vives. However, how could a penitent intent on acquiring perfect contrition or a confessor observing a penitent's signs find this suggestion useful?[103]

While spiritual treatises such as Catherine of Siena's or Ignatius of Loyola's *Spiritual Exercises* focus on the individual's efforts to catch a glimpse of the divine by molding and transforming a private world of feelings, motives, and emotions, the manifestation of tears was by no means limited to the private domain or confined to the narrow space of confession. Tears also had their place in public life. In sixteenth-century Spain, the liturgical calendar offered Christian believers many opportunities to shed abundant tears when participating in collective penitential rituals.[104] Both processions and preaching offered appropriate contexts for this kind of collective manifestation.[105]

Now I turn to an early document written in Mexico and intended for a European audience. The document in question is a letter to the emperor signed by, among others, the Franciscan Fr. Jacobo de Tastera in 1533. The letter, which contains a wildly exaggerated account of the conversion of the Mexican Indians carried out by the Franciscans, responds to the increasingly negative campaign launched by Spanish officials and civilians against the friars. How did the friars endow their inflated version of the evangelization with credibility? How did they explain the alleged success of their enterprise so as to render it plausible? Interestingly enough, the friars ruled out a purely religious explanation.

The letter explains the astonishing progress of the Mexicans in the new religion by postulating the prior existence in Mexican society of certain conditions that made possible the successful task of the friars. The authors explained that Nahua society had reached an important evolutionary stage, evinced by the existence of professional groups, a complex network to collect tribute, and a system to administer justice. Moreover, the Nahuas had elaborate rules, a particularly rich code of reverence that governed the interactions between individuals.[106] Regarding this dimension of the Indians' behavior, the letter mentions the following custom: "[they] go out to welcome honored individuals when they enter their towns, [and have] feelings of sadness *usque ad lacrimas,* when good breeding and gratitude require it."[107] This passage specifically addresses a custom among high-ranking members of the nobility. The letter shows that Spaniards were keen observers, having early on taken notice of the rules of courtesy and hospitality that were an integral part of the symbolic system of interaction and communication governing the relations between different social hierarchies.[108] Decades later, Fr. Bernardino de Sahagún, especially interested in reconstructing the moral world of the ancient Nahua nobility and its conventions, recorded a testimony about the place of gestures and tears in the code of reverence of the elite.[109]

The behavior displayed by the lords when welcoming individuals of similar social status helped the friars explain the achievement of their order among the Nahuas. Evidence of the inroads made by Christianity among the Indians and their children was the frequency of confessions with sobs and tears, pure and very simple confession, together with the correction *nos qui contractavimus de verbo vitae* know it, and that sovereign God, who works miracles hidden in their hearts, knows it, and even those who are not blinded by ignorance or malice will be able to see it in their external acts.[110]

In the continuity between the Nahua past and the colonial present postulated by the religious, the sacrament of penance is conceptualized through the conventions that controlled the behavior of the Indian nobility. That the friars observed similarities between European and Nahua conventions is yet another indication of the advanced development that the friars ascribed to Mexican society.[111] Thus, the Franciscans explained the successful reception of confession among the Nahuas not by resorting to old patterns of religious behavior but rather by looking at the symbolic language of reverence and social hierarchy. Two observations are necessary. First, because this information is limited to the social world of lords and noblemen, we cannot generalize about modes of behavior among the macehuales; nonetheless, it is a clear example of the Franciscans' interest in the behavior and social values of the elite. Second, the description of the confession of the Nahuas opens the possibility of thinking about the meaning of this interaction not from the perspective of the confessors but rather from that of the Indians themselves. From this point of view, the transaction between friars and Mexican Indians could be read as another exchange with "honored persons."

What do these two apparently dissimilar situations have in common? One might be inclined to hold that, in the first case, it is a question of a social convention in which the sincerity of the actors does not determine whether or not the interaction has a felicitous conclusion, while in the second case—confession—the sincerity of the act of repentance is, indeed, fundamental. However, such an explanation is not reflected in the content of the letter, where the Franciscans affirmed that the sentiments shown by the Indians during confession are genuine. Perhaps the key to the connections seen by the friars in such different rituals is the role of the individual's will in the two acts, a sign of reverence and humility in one case, a sign of repentance in the other. We should recall that the act of contrition had been characterized as one originating in the will of the penitent.[112] For these Franciscans, the Indians' participation in confession was ensured by the prior existence of a code of

reverence; in it, gestures were to be taken as the expression of sentiments of humility, a social virtue. This conjunction of sentiment and
nonverbal expression was not, as we have seen, irrelevant to confession.
It is worth recalling the words of the *Catecismo del Santo Concilio de
Trento* on the humility of the penitent during confession:

> Because when we confess sins kneeling at the feet of the priest, heads
> uncovered, face bowed to the ground, hands clasped and raised to
> heaven, and making other signs of Christian humility, although they
> are not necessary for the sacrament, through them we understand
> clearly that we should recognize in the Sacrament a heavenly virtue,
> and that we are to seek and implore with the greatest diligence divine
> mercy.[113]

We should point out two aspects of the relation between penance
and gestures. First, in addition to an appropriate internal disposition,
the sacrament required of the individual to follow certain conventions
that included specific physical gestures and postures associated with the
values of humility and submission. Second, we are also interested in the
external forms linked to contrition. The latter were, in part, codified but
also exceeded the repertory of gestures conceived within the Christian
tradition; such a result is understandable if we keep in mind the common identification of contrition with distinct human emotions and the
variety of expressions that these emotions can find.[114]

When describing the penance of the ancient Mexicans, Bartolomé de
Las Casas included a familiar repertory of external gestures that accompanied their acts of repentance. Such gestures did not differ from those
sanctioned within the Christian tradition: "each person alone went into
a corner of his house and placed his hands as would one who felt very
afflicted, some times wringing them, other times intertwining their
fingers, crying, and, those who could not spill tears, moaning and wail-
ing."[115]

Theologians did indeed consider that there could be situations in
which verbal communication between confessor and penitent was
difficult or simply nonexistent. In the search for a solution to this problem, which threatened the integrity of the sacrament, there arose different opinions about the use of interpreters and written confessions.
Where verbal communication was impossible, the confessor could only
observe the penitent's external signs of remorse to determine this per-

son's degree of contrition and to decide whether to verify the repentance and the sorrow of the sinner. References to reconciliation in extremis abound in the manuals for confessors, especially in the cases of the critically ill who were no longer able to speak and confess their sins vocally. Some of the alternatives that were considered to overcome obstacles of this kind included the use of a set of conventional signs to convey information about the sins to the confessor or the observation of signs of contrition. If the sick individual lost the ability to speak but the confessor was certain that the person had acted as a good Christian throughout his or her life, Anthonino de Florencia, the author of a well-known summa for confessors, thought that the confessor could absolve the penitent.[116] Fr. Francisco de Alcocer, author of a *Confessionario breve* (1568), suggested that if a sick person was able to declare by signs at least one sin, whether mortal or not, the confessor should grant absolution since regardless of that person's disposition the priest's absolution was sufficient for the remission of sins.[117] Here Alcocer was expressing the widespread opinion that the declaration of at least some sin was necessary for the penitent to receive absolution. Zumárraga briefly considered such a situation in the final section of his *Regla cristiana breve:* "If he should have lost speech and retains consciousness, he should show his faith and contrition with signs."[118]

In the last section of the curious *Libro llamado Refugium infirmorum* (1593) of Melchior de Yebra, we find an alphabet attributed to Bonaventure to be used by the sick to communicate with their confessors; it could also be used by confessors with penitents who were deaf (fig. 24).[119] At a later date, an alphabet based on hand gestures to be used by the deaf was included in Juan Pablo Bonet's important treatise published in 1620 (fig. 25).[120] Commenting on a case in which the Eucharist was administered to a sick individual who had lost the ability to speak and, as a consequence, had not confessed, Alcocer wrote that such administration was appropriate under the following circumstances:

> [I]f the penitent had earlier asked for the sacrament of the Eucharist or showed or now shows signs of contrition or of [being a] Christian, because he worships the cross; or, when asking him to repent for his sins against God with the intention of amending his ways, or another holy and good thing, he raises his eyes to heaven or shows another good sign, give him the sacrament of the Eucharist.[121]

Although Alcocer did not explain what he meant by a "good sign" of contrition, he did indicate that the expression on the face of the dying person is of great significance. Such is the kind of gesture that when accompanied by tears, we find in El Greco's paintings of St. Peter and Mary Magdalene as well as in the representation of contrition in Cesare Ripa's *Iconologia*. In Ripa's work, the index finger of the right hand pointing upward conveys the importance of heaven as the divine recipient of contrition (fig. 26).[122] Another gesture with a similar meaning—raising the hands—was also associated with the signs of contrition and was among those the confessor was to consider.[123]

Nonetheless, while Las Casas and other friars such as Mendieta believed that the Mexican Indians had a particular inclination to experience contrition, as demonstrated by abundant external signs, other religious writers did not share their opinions. Fr. Diego Durán complained that the Indians were so poorly prepared for confession that he could not find even signs of attrition in them.[124] As mentioned in the previous chapter, years later Fr. Juan Bautista, a Franciscan, wrote in his *Advertencias para los confessores* that first among the most common complaints from confessors was the lack of true repentance in their penitents.[125] Bautista, who was truly an expert in the Nahuatl language, was keenly aware of the difficulties faced by confessors unfamiliar with the languages spoken around them, such as this:

> Many times a priest is walking along a road and is called to confess an Indian who is ill, but the priest does not know much of the language. What will he do? When there is no other priest nearby who can confess him, he should confess him, seeing signs of contrition in him. No matter how few sins he understands, even if he fails to understand many more, it is enough for him to be able to grant absolution, and that soul is made right.[126]

According to numerous Catholic theologians, in situations of danger or when communication was difficult, an incomplete confession of sins did not invalidate the sacrament. In this particular case, although the signs of contrition were of great importance; there was no information about the specific characteristics of those signs. Bautista did comment about the use of interpreters in confession, saying that the penitent was not obligated to submit to it if he was in any way healthy. If the penitent happened to be close to dying, the Franciscan followed the opinion of those theologians who believed that confession through an interpreter should be obligatory, as long as the secrecy of confession was by no means compromised.[127] Franciscan sources indicate that the concept of contrition was not unknown to Indian converts; in the visits to towns under their jurisdiction, the Franciscans depended on Indians who were entrusted with the baptism of children in danger of dying and with advising the ill of the importance of contrition.[128] When the infirm wanted to confess but could not find a confessor, the Augustinian Fr. Juan de la Anunciación affirmed that contrition was sufficient to obtain absolution of sins.[129]

Bautista presented a similar situation; in this case the obstacle was caused by the penitent's loss of speech:

> It happens that a confessor is called and he goes to confess the ill or wounded person who has requested confession, and when the priest arrives, he finds the sick person unable to speak [but with demonstrations and signs of contrition] and even sometimes unconscious and unable to reason. The same can happen when at the Church. What will he do?[130]

To find a solution to this particular problem, Bautista turned to the authorities examined years earlier by Fr. Juan Focher in his treatise on how to administer confession to the mute.[131] Following Juan de Medina, Focher had advised the priest to absolve the dying person who was showing or had shown signs of contrition. Bautista corroborated this point of view by referring to a well-established opinion on the confession of the mute, which held that if the individual could communicate through signs, he was obliged to confess. However if this was not the case, the obligation did not apply, and the penitent did not receive the priest's absolution.[132]

What do these cases collected by Fr. Juan Bautista tell us? Even though his examples present situations for which theologians had already offered solutions, we should consider the particular context in which Bautista composed his *Advertencias para los confessores*. Dying Indians, confessors who did not understand the language of their penitents, mutes: all these are characters in the same drama that, with variations, tells us how the absence of communication becomes the main obstacle to salvation. The examples, easily found in European treatises, are an eloquent testimony of the attention paid by theologians to every conceivable circumstance that a confessor may encounter. In the Mexican context, the linguistic barrier between Indians and missionaries was an everyday phenomenon. The same could be said of the unfortunate frequency with which friars came upon dying Indians, given the regular occurrence of epidemics that decimated the Mexican population throughout the sixteenth century.[133] The identification of the Mexican Indian with the mute was surely not lost to Bautista: when writing about the use of interpreters, he resorted to the authority of Duns Scotus, who had explicitly linked the deaf and the barbarians.[134] It is safe to say that the cases brought up by Bautista and the specific solutions for each of them are indications of what was a daily reality and anything but isolated events for many confessors who did not know the indigenous languages.

By way of conclusion I summarize here the main points covered in this chapter. On the one hand, we have looked at the consequences derived from the conceptualization of contrition. When the *Catecismo del Santo Concilio de Trento* insisted on not identifying contrition with human emotions, it did not simply repeat a well-established theological notion; it warned against an understanding of contrition that, although erroneous from the scholastic perspective, was widely accepted among believers and priests. That misunderstanding was the direct result of the language used in the first place to conceptualize contrition. On the other hand, after considering the obstacle posed by the indigenous languages to confessors in Mexico, we have seen that, from the beginning of the evangelization, the Spaniards had paid close attention to the postures and gestures of the Indians. Writing at the end of the sixteenth century, Fr. Juan Bautista showed how nonverbal language became a crucial indicator of contrition when verbal communication between confessors and Indians was impossible. Now then, how did the priest recognize those signs? Confessors were familiar with the repertory of signs with which Christian tradition had endowed contrition; could one expect to find those same signs among the Indians? Religious instruction might have made this possible. Catechisms and sermons spoke about contrition and mentioned the tears and feelings of sorrow and sadness that penitents should experience. But when the confessors were faced with concrete situations, what standard guided them as they observed the penitents? For example, did the Indians express sorrow and sadness the same way that Europeans did?

In order to represent human emotional states in painting, Leonardo da Vinci recommended closely studying the gestures of the mute, in particular, those corresponding to laughter and grief.[135] Fr. Jacobo de Tastera seemed to have found in the nonverbal language used by the Mexican nobles to greet their equals an "adunatio linguarum" of sorts, the realization of which the Venerable Bede had imagined, centuries earlier, in the heavens.[136] From the sixteenth to the eighteenth centuries, human gestures were thought to be a distinctive language. In the case of the nonverbal language employed by the mutes, opinions were divided around its specificity: for some, it was a natural language; for others, it was shaped by conventions; there were also those who thought it a combination of the two.[137]

For Leonardo the study of human expressions and emotions was a way to become a better artist; the speculations made about mutes in the centuries that followed were part of a broader search to define the concepts of nature and society. For many a priest and friar exposed to alien languages in Mexico, the attention paid to the faces and the emotions of the Indians was not a speculative exercise. Confessors had to catch glimpses of contrition in elusive gestures that could express both simple and complex human emotions. It was maybe inevitable that contrition, in the context of the Christianization of Mexico, was often considered in terms of human communication. Up to this point we have reconstructed the basics of a small drama in which confessors and penitents participated. We must rely on our imagination to provide the details of those encounters: the gestures and emotions of the Indians and the doubts and solutions of their confessors.

CHAPTER FIVE

The Eucharist and the Ambivalence of the Gift

The Eucharist among the Sacraments

In 1528 in the town of Huexotzinco, Diego, a nephew of the local lord, lay ill waiting to be given the Eucharist. Diego, who had been raised by the Franciscan friars, had requested the sacrament several times after having confessed, but the friars, despite having proof of his devotion, remained reluctant to meet his demand. Nonetheless, the young man's wish was granted when two unidentified men wearing Franciscan garments appeared at his side and handed him the host; afterwards the visitors disappeared. Later on, when Diego was offered some food by his father, he gently declined, explaining that two friars had already fed him, leaving him fully sated. Soon after, the youngster passed away.

For sixteenth-century Spanish theologians and religious writers the multiplicity of names by which the Eucharist was known and referred to was proportionate to the manifold layers of meaning that this sacrament concealed.[1] This richness of meaning spoke to them of the privileged place that the Eucharist had come to enjoy among the other sacraments and in Christianity in general. This is why they often set out to explain the meanings of the sacrament by teasing out the wide variety of expressions traditionally used to make reference to it. They would report that the sacrament of the altar—as it was commonly called—was also known as "gift" (*don*),[2] *manjar* (delicacy), "Communion," "sacrifice,"[3] and "Mass" (*missa*).[4] Because it also condensed the story of Christ's sacrifice with its ultimate promise of salvation, the source of all the sacraments, the Eucharist was sometimes called "memorial y suma de todo el Evangelio."[5] From the viewpoint of the sacramental operation, the Eucharist held a prominent place among the other sacraments because it was the only ritual where the matter (*materia*)— unleavened bread and wine—was transformed into the body and blood of Christ by the words of consecration (*forma*) uttered by the priest.

As established in 1215 by the Lateran Council, Christians were obliged to receive Communion at least once a year at a time determined by the church, generally Easter.[6] The council also determined that it was necessary for the sacramental reception of the host that the individual had previously confessed to a priest, an annual obligation decreed by the same council.[7] In practice, though, things were somewhat more complicated for parishioners and priests alike, as Diego and his friars eventually found out.

Diego's story—as well as another one concerning a consecrated host that found its way into the mouth of an Indian woman attending Mass—was reported in plain style by Motolinía as another example of the successful reception of Christianity among the Mexican Indians.[8] Decades later when another Franciscan chronicler, Juan de Torquemada, revisited the story about Diego, he could not help speculating on the identities of the two mysterious friars as a way to ground his own interpretation of the miraculous incident. He thought that the most likely candidates were St. Francis and St. Bonaventure, two Franciscan saints renowned for the high regard in which they had held the Eucharist. St. Francis's devotion to the sacrament had led him to remain a deacon, never seeking the orders that might have allowed him to celebrate Mass; as for St. Bonaventure, although a priest, his hesitancy to celebrate Mass, "fearing how much preparation is required from the person who is to receive it (the Eucharist)," had brought him much respect among the friars of the order.[9]

In Torquemada's hands the story was slightly transformed; while his contribution highlights the anecdote's original meaning, it inadvertently ends up deepening the paradox that in Motolinía's version remains in the background. First there is the role of the friars who turned down Diego's requests. While Motolinía's version focuses on Diego's devotion, whose exact measure was left to the heavenly envoys to appreciate fully, Torquemada drew harsher conclusions from the friars' act of denying Communion to Diego, going so far as to label it an act of cowardice.[10] Secondly, there is Torquemada's addition of the ambiguous figures of St. Francis and St Bonaventure, with their saintly lives and their saintly, and no less paradoxical, relation to the Eucharist.

The story, as told first by Motolinía and later through Torquemada's embellishment, addresses the friars' uncertainty and disproportionate caution in administering the Eucharist despite the fact that

Diego had confessed and was held to be a devoted Christian. That such uncertainty could only be dispelled by a miraculous intervention highlights in contradictory ways both the friars' limited and questionable ability to come to a judgment and the unbridgeable gap between their knowledge and that of superior spiritual entities. This paradox is compounded by the addition to the story of St. Francis and St. Bonaventure, two friars who had expressed their unworthiness to consecrate the host.

Notwithstanding Torquemada's intention in retelling Diego's story—that devoted Indians should not be left without the Eucharist—his treatment of the story also reveals that the administration of the sacrament was fraught with difficulties that had little to do with the logistics of the ritual itself, but rather with feelings and attitudes arising from the prospect of a direct contact with the sacred. This long-standing set of concerns among European priests came also to haunt the minds of Mexican missionaries.

As had been the case with baptism, the administration of the Eucharist to the Mexican Indians became an occasion for controversy both within and outside the church. While the debate on the baptism of adults had revolved around the question of how the Indians were to be baptized, the disagreement over the Eucharist touched, in its most dramatic manifestation, on whether the sacrament should be made available to the Mexicans at all.[11] However, the questions that for practical reasons needed the more immediate attention of the friars concerned to whom among the Indians and how often the sacrament should be administered. The exchange of opinions on the Eucharist never reached the virulence and divisiveness that had characterized the discrepancies over baptism; nevertheless, while the latter faded away as infant baptism slowly emerged as the new focus of Christianization, the doubts and apprehensions on the part of friars and priests alike surrounding the Eucharist lingered throughout the century.

Those who favored the wide administration of the Eucharist to the Indians were led to revise the principles that informed their position by carefully examining the arguments of the opposite camp. To some extent a serious consideration of those reasons was unavoidable since they reflected wider concerns regarding the course of the evangelization, concerns that were shared and acknowledged by both parties. For the missionaries, dealing with the Eucharist meant posing crucial questions, starting with the basic need to assess the state of the Indians as Christians and the search for explanations regarding perceived shortcomings.

Moreover, if the voices of those reluctant to make the Eucharist available to the Indians were heard—and sometimes prevailed, as was the case in Peru—it was in no small part due to the fact that the doubts and fears that they expressed were familiar, as were the answers to assuage them.

As the discussions over the baptism of adults in Mexico made apparent, theologians and friars had not concerned themselves exclusively with ensuring the efficacy of the sacrament. They were also concerned about questions related to those aspects of the ritual that, if not strictly essential, were nonetheless considered by some indispensable to preserve the reverence owed to it. The administering of the Eucharist to the Indians mobilized in the ministers feelings and sentiments that sacramental theology, despite its thorough treatment of the workings of the sacrament and its penchant to anticipate solutions to foreseeable contingencies, could not altogether prevent from arising. These feelings, often expressed in terms of fear, seem at first rather basic in nature, inspired as they were by the handling of the sacred in a most tangible form, a feature that set the Eucharist apart from all the other sacraments. While the pivotal moment of consecration was quite literally in the hands—and mouth—of the priest, there remained the more delicate instance of the actual administration of the host to the faithful, and with it the concerns attending the proper and orderly transfer of, and the recipient's contact with, the sacred. If the giving of the Eucharist gave way to a certain unease and fear in the officiating priest, these sentiments were often elicited by doubts regarding the spiritual, moral, and even physical condition of the recipient that could taint his or her contact with the host.[12] Religious writers such as the Franciscan Francisco de Osuna warned priests against denying the sacrament to their flock based on unwarranted fears of this nature.[13]

Technically, all that was necessary for an individual to receive the Eucharist was to have been absolved by a confessor and to approach the sacrament with a basic knowledge of its meaning. Indians who had submitted to confession, as the friars expected them to do at least once a year, would then be licensed by their confessors to approach Communion. In practice, as we have seen, a significant number of friars did not think that these basic requirements were enough or commensurate with the unique nature of the mystery that distinguished this particular sacrament.

Religious instruction was to play a central role in conveying to the Indian population the friars' expectations on how best to prepare before accessing the sacrament. The preparation for Communion had been a central preoccupation among different religious groups committed to the reform of Christian devotion and spirituality that had, in their view, become hostage to ritual formalism. It was believed that a systematic reflection on the meaning of the sacrament, which was to take place before, during, and after the individual had received it, would contribute to restoring to the act of Communion the preeminent place that it was meant to have in a Christian's life. For the first archbishop of Mexico, Fr. Juan de Zumárraga, the expectation that the new Indian converts should approach the sacrament by engaging in an elaborate exercise of reflection and contemplation did not seem unrealistic. To this end Zumárraga included in his *Doctrina cristiana* (1546)—a treatise addressed to Indians already familiar with the basic tenets of Christianity—a full section with advice on how to best receive Communion. The guidelines touched exclusively on the preparation of the soul, a preoccupation underlined by a call to shed all concerns with material matters. This disdain for the sensual world permeates the entire work and may explain in part the absence of references to the Mexican context in which it was conceived.

Zumárraga's *Doctrina cristiana,* informed as it was by the desire to project on the Mexican Indians the kind of inner piety that had been taking hold in Spain among the laity, did not acknowledge the more mundane concerns that the friars came to voice when faced with administering Communion among the Indians. As it turned out, these concerns had more to do with fear that the Indians might pollute or desecrate the consecrated host than with their spiritual or mental disposition. If Zumárraga had made the preparation of the soul the most important step for Communion, years later Alonso de Molina would assign an equally significant role to the proper preparation of the body. Before Communion the Indians were to fast, abstain from sexual intercourse for at least two days, wash their bodies, and wear clean clothing when in church. For the actual reception of the host, Molina instructed the Indians not to open their mouths too much, to stick their tongues out a little bit, and never to touch the host with their hands in case it happened to get stuck on their palates.[14] The message conveyed to the Indians was that Communion was a special occasion to partake in the sacred as much as a demanding ritual with rules that, if not correctly followed, could imperil the recipient's spiritual state by incurring new sins.

The Debate

According to the chronicler Jerónimo de Mendieta, the bishops gathered at the episcopal meeting of 1546 in the city of Mexico decided in favor of administering the Eucharist to the Indians at a time when dissenting voices within and outside the church expressed views to the contrary.[15] Among the bishops attending the meeting called by the visitador Tello de Sandoval were Juan de Zumárraga, Vasco de Quiroga, and the recently appointed and controversial bishop of Chiapas, Bartolomé de Las Casas. Although the meeting of Sandoval with the bishops dealt primarily with the future of the *encomiendas* in the light of the New Laws of 1542—in the promulgation of which Bartolomé de Las Casas had played a fundamental role—the situation regarding the Eucharist seems to have become pressing enough to warrant a new pronouncement on the part of the bishops. In it, no new grounds regarding policy were broken, and the bishops limited themselves to reiterating Pope Paul III's recommendation in the bull *Altitudo divini consilii,* which had been carefully examined in the ecclesiastical meeting of 1539 when new guidelines for the baptism of adults had been issued. The resulting document of the 1539 meeting had established that the Eucharist should not be denied to Indians who had been baptized, submitted to confession, and been able to discern the difference between material and sacramental bread.[16] This last point, which directly addressed the Indians' familiarity with doctrinal matters, had been, and would continue to be, a source of contention, and not because it was thought to be unreasonable. Rather, it provided those opposed to admitting Indians to Communion with an occasion to put into question the Indians' capacity to understand the sacramental operation. The authorities also agreed that the Indians were, as other Christians, under the obligation to receive Communion at least once a year.

Writing some years before the episcopal meeting of 1546, Motolinía found remarkably little to say about any existing differences among friars regarding the administration of the Eucharist, except for indicating that they had been settled when Pope Paul III decreed in 1533 that the Indians be admitted to Communion.[17]

In general the Franciscans only admitted to Communion a handful of Indians, having chosen to focus more on other sacraments deemed more urgent for the overall conversion of the population. This is why, when he commented about having witnessed on one occasion how a group of Spaniards had marveled at the eagerness with which the Mexican Indians sought the sacraments, Motolinía did not count the Eucharist among them.[18] Those who did receive Communion were Indians of exceptional devotion, as was the case with a certain nobleman called Juan from Cuauhquechollan in Tlaxcala, who had taken to receiving Communion together with his wife once a year.[19] Mendieta reported that this same Juan was the first Mexican to receive the sacrament.[20]

During the first three or four years after the arrival of the Franciscans, the sacrament had been only available in their monastery in Mexico City, and shortly after in Texcoco. As Motolinía's account suggests, the friars' early efforts appear to have centered less on promoting the actual reception of the Eucharist than on instilling in the Indians the sentiments of respect and reverence due to the sacrament, sentiments that would eventually translate into external forms of devotion and the desire to partake in it. Through religious instruction the Mexican Indians were to become acquainted with the meaning of the Eucharist as a sacrament and also with the significance that the new religion placed on the various symbols and objects associated with it. Religious holidays also became powerful vehicles to instruct and promote particular devotions among the population. Franciscan chroniclers took much pride in the extraordinary participation of the Mexican Indians in the festivities of Corpus Christi, which were celebrated with elaborate theatrical performances.[21] Celebrations also sometimes accompanied the arrival of the sacrament to a church, events that Indian officials often recorded in the annals of the town. The *Codex Aubin,* for example, registered that in 1557 the finishing of a sagrarium (*icaltzin sacramento,* literally, the sacrament's little house) was celebrated with theatrical representations; the arrival of the sacrament to San José in 1590 merited mention as well.[22] The *Anales de Tecamachalco* did not fail to record the inauguration of the sagrarium in 1559.[23]

The Mexican Indians came to learn that the Eucharist, more than any other sacrament that the friars had taught them about, carried a surplus of symbolic power that was not exhausted in, or limited to, the ritual that culminated with its reception. They also learned that the power stemming from its unique sacred status could also be of assistance in serious circumstances, as was the case in 1538 when Viceroy Antonio de Mendoza ordered the closing of Franciscan monasteries with an insufficient number of friars. To prevent this measure from being carried out, a group of Indians knelt in front of the sacrament and pleaded for the religious men to remain with them.[24] These scattered examples reflect in part what by the sixteenth century had become a well-defined trend of European Christian spirituality that placed the utmost importance on the devotion to the sacrament rather than on its actual reception. In Mexico and in other Spanish colonies, the mysterious and alien nature of the sacrament made itself visible to the Indians through the monstrance, the sagrarium, and the altar. As time went on, the sacrament shed some of its strangeness and novelty as Indian artisans and painters began to contribute to the design and decoration of ritual objects.[25]

That the administration of the Eucharist should not have ranked high among the friars' priorities in the early stages of the conversion efforts is not altogether surprising, and there is little reason to think that it could have been otherwise. The baptism of adults alone had posed from the start enough logistical difficulties for the friars to surmount. In addition to imparting religious instruction to large crowds, the friars also needed to determine—albeit often in a hasty fashion—the status of Indian marriages before the actual ritual of baptism could take place.[26] The steps leading to the actual administration of the Eucharist were no less cumbersome since technically the Indians were required to have gone through confession and be familiar with the meaning of the sacrament they were about to receive. In spite of this considerable practical burden, no explicit official directive barring the Mexican Indians from the sacrament seems to have been in place, except for the Franciscans' decision at the beginning of the conversion campaigns to deny the Eucharist to the natives on account of their status as neophytes. After a short period of time, however, this original measure was revised when the Franciscan friars agreed to let confessors decide if the penitent was ready for Communion.[27] The First Mexican Church Council (1555) proceeded along the same lines, this time elaborating in some detail the conditions to be met by the Indians prior to Communion.[28] Sixteenth-century Franciscan chronicles suggest that the recently baptized were not expected to approach the Eucharist anytime soon, as was recommended by Vitoria and the theologians of Salamanca in 1542.

The Franciscans laid out their policy of admitting a reduced number of Indians to Communion in a report from 1571 requested by the visitador Juan de Ovando. The significance of the document lies in the reasons presented in defense of the policy, which were carefully framed to avoid presenting a discouraging portrait of the progress of Christianity among the Indians and that could, in turn, put into question the effectiveness of the friars' activities. Thus, while it states that some Indians, despite their good disposition, lacked the ability to receive the sacrament, those fully equipped for Communion were not always admitted, a measure taken to protect the sacredness of the ritual.[29] We find then the odd formulation of a general rule of restrictive administration, which simultaneously attempts to erase and sanction differences among the converts.

Selective admission seems to have also been intended to awaken and strengthen in the Indians the desire to participate in the sacrament, a disposition that was viewed as necessary for the spiritual preparation of the Christian before reception. The Franciscans' resolution to limit Communion to a select number of individuals was to be implemented by the confessors who had ultimate power to decide who would be licensed. As it happened, the confessor's task was greatly helped by the existence of Indian *cofradías* (brotherhoods) founded to foster religious devotion among their lay members under Franciscan supervision. Reportedly, most of the Indians who received Communion from Franciscan hands came from these associations.[30] The Eucharist was thus linked to membership in a particular social and religious organization, therefore becoming a marker—a sign of prestige even—that distinguished the brotherhood's members from the rest.

The controversy, which seems not to have created any significant divisions among the ecclesiastical authorities in Mexico, together with the position adopted by the Franciscan order, were duly reported by Mendieta in his *Historia eclesiástica indiana*. This chronicler did not directly identify the opposite factions, except for their respectively extreme views: those who sought to keep the Indians away from the sacrament and those who defended its wide administration. Resorting to a basic lesson learned from the jurists who were used to reconciling seemingly disparate precepts by attending to the particular time and place in which they were issued, Mendieta characterized the Franciscan stand on the Eucharist as the correct practical approach.[31] In rejecting a discussion based on abstract principles, Mendieta showed once again how central the insistence on arriving at solutions based on direct missionary experience continued to be for the Franciscans.[32] His order, Mendieta explained, had struck a middle ground between two extreme opinions because those who did not welcome the Indians to Communion were led by ignorance and prejudice, while their opponents failed to acknowledge the lack of religious fervor among the Indians who continued to indulge in drinking and questionable behavior. Mendieta's opinion that only a few Indians with adequate preparation should be given the Eucharist restated the position of the early Franciscans. Despite the friars' desire to see more Indians enjoying the sacrament, little had changed in Mendieta's day.[33] If the Franciscan approach had remained unchanged, it was because to a certain extent the spiritual condition of the Indians had remained unchanged, a view that, as pointed out previously, was central to Mendieta's project of securing the Indians' subjection to Franciscan supervision. In this regard we should note that, while he was certainly aware that the administration of the Eucharist had a history that was subject to change according to times and circumstances, he refused to entertain the possibility of any future change in Mexico. Place and people, then, took precedence over time as determining factors for deciding on policies. In order to allow the Indians to comply with the obligation to receive Communion at least once a year as established by the church, Mendieta and his fellow friars exhorted the Indians to request Communion, although the ultimate decision was left to the confessors.[34]

As was later confirmed by Torquemada, the Franciscans felt comfortable selectively admitting a small number of Indians to Communion, a sacrament that, as he pointed out, was not necessary for salvation ("no es de necesidad precisa").[35] This approach, which seems to have been originally adopted as a means to encourage the commoners to emulate the devotion of those admitted to the Eucharist (Juan, the first Indian to receive Communion, was a nobleman married into Moctezuma's kin), ended up promoting and sanctioning the existence of two distinct kinds of Indian converts, as already noted. Among those who were admitted to Communion, there existed a small number of individuals who enjoyed the privilege of doing so when they wished and not exclusively during the times stipulated by the church. According to the Dominican historian Dávila Padilla, these Indians were known as *Comuniotlacatl*, or the people of Communion.[36] Regarding the sacrament, the Dominican friars appear to have followed the same path as the Franciscans. Their preoccupation with preserving the highest reverence toward the sacrament—especially among the more committed Observant friars—made the creation of differences among Christianized Indians unavoidable. But despite having gathered wide support, not all the friars found themselves in agreement with this restrictive policy and the state of affairs to which it had contributed. In 1578 Philip II issued a decree urging archbishops and bishops in the colonies to administer the Eucharist to all the Indians capable of receiving it.[37]

Father Pedro de Agurto and the Augustinians

In their approach, as detailed by the chronicler Juan de Grijalva, the Augustinians had departed, at least in theory, from their Franciscan counterparts, in that they took Communion to be a sacrament as necessary as baptism.[38] This principle, however, did not prevent Grijalva from finding the policy adopted by the Peruvian church, which had restricted Communion to a small number of Indians, unjustified. The church in Peru, he argued, had exercised its legitimate authority to determine when the sacrament should be administered, a prerogative that had been ratified by the Council of Trent.[39] Although Grijalva was clear about the legal framework that gave power to ecclesiastical authorities for tailoring policies according to particular times and places, he could not avoid finding the reasons behind the decisions to curtail the Indians' access to the Eucharist flawed. He took exception with the common assumption that the Indians were incapable; this label failed to account for their true condition, which was more akin to simplicity—a word dear to Grijalva. To those who had seen the Indians' condition as neophytes an obstacle to their full participation in the sacrament, he responded that the sacrament itself was considered spiritual food to sustain the growth of the faithful.[40]

While Grijalva was respectful of other approaches in so far as ecclesiastical law warranted them, he took special pride in his fellow brothers who had from the very beginning of their activities in Mexico generously made the Eucharist accessible to the Mexican Indians. The practice had been accompanied by teachings that highlighted the connection between the Eucharist and baptism, thus restoring at least symbolically a unity that had been lost in Spain and might never take hold in Catholic Mexico. To this end, the Indians about to be baptized by the Augustinians were often reminded about the need to later prepare to receive the Eucharist.[41]

Not all friars contented themselves with seeing the particular approach to Communion adopted by their respective orders consistently implemented since reality showed that Indians who had been properly baptized continued, by and large, being excluded from the sacrament. This is why the Augustinian Pedro de Agurto published in 1573 his *Tractado de que se deben administrar los Sacramentos de la Sancta Eucharistia y Extremaunction a los indios de esta nueva España* in which he assessed the causes that contributed to the neglect of the Indian population regarding the Eucharist. Agurto taught arts at the University of Mexico, where he also replaced his fellow brother Alonso de la Veracruz in the teaching of theology while the latter was in Spain, but he was known as well for his dedication to the study of canon law.[42] The title unequivocally states the author's position while hinting, through its emphasis on the obligation to administer the Eucharist to the Indians, at the legal perspective that the author would bring to the discussion on the sacrament.

Almost every chapter is aimed at debunking as erroneous and baseless the most common justifications circulating at the time for restricting the Indians' access to the Eucharist. More often than not these justifications assumed the form of charges against the Indians, such as their alleged inclination to drunkenness and incorrigible persistence in sinning. Agurto argued that these charges themselves needed first to be substantiated but, more importantly, that between them and the widespread practice of denying the sacrament to the new converts there stood a body of ecclesiastical regulations and opinions spelling out under which circumstances a Christian could be excluded from the sacrament. It was in the light of this body of ecclesiastical provisions and opinions that Agurto set out to question the validity of the claims in favor of barring the Indians from Communion, a measure that the church had regarded as particularly serious. For instance, when confronting the widespread accusation that Indians were inveterate sinners, Agurto found this characterization wanting in precision since the church had traditionally recognized different categories of sinners and made provisions as to which kind of offender should be excluded from the sacrament. In the particular case of public sinners who persisted in their offenses—persons whose sins were well-known to the entire community and who had failed to make amendment—such exclusion was indeed contemplated.[43] The question was then whether the Indians might accurately be said to fall under this category. Agurto concluded that such judgment could only be reached through a judicial inquiry, and that the exclusion from Communion should be issued and take effect after the individual had been proven to be a notorious sinner, and never before. But the term "sinner," as Agurto argued, was also employed to identify the majority of Christians and referred thus to the vast number of individuals who had sinned but were granted sacramental absolution after confession; if the label was still commonly applied in this case, it was mainly because they had only recently emerged from a sinful state. Communion was to these Christians what medicine was to a sick person and therefore, he noted, should never be denied. If the Indians were thought to be sinners of this particular kind, then there was no reason or legal justification to deny them the sacrament. In a final analysis what Agurto showed was that if one were to closely follow ecclesiastical guidelines, the extreme measure of excluding a Christian from Communion only applied to very restricted cases.

Agurto's argument was not exclusively confined to proving the Indians' right to demand and receive the Eucharist but also called attention to the obligation of priests and friars to administer the sacrament and the legal consequences that they might face for not complying with this obligation. To have considered this often overlooked side of the equation that made up the ritual is perhaps the most salient contribution of Agurto to the debate on the Eucharist, which, as he showed, had rested almost entirely on a variety of opinions regarding the Mexican Indians' moral and cognitive abilities. These opinions had very concrete and mostly negative consequences, such as directly affecting the administration of the Eucharist. But something else besides the Indians being deprived of the benefits of the sacrament was at stake since the exclusion from the Eucharist in turn weakened and undermined the obligations of Indians and priests alike—hence Agurto's decision to examine the decisions by friars and priests from a legal viewpoint.[44] Thus, when rejecting as inadequate the characterization of the Indians as public sinners, Agurto added that the very expression of a statement that was

untruthful amounted to false testimony.[45] The same applied to those
who believed that the lower cognitive capacities of the Indians justified
their separation from the sacrament.[46]

As for drunkenness as a motive for barring Indians from Communion, Agurto once again saw the need to go back to the distinctions
found in ecclesiastical legislation. While he did not minimize the negative consequences of drinking for the moral life of the Christian—drinking as a source of worse sins to come—he found that punishment in the
form of privation of Communion should be limited to those cases in
which drunkenness had become habitual.[47] Even in these cases the decision to impose such an extreme penalty was to be left to a judge once he
had determined without a doubt that the individual was at fault.[48]

Another important argument attacked by Agurto touched directly
on the much debated question on the status of the Indians as neophytes.
At issue was not only whether this label might be applied to the Indians
but also what kind of obligations should a neophyte reasonably be
expected to have. Writing several decades after the first friars arrived in
Mexico, Agurto rejected the by then increasingly popular notion in religious circles of treating the Indians as neophytes, pointing out that most
of the Indians had been baptized in childhood.[49] As he understood it,
neophytes, strictly speaking, were those individuals who embraced
Christianity in adulthood. Showing little patience with labels, Agurto
concluded that whether the Indians were neophytes or not, ecclesiastical law did not warrant their exclusion from Communion; if a restric-
tion regarding the sacraments applied to new converts, this one only
concerned their access to sacred orders and the episcopal office.[50]

The troubling implications of considering the Mexican Indians neophytes were not lost on Agurto. The use of such a notion—which a few
years later would be officially adopted by the Third Mexican Church
Council—had given support to the widespread practice of not administering Communion to the Indians, but what made this use more worrisome was that it contradicted a long-held Christian view of spiritual
progress and perfection that had traditionally served as a guide for friars and priests. In the spiritual as well as the biological world, as the
saying that Agurto quoted goes, "none becomes an adult all of the sudden." If the Indians were living indeed in a sort of spiritual childhood,
as some of Agurto's contemporaries claimed, Communion was then
necessary to help them grow, the same way that Christ did not wait
until after resurrecting to offer his body to the Apostles.[51] For Agurto,

then, the term "neophyte," regardless of whether it accurately described the state of the Mexican Indians as Christians, had become an obstacle to the fulfillment of their obligation to receive Communion at the same time that it freed priests and friars from their own duty to administer the sacrament.

Father Joseph de Acosta on the Eucharist

Toward the end of the sixteenth century the Jesuit Joseph de Acosta took up the issue of the administration of the Eucharist to the Indians in his treatise *De procuranda indorum salute* (1588). Having arrived in Lima in 1572 with the solid theological background expected by then of all ordained Jesuit priests, Acosta came in a relatively short time to a remarkable understanding of the cross-cultural dynamics that were shaping Peruvian Christianity. His treatment of the Eucharist was aimed at showing how early policy on the administration of the sacrament in Peru rested on shaky theological grounds and, more importantly, establishing clear general guidelines to ensure the future access of the Indians to Communion in Peru and elsewhere. His position owed much to contemporary debates among Spanish theologians, as well as to the religious practices promoted by his fellow brothers in the Company of Jesus.

The First Provincial Church Council in Peru, celebrated in Lima between 1551 and 1552, had restricted the sacraments that the Indians were to receive to baptism, confession, and marriage, leaving to the discretion of the prelate whether to recommend confirmation in particular cases. The decision reflected the idea that the new converts "were to be fed spiritual milk, and not the sustenance reserved for the mature."[52] Communion was allowed only with permission of the prelate after he had made sure that the Indian understood the sacrament that he or she was to receive; no provision of this kind, however, was contemplated for the administration of the viaticum to the sick.

The Second Provincial Church Council (1567–68) departed from previous policy, doing away with the exclusion of Indians who were now allowed to receive the Eucharist after having confessed to a priest and shown that they understood the sacramental operation at the heart of the ritual as well as the distinction between the material and sacramental bread.[53] In a similar move toward a less restrictive policy, the council also allowed for the administration of the viaticum to those Indians who were prepared to receive it.[54]

The same approach was ratified by the Third Provincial Church Council held in Lima in 1583, the agenda of which Joseph de Acosta played a decisive role in setting.[55] Despite the changes introduced by the second council, to judge by the words of the third council, little progress had been made in their effective implementation. While the new council restated previous policy, it also found it necessary to explain why the Indians continued being denied the sacrament. Although the church mandated that all Christians receive Communion at least once a year— except in those cases where confessors deemed a delay necessary—the council explained that such obligation had not theretofore been enforced, due mainly to the Indians' lack of Christian instruction and preparedness, a condition attributed to widespread drinking, concubinage, and superstitions.[56] Considering, however, that a growing number of Indians were making progress in the Christian religion, the ecclesiastical authorities at the council recognized that this group could not be denied Communion. With a view to ensuring its wider administration, the council ordered priests and preachers to instruct the Indians in the mystery of the sacrament in order to awake in them the desire to receive it. As we have already pointed out, while Christians were obliged to receive Communion at least once a year, the church also recognized that the desire to do so was a legitimate form of participation, albeit not a sacramental one.

Regarding the viaticum, the situation of the sick, as the council acknowledged, was not much different from that of the general Indian population. It should be noted that the council found that the causes behind the lack of assistance to the infirm were, however, of a very different nature. While the Indians had to be faulted for their lukewarm spiritual condition, the priests themselves were to be blamed for failing to fulfill their duties toward the dying, either by negligence or misplaced zeal. It was then determined that the viaticum be administered to Indians, blacks, and persons who fell under the legal category of "miserable," provided that they had shown the required disposition for its reception, such as faith and repentance.[57] A few years later, these two sets of explanations were revisited and subjected to new scrutiny when Acosta, appointed provincial of his order, set out to write his thoughts on what had gone wrong with the administration of the Eucharist in Peru.

In spite of the commitment on the part of the Third Provincial Church Council to make the Eucharist available to a wider number of Indians, the steps it took in this direction seem to have fallen short of Acosta's expectations. For him, the root of the problem had less to do with the alleged deficiencies of the Indians in matters of faith than with the priests' continued neglect of their religious duties toward their flock. Acosta took pride in the labor of his fellow brothers in the Society when pointing out that thanks to them the Eucharist had reached the Indians of Peru.

There is no direct indication that Acosta had read Pedro de Agurto's small treatise on the Eucharist, although we cannot rule out that he might have come across a copy during his stay in Mexico on his way to Spain. Whatever the case may be, Acosta's approach to what by then had become a source of frustration for all friars urging for a more complete participation of the Indians in Christian life differed from the Augustinian's, despite sharing similar points of view. This becomes apparent in Acosta's careful examination of current ecclesiastical practices in Peru in light of wider theological and legal issues. For instance, before elaborating his own opinion, he wondered whether the sanctioned and widespread practice of not allowing the Indians to accept the Eucharist in Peru should be considered a local custom and therefore be accepted and preserved without challenge.[58] By posing this question, Acosta was anticipating a possible rebuke to his own project of introducing changes in church policies and practices, as well as addressing a larger issue for a church still in gestation that was already showing signs of departing from other churches in the colonies. The issue he raised to clear the ground for his argument—when and under which circumstances does a particular practice become custom—was a crucial one, and it had never been so clearly stated.

Acosta chose to open his observations on the Eucharist by revisiting and taking sides on the long-standing discussion among theologians and canonists over whether the obligation to receive Communion was to be interpreted as a precept pertaining to divine law. Aquinas had answered to this question affirmatively, as did his sixteenth-century followers in Spain, and Acosta found their judgment conclusive.[59] Pedro de Agurto had voiced the same opinion in Mexico.[60] When the Franciscan chronicler Juan de Torquemada reported on the Mexican controversy in his *Monarquía indiana,* he was quick to point out that the arguments of those in favor of admitting the Indians to Communion had rested on the opinion that there was a divine precept to this end. The number of theologians past and present who had held this view was extensive and authoritative, and Torquemada, displaying in typical fashion his thorough familiarity with theological literature, did not fail to make reference to them. However impressive that vast body of opinion was, it did little to compel the Franciscan to take sides, choosing instead to affirm that whether by divine or ecclesiastical law Christians were obliged to receive Communion at least once a year.[61]

As if the weight of the opinions by respected theologians alone was not convincing enough, Acosta—anticipating responses such as Torquemada's—went on to elaborate an independent argument to further confirm his position, the basic premise of which held that the necessity of any sacrament could be inferred from its particular signification.[62] Thus, in the same fashion that the church had affirmed that spiritual rebirth was the true meaning of baptism and no person could be brought to Christian life without it, spiritual life could not be sustained without the nourishment provided by the Eucharist.[63] For Acosta this basic meaning—which stood at odds with the opinions turned into policy in Peru—illustrated in the simplest terms that Communion was to be an integral part of the Christian life. According to Acosta, ecclesiastical law could determine when Christians should receive the sacrament—as the Lateran Council had done in 1215—but had no authority to pronounce which sacraments were necessary.

The meaning of the sacrament as nourishment implied its status as necessary for believers, a point that was not directly reflected in doctrinal teaching on the conditions for salvation. The analogy that explained the function of the sacraments in relation to basic biological functions in human beings also ran the risk of making the sacraments appear too ordinary and, as such, removed from the realm of the sacred to which they belonged. As we will have occasion to see, this tension, which found expression in opposite attitudes regarding the administration of the Eucharist in Mexico and Peru, came to the fore in contemporary discussions over frequent Communion.

Theologians had long recognized that any Christian could actually partake spiritually in the Eucharist by simply desiring it without actually ingesting the consecrated host.[64] Anticipating that such a provision could easily be used to justify the refusal to admit the Indians to Communion, Acosta argued that the Scriptures made a clear distinction between a spiritual and a sacramental Communion and that the church itself had decreed that the obligation applied exclusively to the latter. While divine law dictated that all the faithful had the obligation to receive Communion, and ecclesiastical law granted priests the authority to withhold the sacrament in those instances when such a measure could be fully justified, it was nonetheless difficult for Acosta to reconcile these facts with the outright decision to bar Indians from the sacrament in Peru.

Acosta's assessment of the policy followed by the Peruvian church was carefully paced, progressing almost in half-steps. This kind of exposition, deployed to soften the author's negative view of both past policies and the current state of affairs, allowed him, for example, to salute the changes introduced by the Third Provincial Church Council of Lima and later to express the more radical view that new converts should not be turned away from Communion.

An important notion touching on the once important question of the interrelationship between the sacraments, one that had been put forward by the theologians of Salamanca regarding baptism, reappears in Acosta's proposal. In terms very similar to those found in the 1541 document, the Jesuit made a case for the return to an integrated ritual by which the newly baptized would be immediately ready for Communion, as had been customary in the apostolic ages and certainly not forgotten in Visigothic Spain.[65]

A central assumption in the argument against administering the Eucharist to the Indians had been that they had failed to show any sign of spiritual progress in matters of faith, trapped, as they were, in a condition that relegated them to a perpetual state of neophyte. Were this the case, Acosta counteracted, their weakness could not be helped by denying access to a sacrament that had been precisely intended to foster the spiritual growth of the faithful.[66] Those who kept the Indians away from their source of spiritual nourishment seemed to have forgotten the meaning of the parable of the banquet in Luke 14 in which Acosta found the best illustration of the inclusiveness of Jesus's table.

Despite his deft critique of the stance taken by the Peruvian church on the Eucharist, Acosta's practical proposal was open to a compromise; the strong claim of making the Eucharist accessible to all the Indians who had fulfilled their religious obligations was softened in the end, leaving in the process some unresolved contradictions. The Third Provincial Church Council in Peru had considered all Indians neophytes, a notion that became the guiding principle behind its policies;

the Third Mexican Church Council would shortly follow the same path.[67] By contrast, Acosta found no use for this notion, perceiving how such characterization both froze the Indians into a perpetual state of catechumens and could ultimately encourage priests to neglect their pastoral responsibility. In his alternative view, Christians, new and old alike, were to be subject without distinctions to the same standards when the time came to evaluate their readiness for Communion. This solution, then, put into question the widespread and deep-seated mental habit that had led to the formulation of ecclesiastical and secular policies based on a set of loose generalizations meant to capture the Indians' nature and dispositions. From this perspective, which ultimately sought to restore a sense of moral autonomy to the Indians, particular moral faults—the Indians' so much talked about drunkenness and superstition, for instance—were to be treated as such and corrected appropriately.

Surprisingly, though, Acosta went on to suggest that the administration of the Eucharist could play a part in the moral reform of the Indian population if it were presented to them as a reward. At this point an important shift takes place, and the objections of those opposing the admission of the Indians are addressed by making the sacrament part of the solution to the Indians' alleged moral weaknesses. Hence, Acosta made room for the Eucharist to become a tool to foster appropriate Christian behavior. Whereas for all practical purposes the recommendation seems straightforward enough, when viewed in the light of both Acosta's previous discussion and church opinion, it becomes somewhat more problematic. The difficulty arises from trying to reconcile the impulse to consider Indians as moral agents in equal standing with their Spanish counterparts with the simultaneous attempt to reward them with the Eucharist in exchange for good behavior. Two separate issues seem to have been collapsed into one. In this process the moral faults that were first to be considered as individual lapses have now been ascribed to a large social group. Therefore the Eucharist, whose ultimate meaning as originally spelled out by Acosta rested on its being spiritual nourishment for the sustenance and perfection of the Christian individual, is transformed into a social remedy. It is not hard to see how Acosta's own interpretation of Luke 14 has been lost on the way to formulating a solution sensitive to the concerns of the opposing party.

The proposed use of the Eucharist as a means to improve social mores, which might at first be thought of as a simple additional benefit, had theological consequences. Such a recommendation ran counter to the opinions of theologians and church authorities who had been reluctant to construe the access to the Eucharist as some kind of reward, considering that the church had long and firmly established the means for the faithful to participate fully in the sacraments, which were at everybody's disposal. The Mexican friars were alerted against falling into such temptation to help promote the sacraments. Early on the ecclesiastical authorities gathered at the meeting of 1539 in Mexico had explicitly rejected this very approach, stating that Communion "is not given on the basis of merit but rather as remedy and medicine to those who receive it according to Church precepts; because this said medicine, which brings aid and relief, is not of less benefit to the weak and the sick than to those who enjoy health and perfection."[68] This clarification addressed both the teaching about the sacrament and its administration. But, as we have seen concerning how Franciscans and Dominicans promoted the reception of the Eucharist among a reduced group of Indians, it seems to have had little impact on the ways in which these orders designed their policies.

A last important point on which Acosta paused only briefly was whether the Indians should be expected to receive Communion frequently. For the time being, Acosta stated, such practice should be discouraged lest the Indians lose the respect due to the sacrament, an occurrence bound to happen if the Eucharist became easily available.[69] This kind of reasoning shows once again the inherent tension brought about by the difficulty in reconciling the double perspective that Acosta thought essential for a discussion of the sacrament: one concerning the recipient, the second focused on the preservation of the sacrament's status as an object of reverence.

Although Acosta's position regarding frequent Communion was well in line with his general practical recommendations, the fact that he brought it up at all in his discussion is significant. Why so? Since its beginnings, the Society of Jesus had promoted frequent Communion among its brothers and followers in the laity, a practice that had soon become one of the salient features of the devotions fostered by the order.[70] The promotion of frequent Communion found fertile ground in the congregations of laymen and women affiliated with the order, which had been founded for the spiritual improvement of their members under Jesuit guidance.[71]

This predilection, however, was not exclusive to the Jesuits since frequent Communion had for some time been highly regarded and recommended by religious reformers of widely different extraction, notably proponents of the *devotio moderna* such as Jean Gerson. Ignatius Loyola himself, the founder of the Jesuit order, grew particularly fond of it upon reading the fifteenth-century *Imitation of Christ,* a spiritual treatise that enjoyed a large readership in sixteenth-century Spain, as well as in the rest of the continent.[72] In sixteenth-century Spain, frequent Communion had been praised and recommended by Franciscan contemplative writers such as Fr. Francisco de Osuna, who devoted his tract *Gracioso combite* (1530) to explaining the benefits of the Eucharist.[73] Osuna found authoritative justification in support of frequent Communion in the opinion of another Franciscan, the theologian Duns Scotus.[74] Osuna's works were popular in Spain;[75] in Mexico they seem to have appealed especially to the religious sensibility of those friars sympathetic with the call for spiritual renewal within the Catholic Church.[76]

Very different from Osuna in intellectual outlook, but equally committed to restoring a more intimate connection between believers and their church, the Dominican Bartolomé Carranza de Miranda had also commended the frequent reception of the Eucharist for its spiritual benefits.[77] Besides these vernacular trends, the spread of frequent Communion as a devotional practice in Spain was later furthered by the increasing influence of similar devotions of Italian origin that found their way to Spain through spiritual treatises, some of them penned by Jesuit authors.[78]

Decades before Acosta, the Mexican archbishop Zumárraga thought about how often Christians should receive Communion, and he did so aware that throughout its history the church had made room for change and accommodation. But for Zumárraga the example of the primitive church, when Christians were said to have partaken in the Eucharist, had a special allure, even as he recognized the gap between that world and that of his contemporaries who sometimes failed to comply with their yearly obligation to receive Communion. Still, frequent Communion held for him the key to rekindling the devotion of his fellow contemporaries.[79] Despite this conviction his practical recommendation was rather cautious, calling on Catholics to seek Communion during the most important holidays marked by the church.[80]

The period that runs from Zumárraga and his contemporaries such as Osuna to Acosta saw a radical transformation in the attitude of ecclesiastical authorities toward doctrinal and devotional matters. The controversy about the sacrament of the Eucharist, which exploded in the mid-1520s, marked a turning point for the Catholic Church. The rejection of the doctrine of the real presence was taken by its Catholic defenders to be the ultimate and most disturbing step in the critique of the sacramental system launched by the leading theologians of the Reform, one that sought to devalue and undermine the sacred status of the Eucharist. Certainly for theologians and the populace on both sides of the dispute no other religious issue provided a more dramatic occasion for violent confrontation as the Eucharist, ideological as well as physical. Suspicious of any sign that could be interpreted as an act potentially demeaning to the holiness of the sacraments, Spanish ecclesiastical authorities turned their attention to friars, priests, and laymen and women who, in line with the spiritual reform introduced by Cardinal Ximénez de Cisneros, had embraced various forms of religiosity that exalted the virtues of inner devotion. In 1525 the archbishop of Seville Alonso Manrique, in his role of general inquisitor, produced an edict condemning the views of a small group of individuals active in Toledo as contrary to Catholic teaching. These individuals, whose practices and beliefs were sometimes hard to separate from the ones promoted by other Catholic reformers of the time, came to be known as "alumbrados."[81] The individuals involved were tried, but soon others came to face charges for heresy in different parts of Spain and were given the label of "alumbrados." Manrique's edict did not mention frequent communion; soon, however, ecclesiastical authorities would become less tolerant of this practice that was quickly taking hold among the laity. Reportedly the *beatas* (laywomen living under religious vows without belonging to any religious order) accused as alumbradas in Llerena during the 1570s were used to receiving Communion daily.

In 1559 Osuna's *Gracioso combite* and Carranza's *Comentarios sobre el catecismo cristiano* were among the books banned by the Spanish Inquisition and included in the *Index;* in each case the author's advice in favor of frequent Communion was deemed controversial.[82] Osuna himself had been rumored to be associated with the alumbrados of Toledo. Regarding the frequency for Communion, Carranza left it to the individual's own conscience and the confessor. By the time Carranza was writing on this issue he was well aware of treading on somewhat sensitive terrain, as his remarks on the dangers faced by those who enjoyed frequent Communion make apparent. These dangers were of two kinds, internal and external: those who communicated frequently could fool themselves into claiming some kind of spiritual superiority over their fellow Christians, but they could also fall prey to the suspicion of those who for whatever reason did not approve of their practice.[83] Carranza knew that this latter scenario was all too real since the Inquisition's crackdown on religious groups suspected of heterodoxy was by then well underway, having created a state of affairs of which he disapproved and that would ultimately alter the course of his life. He soon found himself facing charges for religious dissidence. As the Inquisition expanded its list of suspected books, more titles encouraging frequent Communion found their place in the *Index*.

In essence, Acosta's refusal to grant the Indians frequent access to the Eucharist did not depart in its justification from the concerns voiced by theologians in Spain and the colonies. If the consideration of such restricted practice seems of little importance compared with Acosta's central preoccupation with ensuring the administration of a sacrament that by ecclesiastical law all Christians were obliged to receive annually, it remains nonetheless revealing of the doubts—and the selection process—that attended the transmission of religious beliefs and devotions to the Indian populations. To recommend frequent Communion was to assume that this preliminary stage had been accomplished.

The disagreements over frequent Communion shed light on the expectations of the church regarding what kind of relationship Christians should have with the rituals they were obliged to submit to regularly, an issue that goes to the core of sixteenth-century religious discussions. It was argued that frequenting the sacrament too often might somehow diminish its sacred status and the reverence owed by the faithful. From this perspective, the obligation to receive Communion once a year can be read in part as helping preserve the special character of the ritual. Catholic reformers and their followers had reacted in different ways against what they perceived to be the ritual formalism that had taken over the church. Church rituals, they held, had for the most part become meaningless. The reformers' efforts to restore this lost meaning were neatly reflected in the devotional literature dedicated to instructing the laity on how to participate in and listen to Mass and receive Communion.[84] Frequent Communion among the laity—the practice had been mainly restricted to members of the church—was seen by some reformers as central to the reorientation of Christian life that they envisioned because it could bridge the gap between ritual life and spiritual life that they denounced. The reformers presented the laity with a model of existence permeated by the all-encompassing presence of religion, where ordinary and ritual life would be perfectly integrated. While this particular conception had guided religious life in a number of monasteries, some theologians and ecclesiastical authorities thought that when it came to the laity, there was the likely possibility that frequent Communion, for example, would diffuse the importance of the sacrament. Not only was the centrality of the sacrament threatened but also its status as ritual, that is, as a particular action neatly differentiated from everyday activity. As already noted, the friars' preoccupation with ensuring the Indians' recognition of Christian rituals as having clearly distinct identities was the main reason behind repeated attempts to establish ritual uniformity in the administration of the sacraments.[85] In essence the issues brought up in the discussions on frequent Communion were not different from the questions that surfaced around the status and function of church rituals in general.

The examination of policy and opinions concerning the Eucharist in Mexico reveals the emergence and persistence of tensions, conceptual and practical, old and new. It also shows how much thought the friars put into formulating satisfactory policies able to reconcile ecclesiastical law, the most immediate demands of pastoral care, and their own particular agendas regarding the present and future Christianity of Indian peoples.

Acosta's analysis of the situation in Peru taught him that because of misguided policies the basic steps toward establishing appropriate conditions for the reception of the Eucharist among the Indians had been seriously compromised. Lack of instruction compounded by the exclusion of the Indians from the sacrament had kept the Eucharist from emerging in the Indians' minds as a necessary ritual with its own identity. In a different context, Fr. Alonso de Molina had faced a similar problem in relation to the sacrament of confirmation. Acosta acknowledged that in preventing the majority of the Indians from accessing Communion, the original meaning of the sacrament had been altered.

The selective administration of the Eucharist embraced by a significant number of friars in Mexico did somehow upset the natural progression of spiritual life that, as the friars had learned, gave unity to the sacramental system. In the analogy of the sacraments with the human life cycle the Mexican friars had come to see not only the ideal development of a Christian life but also the not-less-ideal consolidation and growth of Christianity among Indian peoples. When religious chroniclers shaped a historical narrative of Christianity in Mexico punctuated by the introduction of each sacrament they did more than report on their orders' activities and successes; to a great extent their choice amounted to symbolically sanctioning as irrevocable the setting in motion of a spiritual cycle that could only go forward. Along the way the assurances that guided and found expression in historical writings no longer coincided with the friars' increasingly hesitant assessment of the conversion enterprise. It was then possible to think that the growth of Christianity could stall, leaving the Indians in a state of arrested development and the friars attending to the needs that such a stage demanded. The completion of the full cycle of spiritual progress was left for a better future and so, in part, was the promise of change that the sacramental rituals had once contained.

Spanish friars writing on the religious practices of the Mexicans noticed how close some ceremonies came to resembling Christian Communion. One early account from Motolinía described a celebration in honor of Tezcatlipoca in which a group of youngsters ate small pieces of boiled dough made out of maize and seeds, which were said to become the flesh of the god.[86] Motolinía was probably referring to the feast of Panquetzaliztli dedicated to Huitzilopochtli and held during the month of November, an important ceremony in the Nahua ritual calendar about which later writers gathered more complete and detailed information. We learn that during this festival dough prepared from finely floured seeds was used to build the figure of the god, which was later cut into pieces, distributed, and finally eaten by the lord, priests, and a select group of young men.[87] For the youngsters who happened to eat the body of Huitzilopochtli, it was the start of an onerous and taxing obligation. They were expected to serve the god in the temple, make penance, and offer costly goods as tribute for a full year.[88] Reporting on the same festival, the Dominican Fr. Diego Durán was puzzled by the apparent coexistence of ritual actions that recalled the Eucharist—that is, actions that he deemed intelligible—with fanciful inventions introduced by the Mexican Indians themselves.[89] Other rituals, he reported, involved eating dough made into figures of birds[90] or mountains representing particular deities.[91]

The preparation and consumption of edible figures that stood for religious forces was just one particular manifestation of a feature that dominated the religion of the Nahuas: the reproduction of the sacred in varied scales in which both humans and natural elements were called to play the roles of gods or goddesses. In religious rituals sacrificial victims were often god impersonators, and sometimes priests themselves were required to slip into the identity of a god. The Nahuas referred to all these diverse genres of representation as *ixiptlas*.[92]

To a very limited extent Motolinía and Durán could, based on their familiarity with the Eucharist, make sense of the Mexican Indians ritual eating of their gods, even when they found in the native gods little worth commending in either moral or ceremonial matters. At the same time, an outright identification of the reception of the host with the consumption of a god figure was a rather precarious proposition. The Nahuas did not seem particularly invested in hiding the process of selecting, cleaning, and grinding the seeds and kernels that later led to the preparation of the dough that would finally become the flesh of the god. These communal activities were themselves an integral part of the ritual. Moreover, there was the issue of what the participants believed they were eating. At the moment of consecration in the Catholic Mass, the priest's words made reference to the body and blood of Christ. In the ceremony of Panquetzaliztli, for example, it was noted that those who participated were not eating merely the body or the flesh of the god but "the bones of Huitzilopochtli," a body part that enjoyed a prominent role in the religious imagination of the Nahuas but was not part of the basic vocabulary of Communion.[93] The blatant, almost unmediated correspondence of the idea of eating the body of the god with the figure of the god materialized as food betrayed in the Spaniards' eyes a rather poor conceptualization of the sacred that extended to every single aspect of the local religion and beyond.[94] The friars who took notice of the Nahuas' pervasive desire to make visually manifest the different religious forces at work in the world were equally uncomfortable with the Indians' proclivity to indulge in food during their too frequent religious celebrations—anthropophagy being an extreme example of a seemingly unstoppable appetite.[95] The Nahuas' alleged need to rely on multiple representations of their gods and goddesses to propitiate the embodiment of the sacred was taken by the friars to run contrary to the far more restricted symbolical economy of Christianity achieved in the Eucharist. In similar fashion the theophagy practiced by the Nahuas, when seen against the widespread occurrence of eating in ritual settings, seemed to tell the friars more about the participants' excessive concern with their own inclinations and their efforts to channel them than about any easily recognizable sign indicative of a realm worth calling sacred.

Missionaries were certainly good at describing in great detail the intricate tapestry of Nahua rituals. When it came to commenting on their meaning or meanings, however, they tended to be less thorough. This circumspection may be sometimes attributed to a calculated refusal to deal with potentially dangerous material, elsewhere, to the limitations of their native sources. Nonetheless, exceptions were made when the rituals in question happened to closely resemble the Christian sacraments, as was the case with baptism or confession. To deal with this limited number of rituals, sacramental theology provided the missionaries with some guidance both for describing ritual actions and emotions as well as for venturing into discussions about meaning. But sacramental theology, because of its powerfully economic way of explaining how sacraments work, also offered too restricted a model to think about ritual performance, meaning, and ritual efficacy.

The ritual excess, perceived both in the complexity of the over-scripted Nahua ceremonies as well as in their frequency, appeared to be one side of a troubling deficiency in the Indians' conceptualization of ritual that undermined its sacred status. The friars noted that at a symbolic level the multiple representations of sacred forces and actions were governed by a crude literalism or mimesis that made the search for a unifying meaning either difficult or irrelevant. Moreover, the meaning as well as meaningfulness of ritual seemed to be undone by the sheer omnipresence of ceremonies that overwhelmed the lives of the Nahuas, as if a minimum distance or tension between the ordinary happenings of everyday life and religious participation in order to preserve the identity of the sacred order would be needed. This particular concern—to which we could add the friars' objections to the coercive nature of Nahua religion in so far as it engendered empty ritualism—was an important part of the constellations of questions that underlined the discussions on the role of ritual in Christian religion both in Europe and Mexico.

Conclusion

In chapter 5 I delve into the variety of reasons that contributed to keeping a majority of Mexican Indians separated from the Eucharist; these same reasons, when examined in a wider context and in search of a unifying problematic, reveal a not so surprising correspondence with questions that went to the core of the colonial enterprise, understood as ideological project and historical reality. Among the seven sacraments, the channels of grace opened to all people for their salvation, the Eucharist was the only one to be also known as "don" (gift). Jesus's sacrifice as the ultimate gift for all humankind. Yet somehow that gift eluded for quite some time the Indians in Mexico and elsewhere in the colonies.

Questions about what to give, to whom, in what circumstances, and to which end—and the concomitant set of obligations that went with the giving—enmeshed as they were in the very fabric of Christian theology—were also the questions that Spanish jurists and theologians faced both to justify and keep the colonial process in motion. This is how the theological language of the gift crept up refracted in the opinions of the letrados and in the policies of the Crown regarding the Indians' need to adopt a variety of European cultural features such as language, religion, and custom.

However limited the focus on the colonizer's rhetoric of the gift may appear, it nonetheless allows us to raise an issue that when looking back to the ground covered in this book, could well be identified as the reluctance of the giver, an instance that points to the limits or resistances of such rhetoric. I am not referring here to the claims on the impossibility of giving as a founding paradox in Christian theology[1] but rather to what seems to be at stake in the self-figuration of the colonial enterprise as an act of giving—cultural and religious: the preservation of the original meaning of the gift during and after its transmission and, ultimately, the identity of the giver.

Sixteenth-century Spain abounds with examples that could serve as a starting point to further explore the interplay of identities—religious, cultural, national—in the context of the conversion of Jews and Muslims with its changing policies and the concomitant creation of legal labels to deal with the emergence of minoritarian groups. In a more direct way the question could be posed as follows: to what extent is the giver's identity (religious? national?) thought to be compromised in the process of transferring that accompanied colonial domination?[2]

It was in the religious area where the engagement by priests, friars, and ecclesiastical authorities with almost everything pertaining to the transmission of beliefs, values, and practices took shape and persisted for a long time. As shown in the previous chapters, the administration of the sacraments to the Mexican Indians was not an easy task. Both at a practical and abstract level, the fulfillment of this task was fraught with difficulties of widely different nature, as historical antecedents, legal guidelines, and ecclesiastical precepts were ultimately measured against what the friars came eventually to value as their most important source of authority: their own experience. But experience itself was multifaceted and shaped in no small part by the friars' allegiance to the agendas of their respective orders.

A basic feature of the sacraments, which distinguished them from all other Christian rituals, was their power to bring about certain transformations that were themselves signified by each ritual. Much thought and effort were put into making sure that the conditions for the successful reception of the sacraments were in place, and into trying to arrive at a consensus as to which conditions were to be considered acceptable in the new Mexican context. Regarding this consensus, the attitudes of the friars varied as they strove to reconcile church teaching, their perception of the Nahuas' response to Christianity, and their own expectations regarding the success of conversion.

Ritual integrity and uniformity are but two examples of the friars' more general concern with the preservation of the identity of each sacrament and its status as a sacred event to which the Indians were expected to accord due reverence. As discussed, this special attention did not necessarily imply a merely legalistic or formalistic approach to the administration of the sacraments on the part of the missionaries. Although the accusation of ritual formalism was certainly heard during the discussions on the baptism of adults, it is fair to say that in general the friars' positions shared the same desire to avoid hurriedly equating success in the conversion with ritual compliance. This is why church guidelines regarding the sacraments were sometimes perceived by the missionaries to fall short of the Christian standards that they had set up for the Nahuas. Often the solution to this particular problem was thought to lie in a more sustained doctrinal preparation of the Indian population and delaying the reception of certain sacraments, as was the case with the Eucharist. But the renewed calls to strengthen and improve the instruction received by the Nahuas concentrated on one partial aspect of religious conversion. There remained other essential elements of Christianity that could only be accessed and made known to the new subjects through ritual experience.

Early on, the friars, struck by the omnipresence of the ceremonial in Nahua social life, had ciphered in ritual their hopes of finding a common ground. This optimism was not without its problematic side since the ritual excess of the Nahuas was frequently seen as the counterpart of what the friars construed as a deficiency in doctrinal sophistication. This suspicion partially explains the attitudes that often informed the description of Nahua rituals, either derision at their alleged mimetic nature or perplexity at their apparent lack of meaning.

Unhappy with the lack of diffusion of the sacraments, some religious writers noted that excessive worries about ritual procedure and standards had led the ministers to forget the spiritual needs of the Indian population. As it happened, the friars were caught between two impulses: to fully trust ritual, thus leaving the sacraments to unleash their power to bring about the desired transformation of the Nahuas into full fledged Christians, and to fight the routinization that the administration of the sacraments would ultimately produce.

The friars in Mexico, like their European predecessors, were also tuned in to the dynamic dimension of the sacraments and ready to explore their adaptability both in action and meaning. One could say that the sacramental system, which symbolically comprised the human cycle from birth to death, provided the friars with a basic scheme against which they could project a figure by filling out the dots that led from sacrament to sacrament in order to conjure up different kinds of Christians. In this sense the sacraments were tools with which to think about conversion and a whole constellation of issues, religious as well as social. Ultimately, the version of the Christian Indian that prevailed, and was officially sanctioned by the Third Church Council of Mexico in 1585, was that of a neophyte, a close cousin of the new Christian. In a paradoxical way, the confinement of the Nahuas to this category ended up inadvertently devaluing the hope in the transformative powers of the sacraments.

In the last two decades much of the research on the evangelization of the Mexican Indians has sought to explore and determine the limits of such historical transformation. It has done so by placing an altogether new emphasis on native sources, which revealed that the reception of Christianity among the Nahuas took place over a long period of time through accommodations, negotiations, and not infrequent misunderstandings between Indians and friars. I have dealt mainly with one side of this contact, focusing more on how Europeans engaged with the very set of rituals that they intended the Mexican Indians to grasp, participate in, and hopefully, grow fond of, than on the ways in which these Indians lived up or failed to live up to these expectations. It would be a mistake to assume that by knowing the basic motives behind the friars' presence in Mexico their policies, actions, and discussions would become transparent. All these become more intelligible if we have access to the intellectual infrastructure that was part and parcel of the exchange between friars and Indians. In this case, it was sacramental theology that furnished the basic vocabulary that allowed missionaries to describe and pose questions about Christian and Nahua rituals.

Far from reinforcing traditional views about the evangelization that recent scholarship has helped correct, the study of the conceptual apparatus—and its unsolved problems—to which the friars resorted tells us a good deal about the way they made sense of the impact of Nahua culture on their own. An inquiry into the friars' everyday chores and theological preoccupations may appear less appealing than the missionaries' occasional confrontation with idolatry. However, early on, the administration of the sacraments was among the most immediate issues that friars and ecclesiastical authorities had to confront. They wrote about them, implemented policies, disagreed, and even made enemies during the process. The sacraments were, in short, a fundamental part of their trade. The more we understand the particular nature of this trade and the missionaries' exclusive role as technicians and sometimes ad hoc theorists of ritual, the better prepared we will be to assess the brand of Christianity that eventually emerged from the Mexican colonial experience.

Notes

Introduction

1. Emile Mâle, *Religious Art in France: The Thirteenth Century* (Princeton: Princeton University Press, 1984), 102.

2. Mâle, *Religious Art,* 111; in this shift Michael Camille perceived the new impulse toward interiorization that accompanied the obligation for all the faithful to submit to private penance once a year. See Camille, *The Gothic Idol: Ideology and Image-Making in Medieval Art* (Cambridge: Cambridge University Press, 1989), 9–15.

3. Prior to Cisneros's intervention, the Franciscan and Dominican orders had witnessed their own organized attempts at reforming the cloisters, leading to the establishment of reformed monasteries that coexisted alongside religious houses that remained untouched by the reform. Such changes inside religious orders did not occur without strong opposition from friars reluctant to embrace the strict observance of their rules; the practice of poverty, for instance, did not prove appealing to everyone. For a general account of the reform of the religious orders under Cisneros, with a rich selection of transcribed documents, José García Oro, *La reforma de los religiosos en tiempo de los Reyes Católicos* (Valladolid: Instituto "Isabel La Católica" de Historia Eclesiástica, 1969), 91–125 for Castile.

4. G. Baudot, *Utopía e historia en México. Los primeros cronistas de la civilización mexicana (1520–1569)* (Madrid: Espasa Calpe, 1983), 92–94; the early presence of Observant Franciscan friars in the Antilles was brought to light by Lino Gómez Canedo, "Conventuales, observantes y reformados (Política indigenista y filiación espiritual de los primeros franciscanos en Indias)," *Anuario de Estudios Americanos* 23 (1966): 611–22.

5. Toribio de Benavente (Motolinía), *Historia de los indios de Nueva España,* ed. Georges Baudot (Madrid: Castalia, 1985), treat. 3, chap. 2, 282–83.

6. Baudot, *Utopia e historia,* 95–102; on Joachim de Fiore's interpretation of history and its influence into the Renaissance, see Marjorie Reeves, *Joachim of Fiore and the Prophetic Future. A Medieval Study in Historical Thinking* (Stroud: Sutton, 1999); for his influence on the Franciscans, 29–58. On the differences between Franciscan notions of mission and conversion as spiritual renewal and Joachimist eschatology, E. Randolph Daniel, *The Franciscan Concept of Mission in the High Middle Ages* (Lexington: University of Kentucky Press, 1975), 27.

7. John Leddy Phelan, *The Millennial Kingdom of the Franciscans of the New World*, 2nd. ed. (Berkeley: University of California Press, 1970), 92–102.

8. Despite contemporary testimonies about his abrasive personality and harsh views on the Indians' intellectual capacities, Betanzos cultivated a close friendship with Archbishop Juan de Zumárraga and other Franciscans. On the history and controversies that accompanied the foundation of the Dominican province of Santiago, see Daniel Ulloa, *Los predicadores divididos (Los Dominicos en Nueva España, siglo XVI)* (Mexico City: El Colegio de México, 1977). On the debate about the incapacity of the Mexican Indians, and Betanzos's role in it, Lino Gómez Canedo, "Hombres o Bestias? (Nuevo examen crítico de un viejo tópico)," *Estudios de Historia Novohispana* 1 (1966): 29–51.

9. A detailed account of Augustinian organization and activities can be found in Antonio Rubial García, *El Convento Agustino y la Sociedad Novohispana (1533–1630)* (Mexico City: Universidad Nacional Autónoma de México, 1989).

10. Charles Gibson, *The Aztecs under Spanish Rule* (Stanford: Stanford University Press, 1964), 105–11.

11. G. Baudot, "La 'conspiración' franciscana contra la primera Audiencia de México," in *La pugna franciscana por México* (Mexico City: Alianza Editorial Mexicana, 1990), 37–58; see also Robert Ricard, *La "conquête spirituelle" du Mexique* (Paris: Institut D'Ethnologie, 1933), 303–8; on the internal dissension among the Dominicans around Nuño de Guzmán, Ulloa, *Los predicadores divididos*, 108.

12. Inga Clendinnen coined this expression to characterize the missionaries' basic approach to conversion as a process of replacing isolated native beliefs and practices with new ones. See Clendinnen, "Franciscan Missionaries in Sixteenth-Century Mexico," in *Disciplines of Faith. Studies in Religion, Politics and Patriarchy*, ed. Jim Obelkevich, Lyndal Roper, and Raphael Samuel (London: Routledge and Kegan Paul, 1987), 231.

13. John H. Elliott, "The Discovery of America and the Discovery of Man," in *Spain and Its World, 1500–1700* (New Haven: Yale University Press, 1989), 43. A reworking of Elliott's statement can be found in Michael T. Ryan, "Assimilating New Worlds in the Sixteenth and Seventeenth Centuries," *Comparative Studies in Society and History* 23, no. 4 (October 1981); also in dialogue with Elliott, Sabine MacCormack, "Limits of Understanding. Perceptions of Greco-Roman and Amerindian Paganism in Early Modern Europe," in *America in European Consciousness, 1493–1750*, ed. Karen Ordahl Kupperman, Institute of Early American History and Culture, Williamsburg, VA (Chapel Hill: University of North Carolina Press, 1994), 79–129.

14. Roland H. Bainton, *Erasmus of Christendom* (New York: Charles Scribner's Sons, 1969), 242. On Erasmus's edition of Ptolemy's work, see A. de Smet, "Érasme et la cartographie," in *Scrinium Erasmianum*, ed. J. Coppens (Leiden: Brill, 1969), 1: 277–91. The Latin editions of the *Geography* published in the sixteenth century contained maps that often incorporated new discoveries; Erasmus was well acquainted with the geographers of his time who were involved in these

editions, Anthony Grafton, *New Worlds, Ancient Texts* (Cambridge, MA.: Belknap Press of Harvard University Press, 1992), 51–54.

15. Erasmus, *Paráfrasis del Evangelio de San Lucas* in *Obras escogidas* (Madrid, 1964), 787–88. "[E]t ait dominus servo exi in vias et sepes et conpelle intrare ut impleatur domus mea," Lk 14: 5–23, *Biblia Sacra Iuxta Vulgatam Versionem* (Stuttgart: Deutsche Bibelgesellschaft, 1983). The *Paraphases* was among the works by Erasmus reprinted in 1525 in Alcalá, Marcel Bataillon, *Erasmo y España. Estudios sobre la historia espiritual del siglo XVI,* trans. Antonio Alatorre (México: Fondo de Cultura Económica, 1966), 164; a useful commentary on the work can be found in Roland H. Bainton, "The Paraphrases of Erasmus," *Archiv für Reformationsgeschichte* 57 (1966): 67–76.

16. Fr. Gerónimo de Mendieta, *Historia eclesiástica indiana,* bk. 1, chap. 4, 1: 27–28 (Mexico City: Salvador Chávez Hayhoe, 1945). Mendieta interpreted the lord's three calls as three different ways to convert non-Christian peoples; on Mendieta's interpretation, see Phelan, *The Millennial Kingdom,* 6–8, and see 9–10 on Sepúlveda's reading of the same passage to support the use of coercion.

17. José Miranda, "La fraternidad cristiana y la labor social de la primitiva iglesia mexicana," *Cuadernos Americanos* 141, no. 4 (1965): 151.

18. "[L]o que no querrias para ti, no lo quieras para tu proximo, y lo que querrias para ti, esso quiere para tu proximo," Juan Bautista, *Advertencias para los confessores de los naturales* (Mexico City: Pedro Ocharte, 1600), 35.

19. Juan de Grijalva, *Crónica de la orden de N. P. S. Agustín en las provincias de la Nueva España* (Mexico City: Porrúa, 1985), 106.

20. On literacy in colonial Mexico, see Frances Karttunen, "Nahuatl Literacy," in *The Inca and Aztec States, 1400–1800,* ed. George A. Collier, Renato Rosaldo, and John Wirth (New York: Academic Press, 1982), 395–417; on the evolution of alphabetic writing in Nahuatl, see James Lockhart, *The Nahuas after the Conquest: A Social and Cultural History of the Indians of Central Mexico, Sixteenth through Eighteenth Centuries* (Stanford: Stanford University Press, 1992), 330–73.

21. Richard E. Greenleaf, *Zumárraga and the Spanish Inquisition, 1536–1543* (Washington, DC: Academy of American Franciscan History, 1961), 53–56; Serge Gruzinski, *Man-Gods in the Mexican Highlands: Indian Power and Colonial Society, 1520–1800* (Stanford: Stanford University Press, 1989), 31–62.

22. On Nahua testaments and religious beliefs, see Lockhart, *The Nahuas after the Conquest,* 251–55; for the Mixtec area, Kevin Terraciano, "Native Expressions of Piety in Mixtec Testaments," in *Dead Giveaways: Indigenous Testaments of Colonial Mesoamerica and the Andes,* ed. Susan Kellogg and Matthew Restall (Salt Lake City: University of Utah Press, 1998), 115–40.

23. On the notion of tradition in the Catholic Church, see the first part of Yves M.-J. Congar's classic work *Tradition and Traditions: An Historical and a Theological Essay* (New York: MacMillan Company, 1967).

24. Lockhart, *The Nahuas after the Conquest,* 203.

25. In 1529, Fr. Pedro de Gante was said to have baptized together with

another brother more than two hundred thousand people, *Cartas de Pedro de Gante,* ed. Fidel J. Chauvet (Mexico City: Provincia del Santo Evangelio de México, 1951), 14. Motolinía ventured that fifteen million Indians had received baptism by the year 1537, *Historia de los indios,* treat. 2, chap. 4, 229. This picture has been challenged by new documentation that shows that a significant number of nonbaptized Indians lived side by side with baptized individuals between 1535 and 1540: see S. L. Cline, "The Spiritual Conquest Reexamined: Baptism and Christian Marriage in Early Sixteenth-Century Mexico," *Hispanic American Historical Review* 73, no. 3 (1993): 453–80.

26. Fr. Agustín Dávila Padilla, *Historia de la fundación y discurso de la Provincia de Santiago de México, de la Orden de Predicadores* [1596] (Mexico City: Academia Literaria, 1955), 4. The scope of Plutarch's influence in colonial historiography remains to be assessed. Sabine MacCormack persuasively showed Garcilaso de la Vega's use of this Greek historian in his *Comentarios reales,* MacCormack, "The Incas and Rome," in *Garcilaso de la Vega. An American Humanist. A Tribute to José Durand,* ed. José Anadón (Notre Dame: University of Notre Dame, 1998), 8–31.

27. Fr. Diego Durán, *Historia de las Indias de Nueva España e Islas de la Tierra Firme,* ed. Angel Ma. Garibay (Mexico City: Porrúa, 1967), 1: 6.

28. Fr. Antonio de Remesal, *Historia general de las Indias Occidentales, y particular de la gobernación de Chiapa y Guatemala,* ed. Carmelo Sáenz de Santa María, (Madrid: Biblioteca de Autores Españoles, 1964–66), bk. 10, chap. 3, 2: 276–77.

29. On Sahagún's criticism of other writers' choice of *tlacatecolotl* to convey the Christian idea of devil, Louise M. Burkhart, *The Slippery Earth: Nahua Christian Moral Dialogue in Sixteenth-Century Mexico* (Tucson: University of Arizona Press, 1989), 40–42. On Sahagún's linguistic project and ideas on translation, see Jesús Bustamante García, "Retórica, traducción y responsabilidad histórica: claves humanísticas en la obra de Bernardino de Sahagún," in *Humanismo y visión del otro en la España Moderna: cuatro estudios,* ed. Berta Ares, Jesús Bustamante, et al. (Madrid: Consejo Superior de Investigaciones Científicas, 1992), especially 332–64.

30. The translation of religious material into the native languages was subject to supervision and official approval; we know that by the year 1573 the Mexican Inquisition was inspecting copies of Molina's *Vocabulario* for which it had ordered some deletions, Francisco Fernández del Castillo, ed., *Libros y libreros en el siglo XVI* [1914] (Mexico City: Fondo de Cultura Económica, 1982), 482, 484, and 493. I am not aware of the exact nature of the Inquisition's objections.

31. Motolinía employed these three terms ("ritos, costumbres y ceremonias") when referring to contemporary comparisons of the Mexicans with other peoples such as the Jews or the Moors, *Historia de los indios, Epistola,* 113.

32. "Rito es publica costumbre del pueblo, et fabla aprovada." Alfonso de Palencia, *Universal Vocabulario en Latín y en Romance,* 2 vols. (Seville, 1490; Madrid: Comisión Permanente de la Asociación de Academias de la Lengua Española, 1967); see also the entry for *rite.* Sebastián de Covarrubias defined *rito*

as follows: "Costumbre o ceremonia." *Tesoro de la lengua castellana o española,* ed. Martín de Riquer (Madrid, 1611; Barcelona: Horta, I.E., 1943).

33. "Se nombravan los libros de los toscanos en que estaba escripta la costumbre como devian fundar cibdades y consagrar los templos y distribuyr las cortes y las tribus las centurias." Palencia, *Universal Vocabulario.* Palencia translated the Latin *ritus* as "costumbre."

34. On the liturgical usage of these terms, Pierre-Marie Gy, "Typologie et ecclésiologie," in *La liturgie dans l'histoire* (Paris: Cerf/Saint-Paul, 1990), 75–89. For an overview of ritual in the Renaissance, Edward Muir, *Ritual in Early Modern Europe* (Cambridge: Cambridge University Press, 1997); the centrality of ritual in Renaissance literature has been convincingly analyzed by Thomas M. Greene, "Ritual and Text in the Renaissance," *Canadian Review of Comparative Literature* (June–September 1991): 179–97. On the notion of ritual and its evolution in English discussed from an anthropological perspective, Talal Asad offered interesting observations in the opening section of his "Toward a Genealogy of the Concept of Ritual," in *Genealogies of Religion. Discipline and Reasons of Power in Christianity and Islam* (Baltimore: Johns Hopkins University Press, 1993), 55–62. More recently, Philippe Buc brilliantly showed the inadequacy of well-established approaches to the study of medieval rituals, *The Dangers of Ritual: Between Early Medieval Texts and Social Scientific Theory* (Princeton: Princeton University Press, 2001), especially 164–202.

35. A. D. Nock, *Conversion. The old and new in religion from Alexander the Great to Augustine of Hippo* (1933; Lanham, MD: University Press of America, 1988).

36. Peter Lombard's *Liber Sententiarum,* which became one of the most popular works for students of theology, was progressively replaced in Spanish universities in the sixteenth century. At the direction of Cardinal Cisneros, the authors who were read and studied at the University of Alcalá de Henares were Thomas Aquinas, Johannes Duns Scotus, and Gabriel Biel: they represented the three major theological schools of the time. In 1561 the traditional commentary on Lombard's text in university classrooms was replaced once and for all by Aquinas's *Summa,* Melquíades Andrés, *La teología española en el s. XVI* (Madrid: Biblioteca de Autores Cristianos, 1976), 1: 44. In any case, Lombard's work continued attracting the interest of commentators such as Domingo de Soto and was widely read by Mexican friars.

37. J. Pelikan, *Reformation of Church and Dogma (1300–1700)* (Chicago: University of Chicago Press, 1984), 291. Although it is not totally clear when the list of what is now known as the seven sacraments took form, the traditional sequence already appears in an anonymous text known as *Sentences of Divinity,* from approximately 1145, J. Pelikan, *The Growth of Medieval Theology (600–1300)* (Chicago: University of Chicago Press, 1978), 209. For the development of Peter Lombard's sacramental theology, with special attention to the theological traditions from which it emerged, see Marcia Collish, *Peter Lombard* (Leiden: E. J. Brill, 1994), 2: 516–32.

38. Thomas Aquinas, *Summa Theologiae,* 61 vols. (Blackfriars, NY:

McGraw Hill, 1964–81), 3a, q. 65, art. 1, res. In his treatment of the virtues Aquinas distinguished three stages in the development of charity in humans: "incipiens, proficiens et perfecta." To illustrate these distinctions, Aquinas referred to the physical development of humans, where he found a stage in which they do not speak ("aetus infantilis"), another characterized by the acquisition of speech and reason, and a third, puberty, marked by the capacity to procreate as a prior step to full maturity, *Summa,* 2a2ae, q. 24, art. 9, res.

39. Fr. Luis de Granada, *Compendio y explicación de la doctrina cristiana,* vol. 3 in *Obras de Fr. Luis de Granada* (Madrid: Biblioteca de Autores Españoles, 1945), 148. The *Compendio* was first published in 1559 in Portugal and in the Portuguese language.

40. In European iconography this parallel coexisted with other forms of representation of the sacraments; in some cases the artists expressed their preference for the association of the sacraments with the seven virtues, an idea already present in Aquinas's work, Servus Gieben, *Christian Sacrament and Devotion* (Leiden: E. J. Brill, 1980), 1. For the correlation between the seven sacraments and the seven virtues by Aquinas, *Summa,* 3a, q. 65, art. 1, res.

41. James Snyder, *Northern Renaissance Art* (New York: Harry N. Abrams, 1985), 129.

42. Gertrude Schiller, *Ikonographie der christlichen Kunst: Die Kirche* (Gütersloh: Güterloher Verlagshaus Gerd Mohn, 1976), 157.

43. The artist seems to have found inspiration in a 1569 engraving by Bartolomeo Olmo o Lulmus, Santiago Sebastián López, "El arte iberoamericano del siglo XVI," in *Summa Artis* (Madrid: Espasa-Calpe, 1985), 28: 194. On the mural paintings in the convent of Los Santos Reyes, the reader may consult José Guadalupe Victoria, *Arte y arquitectura en la Sierra Alta, siglo XVI* (Mexico City: Universidad Nacional Autónoma de México, 1985), 129–48; on the convent's architecture, Juan B. Artigas, *Metztitlán, Hidalgo: arquitectura del siglo XVI* (Mexico City: Gobierno del Estado de Hidalgo/Universidad Nacional Autónoma de México, 1996), 75–91.

44. Historically the sacramental nature of marriage has been much debated between canon lawyers and theologians; for an overview of the positions adopted by theologians from the Middle Ages to the Council of Trent, see Theodore Mackin, *The Marital Sacrament* (New York/Mahwah, NJ: Paulist Press, 1989), 325–436; for the development of ecclesiastical law regarding marriage, see James A. Brundage's classic study *Law, Sex, and Christian Society in Medieval Europe* (Chicago: University of Chicago Press, 1987). A partial account on the missionaries' approach to marriage regarding the Mexican Indians can be found in Pierre Ragon, *Les Indiens de la découverte: evangelisation, mariage et sexualité. Mexique, XVIe siècle* (Paris: L'Harmattan, 1992).

45. Mary Douglas stands, as far as I know, as an exception. See her *Natural Symbols. Explorations in Cosmology* (London and New York: Routledge, 1996), 1–19, and her somehow idiosyncratic take on the issue of women's ordination in the Catholic Church, "Sacraments and Society: An Anthropologist Asks, What Women Could Be Doing in the Church?" in *Anthropology and Theology: Gods, Icons, and God-Talk,* ed. Walter Randolph Adams and Frank Salamone (Lan-

ham, MD: University Press of America, 2000), 391–406. Asad approached Christian rituals by focusing on monastic practices in a flawed yet suggestive study, *Genealogies of Religion*, 125–67. Theologians, on the other hand, have not shied away from resorting to other disciplines to rethink aspects of theology. In the case of the sacraments, theologians who have delved into anthropology—among other disciplines—have done so guided by the desire to renew or update the language of sacramental theology in order to prove the relevance of the sacraments and ritual life for contemporary Christians. They seem fully aware of the general tendency "away from ritual" analyzed by Douglas. Among these works, see George S. Worgul, *From Magic to Metaphor* (Lanham, MD: University Press of America, 1985), 70–110, and Louis Marie Chauvet's semiotic-anthropological approach, *Du symbolique au symbole: essai sur les sacrements* (Paris: Les Éditions du Cerf, 1979).

46. James Lockhart, "The Social History of Colonial Spanish America: Evolution and Potential." *Latin American Research Review* 7, no. 1 (Spring 1972): 11; this piece was reprinted with a short epilogue in *Of Things of the Indies. Essays Old and New in Early Latin American History* (Stanford: Stanford UP, 1999).

47. A few of the most representative are Jorge Klor de Alva, "Spiritual Conflict and Accommodation in New Spain: Toward a Typology of Aztec Responses to Christianity," in *The Inca and Aztec States*, 345–66; Burkhart, *The Slippery Earth*, and *Ash Wednesday: A Nahua Drama from Early Colonial Mexico* (Philadelphia: University of Pennsylvania Press, 1996); Jeanette Favrot Peterson, *The Paradise Garden Murals of Malinalco* (Austin: University of Texas Press, 1993); and Lockhart, *The Nahuas after the Conquest*.

48. Burkhart moved toward this direction in her superb study on Nahua drama, *Ash Wednesday*.

49. With characteristic insight, Richard Morse called attention to this particular kind of reductionism when he wrote: "Religion, after all, takes hold in many realms, one of them being a shared instinct for behavior. In other words, we may take religion not simply as an ideological bulwark for a political structure but also as a pliant set of beliefs, social as well as theological, entertained by common folk." *New World Soundings: Culture and Ideology in the Americas* (Baltimore: Johns Hopkins University Press, 1989), 100–101.

Chapter 1

1. Ricard, *La "conquête spirituelle,"* 103–16.

2. For biographical information on Diego Muñoz Camargo I rely on Luis Reyes Garcia's introduction to his edition of Muñoz Camargo's *Historia de Tlaxcala* (MS 210 de la Biblioteca Nacional de París) (Tlaxcala: Gobierno del Estado de Tlaxcala/Centro de Investigaciones y Estudios en Antropología Social, Universidad Autónoma de Tlaxcala, 1998).

3. Charles Gibson, "The Identity of Diego Muñoz Camargo," *Hispanic American Historical Review* 30, no. 2 (1950): 202–3.

4. Muñoz Camargo compiled and wrote an extensive report on Tlaxcala requested by the Crown in 1579. The report is part of the massive documentary

collection known as *relaciones geográficas* (see chap. 4). The reader may consult René Acuña's facsimile edition of Muñoz Camargo's *Descripción de la ciudad y provincia de Tlaxcala* (Mexico City: Instituto de Investigaciones Filológicas, Universidad Autonóma de México), 1981.

5. Muñoz Camargo, *Historia de Tlaxcala,* 195–96.

6. Muñoz Camargo, *Historia de Tlaxcala,* 198.

7. A similar reaction was attributed to the Mexica priests addressing the first Franciscan friars in Mexico in a doctrinal dialogue composed by the Franciscan Bernardino de Sahagún, *Coloquios y doctrina cristiana,* ed. Miguel León-Portilla (Mexico City: Universidad Nacional Autónoma de México, 1986), chap. 7, 89.

8. Muñoz Camargo, *Historia de Tlaxcala,* 205.

9. Juan de Torquemada, *Monarquía indiana* [1614], int. Miguel León-Portilla (Mexico City: Porrúa, 1986), bk. 16, chap. 13, 3: 166–69.

10. The *Monarquía indiana* was first published in Seville in 1615. It was later reprinted between 1723 and 1725 at a time that saw a renewed interest in Indian antiquities and the early history of the Spanish colonies on both sides of the Atlantic. The authority that Torquemada's work enjoyed as a historical source in the eighteenth century can be gathered from the documents related to Boturini's collection. See Manuel Ballesteros Gaibrois, *Papeles de Indias* (Madrid: Mestre, 1947), 1: 119–20. Equally instructive in this regard is the exchange between the Valencian historian Juan Bautista Muñoz and Ramón Diosdado Caballero regarding Francisco Javier Clavigero's *Historia de la nación mexicana.* See Carlos de Onís, *Las polémicas de Juan Bautista Muñoz* (Madrid: José Porrúa Turanzas, 1984).

11. On the diffusion of this legend in Tlaxcalan indigenous traditions, see S. Wood, *Transcending Conquest: Nahua Views of Spanish Colonial Mexico.* Norman: University of Oklahoma Press, 2003, 85–94. The composition of an *auto sacramental* on the baptism of the four lords of Tlaxcala suggests that the story appealed to Spaniards as well. This religious play known as *Coloquio de los cuatro reyes de Tlaxcala,* was written sometime between the end of the sixteenth and the beginning of the seventeenth centuries; the text can be found in J. Rojas Garcidueñas and José Juan Arrom, *Tres piezas teatrales del virreinato.* México: Universidad Nacional Autónoma de México, 1976, 187–219. The most comprehensive study of the early transformation of Tlaxcala under the Spaniards remains Charles Gibson, *Tlaxcala in the Sixteenth Century* (Stanford: Stanford University Press, 1952). See pp. 28–31 where Gibson discussed the legends about the arrival of Christianity to the province.

12. Gibson, *Tlaxcala,* 29.

13. On Franciscan origins in Mexico, Ricard, *La "conquête spirituelle,"* 80–87.

14. Motolinía, *Historia de los indios,* treat. 2, chap. 3, 226. On the role of exorcism in baptism, see Henry Angstar Kelly, *The Devil at Baptism* (Ithaca: Cornell University Press, 1985), 106–22.

15. In order to validate the truthfulness of his account Motolinía included the names of other witnesses, a fact that may well indicate that what is being con-

veyed is the story behind the foundation of the Church of San Hipólito. The holiday of San Hipólito, patron saint of Mexico City, was celebrated in August to commemorate Cortés's victory over the Mexicans. The celebration seems to have been instituted in 1526, *Actas de cabildo de la ciudad de México,* ed. Ignacio Bejarano, paleography by Manuel Orozco y Berra (Mexico City, 1862), 5: 147. For Sahagún this celebration commemorated the day when the Mexican Indians had been delivered from the devil, Bernardino de Sahagún, *Psalmodia Christiana* [1583], trans. Arthur J. O. Anderson (Salt Lake City: University of Utah Press, 1983), 243–47. Spaniards were required to observe this holiday, Francisco Antonio Lorenzana y Buitrón, *Concilios provinciales primero y segundo celebrados en la muy noble y leal ciudad de México* (México: Joseph Antonio de Hogal, 1769), 66; Francisco Antonio Lorenzana y Buitrón, *Concilium Mexicanum Provinciale III,* bk. 2 (Mexico City, 1770), chap. 3, § 1, 112.

16. Martín de León, *Manual breve y forma para administrar los santos Sacramentos a los Indios universalmente* (Mexico City: María de Espinosa, 1614), 213–14.

17. In Western Europe the appearance of prebaptismal exorcism seems to have taken place in the third century A.D., Kelly, *The Devil at Baptism,* 81. And see pp. 232–53 for developments in Spain. A fundamental study on the evolution of baptismal liturgy in Spain remains, T. C. Akeley, *Christian Initiation in Spain* (London: Darton, Longman and Todd, 1967), 123–58.

18. For a recent contribution on the symbolic transformations of the sacrament, see Peter Cramer, *Baptism and Change in the Early Middle Ages, c. 200–c. 1150* (Cambridge: Cambridge University Press, 1993).

19. Evidence of baptized and nonbaptized Indians living in the same household can be found in S. L. Cline, *The Book of Tributes. Early Sixteenth-Century Nahuatl Censuses from Morelos* (Los Angeles: UCLA Latin American Center Publications/University of California, 1993). On the naming system in place among the Indians of Toluca at the end of the sixteenth century, James Lockhart, "Spaniards among Indians: Toluca in the Later Sixteenth Century," in *Nahuas and Spaniards: Postconquest Central Mexican History and Philology* (Stanford: Stanford University Press/UCLA Latin American Center Publication, 1991), 237–39.

20. On the development of spiritual kinship in the Christian tradition, Joseph H. Lynch, *Godparents and Kinship in Early Medieval Europe* (Princeton: Princeton University Press, 1986). For the Mexican case, the literature on the institution of compadrazgo is extensive; see the collection *Essays on Mexican Kinship,* ed. Hugo Nutini, Pedro Carrasco, and James Taggart (Pittsburgh: University of Pittsburgh Press, 1976), and Nutini's classic ethnographic study *Ritual Kinship: Ideological and Structural Integration of the Compadrazgo System in Rural Tlaxcala.* 2 vols. (Princeton: Princeton University Press, 1984).

21. The annals from Tecamachalco record that the Franciscan Francisco de las Navas baptized the commoners (*macehualtin*) in 1541 and a group of non-Nahuatl speakers (*popoloca*) in 1542, *Anales de Tecamachalco, 1398–1590,* ed. Eustaquio Celestino Solís and Luis Reyes García (Mexico City: Fondo de Cultura Económica, 1992), 27. The historical records from San Gregorio Acapulco men-

tion that baptism was first administered in 1525, "Anales de San Gregorio Acapulco, 1520–1606," *Tlalocan* 3 (1949–57): 106.

22. A recent retelling of the events surrounding Moctezuma's death can be found in Hugh Thomas, *Conquest: Moctezuma, Cortés and the Fall of Old Mexico* (New York: Simon and Shuster, 1993), 401–6. The trial and execution of the *cazonci* (lord) of Michoacán presided over by Nuño de Guzmán in 1529 proved even more controversial. The trial documentation can be found in Olmedo Armando Escobar, ed., *Proceso, tormento y muerte del Cazonci, último gran señor de los tarascos por Nuño de Guzmán, 1530* (Morelia: Michoacán, 1997). For an account of the trial, Benedict Warren, *The Conquest of Michoacan* (Norman: University of Oklahoma Press, 1984), chap. 11. The different historical versions on the burial of the cazonci have been analyzed by Cynthia Leigh Stone, "Rewriting Indigenous Traditions: The Burial Ceremony of the Cazonci," *Colonial Latin American Review* 3, nos. 1–2 (1994): 87–114.

23. The Reformation launched a strong attack on exorcism and the superstitions associated with it, Keith Thomas, *Religion and the Decline of Magic* (New York: Charles Scribner's Sons, 1971), 55–56.

24. "Catechismus et exorcismus neophytorum sunt, magisque sacramentalia quam sacramenta dici debent," Peter Lombard, *Sententiae in IV libris distinctae,* (Grottaferrata [Romae]: Editiones Colegii S. Bonaventurae Ad Claras Aquas, 1981), 4. d. 6. c. 7. 3, 2: 276. Aquinas paid closer attention to the relationship between the pair instruction/exorcism and baptism. According to him, both instruction and exorcism were preparatory stages for baptism. Instruction had to precede the baptism of adults, Aquinas, *Summa*, 3a, q. 71, art. 2, ad. 3; exorcism's function was to remove the obstacles that demonic forces may pose against the reception of the sacrament, Aquinas, *Summa*, 3a, q. 71, art. 2, res. Lombard's distinction between essential and nonessential elements of the sacrament was preserved in Diego Valadés's compendium of Lombard's *Sentences* in his *Retórica cristiana* [1579], int. Esteban J. Palomera, trans. Tarsicio Herrera Zapién (Mexico City: Fondo de Cultura Económica, 1989), 797.

25. Lombard, *Sententiae*, 4. d. 3. c. 1. 2, 2: 243.

26. Lombard, *Sententiae*, 4. d. 3. c. 1. 3, 2: 244.

27. Aquinas, *Summa*, 3a, q. 66, art. 3, res., and art. 5, res., respectively.

28. Mariano Cuevas, ed. *Documentos inéditos del siglo XVI para la historia de México,* 2nd ed. (Mexico City: Porrúa, 1975), 65.

29. "Item, que en el bautizar de los adultos se guarden y renueven decretos antiguos, como se guardaban y guardaron y mandaron guardar y renovar en la conversión del Alemania e Inglaterra cuando se conviertieron en tiempo del Papa Grigorio y del Emperador Carlo Magno y Pepino, pues tenemos el mesmo caso entre las manos e hay la mesma razón que cuando se establecieron los dichos decretos había," Joaquín García Icazbalceta, *Don Fray Juan de Zumárraga, primer obispo y arzobispo de México,* ed. Rafael Aguayo Spencer and Antonio Castro Leal (Mexico City: Porrúa, 1947), 3: 153. Cramer, *Baptism and Change,* 130; and Jean-Paul Bouhot, "Explications du rituel baptismal à l'époque carolingienne," *Revue de études augustiniennes* 24 (1978): 280. For an overview, Peter Brown, *The Rise of Western Christendom* (Oxford: Blackwell, 1997), chap.

16. On baptism, pp. 288–90. On the political dimension of the conversion campaigns launched by Charlemagne, Richard E. Sullivan, "The Carolingian Missionary and the Pagan," *Speculum* 28, no. 4 (October 1953): 714. And see pp. 718–20 on baptism and instruction.

30. Motolinía, *Historia de los indios,* treat. 2, chap. 4, 229.

31. These times were set up by what the eighteenth-century archbishop Lorenzana referred to as the "primera junta apostólica," which took place in 1525. The document issued from that meeting was published by Lorenzana in his edition of the first two Mexican councils, *Concilios provinciales primero y segundo,* 1.

32. "[A]l tiempo del bautismo ponían todos juntos los que se habían de bautizar poniendo los niños delante, y hacían todos el oficio del bautismo, y sobre algunos pocos la ceremonia de la cruz, flato, sal, saliva, alba. Luego bautizaban a los niños cada por sí en agua bendita, y esta orden siempre se guardó en cuanto yo he sabido." Motolinía, *Historia de los indios,* 231.

33. Motolinía's point is made fully clear in the following passage, where we encounter an identical sequence: "Acá en esta conversión, ¿cómo podía un solo sacerdote bautizar a dos y tres mil en un día, y dar a todos saliva, flato, y candela, y alba, y hacer sobre cada uno particularmente todas las ceremonias, y meterlos en la iglesia donde no las había?" Motolinía, *Historia de los indios,* 231.

34. Motolinía, *Historia de los indios,* treat. 3, chap. 14, 359; on noble Indian girls educated by Spanish women, treat. 3, chap. 15, 372–73; Gante, *Cartas de Pedro de Gante,* 42; Mendieta, *Historia eclesiástica indiana,* bk. 3, chap. 15, 2: 59–61. The role of Indian children in the evangelization has been studied by Richard Trexler, "From the Mouth of Babes," in *Church and Community, 1200–1600* (Rome, 1987), 549–73.

35. Cuevas, *Documentos inéditos,* 67.

36. "Iudaeorum filios uel filias, ne parentum ultra inuoluantur erroribus, ab eorum consortio separari decernimus deputatos aut monasteriis aut Christianis uiris ac mulieribus Deum timentibus, ut sub eorum conuersatione cultum fidei discant atque in melius instituti tam in moribus quam in fide proficiant." *La Colección Canónica Hispana* (Madrid, 1992), tit. LX, 5: 238.

37. Juan Focher, *Manual del Bautismo de Adultos* [1544] (Mexico City, 1997), 33.

38. Mendieta, *Historia eclesiástica indiana,* bk. 3, chap. 36, 2: 115; Torquemada followed Mendieta, *Monarquía indiana,* bk. 16, chap. 7, 3: 153.

39. Motolinía, *Historia de los indios,* treat. 2, chap. 4, 231. Church law allowed baptisms to be administered in cases of impending death, illness, persecution, and shipwreck, E. Friedberg, ed. *Decretum Magistri Gratiani, Corpus iuris canonici.* 1 [1879] (Graz, 1955), de cons., d. 4, c. 16. Given a case of necessity, if no religious minister was available, a layperson could baptize, *Decretum,* de cons., d. 4, c. 21.

40. García Icazbalceta, *Don Fray Juan de Zumárraga,* vol. 3, doc. 32, 111.

41. "Y los indios, que no distinguían entre lo esencial y ceremonial, turbábanse de ver que ejercitasen los santos Sacramentos, unos con más y otros con menos ceremonias." Grijalva, *Crónica de la orden de N. P. S. Agustín,* 115.

42. The Mexican Indians were frequently labeled *ceremoniáticos,* inclined both to observe and participate in ceremonies, see Joaquín García Icazbalceta, ed., *Códice Mendieta* [1892] (México: Edmundo Aviña Levy, 1971), 2: 11. The idea was not new, although it would play a significant part in the religious orders' argument against entrusting parish priests to the Indians. The change that the priests would bring with them would not pass unnoticed by the Indians whose Christianity would be adversely affected since, as the friars wrote, "no son los indios intelectuales ni usan de discursos sino *omnino* sensuales, que no perciben sino lo que ven." *Cartas de religiosos de Nueva España* (México, 1941), 173; the same point is made in a set of opinions compiled by Torquemada, *Codice Mendieta,* 2: 171.

43. References to this ceremony are numerous. The reader can consult Motolinía, *Historia de los indios,* treat. 2, chap. 3, 227; Durán, *Historia de las Indias,* 1: 57; Mendieta, *Historia eclesiástica indiana,* vol. 1, bk. 2, chap. 19, 117; and Bernardino de Sahagún, *Florentine Codex: General History of the Things of New Spain,* ed. and trans. Charles Dibble and Arthur J. O. Anderson,, bk. 4, chap. 35 (Santa Fe: School of American Research and the University of Utah, 1950–82), 113, among others. Some sources refer to two separate ablutions, the one immediately after birth and the second one a few days later, Torquemada, *Monarquía indiana,* bk. 13, chap. 16, 2: 445; chap. 20, 2: 450.

44. Sahagún, *Florentine Codex,* bk. 4, chap. 35, 114–15; Torquemada, *Monarquía indiana,* bk. 13, chap. 20, 2: 450–51.

45. Motolinía, for example, saw in the Nahua ceremony a *figura* of Christian baptism, *Historia de los indios,* treat. 2, chap. 3, 227; although overall Mendieta showed a more ambiguous attitude, he referred to the ancient ceremony as an *execramento, Historia eclesiástica indiana,* bk. 2, chap. 19, 1: 116–17 (on execramentos, see chap. 3, n. 43). The best account on the missionaries' interpretation of Nahua rituals in relation to baptism can be found in Burkhart, *The Slippery Earth,* 110–21.

46. It is still unclear exactly how many of these meetings were held prior to 1555; the number has been periodically subjected to revision in recent years and is likely to be modified as more archival research is conducted. For the most recent contributions, see Fernando Gil, "Las 'Juntas eclesiásticas' durante el episcopado de Fray Juan de Zumárraga (1528–1548). Algunas precisiones históricas," *Teología. Revista de la Facultad de Teología de la Pontificia Universidad Católica Argentina* 26 (1989): 3–20. A more in-depth treatment of the issues discussed in the juntas during Zumárraga's tenure as bishop can be found in Gil's richly documented study *Primeras "Doctrinas" del Nuevo Mundo. Estudio histórico-teológico de las obras de Juan de Zumárraga († 1548)* (Buenos Aires: Facultad de Teología de la Pontificia Universidad Católica Argentina Santa María de los Buenos Aires, 1992), chap. 3; Helen-Rand Parish and Harold E. Weidman, *Las Casas en México. Historia y obras desconocidas* (Mexico City: Fondo de Cultura Económica, 1992), especially the first part; and Ernest J. Burrus, "Key Decision of the 1541 Mexican Conference," *Neue Zeitschrift für Missionswissenschaft* 28 (1972): 253–63.

47. Fidel Chauvet was the first one to establish the existence of this meeting

and included a Spanish translation of its minutes in *Fray Juan de Zumárraga, O.F.M.* (Mexico City: Beatriz de Silva, 1948), 153–54; on problems in determining the exact date arising from documentary inconsistencies, Gil, *Primeras "Doctrinas,"* 205–6, and Parish and Weidman, *Las Casas en México,* 24–26.

48. "[E]xplíquese que esas ceremonias sólo pertenecen a la solemnidad del sacramento, pero no a su sustancia, ni son de necesidad," Chauvet, *Fray Juan de Zumárraga,* 154.

49. Pope Paul III issued the convocation for the general council in the bull *Ad dominici gregis curam* on May 23, 1537. On the motives behind the call for a general council in Mantua and the political difficulties that conspired against its realization, see Hubert Jedin, *A History of the Council of Trent,* trans. Dom Ernest Graf (St. Louis, MO: B. Herder Book Co., 1957), 288–354.

50. In an important letter to the Consejo de Indias from February 1537, Zumárraga commented briefly on Mendoza's decision, Cuevas, *Documentos inéditos,* 72–73. The Spanish colonies, however, did not have direct representation at the Council of Trent.

51. Pedro de Oseguera was among the first Augustinians to arrive in Mexico in 1533. It has been assumed that he was present at the junta of 1536 to voice his order's position regarding the baptismal ritual, on which he wrote a treatise now lost rejecting the use of aspersion, Parish and Weidman, *Las Casas en México,* 25; a document about the baptismal debate signed by Cristobal de Almazán and addressed to the Council of the Indies can be found in the same work, pp. 326–27.

52. "Lo 30.: que se ha de procurar con mucha diligencia es que entre todos los que en estas partes entienden en la conversión e instrucción de los naturales dellas, haya conformidad y uniformidad así en la doctrina e administración de los sacramentos , como en el criarlos y edificar en nuestra religión cristiana," Cuevas, *Documentos inéditos,* 64.

53. On the Franciscan move to have their view validated, and the role of the Fr. Francisco Castillo, the order's representative in the papacy, Parish and Weidman, *Las Casas en México,* 26.

54. "[Y] envío a ese alto Consejo, la opinión persuasiva de los franciscos sobre las ceremonias del baptismo, que en el capítulo que en principio del año tuvieron juntos, me lo dieron. Y los otros padres dominicos y agustinos tienen y defienden la contraria opinión que no se deben dejar las cerimonias por la Iglesia ordenadas, si no es en caso o peligro de muerte." Cuevas, *Documentos inéditos,* 73.

55. Motolinía, *Historia de los indios,* treat. 2, chap. 4, 230–31.

56. Motolinía, *Historia de los indios,* 230. Records of books confiscated by the Mexican Inquisition for examination show that the *Tercer Abecedario Espiritual,* vol. 2 of *Místicos franciscanos españoles* (Toledo, 1527; Madrid: Biblioteca de Autores Cristianos, 1998), by the Franciscan observant Francisco de Osuna was widely read in the colonies, especially among members of his order (see Fernández del Castillo, *Libros y libreros,* 474–75). In this work Osuna discerned two kinds of theology, the speculative and the hidden—which corresponds to the mystic. Speculative theology, Osuna explained, "usa de razones y argumentos y discursos y probabilidades según las otras ciencias; y de aquí es que se llama teología escolástica y de letrados," Osuna, *Tercer Abecedario Espiritual,* 200. On

the rejection of the letrados by religious visionaries in Spain, Geraldine McKendrick and Angus MacKay, "Visionaries and Affective Spirituality during the First Half of the Sixteenth Century," in *Cultural Encounters: The Impact of the Inquisition in Spain and the New World,* ed. Mary Elizabeth Perry and Anne J. Cruz (Berkeley: University of California Press, 1991), 98–99. On the letrados as a class and the pivotal role they came to play in Spanish political and administrative circles, see José A. Maravall, "Los hombres de 'saber' o letrados y la formación de su conciencia estamental," in *Estudios de historia del pensamiento español. Edad Media. Serie primera* (Madrid: Ediciones Cultura Hispánica, 1967), 345–80, and Jean-Marc Pelorson, *Les Letrados juristes castillans sous Philippe III* (Poitiers: Université de Poitiers, 1980).

57. Gante, *Cartas de Pedro de Gante,* 15. The intellectual background of the three Flemish friars was discussed by Geertrui van Acker, "El humanismo cristiano en México: los tres flamencos," in *Historia de la evangelización de América. Simposio Internacional, Ciudad del Vaticano, 11–14 de mayo de 1992,* coord. José Escudero Imbert (Ciudad del Vaticano: Libreria Editrice Vaticana, 1992), 795–819.

58. Although the reaction against formal theology as represented by the university curriculum was a common theme in reform movements, the Franciscan Observants who emerged at the end of the fourteenth century showed an unmistakable contempt toward theological speculation of the types found in nominalism and the humanist variety, Melquíades Andrés, *La teología española en el siglo XVI* (Madrid: Biblioteca de Autores Cristianos, 1976), 1: 84.

59. "Fueron estos celadores (que presumían de letrados) de harta inquietud y turbación a los que primero habían venido, y tenían con su sudor plantada esta viña del señor: que aunque por su humildad y propio menosprecio holgaban de ser tenidos por simples y sin letras, todos ellos habían oído, unos el derecho canónico, y otros la sacra teología." Mendieta, *Historia eclesiástica indiana,* bk. 3, chap. 36, 2: 116. In so doing, Mendieta was actually leveling the ground for the dispute instead of downplaying the knowledge of the letrados who criticized the baptismal practices of the Franciscans. Mendieta concluded his *Historia* with a catalogue of Franciscans writers that summed up the tradition developed since the arrival of the first Franciscans.

60. "Oído he yo por mis oídos a algunas personas decir que sus veinte años o más de letras no las quieren emplear con gente tan bestial. En lo cual me parece que que no aciertan, porque a mi parecer no se pueden las letras mejor emplear que en amonestar al que no lo sabe el camino por donde se tienen de salvar y conocer a Dios." Motolinía, *Historia de los indios,* treat. 2, chap. 4, 236.

61. "Solamente supe de un letrado que pensaba que sabía lo que hacía, que bautizó con hisopo, y éste fue después uno de los que trabajaron en estorbar el bautismo de los otros." Motolinía, *Historia de los indios,* 231.

62. Mendieta, based on Motolinía's testimony denied the accusation, Mendieta, *Historia eclesiástica indiana,* vol. 2, bk. 3, chap. 32, 2: 104.

63. Despite its prominent place in sixteenth-century religious writings, a detailed study of how different writers thought of the primitive church is still lacking. Often, competing claims to the primitive church from the religious

orders have been overlooked and replaced by a single vision, as is the case with Miranda, "La fraternidad cristiana"; Antonio Rubial García, "Evangelismo y evangelización. Los primeros franciscanos en la Nueva España y el ideal del cristianismo primitivo," *Anuario de Historia* 10 (1979): 95–124.

64. Cuevas, *Documentos inéditos*, 64–65.

65. The same February Zumárraga wrote about the split of opinions: "E yo no basto conformarlos ni alcanzo lo que debo mandar ni consentir en esto con las auctoridades y decretos de una parte, y razones con la experiencia de la otra." Cuevas, *Documentos inéditos*, 73.

66. "Pero gran ciencia es saber la lengua de los Indios y conocer esta gente, y los que no se ejercitasen primero a lo menos tres o cuatro años, no deberían hablar absolutamente en esta materia." Motolinía, *Historia de los indios*, 232.

67. Phrases such as "fue de razonable ciencia," "hombre de mediana ciencia," and "religiosos de medianas letras" are sprinkled to quickly characterize his brothers. The centrality of study in the formation of Dominican preachers did not pass unmentioned either, Juan de Córdova, *Relación de la Fundación, Capítulos y Elecciones, que se han Tenido en esta Provincia de Santiago de ésta Nueva España, de la Orden de Predicadores de Santo domingo. 1569* (Mexico City: Vargas Rea, 1944), 38. For an overview of the principal trends of Dominican spirituality in Spain during this period with special emphasis on the reform movement within the order, V. Beltrán de Heredia, *Las corrientes de espiritualidad entre los dominicos de Castilla durante la primera mitad del siglo XVI* (Salamanca, 1941).

68. Juan Garcés and Marroquín, bishops of Tlaxcala and Guatemala, respectively, were not present at this meeting. The minutes of the meeting were first published in Lorenzana's edition of the first and second councils; García Icazbalceta included them in *Don Fray Juan de Zumárraga*, 3: 149–84.

69. The bull was reproduced by Lorenzana, *Concilios provinciales primero y segundo*, 31. A partial reproduction can be found in Francisco J. Hernáez, *Colección de bulas, breves y otros documentos* (Bruselas: Imprenta de Alfredo Vromant, 1879; Vaduz, 1964), 1: 65–67. A complete transcription of the bull can be found in Parish and Weidman, *Las Casas in México*, 306–7.

70. Lorenzana, *Concilios provinciales primero y segundo*, 30. The distinction between Christian baptism and body cleansing was clearly spelled out in 1 Peter 3:21–22.

71. García Icazbalceta, *Don Fray Juan de Zumárraga*, 3: 152 and 163, for the regular times; on the distinction between extreme and urgent necessity, 162. In 1537 Zumárraga informed the Council of the Indies that Bishop Quiroga favored the observance of the traditional times reserved by the church when dealing with the baptism of adults, Cuevas, *Documentos inéditos*, 74.

72. Motolinía, *Historia de los indios*, treat. 2, chap. 4, 234.

73. Juan Focher, *Manual del bautismo de adultos y del matrimonio de los bautizandos (Enchiridion Baptismi Adultorum et Matrimonii Baptizandorum)*, trans. José Pascual Guzmán de Alba (México: Frente de Afirmación Hispanista, A.C., 1997); Juan Focher, *Itinerario del misionero en América* [1574], ed. Antonio Eguiluz. (Madrid: Librería General Victoriano Suárez, 1960).

74. Focher did not hesitate in suggesting that baptism could be celebrated

dispensing with the required solemnity even in those two times reserved by the church, *Manual del bautismo de adultos,* 20–21.

75. "En mi Orden no hallo relación del modo que tuvieron de bautizar hasta este año de 40, en que el santo Coruña escribe la multitud de los bautizados en todas partes, la solemnidad con que se hacía y el inmenso trabajo que en esto tenían." Grijalva, *Crónica de la orden de N. P. S. Agustín,* 103.

76. Grijalva, *Crónica de la orden de N. P. S. Agustín,* 103. On the times allowed traditionally by the church for the administration of baptism, Friedberg, *Decretum,* de cons., d. 4 c. 12, col. 1365.

77. "Pues de haber a tiempo diferencias entre los obispos y religiosos, o los religiosos entre sí mismos, sobre la administración de la doctrina y los sacramentos, ninguno se debe espantar, ni menos escandalizar, que no son cosas nuevas entre siervos de Dios y muy perfectos, ni se fundan en malicia, sino en toda sinceridad de conciencia, porque grandes varones y prelados santos de la Iglesia tuvieron entre sí discordias, movidos cada uno de ellos por santísimo celo." *Cartas de religiosos,* 7.

78. The detailed study of C. Ceccherelli is a case in point; that the old dispute carries still to the present can be gathered from the author's insistence in defending the Franciscan solution as rooted in church tradition, "El bautismo y los franciscanos en México (1524–1539)," *Missionalia hispánica* (Madrid) 12, no. 35 (1955): 209–89.

79. While Motolinía did not make much of the papal bull containing the new guidelines that he opposed, Mendieta, writing much later, would choose to include a full translation of it. Here Mendieta used the papal document to suggest that the exceptions it made for the modification of the baptismal ritual in cases of necessity fully justified the Franciscans' approach to baptism, *Historia eclesiástica indiana,* bk. 3, 2:122. Both in the *Historia de los indios* and *Memoriales,* Motolinía avoided the transcription of official documents, including those issued by the papacy on matters of direct interest for the Franciscans. This was not the case with later Franciscan chroniclers, such as Mendieta and Torquemada, who were pressed to include in their historical writings a defense of their order based on the original privileges granted by the pope. Regarding the bull *Altitudo divini consilii,* Mendieta and Torquemada offered Spanish translations.

80. Thus, the baptisms were deemed valid, although the bull does not employ this term; instead, the papal document declares that if the ministers had baptized in the name of the Holy Trinity, they had not incurred in mortal sin, Mendieta, *Historia eclesiástica indiana,* bk. 3, chap. 37, 2: 120. The emergence of the usage of the expressions *validus/invalidus* in sacramental theology, and their place in canon law, was analyzed by Gy in "La validité sacramentelle. Développement de la notion avant le Concile de Trente," *La liturgie dans l'histoire,* 165–75.

81. The issue went back to the situation created by the forced conversion of Jews under Sisebut in Visigothic Spain. The Fourth Council of Toledo declared that the baptisms of those who converted to Christianity to avert expulsion were to be considered valid since the person's freedom to choose had not been entirely compromised: see S. Monzó, "El Bautismo de los judíos en la españa visigoda. En torno al canon 57 del Concilio IV de Toledo," *Cuadernos de Trabajos de Dere-*

cho (Roma) 2 (1953): 111–55; on King Ervig's measures regarding baptized Jews, and the legal distinction between baptism and conversion, see P. D. King, *Law and Society in the Visigothic Kingdom* (Cambridge: Cambridge University Press, 1972), 133–45. For a recent interpretation of Visigothic conciliar legislation concerning the Jews, Rachel L. Stocking, *Bishops, Councils, and Consensus in the Visigothic Kingdom, 589–633* (Ann Arbor: University of Michigan Press, 2000).

82. On the economic and social conditions that made the revolt possible, see Ricard Garcia Càrcel, *Las Germanías de Valencia* (Barcelona: Península, 1975), especially chaps. 3 and 5; on the economic motivation behind the baptisms of the Mudejars, Ricard Garcia Càrcel and Eduard Císcar Pallarés, *Moriscos i Agermanats* (Valencia, 1974), 125–30.

83. Between 1500 and 1502 the Mudejars of Castile came under the increasing pressure of the Crown to convert to Christianity after the violent uprisings witnessed in Granada in 1499. In 1502 they were given the choice of converting or facing exile: see A. Domínguez Ortíz and Bernard Vincent, *Historia de los moriscos* (Madrid: Alianza Universidad, 1989), 19.

84. Manuel Danvila y Collado, *La germanía de Valencia* (Madrid: Tipografía de Manuel G. Hernández, 1884), 155.

85. After Hurtado de Mendoza's military victory over the rebel forces, Germana de Foix, widow of Ferdinand the Catholic, was appointed *virreina* of Valencia on March 27, 1523. The new viceroy's attitude toward the defeated was uncompromising: several participants in the revolt were executed, and cities, guilds, as well as individuals faced severe fines, García Cárcel, *Las Germanías de Valencia,* 147–55.

86. Pascual Boronat y Barrachina, *Los moriscos españoles y su expulsión* (Valencia: Imprenta de Francisco Vives y Mora, 1901), 1: 401. With regard to the extent of coercion that went into these baptisms, the first comprehensive historical assessments wildly differ along national and religious lines. Charles Lea emphasized the illegality of the actions, *The Moriscos of Spain: Their Conversion and Expulsion* [1901] (Westport, CT: Greenwood Press, 1968), 57–81; Danvila y Collado tried to show that the irregularities were circumscribed to isolated episodes and that most of the conversions were carried out within the legal norms adopted by the church, *Las Germanías de Valencia,* 471–482; for a similar view, Boronat y Barrachina, *Los moriscos españoles,* 1: 128–29.

87. Boronat y Barrachina, *Los moriscos españoles,* 1: 402.

88. García Icazbalceta, *Don Fray Juan de Zumárraga,* vol. 3, doc. 27, 71–73.

89. For a roster of authorities attending the meeting, Boronat y Barrachina, *Los moriscos españoles,* 1: 409. On Cardinal García de Loaysa's intervention in favor of Indian slavery, an issue on which he sided with Betanzos, Parish and Weidman, *Las Casas en México,* 30 and 39.

90. Documentation related to Guevara's activities in Valencia can be found in Ángel Uribe's partisan contribution "Guevara, inquisidor del Santo Oficio," in *Estudios acerca de Fray Antonio de Guevara en el IV centenario de su muerte.* (Madrid: Archivo Ibero-Americano, Revista de Estudios Históricos, 1946).

91. Domínguez Ortíz and Vincent, *Historia de los moriscos,* 24–25.

92. Franz Kafka, *Parables and Paradoxes* (New York, 1961), 92–93. To what

extent the endeavors of sacramental theology to produce satisfying explanations of how the sacraments work could be reinterpreted as attempts to minimize and control the possible disruption of unforeseen contexts is a question that, although worth exploring, falls outside the scope of this study.

93. On ritual violence in the Spanish interreligious context, see David Nirenberg's analysis in his *Communities of Violence* (Princeton: Princeton University Press, 1996), chap. 7. Nirenberg's starting point for his reflections is Natalie Z. Davis, "The Rites of Violence," in *Society and Culture in Sixteenth-Century France* (Stanford: Stanford UP, 1965), 152–87.

94. Lea, *The Moriscos of Spain*, 74.

95. Torquemada, *Monarquía indiana*, vol. 3, bk. 16, chap. 1, 140.

96. Robert Ricard was among the first to pursue this line of inquiry and pointed to the likely influence of Pedro de Alcalá's *Arte para ligeramente saber la lengua araviga* (Granada, 1505) on Alonso de Molina's doctrinal manuals for the Nahuas: Ricard, "Indiens et Morisques (Note sur quelques procédés d'evangelisation)," and "Remarques sur l' *Arte* et la *Vocabulista de* Fr. Pedro de Alcalá," compiled in *Etudes et documents pour l'Histoire missionaire de l'Espagne et du Portugal* (Louvain, A.U.C.A.M./Paris: J. M. Peigues, 1931), 209–19 and 220–28, respectively. Ricard's call for further investigation was taken up by Antonio Garrido Aranda, *Moriscos e Indios. Precedentes hispánicos de la evangelización en México* (Mexico City: Universidad Nacional Autónoma de México, 1980). Although not an entirely satisfying work, Garrido Aranda's comparison of conciliar legislation is instructive.

97. The importance assigned to the Moriscos in missionary thought was not limited to a search for a model of religious conversion. Early on, Zumárraga envisioned the transformation of the Mexican Indians into productive peasants by having them live next to Morisco families that were to be transplanted to Mexico to produce silk, García Icazbalceta, *Don Fray Juan de Zumárraga*, 3: 142–43. Regarding their dispositions, Mendieta rejected a comparison between the Mexican Indians and the Moriscos, García Icazbalceta, *Códice Mendieta*, 2: 11. A more precise picture of the relationship between the conversion of the Moriscos and the Mexican Indians has yet to emerge. A sometimes too restricted focus on questions of missionary methods has somehow led to losing sight of the fact that the religious campaigns aimed at the Moriscos took place over a long period of time with frequent changes in policy. For Mendieta the conversion of the Moriscos had failed; in 1564 he attributed this failure to the Crown's decision to entrust the spiritual care of the Moriscos to parish priests, García Icazbalceta, *Códice Mendieta*, 2: 27. We find a similar reasoning in a document dating from 1584 by Alonso de Zurita, Cuevas, *Documentos inéditos*, 334.

98. With regard to instruction the junta of 1539 limited itself to discouraging the use of physical punishment as a corrective; it favored instead as a model the kind of reprehension that a pupil might expect from a tutor, García Icazbalceta, *Don Fray Juan de Zumárraga*, 3: 158–59.

99. *Colección de documentos inéditos relativos al descubrimiento, conquista y organización de las antiguas posesiones españolas de ultramar* (Madrid: "Suce-

sores de Rivadeneyra," 1923–24), 14: 42. The instructions in question, as the reader may recall, had been drafted by Zumárraga and entrusted to Oseguera for his European mission in 1537.

100. The *Relectiones de Indiis* was written between 1537 and 1538 and delivered in lecture form in January 1539, V. Beltrán de Heredia, "Personalidad del maestro Francisco de Vitoria," in Francisco de Vitoria, *Relectio de Indiis o libertad de los indios*. ed. L. Pereña and J. M. Pérez Prendes (Madrid: Consejo Superior de Investigaciones Científicas, 1967), xxviii.

101. *Colección de documentos inéditos de ultramar,* 14: 114.

102. Henry Raup Wagner, *The Life and Writings of Bartolomé de las Casas* (Albuquerque: University of New Mexico Press, 1967), 99. Las Casas left Mexico in 1540; Zumárraga informed the king about his departure and the Dominicans' intentions to inform him about Mexican matters, *Colección de documentos inéditos, relativos al descubrimiento, conquista y organización de las antiguas posesiones españolas de América y Oceanía, sacados de los archivos del reino, y muy especialmente del de Indias* (1884), 41: 183. At the time of Wagner's study not much was known about Las Casas's activities in Mexico; thanks to the work of Parish and Weidman, who have described the Dominicans' role in the baptismal controversy, this is no longer the case.

103. For an analysis of the resulting document, Dionisio Borobio, "Los teólogos salmantinos ante el problema bautismal en la evangelización de América (s. XVI)," *Salmanticensis* 33 (1986): 179–206.

104. Vitoria's comments applied to Aquinas's *Secunda secundae*, q. 10. 8, in Francisco de Vitoria, *Political writings,* ed. Anthony Pagden (Cambridge: Cambridge University Press, 1991), 346; on the difference between involuntary and nonvoluntary acts, p. 341. For related questions concerning the baptism of the offspring of unbelievers, see Vitoria's comments about Aquinas's article 12 in *Comentarios a la Secunda secundae de Santo Tomás,* ed. Vicente Beltrán de Heredia (Salamanca: Biblioteca de Teólogos Españoles, 1932), 2: 203–12.

105. "Barbari illi infideles, non antea sunt baptizandi, quam sint sufficienter instructi, non solum in fide, sed etiam in moribus christianis," *Colección de documentos inéditos, relativos* (1865), 3: 545.

106. "Constat autem de istis barbaris quod sunt omnes in peccato mortali, non solum infidelitatis, sed in multis aliis pecatis mortalibus, a quibus liberari non possunt, nisi saltem proponant relinquere perversos et impios mores prioris vite et consuetudinis, quod facere non possunt, nisi prius diligenter instruantur de fide et moribus christianis et de iniquitate morum preteritorum." *Colección de documentos inéditos, relativos* (1865), 3: 546. In Spain, the church showed a similar preoccupation regarding the customs of the rural population. The Provincial Chapter of Burgos from 1553 expressed the need to remedy the populace's ignorance in matters of faith and customs ("doctrina circa fidem at mores"), Beltrán de Heredia, *Las corrientes de espiritualidad,* 45.

107. "Ex quo constat in primitiva ecclesia neminem admiti ad baptismum, quid non existimaretur dignus eucharistia." *Colección de documentos inéditos, relativos* (1865), 3: 548. For an overview of the positions adopted regarding the

administration of the Eucharist to the American Indians, see Constantino Bayle, "La comunión entre los indios americanos," *Missionalia hispánica* (Madrid) 1 (1944): 13–72.

108. Lorenzana, *Concilios provinciales primero y segundo,* 42.

109. Parish and Weidman, *Las Casas en México,* 30–34.

110. Dávila Padilla described how Betanzos envisioned the ways in which the Indians ought to familiarize themselves with doctrinal truths: "dándoselas a entender a su modo: para que no solamente las recitassen por el hilo de la memoria, sino que las tuviessen assentadas en la voluntad amando a un Dios tan bueno," *Historia de la fundación,* 65. In describing the general approach of the Dominican friars, Dávila Padilla noted: "Ocupavanse los ministros de Christo, en dar asiento en la voluntad por pia afeccion, y en el entendimiento por firmeza a las verdades que la Fe Christiana propone," *Historia de la fundación,* 66. Of special interest is Dávila Padilla's reference to baptisms administered secretly by Dominicans, some of them prominent, such as the second archbishop of Mexico, Alonso de Montúfar. There is a hint that such practices took place as a consequence of inadequate Christian teaching that prevented the Indians from accessing baptism, p. 118.

111. "Dicen que quieren los diezmos para que haya ministros, y que por esta causa muchos niños y adultos se mueren sin los Sacramentos. Para poder confesar a todos, verdad es que faltan ministros; pero para todos los otros Sacramentos hay todo recaudo, porque un solo sacerdote basta en una Tlaxcalla o México para baptizar cuantos niños nacen y para entender en los matrimonios y decir misa y predicar, y son muchos los que se confiesan." García Icazbalceta, *Códice Mendieta,* 1: 4. This document was a direct response to a long letter on the need to collect tithes from the Indians addressed by Archbishop Montúfar to the Council of the Indies in 1556, Luis García Pimentel, ed., *Descripción del Arzobispado de México hecha en 1570 y otros documentos* (Mexico City: José Joaquín Terrazas e Hijas, 1897), 421–48. In his letter, Montúfar pointed to the endemic shortage of ministers for the administration of the sacraments, *Descripción,* 423–25; on Montúfar's document, see chap. 2. In 1568, the cabildo of the city of Mexico ordered that four parishes be finished to administer the sacraments more efficiently, *Actas de cabildo de la ciudad de México,* 7: 401.

112. It is outside the scope of this chapter to offer a detailed analysis of Mendieta's thought; I have limited myself to highlighting those elements that are directly relevant to my discussion of Christian initiation. The Franciscan political project was first analyzed by José A. Maravall in "La utopía político-religiosa de los Franciscanos en Nueva España," reprinted in *Utopía y reformismo* (México, 1982), 79–110. For a thorough study of Mendieta's thought, Phelan, *The Millennial Kingdom;* for a more recent contribution on Mendieta's *memoriales* (reports), Carlos Sempat Assadourian, "*Memoriales* de Fray Gerónimo de Mendieta," *Historia Mexicana* 37, no. 3 (1988): 357–422.

113. In a memorial to Felipe II written in 1586, Mendieta equated the Indians with "mozuelos de hasta diez o doce años"; in other documents they were considered "muchachos como de nueve o diez años" and "párvulos," García Icazbalceta, *Códice Mendieta,* 2: 8, 28, and 29, respectively. The memorial from 1586 pre-

sents a fully elaborated version of the Franciscan's designs regarding the governance of Mexican Indians under religious authority. An interesting feature of the document is that the idea of the Mexican Indians as children is not simply assumed but presented as the most apt after other current comparisons have been considered, such as the Indians with Spanish peasants, *Códice Mendieta*, 2: 9.

114. In 1529 Pedro de Gante expressed the opinion that the Indians were used to responding to the use of force, *Cartas de Pedro de Gante*, 12; Zumárraga, making no distinction between nature and custom, declared that in spiritual matters the Indians needed to be compelled, Cuevas, *Documentos inéditos*, 68.

115. The parental metaphor also found a more explicit elaboration in the claim that the friars, through conversion and baptism, had in fact regenerated the Indians, the spiritual equivalent of bringing them to life, and therefore had the obligation to raise and watch after them as expected from biological fathers. García Icazbalceta, *Códice Mendieta*, 2: 163.

116. "Cuanto más que yo no sé que motivo se pudo tener para que el Virrey de esta tierra esté en todo sujeto y atado a tres o cuatro oidores, por ser letrados en el Derecho Civil; porque es verdad que es de tan poca importancia y necesidad para el gobierno destos reinos, que pluguiera a Dios que ni Código ni Digesto, ni hombre que había de regir a estos indios por ellos pasara a estas partes; porque ni Justiniano hizo leyes, ni Barthulo ni Baldo las expusieron para este nuevo mundo y su gente, porque toda ell es de los que *non sunt sui, sed alieni juris*," *Cartas de religiosos*, 17. The letrados were perceived as instigators of lawsuits and legal disputes among Indians, *Cartas de Pedro de Gante*, 32; Mendieta, expressing a similar view to Philip II, argued that the written legal tradition was entirely alien to the Indians, *Cartas de religiosos*, 38, and also García Icazbalceta, *Códice Mendieta*, 2: 110. The negative social effects associated with the proliferation of lawsuits and the increasing influence of lawyers were repeatedly discussed in sixteenth-century Spain, Richard Kagan, *Lawsuits and Litigants in Castile, 1500–1700* (Chapel Hill: University of North Carolina Press, 1981), 17–20.

Chapter 2

1. Motolinía, *Memoriales*, pt.1, chap. 51, 161–62.

2. Motolinía, *Memoriales*, 162, and *Historia de los indios*, treat. 2, chap. 9, 259.

3. "[Y] como ya es otro el sentimiento de agora que el de entonces, dicen que en aquel tiempo estaban como niños." Motolinía, *Memoriales*, 162.

4. 1 Corinthians 3:2.

5. The Third Mexican Church Council ordered, "Inde etiam, nec Mixti, tam ab Indis, quam a Mauris, nec non ab illis, qui ex altero parente Aetiope nascuntur, descendentes in primo gradu, ad Ordines sine magno delectu admittantur." Lorenzana y Buitrón, *Concilium Mexicanum Provinciale III*, bk. 1, tit. 4, § 3, 31. The phrasing is not free of ambiguity; the text of this decree went through various transformations in which there was an attempt to weaken the prohibition, José A. Llaguno, *La personalidad jurídica del indio y el III Concilio Provincial Mexicano (1585)* (Mexico City: Porrúa, 1963), 123–24. On the question of

indigenous clergy in the sixteenth century, Ricard, *La "conquête spirituelle,"* 273–78; for legislation related to the ordination of Indians issued by the Third Mexican Church Council of 1585, Stafford Poole, "Church Law on the Ordination of the Indians and *Castas* in New Spain," *Hispanic American Historical Review* 61, no. 4 (1981): 637–50.

6. "[U]n natural extraño que tienen por la mayor parte los indios, diferente del de otras naciones (aunque no sé si participan de él algunos de los griegos) que no son buenos para mandar ni regir, sino para ser mandados y regidos." Mendieta, *Historia eclesiástica indiana,* bk. 4, chap. 23, 3: 103. Mendieta also briefly mentioned the case of the indigenous youth reported by Motolinía, 3: 105. We find a similar opinion in two memoriales sent by Mendieta to Fr. Diego Valadés and the *custodio* of Zacatecas, García Icazbalceta, *Códice Mendieta,* 1: 258 and 270, respectively. The references to the childlike state of the Mexicans are, as we pointed out in chap. 1, a recurring theme in Mendieta's writings.

7. Mendieta, *Historia eclesiástica indiana,* bk. 4, chap. 23, 3: 104.

8. Mendieta, *Historia eclesiástica indiana,* bk. 2, chap. 24, 1: 135–36.

9. Mendieta, *Historia eclesiástica indiana,* 3: 104.

10. Mendieta, *Historia eclesiástica indiana,* 3: 103.

11. "[S]e les deben los sacramentos fiar, pues se les fía el bautismo, que no es menor que el sacerdocio." García Icazbalceta, *Don Fray Juan de Zumárraga,* 3: 153.

12. García Pimentel, *Descripción,* 485.

13. "Faltando todo esto, nueva teología es menester para decir y creer que algunos de los adultos se salvan." García Pimentel, *Descripción,* 426.

14. Llaguno, *La personalidad jurídica,* 144–46.

15. The evidence in documents about these meetings is fragmentary.

16. The *Doctrina cristiana* published by Zumárraga mentions the decision of the meeting of 1546 in which "fuessen ordenadas dos doctrinas para los indios incipientes y proficientes." Fr. Juan de Zumárraga, *Doctrina cristiana: mas cierta y verdadera para gente sin erudicion y letras: en que se contiene el catecismo o información para indios con todo lo principal y necessario que el cristiano debe saber y obrar* (Mexico City: 1546). The colophon to the *Doctrina cristiana* by Pedro de Córdoba, published in 1544, referring to the wishes of Inquisitor General Tello de Sandoval, who had approved the publication, reads, "El cual pide y ruega mucho a los padres religiosos que entienden en la instrucción y conversión de los indios, ante todas cosas procuren de les predicar y hacer entender esta doctrina breve y llana, pues conocen su capacidad, y que tienen más necesidad de ella que de otros sermones que se les predican. Y esta servirá más para incipientes y la otra con el tripartito de Juan Gerson para proficientes." Pedro de Córdoba, *Doctrina cristiana para instrucción y información de los indios, por manera de historia* [1544] (Ciudad Trujillo: Universidad de Santo domingo, 1945), 122. Jean Gerson's *Tripartito del Christianisimo y consolatorio doctor Juan Gerson de doctrina Christiana,* published by Zumárraga the same year, was printed by Juan Cromberger. This "other" work for proficient Indians is the *Regla cristiana breve,* published by Zumárraga in 1547. The First Mexican Church Council of 1555 ordered that two catechisms be written, "la una breve, y sin glosa . . . , y la

otra con declaracion substancial de los Artículos de la Fé, y Mandamientos, y Pecados mortales, con la declaracion de el *Pater noster,*" Lorenzana, *Concilios provinciales primero y segundo,* 45. In 1570 the Franciscans characterized the two kinds of catechisms in circulation in this way: "Es de saber que muchas maneras de Doctrinas se han compuesto ya en esta tierra en las lenguas de los naturales, mayormente en la lengua mexicana, que es la general, así Doctrinas menores o breves, por donde se enseñan los niños, como otras mayores, en que por extenso pueden entender los adultos y más hábiles las cosas de nuestra fe." Joaquín García Icazbalceta, ed., *Códice franciscano, siglo XVI* (Mexico City: Salvador Chávez Hayhoe, 1941), 29.

17. Aquinas, *Summa,* 3a, q. 72, art. 2, ad. 2, ad. 3.

18. Aquinas, *Summa,* 3a, q. 72, art. 2, ad. 3.

19. Aquinas, *Summa,* 3a, q. 72, art. 8, ad. 2.

20. A study on the relation of the spiritual and physical ages of humans in the work of Saint Ambrose can be found in Émilien Lamirande, "Âges de l'homme et âges spirituels selon Saint Ambroise. Le Commentaire du psaume 36," *Science et Esprit* 35, no. 2 (1983): 211–22. For an overview of the traditional versions of the ages of humans mainly based on English sources, see J. A. Burrow, *The Ages of Man. A Study in Medieval Writing and Thought* (Oxford: Clarendon Press, 1986). A detailed study of iconography on the relationship between the ages of humans and religious conversion can be found in Elizabeth Sears, *The Ages of Man: Medieval Interpretations of the Life Cycle* (Princeton: Princeton University Press, 1986), chap. 4.

21. J. D. C. Fischer, *Confirmation: Then and Now* (London: Alcuin Club/S.P.C.K., 1978), 126–27.

22. J. D. C. Fischer provided evidence concerning the extent of this practice in Spain. *Christian Initiation: Baptism in the Medieval West* (London: Alcuin Club/S.P.C.K., 1965), 93.

23. Fischer, *Christian Initiation,* 121.

24. For the development of confirmation as a separate sacrament and the reasons offered in response to the problems created by the disintegration of the original rite of initiation, see Fischer, *Confirmation,* chap. 9.

25. Fischer, *Christian Initiation,* 122.

26. José Luis Martín and A. Linaje Conde, *Religión y sociedad medieval: el catecismo de Pedro de Cuéllar (1325)* (Salamanca: Junta de Castilla y León, 1987), 189–90.

27. "[P]ara estar mas rezio e mas armado contra los diablos." Martín and Linaje Conde, *Religión y sociedad medieval,* 190.

28. "[L]os pequeñuelos non los embían a la batalla contra los enemigos fasta que sean mayores e robustos: assí dezimos de los baptizados." Martín and Linaje Conde, *Religión y sociedad medieval,* 191.

29. Martín and Linaje Conde, *Religión y sociedad medieval,* 191.

30. Fischer, *Christian Initiation,* 137.

31. "Tambien se ha de observar, que despues del Bautismo puede administrarse a todos el Sacramento de la Confirmacion; pero que no es lo mas conveniente darlo a los niños antes que tengan uso de razon. Y así si no pareciere que

deba dilatarse hasta los doce años, por lo menos hasta los siete, es cierto que conviene muchísimo dilatar este Sacramento." *El Sacrosanto y Ecuménico Concilio de Trento traducido al idioma castellano por Don Ignacio López de Ayala* (Madrid: Imprenta Real, 1785), 121. The *Catecismo Romano* was first published in Rome in 1566 by Aldus Manutius. The first edition printed in Spain dates from 1577. However, the first edition translated into Spanish did not appear until 1777. On the controversy surrounding the publication of the *Catecismo Romano* in Spain in the sixteenth century, see Pedro Rodríguez, *El Catecismo Romano ante Felipe II y la Inquisición española* (Madrid: Rialp, 1998).

32. A. Mostaza Rodríguez, "La edad de los confirmandos," *Anthologica Annua* 4 (1956), 356–60.

33. Mostaza Rodríguez, "La edad," 357.

34. The Dominican theologian Bartolomé Carranza de Miranda played a prominent role at the Council of Trent, which he attended on two occasions. In 1557, he was appointed archbishop of Toledo. In 1559, he was imprisoned by the Spanish Inquisition in connection with the inquisitorial proceedings against a group of individuals suspected of Lutheranism in Valladolid. He was later moved to Rome, where his case continued; he died there in 1576. The complicated trial of Carranza was studied in depth by José Ignacio Tellechea Idígoras in several works. For the circumstances of Carranza's arrest and the formulation of the initial charges, see in particular "Los prolegómenos jurídicos del proceso de Carranza," in *El arzobispo Carranza y su tiempo* (Madrid: Ediciones Guadarrama, 1968), 1: 105–243, and appendix of documents. Carranza's *Comentarios sobre el catecismo cristiano* appeared on the *Index* of books prohibited by the Inquisition in 1559, J. M. De Bujanda, ed., *Index de L'Inquisition Espagnole, 1551, 1554, 1559* (Centre d'Études de la Renaissance. Éditions de l'Université de Sherbrooke/Librairie Droz, 1984), 471. The obstacles to the publication of the *Catecismo Romano* in Spain were, in large part, related to the influence of Carranza's *Comentarios* on the Tridentine catechism, Rodríguez, *El Catecismo Romano*, 38–45; on the question of books of theology in vulgar languages, 139–64.

35. Fr. Bartolomé Carranza de Miranda, *Comentarios sobre el catecismo christiano*, ed. José I. Tellechea Idígoras (Madrid: BAC, 1972), 2: 197.

36. "A mi siempre me pareció que se habían de esperar a los años de discreción y guardarse la costumbre más antigua de la Iglesia, de manera que fuesen enseñados en la religión que profesaron en el bautismo: y después examinados y confirmados, siendo a lo menos de doce o quince años." Carranza, *Comentarios sobre el catecismo*, 2: 198.

37. Aquinas, *Summa*, 3a, q. 72, art. 5, ad. 2.

38. "Agora se usa confirmar los niños en los brazos de sus madres; parecía más conveniente aguardar los años de discreción, así porque se acordasen, como porque supiesen siquiera la doctrina cristiana, y así se solía usar antiguamente. Y cuando tenían ya entendimiento bastante, los llevaban delante del obispo, y allí hacían la confesión de toda la fe, y la obediencia católica; y con esto libraban a los padrinos del cuidado que prometen tener los ahijados." Granada, *Compendio*, 151.

39. G. W. H. Lampe, *The Seal of the Spirit* (London: S.P.C.K., 1967), 310–15; Thomas, *Religion and the Decline*, 56–57.

40. Mendieta, *Historia eclesiástica indiana*, bk. 3, chap. 40, 2: 129; García Icazbalceta, *Códice franciscano*, 85. On July 28, 1525, the cabildo of Mexico City placed the episcopal authority of Motolinía in doubt until it could examine the pertinent bulls. *Actas de cabildo de la ciudad de México* (Mexico City: Imprenta y Librería de Aquilar e Hijos, 1880), 1: 49.

41. "[N]ecnon in casu necessitatis, Episcopis in provincia non existentibus, Confirmationis Sacramentum et Ordinationes usque ad minores Ordines fidelibus ministrare." Hernáez, *Colección de bulas*, 1: 378.

42. *El Sacrosanto y Ecuménico Concilio de Trento,* session 7, "De la confirmación," can. 3, 118.

43. For a concise commentary on Valadés's engravings, see Francisco de la Maza, *Fray Diego Valadés, escritor y grabador franciscano del siglo XVI* (Mexico City: Instituto de Investigaciones Estéticas, 1945). On the architectural innovations introduced for the conversion of the Mexican Indians, see John McAndrew, *The Open-Air Churches of Sixteenth-Century Mexico* (Cambridge: Harvard University Press, 1965), 202–54.

44. Mendieta, *Historia eclesiástica indiana*, bk. 3, chap. 40, 2: 130. A historical document from Tecamachalco in the province of Tlaxcala records Hojacastro confirming Indians in the year 8 tecpatl, (1552); it also describes his successors, Hernando de Villagómez and Diego Romano de Mendoza, doing the same in May of 1565 and on August 14, 1581, respectively, *Anales de Tecamachalco,* 32, 50, and 86.

45. "[Y]es verdad que había cuarenta días que con ayuda de religiosos comencé a confirmar los indios desta ciudad, é muy examinados que no recibiesen más de una vez la confirmación, pasaron de cuatrocientas mill ánimas los que recibieron el ólio y se confirmaron, é con tanto hervor, que estaban por tres días e más en el monasterio, esperando recibirla, é aún no parece que comenzaban a venir, a lo cual atribuyen mi muerte, é yo la tengo por vida," García Icazbalceta, *Don Fray Juan de Zumárraga,* 3: 273–74. The same information was later used by Mendieta.

46. *Tira de Tepechpan,* ed. Xavier Noguez (Mexico City: Biblioteca Enciclopédica del Estado de México, 1978), 2: fol. 17.

47. García Icazbalceta, *Don Fray Juan de Zumárraga,* 3: 111.

48. "Fortifica la virtud del ánimo y es justo y conveniente que todos gocen de ello."

49. "[P]ues es licor natural estilado de los árboles, maravilloso y de mucha virtud para enfermedades y heridas." On August 23, 1538, the Crown informed the bishops that it had requested a papal license to allow the use of balsam of the Indies. Francisco González de Cosío, ed., *Un cedulario mexicano del siglo XVI* (México: Frente de Afirmación Hispanista, 1973), 79.

50. *Colección de documentos inéditos, relativos,* 3: 528.

51. "Quam arborem Pannucini Chucte vocant, nostri Indici Balsami arborem, Mexicenses *Hoitziloxitl,* seu affluentem resina nuncupare consueverunt, quia liquorem effundit Syriaco Balsamo simillimum, neque odore aut

viribus inferiorem." Francisco Hernández, *Nova plantarum, animalium et miner-alium mexicanorum historia* (Romae: Vitali Mascardi, 1651), bk. 3, chap. 9, 51. Tomás López Medel, like Hernández, noted the properties of this balsam to cure stomach pains; regarding the comparison of this balsam to its Middle Eastern counterpart, Medel pointed out, "Y ansí, por estas muchas excelencias este licuor alcanzó por nombre bálsamo, no porque verdaderamente sea como lo de Alejan-dría, sino porque en el efecto y operación lo remeda mucho. Y por esta mesma razón y por no hallarse el bálsamo de Alejandría tan fácilmente en las Indias, para el uso de los sacramentos, está dispensado que puedan usar de él en lugar del ale-jandrino en todos sacramentos donde es necesario el bálsamo, por todos los obis-pados y diócesis de México y Guatimala y en otros comarcanos." López Medel, *De los tres elementos. Tratado sobre la naturaleza y el hombre del Nuevo Mundo,* ed. Berta Ares Queija (Madrid: Alianza, 1990), 173.

52. Hernáez, *Colección de bulas,* 1: 181.

53. "Yo bautizo tres días a la semana y confirmo juntamente los que bautizo, *quoniam episcopus nunquam baptizat nisi confirmat.* Cada semana bautizo tre-scientos y veinte o treinta, nunca menos de trescientos y siempre más. A dónde tantos nacen y sin comparación muchos menos mueren ¿qué gente había?" Quoted by Mariano Cuevas, *Historia de la Iglesia de México,* 5 vols. (Mexico City: Imprenta del Asilo "Patricio Sanz," 1921), 1: 334.

54. "Y aunque por mi persona baptizo y he baptizado y confirmado una infinidad, no puedo hacer todo lo que se requiere para tales sacramentos, porque no se sufre estar mucho en cada pueblo, sino que he de andar corrido y de cor-rida, que la gente es pobre y no me puede sustentar." Cuevas, *Historia de la Igle-sia,* 1: 337.

55. "[Y] está tan puesta en adquirir y guardar, cuanto los que más: y no es el tiempo que solía que daban comidas y presentes." *Historia de la Iglesia,* 1: 337.

56. *El Sacrosanto y Ecuménico Concilio de Trento,* 426. The *Memoriales* by Fr. Alonso de la Mota y Escobar, bishop of Tlaxcala, provides interesting infor-mation about visits carried out from 1608 to 1624. Concerning the 1609 visit to Santiago, in Tzauctlan, we read, "Confirme en él 525 criaturas, hize platica a los yndios acerca denque pidiesen ante mi si les hazian algunos agravios sus ministros eclesiasticos y acerca del servicio y comida que le dan de lo hizo processo mi vis-itador. Pregunteles si avian dado al clérigo algun dinero para mi comida dixeron que no havian dado nada, mas que algunas aves y carnero que se comieron el tiempo que duro la visita y confirmacion." "Memoriales del Obispo de Tlaxcala Fray Alonso de la Mota y Escobar," *Anales del Instituto Nacional de Antropología e Historia* 1 (1945): 196.

57. Stafford Poole, *Pedro Moya de Contreras. Catholic Reform and Royal Power in New Spain, 1571–1591* (Berkeley: University of California Press, 1987). The annals of San Gregorio Acapulco record that Indians were confirmed in 1576, possibly the second time that this sacrament had been administered there since 1536, "Anales de San Gregorio Acapulco," 116.

58. "Baptizaronse muchos yndios adultos y viejos, y confirmaronse todos, con que reçiviron gran devoçion y consolaçion, y de ver vendezir sus yglesias, que, como gente nueva y de sumario entendimiento, gusta de çeremonias y actos

exteriores, y assi se les correspondió con las demostraçiones posibles, para más confirmarlos en la fee." *Cartas de Indias* (Madrid: Biblioteca de Autores Españoles, 1974), 1: 219.

59. "[P]orque no ay en trezientas leguas quien consagre un ara ni un caliz, ni quien confirme un yndio." *Cartas de Indias,* 1: 133.

60. "[E]s mas seguro y aprovado que sean confirmados en su niñez porque no permanezcan imperfectos cristianos: y faltandoles la gracia de aquel sacramento: tengan menos gracia: un solo grado de la cual vale mas que todas las riquezas deste mundo." Juan de Zumárraga, *Doctrina breve muy provechosa de las cosas que pertenecen a la fe catholica y a nuestra cristiandad en estilo llano para comun inteligencia* (Mexico City: 1544; reprinted as *The Doctrina Breve,* New York: United States Catholic Historical Society, 1928), B2v. Years after Zumárraga's death, this work, suspected of containing heretical propositions, was examined by the Inquisition, Fernández del Castillo, *Libros y libreros,* 1–3.

61. "Quisiera que passaramos a la doctrina de los sacramentos: mas estas cosas requieren reposo. Diremos agora en pocas palabras que manera se ha de tener en la confesion y en la comunion: y en el oyr de la misa. Lo demas quedarse ha para otro dia como materia mas larga y aun no tan necessaria ni tan cotidiana." Zumárraga, *Doctrina cristiana,* I6v.

62. The *Suma,* which lacks overt displays of erudition, was written primarily for young people and adults. For the impact of Dr. Ponze de la Fuente's work on the development of catechisms in Spain, see José Ramón Guerrero, *Catecismos españoles del siglo XVI. La obra catequética del Dr. Constantino Ponce de la Fuente* (Madrid: Instituto Superior de Pastoral, 1969). On Ponze de la Fuente and Erasmian thought, Bataillon, *Erasmo y España,* 522–29. The *Suma,* together with other catechetical works and commentaries by the author, were included in the *Index* in 1559, De Bujanda, *Index de L'Inquisition Espagnole, 1551, 1554, 1559,* 458–62. Useful information on the development of Spanish catechisms can be found in Alvaro Huerga, "Sobre la catequesis en España durante los siglos XV–XVI," *Analecta Sacra Tarraconensia* 61, no. 2 (July–December 1968): 302–11.

63. C. Ponze de la Fuente, *Suma de doctrina cristiana* (Barcelona: Librería de Diego Gómez Flores, 1983), h. iiii, v.

64. For the model of instruction of young persons provided by the Church of Alexandria, see Ponze de la Fuente, *Suma,* H5v.

65. On the autonomous development of the reform movements in Spain and the limits of Bataillon's work, see Eugenio Asensio's classic article "El erasmismo y las corrientes espirituales afines. Conversos, franciscanos, italianizantes," *Revista de Filología Española* 36 (1952): 31–99. Asensio's thesis guided the work of José C. Nieto, *El Renacimiento y la otra España* (Geneva: Librairie Droz, 1997); see especially the sections dedicated to Ponze de la Fuente. An earlier response to Bataillon's work can be found in Beltrán de Heredia, *Las corrientes de espiritualidad.*

66. Guerrero, *Catecismos españoles,* 312. Guerrero's opinion appears to be based fundamentally on the catechisms in circulation at that time. Information from the Inquisition of Toledo reveals that the sacrament was very popular among the inhabitants of that city, Jean Pierre Dedieu, " 'Christianization' in

New Castile: Catechism, Communion, Mass, and Confirmation in the Toledo Archbishopric, 1540–1650," in *Culture and Control in Counter-Reformation Spain,* ed. Anne J. Cruz and Mary Elizabeth Perry (Minneapolis: University of Minnesota Press, 1992), 21.

67. An example of this kind of cartilla is the *Cartilla para enseñar a leer,* published by Pedro Ocharte in 1559 and reproduced by Emilio Valton, *El primer libro de alfabetización en América* (Mexico City: Antigua Librería Robredo, 1947).

68. For the production of catechisms in New Spain, see Fidel Chauvet, "Catecismos franciscanos del siglo XVI en México," in *Catecismos y métodos evangelizadores en México del siglo, XVI* (Guadalajara, México: Imprenta Lumen, 1977), 113–40, and Ernesto de la Torre Villar, "Los catecismos, instrumentos de evangelización y cultura," 141–89, in the same volume; see also the first volume of Juan Guillermo Durán, *Monumenta Catechetica Hispanoamericana (Siglo XVI–XVIII),* 2 vols. (Buenos Aires: Facultad de Teología de la Pontificia Universidad Católica Argentina "Santa María de los Buenos Aires," 1984).

69. José Miranda, *El erasmista mexicano Fray Alonso Cabello* (Mexico City: Universidad Nacional Autónoma de México, 1958), 22. In the appendix to the *Paraphrase of the Gospel of Matthew,* Erasmus recommended a ceremony for young people to renew their baptismal vow; the ceremony was intended for young people who had previously passed an examination of Christian doctrine. Contemporary critics considered the suggestion to be an attack against the sacrament of baptism, which could not be repeated, John B. Payne, *Erasmus: His Theology of the Sacraments* (n.p.: M. E. Bratcher, 1970), 172–73. It is probable that Alonso Cabello identified Erasmus's proposal as an attempt to modify the sacrament of confirmation.

70. Molina's *Doctrina breve* was modeled after other catechisms circulating at the time in Spain, Ricard, *La "conquête spirituelle,"* 125.

71. García Icazbalceta, *Códice franciscano,* 39.

72. García Icazbalceta, *Códice franciscano,* 71.

73. "Se da para que el cristiano sea más fuerte y firme en la fe." *Doctrina cristiana para instrucción y información de los indios,* 102. Fr. Pedro de Córdoba worked in Santo Domingo, where he arrived with his Dominican brother Antonio Montesino in 1510; Pedro de Córdoba died in 1521. The title of the 1541 catechism that carries his name mentions that there were additional authors: "otros religiosos doctos de la misma orden." This catechism probably had its origin in a manuscript used by religious in the islands. See Luis Resines, *Catecismos americanos del siglo XVI* (Madrid: Junta de Castilla y León, Consejería de Cultura y Turismo, 1992), 1: 97–100.

74. *Doctrina cristiana en lengua española y mexicana por los Religiosos de la Orden de Santo Domingo* (México: Juan Pablos, 1548; Madrid: Ediciones Cultura Hispánica, 1944), 95. For the relationship between this catechism and Pedro de Córdoba's 1544 *Doctrina cristiana,* Resines, *Catecismos americanos,* 1: 102–6.

75. *Doctrina cristiana por los Religiosos de Santo Domingo,* 96v.

76. Poole, *Pedro Moya de Contreras,* 162.

77. J. Sánchez, *Doctrina cristiana del P. Jerónimo de Ripalda e intento bibliográfico de la misma. Años 1591–1900* (Madrid: Imprenta Alemana, 1909), 26v.

78. *Doctrina cristiana por los religiosos de Santo Domingo,* 95v.

79. Fr. Juan Bautista, *Confessionario en lengua mexicana y castellana* (Mexico City: Melchior Ocharte, 1599), 57.

80. *Catecismo del Santo Concilio de Trento para los párrocos* (Madrid: Imprenta Real, 1785), 116.

81. In the "Epistola nuncupatoria," Molina said that his reason for writing his manual on confession was to help not only penitents and confessors but also preachers; perhaps he was anticipating possible criticism for including "unrelated" material. The sermon on confirmation can be placed in that category. Alonso de Molina, *Confesionario mayor en lengua mexicana y castellana,* int. R. Moreno (México: Antonio de Espinosa, 1569; México: Universidad Nacional Autónoma de México, 1984), 2v.

82. Alonso de Molina, *Vocabulario en lengua castellana y mexicana y mexicana y castellana* [1571] (Mexico City: Porrúa, 1977); for references to Molina and the *Doctrina de los dominicos,* see Fr. Juan de la Anunciación, *Doctrina christiana muy cumplida donde se contiene la exposición de todo lo necesario para doctrinar a los yndios, y administralles los Sanctos Sacramentos* (Mexico City: Pedro Balli, 1575), 138–39.

83. In the Nahuatl version, Molina used Spanish for "oil," "balsam," and "chrism." There is also a reference to the olive tree that produced the oil and a comparison between that oil and *chía* oil.

84. In Molina's *Vocabulario, totonal* is said to correspond to the calendrical sign under which a person is born and also to the soul ("el signo, en que alguno nasce, o el alma y espiritu"). On the relationship between *tonalli* and *chicahualiztli* explained by his informants, Alan R. Sandstrom wrote: "Much of the sun's energy comes to us in the form of heat that the Nahuas call *tona* or *tonatl* in Nahuatl and is experienced by us as body heat. In fact one of the souls possessed by human beings is called the *tonali* in Nahuatl, a term that derives from the word for the divine heat. . . . Once inside the body, this heat is transformed into *chicahualistli,* Nahuatl for a kind of energy or force that gives humans vigor and the power to act." *Corn Is Our Blood: Culture and Ethnic Identity in a Contemporary Aztec Indian Village* (Norman and London: University of Oklahoma Press, 1991), 247; see also 257–60. The literature on tonalli is both extensive and controversial; for a study based on Nahuatl sources see Alfredo López Austin, *The Human Body and Ideology. Concepts of the Ancient Nahuas,* trans. Thelma Ortíz de Montellano and Bernard Ortíz de Montellano (Salt City: University of Utah, 1988), 1: 204–29; the manifold aspects of tonalli are elegantly explored in Jill McKeever Furst, *The Natural History of the Soul in Ancient Mexico* (New Haven: Yale UP, 1995), 63–130.

85. Molina, *Confesionario,* fol. 83v.

86. Aquinas, *Summa,* 3a, q. 72, art. 5, res.

87. Aquinas, *Summa,* 3a, q. 72, 9, ad. 3.

88. "In baptismo regeneramur ad vitam, post baptismum confirmamur ad

pugnam. In baptismo abluimur post baptismum roboramur." L. A. van Buchem, *L'homelie pseudo-eusebienne de Pentecote* (Nijmegen: Drukkerij Gebr, Janssen N. V., 1967), 63.

89. Ronald G. Murphy, *The Saxon Savior: The Germanic Transformation of the Gospel in the Ninth-Century Heliand* (New York: Oxford University Press, 1989).

90. Aquinas, *Summa*, 3a, q. 72, art. 4, res. For the growing importance of vocabulary associated with war and the military world in the first three centuries of Christianity, see the classic work by Adolf Harnack, *Militia Christi*, trans. David Mc Innes Gracie (Philadelphia: Fortress Press, 1981), 27–64.

91. "[L]as insignias y armas para la guerra." Molina, *Confesionario mayor*, 87v.

92. Patricia R. Anawalt, *Indian Clothing before Cortés* (Norman and London: University of Oklahoma Press, 1981), 55.

93. Anawalt, *Indian Clothing before Cortés*, 57.

94. Ross Hassig, *Aztec Warfare: Imperial Expansion and Political Control* (Norman and London: University of Oklahoma Press, 1988), 39–41.

95. *Anales de Tlatelolco y Códice de Tlatelolco*, ed. Heinrich Berlin, with commentary by Robert H. Barlow (Mexico City: Antigua Librería Robredo, 1948), 120–22.

96. Molina, *Confesionario mayor*, 89v.

97. Molina, *Confesionario mayor*, 87v. See Harnack, *Militia Christi*, 32.

98. Hassig, *Aztec Warfare*, 29.

99. For Aquinas, all the sacraments confer grace, but baptism, confirmation, and holy orders also produce another effect called "character," a spiritual mark imprinted upon the soul of the recipient, Aquinas, *Summa*, 3a, q. 63, art. 6, res. Upon explaining the spiritual nature of sacramental character as a mark, Aquinas used Augustine's comparison with the visible mark that identified Roman soldiers, Aquinas, *Summa*, 3a, 63, 1, res; and 3a, 63, 5, sed.

100. Molina, *Confesionario mayor*, 92v.

101. Molina, *Confesionario mayor*, 90v.

102. "Que el hombre bajo que en armas se aventajaba y hacía algún señalado hecho, llegado a la corte a la vuelta de la guerra, era presentado al señor. El cual, alabándole su hecho, le mandaba cercenar la coleta por encima de las orejas y le daba un jubón estofado, con un cuero por haz, de tigre o de venado, blanco, gamuzado, nomás de hasta la cintura y un braguero galano y ancho que le cubría todos los muslos. Dábanle una rodela blanca con cinco pegujones de plumas." Durán, *Historia de las Indias*, 1: 115.

103. Durán, *Historia de las Indias*, 1: 116.

104. Fischer, *Christian Initiation*, 128. This question is treated extensively by Lampe in *The Seal of the Spirit*.

105. "Es propio de este sacramento dar los dones del Espíritu Santo." Carranza, *Comentarios sobre el catechismo*, 2: 200.

106. "Se nos infunde la gracia y acrecentamiento de todos los dones del Espíritu Santo." Granada, *Compendio*, 151.

107. Lombard, *Sententiae*, bk. 4, d. 7, c. 4.1, 2: 278. For Aquinas's view on the same point, see Aquinas, *Summa*, 3a, q. 72, art. 7, ad. 1.

108. Molina, *Confesionario mayor,* 91.

109. "[T]endrán mucha honra, alla en parayso y gloria del cielo, y no seran assi tan afamados ni honrados aquellos que no le recibieron" and "macehuales y gente baja." Molina, *Confesionario mayor,* 92.

110. Molina, *Confesionario mayor,* 92v.

111. Sahagún, *Florentine Codex,* bk. 3, appendix, chap. 3, 49.

112. "[Q]ue traygas una candela, y una venda de lienzo blanco, que no este suzia." Molina, *Confesionario mayor,* 84.

113. H. B. Nicholson, "A 'Royal Headband' of the Tlaxcalteca," *Revista mexicana de estudios antropológicos* 21 (1967): 71–106.

114. For the changes that affected the privileged place of the Aztec elite under the Spaniards and the role played by the macehuales in that process, see Charles Gibson, "The Aztec Aristocracy in Colonial Mexico," *Comparative Studies in Society and History* 2 (1959–60): 169–96.

115. "Cosa digna de loar y aun de notar y no de gente tan bruta y bárbara, como nosotros la queremos hacer, pues tuvieron en su infidelidad tanta polecía y buen gobierno, con tanto orden y concierto como gente en el mundo la pudo tener, y muy en particular, en esto de que los grandes fuesen conocidos y señalados y honrados con particulares honras que los caballeros, y los caballeros, de los hidalgos, y los hidalgos de los escuderos, y los escuderos, de los oficiales y gente plebeya de baja suerte." Durán, *Historia de las Indias,* 2: 112. The connection between the Spaniards' interest in the forms of government found in the Americas and the European debates about liberty and order in the political community was rightly pointed out by Elliott, "The Discovery of America," 58.

116. Durán, *Historia de las Indias,* 1: 112 and 115.

117. For the transformation of the Spanish nobility and the survival of the symbolic value of coats of arms as a sign of social distinction once the role of the aristocracy in the wars was steadily reduced by the ever-increasing participation of other social groups, see José A. Maravall, *Poder, honor y élites en el siglo XVII* (Madrid: Siglo XXI, 1979), 32–41.

118. For a suggestive work on the role of women in the warrior ideology of the Nahuas, see Cecelia F. Klein, "Fighting with Feminity: Gender and War in Aztec Mexico," in *Gender Rhetorics. Postures of Dominance and Submission in History,* ed. Richard Trexler (Binghampton, NY: Medieval and Renaissance Texts and Studies, 1994), 107–46.

119. In a letter Boniface advised the Abbess Bugga in the following way: "Scorn earthly trials with your whole soul; for all soldiers of Christ of either sex have despised temporal troubles and tempests and have held the frailties of this world as naught." Boniface, *The Letters of Saint Boniface,* trans. Ephraim Emerton (New York: Octagon Books, 1973), 171.

120. Aquinas clarified this point in the face of possible problems of interpretation by pointing out that, in the spiritual battle, there are no differences of sex, social status, or age and that numerous female martyrs demonstrated greater strength than did males. Aquinas, *Summa,* 3a, q. 72, 8, ad. 3.

121. López Austin, *Human Body and Ideology,* 1: 283–84. Although López Austin's treatment of this question is useful, it remains, nonetheless, somewhat deceiving, especially if one considers the Marxist framework adopted by the

author. Aiming to demonstrate how the conceptualization of the body and its functions was intimately linked to the ideology of the dominant classes in the Aztec state, it fails to take into account the role played by warfare institutions in the reproduction of state ideology. There seems to exist in López Austin's work a tension between a descriptive perspective of a biological kind and its integration within a Marxist interpretation of functionalist bent. From this point of view, as López Austin himself indicated, the analysis of age groups comes up against the heterogeneity of the information provided by the sources. It also lacks another kind of analysis, one that would account for two important relationships: one between the stages of youth in light of the institutions that defined them, that is, through the progressive specification of the activities and obligations that marked the formation of the warrior, and the other between the attributes of the youth and Nahua cosmology. For this last point, see Inga Clendinnen's analysis of the ceremony of Toxcatl in *Aztecs* (Cambridge: Cambridge University Press, 1991), 104–10 and 141–52.

122. Sahagún, *Florentine Codex,* bk. 3, appendix, chap. 9, 51. For a good synthesis of the formation of Aztec warriors, Hassig, *Aztec Warfare,* 27–47.

123. Sahagún, *Florentine Codex,* bk. 3, appendix, chap. 5, 55.

124. Sahagún, *Florentine Codex,* bk. 8, chap. 20, 71–72.

125. López Austin, *Human Body and Ideology,* 1: 289.

126. "En muchas partes de este tierra tuvieron los indios en su infidelidad una manera como de baptismo para los niños, y era que a los ocho o diez días después de nacidos los bañaban, llevándolos a las fuentes, donde las había, o al río, y después de bañado el niño, el varón poníanle una rodela pequeñita en la mano izquierda, y una saeta en la mano derecha, dando a entender que como varón había de ser valiente y pelear varonilmente contra sus enemigos. . . . Y si lo aplicaran al espiritual y verdadero significado, con harta propiedad les pudieran poner en el bautismo de la Iglesia estas mismas insignias, significando que los bautizados habían de pelear varonilmente contra los enemigos del ánima." Mendieta, *Historia eclesiástica indiana,* bk. 3, chap. 35, 114–15.

127. Hernando Ruiz de Alarcón, *Tratado de las supersticiones y costumbres gentílicas que oy viven entre los indios naturales de esta Nueva España. 1629, Tratado de las idolatrías, supersticiones, dioses, ritos, hechicerías y otras costumbres gentílicas de las razas aborígenes de México,* ed. Francisco del Paso y Troncoso (Mexico City: Fuente Cultural, 1953), 2: 28.

128. Motolinía, *Memoriales,* p. 2, chap. 3, 308.

129. Durán, *Historia de las Indias,* 1: 50.

130. "Y así tenían estos indios cuatro vocablos para diferenciar sus edades: el primero era *piltzintli,* que es como nosotros decimos 'puericia.' El segundo era *tlamacazqui,* que quiere decir tanto como 'juventud.' El tercero era *tlapaliuhqui,* que quiere decir la 'edad madura y perfecta,' y *huehuetqui,* que quiere decir 'vejez.'" Durán, *Historia de la Indias,* 1: 50. Durán's lexicon to refer the different ages of humans is particularly rich and full of nuances.

131. The lack of references in Molina to sponsors in confirmation is noteworthy. In the development of the parallel between the confirmed person and the soldier found in the *Catecismo Romano,* the sponsor is assigned a symbolic role that

recalls the military world: "Tambien aquí se busca Padrino en la misma forma que se declaró tratando del Sacramento del Bautismo. Porque si los luchadores necesitan de alguno, que con arte y destreza les enseñe en qué manera podrán herir y matar al contrario, salvándose a sí mismos; ¿quánto mayor necesidad de Maestro y Director tendrán los fieles, quando escudados y fortalecidos con el Sacramento de la Confirmacion, como con unas armas muy seguras, baxan al combate espiritual, cuya corona es la vida eterna?" *Catecismo del Santo Concilio de Trento,* 120–21.

132. The *Catecismo del Santo Concilio de Trento,* 121, recommends that, although everyone could be confirmed immediately after being baptized, children should not be confirmed until they reach the age of reason, "[p]orque la Confirmación no fué instituida por ser necesaria para la salud; sino porque nos hallemos con su gracia bien armados y apercibidos, quando se hubiere de pelear por la fe de Christo. Y para este linage de pelea es cierto que ninguno juzgará que sean propósito los niños que aun carecen de uso de razón."

133. For the controversies surrounding the administration of the sacraments to the Indians, see Ricard, *La "conquête spirituelle,"* 133–60; McAndrew, *The Open-Air Churches,* 77–85. Fr. Juan Bautista was obligated as late as 1600 to prepare a detailed rebuttal of the ideas on which other religious based their opposition to administering the sacrament of the Eucharist to the Indians. *Advertencias para los confessores,* 56v. and ff.

134. The question concerning what constituted so-called explicit faith was vigorously debated in both Europe and the Americas. Bautista adopted the opinion of Bañez and Constantino in the case of the sacraments: "[el fiel] esta obligado a creer explicitamente todos los articulos de la fee, y tres de los Sacramentos de la Yglesia, que son, Baptismo, Eucharistia y Penitencia: porque destos ay particular precepto que nos obliga a recebirlos: de los demas Sacramentos, dize que el fiel esta obligado a saberlos, quando los quiere recebir." *Advertencias para los confessores,* 34. Concerning the sacraments and their relationship with evangelization in the European context, see the brief study by Gy, "Évangélisation et sacrements au moyen âge," in *La liturgie dans l'histoire,* 151–63.

135. "Confirmatio autem Eucharistia sunt quidem homini necessaria, quod robur et nutrimentum spirituale homini conferant. Sine ipsis tamen, si absit contemptus, homo salvabitur, quod videre apud Indos, quorum maxima pars neutrum hactenus est assecuta." Focher, *Itinerario del misionero en América,* 381.

136. "At the confirmation ceremony the bishop would lay his hands on the child and tie around its forehead a linen band which he was required to wear for three days afterwards. This was believed to strengthen him against the assaults of the fiend, and the notion became current that it was extremely bad luck to untie the band under any circumstances. Here too physical effects were vulgarly attributed to the ceremony: a belief that survived until the nineteenth century." Thomas, *Religion and the Decline,* 38. The superstitions linked to the linen band of the confirmed individual did not go unnoticed within the church. The Third Mexican Church Council ordered that the cloths used in confirmation be burned to keep them from being used profanely. Lorenzana, *Concilium Mexicanum Provinciale III,* bk. 1, tit. 6, § 2, 40.

137. Martin Luther, "The Babylonian Captivity of the Church," in *Works,* ed. Jaroslav Pelikan, American edition (Saint Louis: Concordia Pub. House/ Philadelphia: Fortress Press, 1955), 36: 91.

138. Luther, "The Babylonian Captivity," 92.

139. *El Sacrosanto y Ecuménico Concilio de Trento,* 118.

Chapter 3

1. According to John Bossy's suggestive yet debatable thesis, between the fifteenth and seventeenth centuries penance underwent an important transformation: from a sacrament with an unmistakable social function, it became one increasingly focused on individuals and their mental health. "The Social History of Confession in the Age of Reformation," *Transactions of the Royal Historical Society,* 5th ser., 25 (1975), 21–38. I suspect that a reading of the Molina's *Confesionario mayor* in the light of Bossy's thesis would reveal a somewhat more complete picture of the relationship between penitent and community.

2. Among the works that assume this perspective are J. Jorge Klor de Alva, "Contar vidas: la autobiografía confesional y la reconstrucción del ser nahua," *Arbor* 131, nos. 515–16 (1988): 49–78, and also "Sin and Confession among the Colonial Nahuas: The Confessional as a Tool for Domination," in *La Ciudad y el Campo en la Historia de México. Papers Presented at the VII Conference of Mexican and United States Historians, Oaxaca, 1985,* vol. 1 (Mexico City: Universidad Nacional Autónoma de México, 1992); Serge Gruzinski, "Individualization and Acculturation: Confession among the Nahuas of Mexico from the Sixteenth to the Eighteenth Century," in *Sexuality and Marriage in Colonial Latin America,* ed. Asunción Lavrín (Lincoln and London: University of Nebraska Press, 1989), 96–117; and "Confesión, alianza y sexualidad entre los indios de Nueva España," in *El placer de pecar y el afán de normar,* ed. Sergio Ortega (México: Joaquín Mortíz, 1988), 169–215. Along the same lines, Sonia Corcuera de Mancera, *Del amor al temor. Borrachez, catequesis y control en la Nueva España (1555–1771)* (Mexico City: Fondo de Cultura Económica, 1994), chap. 4; a more recent work offering an overview of the production of manuals for confessors in the Spanish colonies is Martine Azoulai, *Les péchés du Nouveau Monde* (París: Albin Michel, 1993). To a greater or lesser degree, these works are indebted to Michel Foucault's views on sexuality and control elaborated in his *Histoire de la sexualité,* vol. 1 (París: Gallimard, 1976); see in particular "L'hypothèse répressive," 25–67, where he considered the function of the examination of conscience in the sixteenth century. For confession as a form of control, see Thomas Tentler, "The Summa for Confessors as an Instrument of Social Control," in *The Pursuit of Holiness in Late Medieval and Renaissance Religion,* ed. Charles Trinkaus and Heiko Oberman (Leiden: E. J. Brill, 1974), 101–26.

3. J. Jorge Klor de Alva, "Sahagún and the Birth of Modern Ethnography: Representing, Confessing, and Inscribing the Native Other," in *The Work of Bernardino de Sahagun. Pioneer Ethnographer of Sixteenth Century Aztec Mexico,* ed. J. Jorge Klor de Alva, H. B. Nicholson, and Eloise Quiñones Weber (Albany: Institute for Mesoamerican Studies, SUNY, 1988), 31–52.

4. On the linguistic solutions found by the missionaries to convey to the Nahuas the notion of sin, Burkhart, *The Slippery Earth,* especially chaps. 4 and 6.

5. For Klor de Alva, the practice of penance is, in the specific case of the restitutions made by the Indians, a kind of economic intervention, which he called "the forced leveling of social statuses." Such identification of religious with economic control based on Motolinía's examples, whose edifying character is recognized by Klor de Alva himself, seems unwarranted since these highly conventional stories were designed to suggest the influence of St. Francis's original ideals of poverty over the Indians. Klor de Alva, "Sin and Confession," 93; also Gruzinski, "Individualization and Acculturation," 97.

6. "[O]rdenamos, y mandamos, que todos los Curas tenga Biblias, y algunas Sumas de casos de conciencia en latin o romance, assí como la Suma de Navarro, o *Defecerunt* de S. Antonino, o Silvestrina, o Angelica, y algun Libro Sacramental, en que lean," Lorenzana, *Concilios provinciales primero y segundo,* 199.

7. "Y no se contenten [los ministros] con decir que ya saben un poco dela lengua para confesar y que aquello les basta, lo cual es error intolerable, porque para este sacramento es menester más lengua e inteligencia de ella que para otro ninguno, para saber examinar la enmarañada conciencia en idolatrías encubiertas de muchos años de algunos penitentes." Durán, *Historia de las Indias,* 1: 92; for a similar judgment, p. 77.

8. "Donde creo se cometen muchos sacrilegios de confesiones informes, sin tener las partes que el sacramento pide, que es dolor, arrepentimiento, propósito de enmienda y satisfacción y declaración verdadera de todas las culpas." Durán, *Historia de las Indias,* 1: 162.

9. Molina's *Doctrina cristiana breve* lists four conditions necessary to receive forgiveness for mortal sins: contrition, confession, satisfaction, and a "firme propósito y determinación de no tornar otra vez a cometer algún pecado." García Icazbalceta, *Códice franciscano,* 42.

10. During this period there began what Bernhard Poschmann identified as "the formation of a theoretical doctrine of penance," *Penance and the Anointing of the Sick* (New York: Herder and Herder, 1964), 3.

11. In Spain, the diffusion of the new kind of penance promoted by the penitentials took place by the beginning of the ninth century. John T. McNeill and Helena M. Gamer, *Medieval Handbooks of Penance* (New York: Columbia University Press, 1938), 26. However, there is evidence that the new penitential practice had reached the peninsula by the end of the sixth century and was condemned by the Third Council of Toledo. Francis Bezler, *Les pénitentiels espagnols. Contribution à l'étude de la civilisation de l'Espagne chrétienne du haut moyen âge* (Münster: Aschendorff, 1994), xxiv.

12. Recent research on visitation records and related episcopal documents has shown the limitations of traditional accounts on the emergence and consolidation of private penance based exclusively on theological sources. In a superb study, Mansfield has convincingly proved the persistence of public penance well beyond the generally accepted dates of its demise; for a critical evaluation of tra-

ditional historiographical views on penance, see Mary Mansfield, *The Humiliation of Sinners. Public Penance in Thirteenth-Century France* (Ithaca: Cornell
University Press, 1995), 1–13.

13. "Although in ancient Celtic penance great emphasis was laid on penitential works, yet the ecclesiastical and sacramental aspect of penance stands forth
clearly. It is only efficacious through the ministry of the priest; as a judge he has
to adapt the punishment to the gravity of the guilt and to individual circumstances in the light of the penitential book." Poschmann, *Penance,* 129.

14. Poschmann, *Penance,* 157. The renewed attempts during the eleventh and
twelfth centuries to arrive at a more satisfactory definition of sacrament were
inextricably linked to the controversies around the Eucharist. See Pelikan, *The
Growth of Medieval Theology,* 205–14; and Brian Stock's thought-provoking
analysis in *The Implications of Literacy* (Princeton: Princeton University Press,
1983), 241–325.

15. Thomas Tentler, *Sin and Confession on the Eve of the Reformation*
(Princeton: Princeton University Press, 1977), 19.

16. The term "attrition" was first used probably in the eleventh or twelfth
centuries; its earliest recorded appearance, dating from the twelfth century, is in
the work of Alain de Lille, J. Périnelle, *L'Attrition d'après le Concile de Trente et
d'après Saint Thomas D'Aquin* (Kain: Le Saulchoir, 1927), 10.

17. Poschmann, *Penance,* 164.

18. Poschmann, *Penance,* 190.

19. Lombard, *Sententia,* 4. d. 16. c. 1. 1, 2: 336.

20. The usage of "compunctio" was already established in the tradition of
the church fathers, dating back to Jerome and Cassian. Pierre Adnès, "Peni-
tence," *Dictionnaire de Spiritualité* (Paris, 1984), vol. 11, fasc. 78–79, 971.

21. "Poenitentia est virtus, qua commissa mala cum emendationis proposito
plangimus et odimus, et plangenda ulterius commitere nolumus. Quia sic poenitentia vera est in animo dolere et odire vitia." Lombard, *Sententiae,* 4. d. 14. c.
3.1, 2: 318.

22. "Sane quod sine confessione oris et solutione poena exterioris peccata
delentur, per contritionem et humilitatem cordis. Ex quo enim proponit, mente
compuncta, se confessurum, Deus dimittit; quia ibi est confessio cordis, etsi non
oris, per quam anima interius mundatur a macula et contagio peccati commissi,
et debitum aeternae mortis relaxatur," Lombard, *Sententiae,* 4. d. 17. c. 1. 11, 2:
345.

23. Lombard, *Sententiae,* 4. d. 18. c. 6.1, 2: 361.

24. Lombard, *Sententiae,* 4. d. 17. c. 4.12, 2: 354. Rejecting the doctrine of the
transmission of the keys to the priests, Peter Abelard had earlier held that the forgiveness of sins could be achieved only by perfect contrition and without any
need to confess. Abelard's doctrine was condemned by the Senonense Council.
What separates Abelard from Peter Lombard is that the latter included the condition that the penitent should have the intention of confessing. Hugh Patton,
*The Efficacy of Putative Attrition in the Doctrine of Theologians of the XVI and
XVII Centuries* (Roma: Herder, 1966), 5; also Poschmann, *Penance,* 158.

25. Lombard, *Sententiae,* 4. d. 17. c. 3.1, 2: 348.

26. Denzinger, *The Sources of Catholic Dogma*, trans. Roy J. Deferrari (St. Louis, MO: B. Herder Book Co., 1957), 437.

27. Aquinas, *Summa*, 3a, q. 84, art. 2, res.

28. Aquinas, *Summa*, 3a, q. 84, art. 3, res. The *Decretum pro Armenis* of 1493 includes Aquinas's solution. Denzinger, *The Sources*, 699.

29. Aquinas, *Summa*, 3a, q. 84, art. 3, ad. 3; 3a, q. 86, art. 2, res.

30. Aquinas, *Summa*, 3a, q. 85, art. 5, res. See Gordon J. Spykman, *Attrition and Contrition at the Council of Trent* (Kampen: J. H. Kok, 1955), 60; also H. Dondaine, *L'attrition suffisante* (Paris: Librairie Philosophique J. Vrin, 1943), 7–10.

31. Spykman, *Attrition and Contrition*, 60.

32. Poschmann, *Penance*, 172–73; Spykman, *Attrition and Contrition*, 68.

33. Spykman, *Contrition and Attrition*, 59. The main problem with this formulation is that contrition is seen as both the result of the infusion of grace and as its very condition: see Poschmann, *Penance*, 175.

34. Johannes Duns Scotus did away with the traditional distinction of the sacrament in three parts; for him, penance, from a strictly sacramental standpoint, consisted exclusively of the priest's absolution, *Quaestiones in Librum Quartum Sententiarum*, in *Opera Omnia* (Parisiis: Apud Ludovicum Vivès, Bibliopolam Editorem, 1894), 18: dist. 16, q. 1, 7; on the confessor's absolution as "sententia definitiva," see dist. 14, q. 4.

35. Poschmann, *Penance*, 185.

36. Poschmann, *Penance*, 187.

37. Spykman, *Attrition and Contrition*, 80.

38. Although with qualifications, Spykman concurred with this characterization, noting the differences between Aquinas's position and the contritionist doctrines of later theologians such as Gabriel Biel. *Attrition and Contrition*, 69–70; Dondaine, *L'attrition suffisante*, 14–15. On Gabriel Biel's theory of penance and its relationship with the doctrines of Duns Scotus and Thomas Aquinas, Heiko A. Oberman, *The Harvest of Medieval Theology* (Durham: Labyrinth Press, 1983), 146–60.

39. Poschmann, *Penance*, 182–83. An overview of their main positions can be found in Patton, *The Efficacy*, 26–33.

40. Périnelle, *L'Attrition d'après le Concile de Trente*, 17.

41. On the ethnographic activities of the Franciscans, Ricard, *La "conquête spirituelle,"* 54–79, and Baudot, *Utopia e historia*.

42. It is not my purpose to present here a detailed discussion of these similarities but rather to briefly point out their differences.

43. The distorted versions of the Christian sacraments hatched by the devil were known as *execramentos,* Fr. Martín de Castañega, *Tratado de las supersticiones y hechicerías* [1529] (Madrid: Sociedad de Bibliófilos Españoles, 1946), 28–29. This treatise was the model for the Franciscan Andrés de Olmos's own treatise on Nahua "superstition," written in Nahuatl in 1553; in that work, he made reference to the existence of execramentos (*execramentotica*), Fr. Andrés de Olmos, *Tratado de hechicerías y sortilegios,* ed. Georges Baudot (Mexico City: Estudios Mesoamericanos, serie 2, 1979), 69. The same idea is found again in the

Tratado de las supersticiones y costumbres gentílicas (1629) by Ruiz de Alarcón. See also Joseph de Acosta, *Historia natural y moral de las Indias* [1590], ed. Edmundo O'Gorman (Mexico City: Fondo de Cultura Económica, 1962), 235. On European demonological thought, S. Clark, "The Scientific Status of Demonology," in *Occult and Scientific Mentalities in the Renaissance,* ed. Brian Vickers (Cambridge: Cambridge University Press, 1984), 351–74. On the notion of devil as reflected in sixteenth- and seventeenth-century accounts on Andean religion, Sabine MacCormack, *Religion in the Andes. Vision and Imagination in Early Colonial Peru* (Princeton: Princeton University Press, 1991); for the Mexican case, Fernando Cervantes, *The Devil in the New World. The Impact of Diabolism in New Spain* (New Haven: Yale University Press, 1994).

44. "[N]o hay poco fundamento para argüir que estos Indios desta Nueva España se tenían por obligados de se confesar una vez en la vida, y esto in lumine natural, sin haber tenido noticias de la fe." Fr. Bernardino de Sahagún, *Historia general de las cosas de Nueva España* (Madrid: Alianza, 1988), bk. 1, chap. 12, 47. Fr. Luis de Granada pointed out the existence of two lights in humans: the light of faith and the light of reason. About the latter, he wrote, "Esta lumbre de razón es una rayo de luz que se derivó en nuestras ánimas de la fuente de aquella luz infinita, por cuya causa confesamos ser el hombre hecho a imagen de Dios: la cual lumbre tanto es mas perfecta, cuanto es mas pura la vida y la conciencia." Granada, *Del símbolo de la fe,* in *Obras,* treat. 1, pt. 3, 1: 400. While the light of faith "es firme, cierta y infalible," the light of reason "ni es tan cierta ni infalible." The latter becomes more perfect when it is complemented by faith, which allows individuals to consider truths such as the immortality of the soul and the salvation of humankind.

45. Durán vacillated between an explanation based on the idea of a prior evangelization and one that attributed the similarities between the two religions to the devil, *Historia de las Indias,* 1: 157–58. Durán recognized the existence of sacraments among the Indians, but he did not resort to using the term "execramento," "porque ellos también tenían sacramentos, en cierta forma y culto de Dios," 1: 6. For the development of theories of the Jewish origin of the inhabitants of the New World (and Durán was an exponent of them), Giuliano Gliozzi, *Adamo e il Nuovo Mondo* (Firenze: La Nuova Italia Editrice, 1976), 49–69. Alcina Franch offered an excellent synopsis of the different theories of the origin of the Indians in his study of Diego Andrés de Rocha, *El origen de los indios* [1681], ed. J. Alcina Franch (Madrid: Historia 16, 1988), 7–34.

46. Motolinía, *Historia de los indios,* treat. 2, 237. This information was repeated by later Franciscan historians such as Mendieta and Torquemada.

47. Motolinía, *Historia de los indios,* 237.

48. Grijalva, *Crónica de la orden de N. P. S. Agustín,* 105.

49. "[C]on lágrimas íntimas de corazón." Motolinía, *Memoriales,* pt. 1, chap. 36, 129. On the classification of tears in Christian devotion, see chap. 4.

50. Motolinía, *Memoriales,* pt. 1, chap. 62, 261.

51. "No saben si recibieron el baptismo con tanta contrición y aparejo como era menester." Motolinía, *Memoriales,* 261. In the case of adults who received baptism, repentance and sorrow were necessary for the remission of sins, but the

priest could not impose any kind of penance, Focher, *Itinerario del misionero en América*, 112–16.

52. "Muchos de estos naturales tienen sus devociones ordinarias, pero lo que más es, cada día tienen un tiempo señalado para una vez o dos al día darse a la oración mental, y tienen repartidos sus ejercicios para cada día; un día piensan sus pecados y trabajan de tener un intenso dolor por ellos." Motolinía, *Memoriales*, p. 1, chap. 51, 161.

53. Sixteenth-century religious writers mentioned the publication in Mexico of John Climacus's *Spiritual Ladder;* there is no extant copy of the work, which may have been the first book printed in the colonies. García Icazbalceta concluded that Climacus's work might have been used exclusively by Dominican friars, *Bibliografía mexicana del siglo XVI* [1886], ed. Agustín Millares Carlo (Mexico City: Fondo de Cultura Económica, 1954), 27–29. The *Spiritual Ladder* probably was published in 1539. Emilio Valton, *Impresos mexicanos del siglo XVI* (México: Imprenta Universitaria, 1935), 18.

54. Fr. Juan José de la Cruz y Moya, *Historia de la Santa y Apostólica provincia de Santiago de Predicadores de México en la Nueva España,* ed. Gabriel Saldívar (Mexico City: Librería de Manuel Porrúa, 1955), 2: 48.

55. Cruz y Moya, *Historia de la Santa y Apostólica provincia,* 64.

56. "En algunas provincias de esta Nueva España usaban los indios en su infidelidad una manera de confesión vocal, y ésta hacían dos veces en el año a sus dioses, apartándose cada uno en un rincón de su casa, o en el templo, o se iban a los montes, o a las fuentes, cada uno donde más devoción tenía, y allí hacían muestras de grandísima contrición, unos con muchas lágrimas, otros juntando las manos, a manera de quien mucho se cuita, o torciendo y encajando los dedos unos con otros, y haciendo visajes, confesando sus culpas y pecados." Mendieta, *Historia eclesiástica indiana,* vol. 2, bk. 3, chap. 41, 2: 130. For Mendieta's source, see Bartolomé de Las Casas, *Apologética historia sumaria,* ed. Edmundo O'Gorman (Mexico City: Universidad Nacional Autónoma de México, 1967), bk. 3, chap. 176, 2: 212. In the introduction to the *Apologética historia sumaria,* O'Gorman pointed out that Mendieta had knowledge of this work by Las Casas, 1: xxxv. The passage was paraphrased by the Augustinian Jerónimo Román y Zamora in *República de Indias* [1575] (Madrid: Victoriano Suárez, 1897), 1: 186–87. Friars were not the only party interested in the apparent similarities between ancient Mexican rites and Christian sacraments; the existence of a vocal confession among the Indians was briefly described by Juan Suárez de Peralta in his *Tratado del descubrimiento de las Indias* [1589] (Mexico City: Consejo Nacional para la Cultura y las Artes, 1990), 55.

57. Mendieta, *Historia eclesiástica indiana,* bk. 3, chap. 41, 2: 130.

58. Mendieta, *Historia eclesiástica indiana,* 131.

59. Mendieta, *Historia eclesiástica indiana,* 130; also Las Casas, *Apologética historia sumaria,* bk. 3, chap. 179, 2: 226. For the relationship of sin and illness, Burkhart, *The Slippery Earth,* 173–76.

60. On the practice of confession in the Old Testament, see Raffaelle Pettazzoni, *La confessione dei peccati* (Bologna: Forni Editore, 1968), 2: chap. 10.

61. Mendieta, *Historia eclesiástica indiana,* bk. 3, chap. 44, 2: 141.

62. Valadés, *Retórica cristiana,* 188.

63. Valadés, *Retórica cristiana,* 364–66.

64. "[Y] el Maestro, en lo de los Sacramentos, pareciendo en lo que dice que en parte cree, torne a la doctrina de San Pedro." Fernández del Castillo, *Libros y libreros,* 473; the document also mentions the existence of a copy in Atzcapotzalco, 475.

65. This goddess was also known by the names Ixcuina and Tlaelquani. "Ixcuina" referred to four sister goddesses, goddesses of lust, Sahagún, *Florentine Codex,* bk. 1, chap. 12, 23.

66. This ceremony, according to A. Estrada Quevedo, was related to a dual deity that included both feminine and masculine aspects, Tlazolteotl and Tezcatlipoca. Estrada Quevedo, "Neyolmelahualiztli," *Estudios de cultura nahuatl* 2 (1960): 163–75.

67. H. B. Nicholson, "Religion in Pre-Hispanic Central Mexico," in *Handbook of Middle American Indians,* ed. Gordon F. Ekholm and Ignacio Bernal (Austin: University of Texas Press, 1971), 10: 421–22.

68. Sahagún, *Florentine Codex,* bk. 1, chap. 12, 24.

69. Sahagún, *Florentine Codex,* bk. 1, 26.

70. Sahagún, *Florentine Codex,* bk. 1, chap. 12, 27.

71. "[P]ensando que, como en el tiempo pasado, por la confesión y penitencia que hacían se les perdonaban aquellos pecados en el foro judicial, también agora, cuando alguno mata o adultera, acógese a nuestras casas y monasterios, y, callando lo que hicieron, dicen que quieren hacer penitencia, y cavan en la huerta, y barren en la casa, y hacen lo que les mandan, y confiésanse de allí algunos días, y entonces declaran su pecado y la causa porque vinieron a hacer penitencia." Sahagún, *Historia general,* bk. 1, chap. 12, 46. The Indians revealed their transgression first through the work they did in the convent and later in confession. This point is significant if one considers that Sahagún emphasized the existence of vocal confession among the ancient rites of purification, while in this description vocal confession could be seen as part of a negotiation with the friars.

72. Lockhart coined the phrase "double mistaken identity" to describe how both Nahuas and Spaniards interpreted and transformed each other's institutions and practices and recognized in them elements that appeared remarkably like their own. Lockhart, "Double Mistaken Identity: Some Nahua Concepts in Post Conquest Guise," in *Of Things of the Indies,* 98–119; for a study of this phenomenon as registered in the interactions between Nahuas and Spanish religious, Lockhart, *The Nahuas after the Conquest,* 203–60.

73. On August 29, 1542, the cabildo of Mexico City denounced the church for deliberately trying to impede the identification of ecclesiastical *alguaciles,* or staff bearers, who carried staffs similar to those of the secular alguaciles, *Actas de cabildo de la ciudad de México,* 4: 300. In 1560 the Crown warned the bishops against imposing pecuniary penalties on secular clergy, Vasco de Puga, *Provisiones, cédulas, instrucciones para el gobierno de la Nueva España* (Mexico City: Pedro Ocharte, 1563; Madrid: Cultura Hispánica, 1945), 210v; that same year the Crown ruled against the imprisonment and physical punishment of Indians by the friars, p. 201v.

74. Woodrow Borah, *Justice by Insurance. The General Indian Court of Colonial Mexico and the Legal Aides of the Half-Real* (Berkeley: University of California Press, 1983), 34–35.

75. On the discussions about the legal jurisdiction that the Indians should be under, Borah, *Justice by Insurance*, 25–30.

76. "Y así todos aquellos días no pedían otra cosa, sino que no fuesen sus delitos manifestados, derramando muchas lágrimas con extraña confusión y arrepentimiento, ofreciendo cantidad de incienso para aplacar a aquel dios." Durán, *Historia de las Indias*, 1: 39.

77. Durán, *Historia de las Indias*, 1: 40. For the place of fear in the Christian tradition, see Ephrem Boularand's article "Crainte" in the *Dictionnaire de Spiritualité*, vol. 2, pt. 2, 2463–2511. It would be worthwhile to study the concept of fear by considering the theological perspective together with the views found in sixteenth-century political thought.

78. "Notanter autem dico displicentiam, & non dico dolorem seu tristitiam: quoniam contritio proprie significat displicentiam quae est causa tristitiae seu doloris, quamvis frequenti usu dicatur, quod contritio est dolor, significando causam ad effectum." Tommasso Di Vio, *Tractatus Quartus*, in vol. 1 of *Opuscula Omnia* (Lugduni: Officina Iuntarum/Hildesheim, 1587; Hildesheim: Georg Olms, 1995), 68.

79. Durán, *Historia de las Indias*, 1: 162.

80. "Y hubo alguno que con impiedad dijo que se debía quitar la obligación de la confesión de los indios, para que no se cometiesen tan graves sacrilegios, y que tenía éste por muy sano consejo." Grijalva, *Crónica de la orden de N. P. S. Agustín*, 105. Grijalva considered the demands of the confessors on indigenous penitents to be excessive; he denounced confessors for embracing a notion of penance rigidly focused on ritual formalism: "porque aunque las demostraciones de dolor no sean tan vivas, el examen tan exacto, el confesar el número y las circunstancias tan cumplidas: con todo queda el confesor más seguro, que con las oraciones de ciego que los bachilleres recitan, ni con las lágrimas de una mujer, ni con las satisfacciones de un mercader, ni con las justificaciones de un fariseo. Porque al fin aquella es confesión sencilla, y esotra toda exterior y compuesta," 106–7.

81. José Miranda, *El erasmista mexicano Fray Alonso Cabello*, 11.

82. Motolinía, *Historia de los indios*, treat. 2, chap. 6, 244–45.

83. "Después de confesado, descansando un poco díjome, que había sido llevado su espíritu al infierno, a donde de sólo el espanto había padecido mucho tormento; y cuando me lo contaba temblaba del miedo que le había quedado." Motolinía, *Historia de los indios*, 244.

84. Durán, *Historia de las Indias*, 1: 156. The practice of bathing to eliminate illnesses was otherwise extensive and not limited to a specific ritual. Motolinía, *Historia de los indios*, treat. 1, chap. 1, 116.

85. Durán, *Historia de las Indias*, 1: 156.

86. Durán, *Historia de las Indias*, 1: 40.

87. "[H]acen mal los ministros que en las confesiones se muestran ásperos y enojados con estos flacos indios, amenazándolos amagándolos con las manos,

conociendo su flaqueza y sabiendo cuán necesaria sea la benignidad y mucha paciencia y muestras de amor en el acto de la confesión. . . . Lo cual se había de castigar como caso de inquisición, dando perpetua privación de aquel oficio al que tal hace." Durán, *Historia de las Indias,* 1: 40.

88. Denzinger, *The Sources,* 744 and 746.

89. Luther called on the friars in monasteries to ignore the authority of their superiors who appropriated the right to confess, preventing confession among brothers. Luther's advice was eloquent: "And so I advise these children, brothers and sisters: if your superiors are unwilling to permit you to confess your secret sins to whom you choose, then take them to your brother or sister, whomever you like, and be absolved and comforted. Then go and do what you want and ought to do. Only believe firmly that you are absolved, and nothing more is needed." Martin Luther, "To the Christian Nobility of the German Nation Concerning the Reform of the Christian Estate, 1520," in *Works,* 44: 180.

90. *El Sacrosanto y Ecuménico Concilio de Trento,* 198. The discussion about the parts of the sacrament brought Thomists and Scotists face to face. The latter held that the acts of the penitent intervened in the sacrament but were not a part of it, unlike absolution, which was the essential element of the sacrament, Spykman, *Attrition and Contrition,* 135 and 176. A similar discussion about the matter of the sacrament divided the same groups. We should recall that, for Duns Scotus, attrition as disposition was neither a part nor the matter of the sacrament, Spykman, *Attrition and Contrition,* 80. The term "quasi materia," used in the final version of the council text, indicates a compromise.

91. *El Sacrosanto y Ecuménico Concilio,* 197.

92. *El Sacrosanto y Ecuménico Concilio,* 199.

93. The text does not specify the characteristics of perfect contrition.

94. *El Sacrosanto y Ecuménico Concilio,* 200.

95. "Si quis dixerit, Absolutionem sacramentalem sacerdotis non esse actum judicialem, sed nudum ministerium pronuntiandi, et declarandi remissa esse peccata confitendi; modo tantum credat, se esse absolutum; aut sacerdos non serio, sed joco absolvat; aut dixerit, non requiri confessionem poenitentis, ut sacerdos ipsum absolvere possit; anathema sit." *El Sacrosanto y Ecuménico Concilio,* 226–27.

96. Imperfect contrition or attrition "non solum non facere hominem hypocritam, et magis peccatorem, verum etiam donum Dei esse, et Spiritus Sancti impulsum." One can note the answer to Luther's attacks. *El Sacrosanto y Ecuménico Concilio,* 201.

97. "Barbaris autem quoniam est sensus natura imbecillior, fides vero non admodum excitata, rarum est valde ut perfectus ille dolor, quem contritionem dicimus, de criminibus commissis haereat." Joseph de Acosta, *De procuranda indorum salute* [1588], vol. 2, bk. 6, chap. 11 (Madrid: Consejo Superior de Investigaciones Científicas, 1987), 420.

98. "Neque obscure tridentini Patres id docuisse videntur, cum ea attritionem, quae per se non iustificat, ad justificationis gratiam in sacramento poenitentiae impetrandam valere declarant." Acosta, *De procuranda,* 2: 422.

99. Fr. Juan Bautista, born in 1555, taught philosophy and theology in the

convent of San Francisco in Mexico City, García Icazbalceta, *Bibliografía mexicana del siglo XVI,* 470.

100. "[S]in dolor ni arrepentimiento de sus pecados." Bautista, *Advertencias para los confessores,* B1r. Juan Bautista was equally tolerant of the indigenous penitents' lack of a rigorous and systematic knowledge of Christian doctrine.

101. "Muchos no acaban de saber, los requisitos para recebir los sacramentos: por ser comunmente gente de cortos entendimientos no alcançan la calidad que ha de tener la contricion." Bautista, *Advertencias para los confessores,* B1v.

102. "[Q]ue al punto que se acaban las palabras sacramentales de la absolucion recibe el penitente el fructo deste sacramento, no por su merecimiento y disposicion, sino por la ordenacion divina que instituyo este sacramento para perdonar los pecados de los hombres." Bautista, *Advertencias para los confessores,* B2r.

Chapter 4

1. Representative works of these motifs include paintings by Zurbarán and Ribera. Of special interest is the striking painting by Zurbarán that captures St. Peter's vision of Christ tied to a column. See Jeannine Baticle, *Zurbarán* (New York: Metropolitan Museum of Art, 1987), and Pérez Sánchez and Nicola Spinosa, *Jusepe de Ribera 1591–1652* (New York: Metropolitan Museum of Art, 1992).

2. For Mary Magdalene as an example of repentance, see Benedicta Ward, *Harlots of the Desert: A Study on Repentance in Early Monastic Sources* (Kalamazoo: Cistercian Publications, 1987), chap. 2. An authoritative study of the representation of Mary Magdalene in Titian can be found in Harold E. Wethey, *The Paintings of Titian: The Religious Paintings* (London: Phaidon, 1969), 143–51. See also Susan Haskins's analysis of Titian's Magdalene and her overview of related iconography in the sixteenth and seventeenth centuries, *Mary Magdalen: Myth and Metaphor* (New York: Harcourt Brace and Co., 1993), chap. 7.

3. Emile Mâle, *L'art religieux du XVIIe. siècle* (Paris: Armand Colin, 1984), 84–86. The figure of Mary Magdalene, no longer in penance, also appears in El Greco's paintings of St. Peter, José López-Rey, "Spanish Baroque: A Baroque Vision of Repentance in El Greco's St. Peter," *Art in America* 35 (1947): 314.

4. There are disagreements among researchers concerning the composition of this work, which currently is in the Bowes Museum. For Wethey, the date of composition is between 1585 and 1590, *El Greco and His School* (Princeton: Princeton University Press, 1962), 2: 143. W. Jordan favored the dates suggested by Gudiol, between 1579 and 1586, "Catalogue," in *El Greco of Toledo,* ed. Jonathan Brown, W. B. Jordan, R. Kagan, and Alfonso E. Pérez Sánchez (Boston: Little, Brown and Co., 1982), 234.

5. In 1570 Molanus's *De picturis et imaginibus* appeared in Louvain. The work is both a defense of the cult of images and a guide for the examination of sacred images following the dictates of Trent. In the treatise, reprinted with additions in 1594, Molanus specified the meaning of the two keys—one of gold, the other of silver—with which St. Peter had been traditionally represented. "Per

auream clavem, intelligo potestatem absolutionis: per argenteam, excommunicationis: Haec enim inferior est, illa dignior." Molanus, *Traité des saintes images,* ed. François Boespflug, Olivier Christin, and Benoît Tassel, vol. 2, bk. 3, chap. 21 (Paris: Cerf, 1996), 296.

6. López-Rey, "Spanish Baroque," 313.

7. "El Señor, pues, estableció principalmente el Sacramento de la Penitencia, quando resucitado de entre los muertos sopló entre sus discípulos, y les dixo: *Recibid el Espíritu Santo: los pecados de aquellos que perdonaréis, les quedan perdonados, quedan ligados los de aquellos que no perdonaréis.* De este hecho tan notable, y de estas tan claras y precisas palabras, ha entendido siempre el universal consentimiento de todos los PP. Que se comunicó a los Apóstoles, y a sus legítimos sucesores el poder de perdonar, y de retener lo pecados al reconciliares los fieles que han caido en ellos después del Bautismo." *El Sacrosanto y Ecuménico Concilio de Trento,* session 14, 194–95.

8. Motolinía, *Historia de los indios,* treat. 2, chap. 5, 237.

9. On the interface of orality and literacy in the American colonial context, Walter Mignolo, *The Dark Side of the Renaissance* (Ann Arbor: University of Michigan Press, 1998), 29–67.

10. "[E]ran tantos los que venían a confesarse que yo no podía darles recado como yo quisiera, y díjeles: 'yo no tengo de confesar sino a los que trajeren sus pecados escritos y por figuras.' Que esto es cosa que ellos saben y entienden porque ésta era su escritura," Motolinía, *Historia de los indios,* treat. 2, chap. 6, 243.

11. "Y no lo dije a sordos, porque luego comenzaron tantos a a traer sus pecados escritos, que tampoco me podía valer, y ellos con una paja apuntando y yo con otra ayudándoles, se confesaban muy brevemente," Motolinía, *Historia de los indios,* 243.

12. On this point I am following Charles Lea, *A History of Auricular Confession and Indulgences in the Latin Church* (Philadelphia: Lea Brothers and Co., 1896), 1: 362–67.

13. "Praecepit enim Dominus mundandis, ut ostenderent ora sacerdotibus (Luc. XVII, 14): docens corporali praesentia confitenda peccata, non per nuntium, non per scriptum manifestanda. Dixit enim, Ora monstrate; et omnes, non unus pro omnibus." *Liber de vera et falsa poenitentia,* in *Patrologia cursus completus,* ed. J. P. Migne, Series latina (Paris, 1844–64), 40: col. 1122. The influence of this work was enduring; in the sixteenth century the *Catecismo Romano* included it as an authority. Lea proposed that the treatise had been composed by two different authors with one part written perhaps in the fifth century and the other in the middle of the twelfth century, *A History of Auricular Confession,*1: 209–10, n. 3. The work is now believed to have been written in the eleventh century, Paul Anciaux, *La Théologie du Sacrement de Pénitence au XIIe siècle* (Louvain: É. Nauwelaerts, 1949), 15, n. 3. Fr. Alonso de Molina drew on the treatise in his *Confesionario mayor.*

14. "Homo ad confessionem peccatorum sicut ad confessionem fidei obligatur. Sed confessio fidei *ore* est facienda: ut patet Rom. 10 [10]. Ergo et confessio peccatorum." Thomas Aquinas, *Supplementum Tertiae Partis Summae The-*

ologiae, vol. 3 in *Summae Theologiae,* ed. Petri Caramello (Taurini: Marietti, 1956), q. 9, art. 3, s. c.

15. Aquinas, *Supplementum,* q. 9, 3, res. Aquinas explained that the confession of sins was obligatory by considering it in the light of the need to determine the *materia,* or matter, of the sacrament. Thus, just as baptism required water as the materia to signify the washing away of sins, confession made the manifestation of sins necessary.

16. "Ad secundum dicendum quod in eo qui usum linguae non habet, sicut mutus vel qui est alterius lingaue, sufficit quod per scriptum, aut per nutum, aut interpretem confiteatur, quia non exigitur ab homine plus quam possit," *Supplementum,* q. 9, 3, ad. 2. Regarding "nutus," Alfonso de Palencia in his *Universal vocabulario* wrote: "es señalar con el ojo alguna cosa. y es nutus volutad: maiestad: mandamiento. y poderio."

17. Lea, *A History of Auricular Confession,* 1: 364–65.

18. [V]i una cosa muy de notar, y es que vinieron a oír los oficios divinos de la Semana Santa y a celebrar la fiesta de la Pascua, Indios y señores principales de cuarenta provincias y pueblos, y algunos de ellos de cincuenta y sesenta leguas, que ni fueron compelidos ni llamados, y entre éstos había de doce naciones y doce lenguas diferentes," Motolinía, *Historia de los indios,* treat. 2, chap. 5, 239.

19. "[E]stos mudos hacían muchos ademanes, poniendo las manos; y encogiendo los hombros y alzando los ojos al cielo, y todo dando a entender la voluntad y gana con que venían a recibir el bautismo." Motolinía, *Historia de los indios,* treat. 2, chap. 4, 236.

20. These reports are an important antecedent of the *Relaciones geográficas,* a project created by Ovando that was carried out by Juan López de Velazco, his secretary. H. F. Cline, "The Relaciones Geográficas of the Spanish Indies, 1577–1648," in *Handbook of Middle American Indians,* ed. Howard F. Cline (Austin: Texas University Press, 1972), 12: 189. The *Descripción* does not contain information from the regular clergy; the friars informed Archbishop Montúfar that they had received royal *cédulas,* or royal orders, separately, so their reports would be sent directly to the Crown, bypassing the archbishop *Descripción,* 17 and 297. The report of the Franciscans was edited by García Icazbalceta and included in *Códice franciscano.* At the time of Ovando's request, Mendieta compiled a list of all the Franciscan friars and their responsibilities; Mendieta's manuscript was published by Jean-Pierre Berthe, "Les franciscains de la province mexicaine du Saint Évangile en 1570: un catalogue de Fray Jerónimo de Mendieta," in *Enquêtes sur l'Amérique Moyenne. Mélanges offerts à Guy Stresser-Péan,* ed. Dominique Michelet (México: Instituto Nacional de Antropología e Historia/Centre d'Études Mexicaines et Centraméricaines, 1989), 213–34.

21. "Y en lo tocante a los prebendados, dicen algunos que se proveen de pocos méritos, ciencia y dotrina, y que algunos apenas saben leer y cuando dicen misa cantada o rezada, lo dan a entender en la pronunciación y acentos: y que se dice públicamente que debieron procurar por vía de interese y negociación las dichas prebendas." García Pimentel, *Descripción,* 9. About the prebendaries, John F. Schwaller pointed out, "The bull of erection for all the Spanish dioceses in the New World provided for the formation of a chapter of twenty-seven mem-

bers generically called prebendaries, *prebendados,*" *The Church and Clergy in Sixteenth-Century Mexico* (Albuquerque: University of New Mexico Press, 1987), 13. Schwaller provided a useful description of the structure and function of the ecclesiastical hierarchy in Mexico.

22. García Pimentel, *Descripción,* 9.

23. For an analysis of the impact of Christianization on the Nahuas that moves beyond the traditional question framed in terms of the success or failure of evangelization efforts, see Lockhart, *The Nahuas after the Conquest,* chap. 6.

24. S. B. Heath, *Telling Tongues: Language Policy in Mexico* (New York: Teachers College Press, 1972), 3. H. R. Harvey wrote an important article about the distribution of languages in New Spain, based on the information in the *Relaciones geográficas,* compiled a few years after the *Descripción.* For the distribution of languages in the area administered by the Archdiocese of Mexico City, the information in García Pimentel's *Descripción* is very close to that found in the *Relaciones geográficas.* Harvey, "The Relaciones Geográficas, 1579–86: Native Languages," in *Handbook of Middle American Indians,* 12: 303.

25. Heath, *Telling Tongues,* 7–8.

26. Baudot, *Utopia e historia,* 111. On the the creation, objectives, and activities of the Colegio de Santa Cruz de Tlatelolco, Ricard, *La "conquête spirituelle,"* 260–81.

27. "A mí paréceme que Vuestra Majestad debe mandar que todos deprendan la lengua mexicana, porque ya no hay pueblo que no hay muchos indios que no la sepan y la deprendan sin ningún trabajo, sino de uso y muy muchos se confiesan en ella." Cuevas, *Documentos inéditos,* 159.

28. "Como una de las principales cosas que nos deseamos para el bien desa tierra es su salvación e instrucción y conversión a nuestra Santa Fe Católica de los naturales della, y que también tomen nuestra policía y buenas costumbres; y así tratando de los medios que para este fin se podrían tener, ha parecido que uno dellos y el más principal sería dar orden como a esas gentes se les enseñase nuestra lengua castellana, porque sabida ésta, con más facilidad podrían ser adoctrinados en las cosas del Santo Evangelio y conseguir todo lo demás que les conviene para su manera de vivir." The warrant, sent to the provincials of the three religious orders, is dated June 7, 1550. Richard Konetzke, comp., *Colección de documentos para la historia de la formación social de Hispanoamérica, 1493–1810* (Madrid: Consejo Superior de Investigaciones Científicas, 1953), 1: 272–73.

29. By the same date a royal warrant with the same content was sent to the provincial of the Dominicans in New Spain, Konetzke, *Colección de documentos,* 1: 273–74. The negative response of the Dominicans in Chiapas to the warrant was reported by Fr. Antonio de Remesal, *Historia general de las Indias Occidentales, y particular de la gobernación de Chiapa y Guatemala,* ed. Carmelo Sáenz de Santa María (Madrid: Biblioteca de Autores Españoles, 1964–66), bk. 6, chap. 6, 1: 418.

30. González de Cosío, *Un cedulario mexicano,* 167–68. This measure was ratified by Philip III in 1619. *Recopilación de leyes de los Reynos de las Indias,* (Madrid: Viuda de Joaquín Ibarra [1791]; reprint, Madrid: Centro de Estudios

Políticos y Constitucionales y el Boletín Oficial del Estado, 1998), bk. 1, tit.13, law 4, 1: 95.

31. Heath, *Telling Tongues*, 24.

32. Harvey, "The Relaciones," 313.

33. Heath, *Telling Tongues*, 35.

34. The Nahuatl language is referred to as both "lengua mexicana" or "nahual" in García Pimentel, *Descripción*.

35. Harvey's study based on the *Relaciones geográficas* identifies three languages all known as Chontal but from different areas. The reference García Pimentel, *Descripción*, seems to point to the language known as Chontal spoken in Guerrero, Harvey, "The Relaciones," 311.

36. This language is also known as *tepuxteca*, Harvey, "The Relaciones," 308.

37. For the group of languages on the Costa Grande, Harvey, "The Relaciones," 309-10.

38. García Pimentel, *Descripción*, 45.

39. García Pimentel, *Descripción*, 238.

40. Schwaller, *Church and Clergy*, 85. The order in question was also the project of Ovando.

41. "Voy dando orden con que todos deprendan la lengua mexicana para que se confiesen de aquí adelante," García Pimentel, *Descripción*, 197.

42. Pedro Infante of Zumpango described the content of such cartillas: "La doctrina que sigo para doctrinar a mis feligreses es la cartilla común donde se les enseñan las cuatro oraciones, los diez mandamientos y los artículos de la fe, y las obras de misericordia y los sacramentos de la Iglesia y los siete pecados mortales y toda la demás doctrina cristiana a los mexicanos, por sí, en latín y en su lengua, y a los otomís por sí, en latín y en su lengua." García Pimentel, *Descripción*, 93.

43. García Pimentel, *Descripción*, 48.

44. Hipólito Farfán comments on the little success of confession among the Otomís: "Procede este tal defecto por el poco tiempo que en este tal partido residen los clérigos, no teniendo ni dándoles lugar y espacio para deprender la lengua otomí que ansí hay entre ellos, para que en la dicha tal lengua otomí se les puedan administrar los sacramentos." García Pimentel, *Descripción*, 143.

45. García Pimentel, *Descripción*, 144.

46. García Pimentel, *Descripción*, 187.

47. García Pimentel, *Descripción*, 115. López de Avalos of Güegüetocan said this about the Otomís: "Los más otomíes no están tan industriados, porque son tan brutos en sus cosas, que se pasa grandísimo trabajo con ellos, que aunque se les dice todos los domingos y fiestas de guardar la doctrina cristiana, y lo que más conviene a la salvación de sus almas, aprovecha poco." García Pimentel, *Descripción*, 262.

48. García Pimentel, *Descripción*, 85.

49. García Pimentel, *Descripción*, 93.

50. García Pimentel, *Descripción*, 88.

51. García Pimentel, *Descripción*, 164.

52. García Pimentel, *Descripción,* 165.

53. García Pimentel, *Descripción,* 168.

54. "La mitad de la gente destas estancias será chontal, y poco o mucho todos estos entienden la lengua mexicana que basta para se confesar, porque vienen y van a los tianguez a los pueblos de alrededor a vender sus granjerías, y se entienden y tratan con los mexicanos," García Pimentel, *Descripción,* 97.

55. García Pimentel, *Descripción,* 197.

56. García Pimentel, *Descripción,* 109.

57. García Pimentel, *Descripción,* 150.

58. García Pimentel, *Descripción,* 153.

59. Lockhart, *The Nahuas after the Conquest,* 195.

60. "Por tanto, suplicamos a V. M., sea servido de mandar que los coadjutores que nos ovieren de dar los Obispos sean tales cuales para este apostolado se requieren, y que sepan muy bien las lenguas, porque no vengan a tratar los Sacramentos del Matrimonio o Baptismo por un muchacho español, mulato, mestizo, indio o negro, y aun tratarán por manos destos el Sacramento de la Confesión, pues es de parecer vuestro Arzobispo que confiesen por intérprete, y así lo ha hecho el que tomando su alguacil por lengua ha confesado algunos, y esto sin necesidad y habiendo quien lo hiciese, porque a la sazón estaban seis Religiosos de la Orden de Sant Francisco, los cuales eran lenguas, confesando." García Icazbalceta, *Códice Mendieta,* 1: 8. The extensive use of interpreters for confession toward the end of the sixteenth century in Guadalajara warranted a complaint from the authorities of that city. P. Castañeda Delgado, "La Iglesia y la Corona ante la nueva realidad lingüística en Indias," in *I Simposio de Filología Iberoamericana (Sevilla: 23 al 30 de marzo de 1990)* (Zaragoza: Libros Pórtico, 1990), 31.

61. "[E]specialmente hay algunas tierras en el obispado de Guaxaca y de Tlaxcalla y en otras partes donde las lenguas de los indios son muy diversas y obscuras; y dícese, como cosa cierta y pública, que han hecho costumbre de contentarse en administrar la doctrina y sacramento de confesión por intérpretes." Cuevas, *Documentos inéditos,* 318. In a 1584 opinion, the former Spanish *oidor* (judge of the *audiencia*) Alonso Zorita expressed his concern about the use of interpreters in the confession of the Indians, pointing out that the practice could endanger the integrity of the sacrament, Cuevas, *Documentos inéditos,* 336.

62. "Quod si Parochus, aut Sacerdos hujusmodi aegroti Idioma non noverit, interpretem adhibeat, ut aegrotum maerentem consoletur, & exhortetur; postquam autem aegrotus admonitus fuerit, se ad id non teneri, valde tamen animae saluti utile esse, tamen per interpretem peccata sua confiteri voluerit, & interpretes spectatae Fidei sit, ea Sacerdos audire poterit." Lorenzana, *Concilium Mexicanum Provinciale III,* bk. 3, tit.2, § 2, 154; on the resolution by the first council, Lorenzana, *Concilios provinciales primero y segundo,* 191.

63. Acosta considered the teaching of doctrine to the Indians through the use of interpreters was not free of problems since the interpreters themselves often did not understand or could not translate what was asked of them, Acosta, *De procuranda,* bk. 4, chap. 7, 2: 52–55.

64. Acosta, *De procuranda*, bk. 4, chap. 7, 2: 54–59, and also bk. 6, chap. 13, 2: 430–33, where Acosta pointed out that even though confession through interpreters was possible, theologians recognized that the penitent was not obligated to submit to an interpreted confession. The Second Provincial Church Council of Lima included this opinion when it prohibited the imposition of such a confession: "Nullus sacerdos per interpretem confessiones audiat; adeo sacratum est hujus sacramenti sigillum, ut non nisi in aure, secrete, clancularieque, ministrandum, suscipendumve sit." R. Vargas Ugarte, ed., *Concilios Limenses (1551–1772)* (Lima, 1951–54), 1: 108.

65. Acosta, *De procuranda*, bk. 6, chap. 13.

66. Mendieta, *Historia eclesiástica indiana*, bk. 4, chap. 44, 3: 212.

67. The psychological dimension of contrition in Aquinas is discussed by Spykman, *Attrition and Contrition*, 56–66; on Gabriel Biel's position in relation to Duns Scotus, Oberman, *The Harvest of Medieval Theology*, 146–60.

68. As seen in the previous chapter, the doctrine of penance of Duns Scotus in which the concept of attrition is a key element made this question moot. The fundamental issue being discussed is whether or not the penitents are certain that they have been absolved. For a detailed analysis of the divided opinions around this question among the Franciscans who attended the Council of Trent, see Valens Heynck, "A Controversy at the Council of Trent Concerning the Doctrine of Duns Scotus." *Franciscan Studies* 9, no. 3 (1949): 181–258.

69. Aquinas, *Summa*, 3a, q. 85, art. 1, res. It is the consideration of the emotions, keeping in mind the intervention of the will and the intellect, that makes it possible to approach the emotions from the moral perspective, 1a, 2ae, q. 24, art. 1 res. On the moral implications of *tristitia* or sadness, 1a, 2ae, q. 39.

70. The *Catecismo Romano* identifies three meanings for "penitencia." The first refers to a feeling of displeasure toward something that earlier was the source of pleasure; however, there is no moral consideration or sadness, "segun el siglo, no segun Dios." The second is the sorrow for sins motivated by selfish reasons. The third, which is penance as virtue and sacrament, is repentance that takes God into consideration. *Catecismo del Santo Concilio de Trento*, 152.

71. "Item proprie loquendo, contritio non est essentialiter dolor, sed potius odium et displicentia peccati, ex quo oritur dolor, et tristitia in appetitu sensitivo, itaque; contritio ab effectu vocatur dolor." Bartolomé de Ledesma, *De septem novae legis sacramentis summarium* (México: Antonio de Espinosa, 1566), 130r. On Ledesma, see Jose-Ignasi Saranyana, "Tres teólogos académicos mexicanos del siglo XVI: Vera Cruz, Ledesma y Pravia," *Hispania sacra* 44 (1982): 561–72.

72. This simplification was considered necessary even for the confessors. Dominican Fr. Bartolomé de Medina clearly indicated the distance separating the abstract treatment of penance in the *summae* for confessors and the concrete reality of confession in the field. The authors of the summae were capable of tirelessly discussing distinctions among sins, "pero no pusieron este negocio en practica, ni enseñaron el modo de aplicar estas medicinas, pareciendose a aquellos de quien dize Plutarcho en el principio de sus Politicas, que adereçan el candil, y despavilan la mecha; pero no le echen azeyte para que arda." Bartolomé de Medina,

Instrucción de como se ha de administrar el sacramento de la penitencia (Alcalá: Iván Gracián, 1591), 8r.

73. One would think that in this kind of literature there would be a greater urgency to promote the obligation of the believers and their adherence to the ritual.

74. "Y la contricion se llama assi porque quire dezir quebrantamiento o dolor juntamente y con voluntad tomado o avido. Ca es menester que todas las potencias del alma: que son: memoria:entendimiento y voluntad. Y los sentidos de fuera con todos los miembros corporales se duelan y ayan contricion de la ofensa hecha a dios," Zumárraga, *Doctrina breve*, B3r.

75. "E si el pecador no se pudiere tanto doler duelase y pesele porque no puede dolerse tanto," Zumárraga, *Doctrina breve*, B3v.

76. "Ca el baptismo se haze en el agua por virtud del spiritu sancto. Y este sacramento por la ggracia de dios se haze en agua de contricion y lloro de compuncion que es agua de lagrimas," Zumárraga, *Doctrina breve*, B2v.

77. Aquinas resolved the question of the matter of penance by broadening its definition. In baptism, water is the matter; in penance, the acts of the penitent are the matter, Aquinas, *Summa*, 3a, q. 84, art. 1, ad. 1; on the distance between Duns Scotus and Aquinas on the question of contrition, see chap. 3.

78. Luke 22:54–62. Ambrose wrote a commentary on Luke's text: "Quare flevit. Quia culpa obrepsit ei. Ego soleo flere, si culpa mihi desit, hoc est, si non me vindicem, si non obstineam quod improbe cupio. Petrus doluit et flevit, quia erravit ut homo. Non invenio quid dixerit, invenio quod fleverit. Lachrymas euis lego, satisfactionem non lego. Sed quod defendi no potest, ablui potest. Lavent lachrymae delictum, quod voce pudor est confiteri." Ambrose, *Omnia Opera* (Basilea, 1527), 4: 748.

79. "[Q]ue quando comensare a sentir semejante dolor de sus Avisole pecados/que entienda que la mano del Señor le despierta y su misericordia le viene a buscar/y le trae en conocimiento de su perdicion." Zumárraga, *Doctrina cristiana*, 18v.

80. Marcel Bataillon, "El 'Enchiridion' y la 'Paraclesis' en México," in *El enquiridión o manual del caballero cristiano*, ed. Dámaso Alonso (Madrid: S. Aguirre, 1932), 527–34.

81. The incomplete treatment of the sacraments in Dr. Constantino's *Suma* appears not to have given greater grounds for disagreement to the censors of his works, Guerrero, *Catecismos españoles*, 311.

82. Payne, *Erasmus: His Theology of the Sacraments*, 192 and ff.

83. In addition to the path represented by the sacrament, Jean Gerson wrote that three truths, if expressed by penitents either "con la boca o con el coraçon," would assure them of a state of grace: repentance for sins, the purpose of sinning no more, and the will to confess according to the requirements set forth by the church. A dying person unable to confess who expressed any of the three truths would be saved, after going through purgatory. *Tripartito del Christianisimo y consolatorio doctor Juan Gerson de doctrina Christiana: a qualquiera muy provechosa* [1544] (Mexico City: Libros de México, 1949), B8v–Cr. For this aspect of Gerson's theology, although the presentation suffers from certain ambiguities, see D. Catherine Brown, *Pastor and Laity in the Theology of Jean Gerson* (Cambridge: Cambridge University Press, 1987), 56–72.

84. *Doctrina cristiana en lengua española,* fol. xcvii v. The entire section deals with sentiments of sadness and the effusion of tears.

85. García Icazbalceta, *Códice franciscano,* 41.

86. López Austin, *Human Body and Ideology,* 1: 208–10; McKeever Furst, *The Natural History of the Soul,* 19–22. The distance between the Christian and Nahua ethical conceptions regarding confession was explored by Klor de Alva, "Contar vidas."

87. López Austin, *Human Body and Ideologyy,* 1: 208–10.

88. "[Y] destas dos cosas [conviene a saber] del conocimiento del pecado, y del temor de dios, tiene principio y procede la contricion y el arrepentimiento de los pecados." Molina, *Confesionario mayor,* 5r.

89. Attrition, as Burkhart correctly observed, did not warrant Molina's attention, *The Slippery Earth,* 34.

90. Molina, *Confesionario mayor,* 13v. Sahagún used the classic distinction between spiritual and earthly sadness, Burkhart, *The Slippery Earth,* 34.

91. "atritio oritur ex timore servili poenarum. . . . At vero contritio oritus ex timore filiali, et est actus virtutis, quia a virtute charitatis elicitur." Ledesma, *De septem novae legis sacramentis summarium,*131v.

92. Molina, *Confesionario mayor,* 15v.

93. Patton, *The Efficacy of Putative Attrition,* 10–11.

94. On the classic episode of the purification of Lazarus and his absolution by the disciples of Christ, Aquinas commented, "Per hoc ergo non ostenditur quod sacerdos non absolvat, aut non debeat dicere 'Ego te absolvo'; sed quod eum non debet absolvere in quo signa contritionis non videt." *De forma absolutionis,* vol. 2 in *Opera Omnia* (Paris, 1875), 7.

95. "Integra, secreta, lachrimabilis, accelerata." Tentler, *Sin and Confession on the Eve of the Reformation,* 106; The sixteenth-century Spanish theologian Martín de Azpilcueta quoted the verses in his *Enchiridion sive Manuale Confessariorum at Poenitentium* (Romae: Georgij Ferraij, 1584), 87.

96. "[P]orque (segun Crisostomo) el pecador deve haver gran dolor y con lagrimas si puede por el pecado que cometio y proponer de jamas no tornar. Y esta condicion es mas necesaria y cumple mas que todas por la qual mas alcançamos de dios y satisfacemos a dios: que siempre que lloramos con deliberacion de confessar estamos en gracia," *Arte para bien confesar,* in civitate Cesarauguste. (Zaragoza, [ca. 1500?]), fol. B ii. Zumárraga's *Doctrina breve* recommends that the penitent who did not feel sufficient sorrow should ponder that deficiency as a way to achieve greater sorrow. The *Arte para bien confesar* makes the same recommendation and introduces the term "attrition" to identify such imperfect sorrow, a notion that does not generally appear in Mexican catechisms and confessionaries.

97. "Y esta contricion o arrepentimiento es de tanto fruto que nunca puede ser que por ella no sean perdonados los pecados que cometio por muchos y grandes que sean / y mayormente quando esta contricion fuere con lagrimas. Ca las nuestras lagrimas son de grande fuerça ante dios." Alonso de Madrigal (El Tostado), *Confessional del Tostado* (Logroño: Miguel de Eguia, 1529), A3r.

98. "Tres condiciones ponen en la contrición, que hacen más a la perfeción de ella que no a la sustancia: Una es que el dolor de los pecados sea con lágrimas y con otros testimonios exteriores, como fue la penitencia de S. Pedro y de la

Magdalena." Carranza de Miranda, *Comentarios sobre el catechismo christiano,* 2: 256.

99. Cassian, *Conlationes XIIII,* ed. Michael Petschenig, Corpus scriptorum ecclesiasticorum latinorum, vol. 13 (Vindobonae: apud C. Geroldi filium, 1886), conlatio 9, 274–75.

100. Catherine of Siena's *Epistolas y oraciones* were published by the initiative of Cardinal Cisneros in Alcalá in 1512, Bataillon, *Erasmo y España,* 49, and James P. R. Lyell, *Early Book Illustration in Spain* (New York: Hacker Art Books, 1976), 264–65. Another widely read work in sixteenth-century Spain was John Climacus's *Spiritual Ladder,* whose seventh chapter deals with weeping. The *Spiritual Ladder*'s second translation into Spanish was the work of Fr. Luis de Granada.

101. Catherine of Siena, *The Dialogue,* ed. Suzanne Noffke (New York: Paulist Press, 1980), 161.

102. "I want you to know that all tears come from the heart. Nor is there any other bodily member that can satisfy the heart as the eyes can." Catherine of Siena, *The Dialogue,* 161. In addition to bodily tears, there are souls consumed by love that have tears of fire, pp. 168–69.

103. For the appearance of tears in European iconography, which was a very late development given the wide circulation of Christian sources that discussed the theme, see Moshe Barasch's excellent article "The Crying Face," in *Imago Hominis: Studies in the Language of Art* (Vienna: IRSA, 1991), 85–99. Barasch also dealt with the gestures of the damned in European art in *Gestures of Despair in Medieval and Early Renaissance Art* (New York: New York University Press, 1976).

104. William Christian Jr. briefly touched upon this phenomenon in "Provoked Religious Weeping in Early Modern Spain," in *Religious Organization and Religious Experience,* ed. J. Davis, A.S.A., Monograph 21 (London: Academic Press, 1982), 97–114. On the public dimension of contrition in penitential rituals, see Maureen Flynn, "The Spectacle of Suffering in Spanish Streets," in *City and Spectacle in Medieval Europe,* ed. Barbara A. Hanawalt and Kathryn L. Reyerson (Minneapolis: University of Minnesota Press, 1994).

105. Although Christian did not elaborate on this difference, I believe that the two contexts allow us to think about two somewhat different dynamics. Preaching is intended to move the spirit and the emotions of the faithful; in the case of processions, the presence of the ecclesiastical authority takes on a decidedly different character.

106. *Cartas de Indias,* 1: 65. The argument evident in this letter forms the basis of positive characterizations of indigenous society that inform not only discussions surrounding the nature of the Indians but also the practical approaches used by the religious to convert them. The most developed example of this line of defense is, of course, the *Apologética historia sumaria* by Las Casas.

107. "[S]alir a reçebir a las personas honrradas quando entran en sus pueblos, sentimientos de tristeza *usque ad lacrimas,* quando buena criança lo requiere e buen agradeçimiento," *Cartas de Indias,* 1: 65.

108. This document ends up confirming Richard Trexler's subtle analysis of European ideas of reverence in the context of New Spain, "Aztec Priests for Christian Altars: The Theory and Practice of Reverence in New Spain," in *Church and Community, 1200–1600: Studies in the History of Florence and New Spain* (Roma: Edizioni di Storia e Letteratura, 1987), 469–92.

109. In a speech by a noble father to his son to teach him the virtue of humility, there is a reference to the exemplary conduct of their ancestors: "They [practised] the bowing of the head, the lowering of the head, the bending of the neck, the weeping, the tears, the sighs." And later, "The more they were honored, the more they wept, suffered affliction, sighed; they became most humble, most meek, most contrite." Sahagún, *Florentine Codex*, bk. 6, chap. 20, 106–7.

110. "[L]a frequencia de las confesiones con solloços e lagrimas, la confesion pura e simplicima, la emienda junta a ella nos qui contractavimus de verbo vitae lo sabemos, y ese soberano Dios, que obra milagros ascondidos en sus coraçones, lo sabe, e aun en los actos de fuera lo podrán ver aquellos a quien o ignorancia o maliçia no çiega," *Cartas de Indias,* 1: 9.

111. Trexler, "Aztec Priests for Christian Altars," 478.

112. "Mas en orden a haberse difinido la contricion por el dolor, se ha de advertir a los fieles, que no piensen acaso que este dolor es de los que se perciben por alguno de los sentidos del cuerpo. Porque la contricion es accion de la voluntad," *Catecismo del Santo Concilio de Trento,* 159.

113. "Porque quando confesamos los pecados arrodillados a los pies del Sacerdote, descubierta la cabeza, inclinado el rostro a la tierra, las manos puestas y enderezadas al Cielo, y dando otras señales semejantes de humildad Christiana, aunque no son necesarias para el sacramento, por ellas entendemos claramente que debemos reconocer en el Sacramento virtud celestial, y que hemos de buscar e implorar con suma diligencia la misericordia divina," *Catecismo del Santo Concilio de Trento,* 165–66.

114. For penance as gesture within the discussion of the concept of "discipline" according to Hugue of Saint Victor, see Jean-Claude Schmitt, *La raison des gestes dans l'Occident médiéval* (Paris: Gallimard, 1990), 194. Schmitt's work gives a comprehensive and intelligent treatment of the function of gestures in medieval society. On Hugue's notion of discipline and theories of ritual in contemporary anthropology, Asad, *Genealogies of Religion,* 125–67.

115. "[C]ada uno se apartaba en un rincón de su casa y ponía las manos a manera de quien mucho se acueita, a veces torciéndoselas, otras, encasando los dedos unos con otros, llorando, y los que no podían derramar lágrimas, gimiendo y acueitándose," Las Casas, *Apologética historia sumaria,* bk. 3, chap. 176, 2: 212. Durán paid close attention to the bodily postures of the Nahuas when they engaged in prayer, noting that they favored squatting over kneeling, *Historia de las Indias,* 1: 121. On the role of the body in Christian prayer, see Trexler's preliminary study to Peter the Chanter's treatise, *The Christian at Prayer: An Illustrated Prayer Manual Attributed to Peter the Chanter (d. 1197)* (Binghampton: Medieval and Renaissance Texts and Studies, 1987). For the narrative function of weeping derived from a contemporary oral testimony in Nahuatl, see Jane H.

Hill, "Weeping as a Meta-signal in a Mexicano Woman's Narrative," in *Native Latin American Cultures through Their Discourse,* ed. Ellen B. Basso (Bloomington: Folklore Institute, Indiana University, 1990), 29–49.

116. "Y si el enfermo tiene perdida ya la fabla: y el uso dela razon: y havia acostumbrado bevir como buen cristiano: y confessava y comulgava y iba a missa y fazia semejantes obras de cristiano, como quiera que entonces por el tal caso no pensando que le acaescio no demande los sacramentos. deve empero ser absuelto de toda sentencia y de todo pecado como dicho es." Anthonino de Florencia, *La summa de confession llamada defecerunt de fray Anthonino arçobispo de florencia del orden de los predicadores. En romance* (Salamanca: Hans Gieser, [1500?]), 71.

117. Fr. Francisco de Alcocer, *Confessionario breve y muy provechoso para los penitentes* (Salamanca: Juan de Canova, 1568), 36v.

118. Juan de Zumárraga, *Regla cristiana breve* [1547], ed. José Almoina (Mexico City: Editorial Jus, 1951), 463.

119. Melchior de Yebra, *Libro llamado Refugium infirmorum* (Seville, 1593), Y5r. The education of mutes in sixteenth-century Spain was primarily the responsibility of friars, one of whom, Benedictine Ponce de León, stands out; for this theme, see the comprehensive study by Susan Plann, *A Silent Minority. Deaf Education in Spain, 1550–1835* (Berkeley: University of California Press, 1997), 13–35.

120. Juan Pablo Bonet, *Reducción de las letras y arte para enseñar a hablar a los mudos* (Madrid: Francisco Beltrán, 1930).

121. "[S]i el penitente antes pidio el sacramento de la eucharistia, o mostro, o agora muestra señales de contricion o de cristiano, porque adora la cruz, o diziendo le que se arrepienta de sus pecados por la offensa de dios, con voluntad de se emendar, o otra cosa sancta y buena: alça los ojos al cielo, o muestra otra buena señal, desele el sacramento de la eucharistia," Alcocer, *Confessionario breve y muy provechoso,* 37.

122. The symbolism of the image is as follows: "Donna vestita di cilicio, addolorata, con la bocca aperta in atto di parlare, con gl'occhi rivolti al Cielo, che versino copiose lagrime, con una corona di pungenti spine in capo tenendo con la sinistra mano un cuore parimente ornato di spine, terrà la destra mano alta, e il dito indice verso il Cielo." Cesare Ripa, *Iconologia,* bk. 1 (Venice: N. Pezzana, 1669), 95. The *Iconologia* was first published in Rome in 1593; the first illustrated edition was published in the same city in 1603.

123. "Se ho enfermo ha perdido ha fala, sentido e entendimento, e antes mostrou sinaes de contriçam, porque levantava as mãos, feria os peytos, dezia Miserere mei deus. Deus propitius esto mihi peccatori: e palabras semelhantes, e pedio os sacramentos." *Manual de confessores, e penitentes em ho qual breve e particular, e muy verdadeyramente se decidem* (Coimbra, 1549), 524.

124. Durán, *Historia de las Indias,* 1: 162.

125. Bautista, *Advertencias para los confessores,* 1r.

126. "Muchas vezes va un sacerdote por un camino, y llamanle a confessar a un indio que esta malo, y no sabe el sacerdote mucha lengua, que hara? Confiessele no haviendo muy cerca otro sacerdote que lo pueda confessar, viendo señales de contricion en el: que por pocos pecados que le entienda, aunque dexe

de entender otros muchos, basta para poderle absolver, y aquella alma queda remediada," Bautista, *Advertencias para los confessores, 9v.* He continued, adding this about sacramental power: "Por que si estava attrita, con el sacramento se haze contrita, y por el consiguiente digna de vida eterna."

127. Bautista, *Advertencias para los confessores,* 11r.

128. García Icazbalceta, *Códice Mendieta,* 1: 4.

129. Fr. Juan de la Anunciación, *Doctrina christiana muy cumplida donde se contiene la exposición de todo lo necesario para doctrinar a los yndios, y administralles los Sanctos Sacramentos* (Mexico City: Pedro Balli, 1575), 108.

130. "Succede que llaman a un Confessor que va ya a confessar a un enfermo, o herido, que pide Confession, y quando llega el Sacerdote halla al enfermo sin habla, [pero con muestras y señales de contricion] y aun algunas vezes sin sentido, ni conoscimiento de hombre, otra yendola a confessar a la Yglesia, succede lo proprio. Que hara?" Bautista, *Advertencias para los confessores,* 17r.

131. The title of Focher's now-lost treatise on the absolution of the infirm who are unable to speak, *Antidotus infirmorum, hoc est, quomodo absolvendi sint infirmi loquela privati,* is given by Mendieta, *Historia eclesiástica indiana,* bk. 5, chap. 96, 4: 131.

132. Bautista, *Advertencias para los confessores,* 114; see Juan de Medina, *De Penitentia, Restitutione & Contractibus* (Ingolstadii: Davidi Sartorii, 1581; reprint, Hants: Gregg Press Limited, 1967), q. xxxix, sed., 206.

133. Gibson, *The Aztecs under Spanish Rule,* 137–38 and app. 4.

134. On mutes not being obligated to confess, Duns Scotus pointed out, "Nullus obligatur ad imposibile; sed mutus non potest loqui." And in the following argument, "Item, omnis extraneus inter illos, quibus est barbarus est mutus; ergo non tenentur confiteri." Duns Scotus, *Quaestiones in Librum Quartum Sententiarum,* dist. 17, q. unica, 504.

135. Leonardo Da Vinci, *Treatise on Painting [Codex Urbinas latinus 1270],* trans. A. Philip McMahon (Princeton: Princeton University Press, 1956), 2: 125 and 403.

136. Bede, *De Tabernaculo, De Templo, In Ezram et Neeiam,* Corpus Christianorum, Series Latina (Turnholt: Brepols, 1969), 119A: 167.

137. James R. Knowlson, "The Idea of Gesture as a Universal Language," *Journal of the History of Ideas* 26 (October–December 1965): 500.

Chapter 5

1. Aquinas himself tackled the issue of the different expressions in use to refer to the Eucharist, *Summa,* 3a, q. 73, art. 4.

2. Francisco de Osuna, *Gracioso combite de las gracias del sancto sacramento del altar* (Sevilla, 1543), B2r. A comment on the different names can also be found in Carranza de Miranda, *Comentarios sobre el catecismo cristiano,* 2: 207–8.

3. Osuna, *Gracioso combite,* B2v.

4. Osuna, *Gracioso combite,* B3r.

5. Carranza de Miranda, *Comentarios sobre el catecismo cristiano,* 2: 208.

6. Denzinger, *The Sources of Catholic Dogma,* 173.

7. For a historical overview of the relation between confession and Eucharist as reflected in canon law and sacramental theology, Louis Braeckmans, *Confession et communion au moyen âge et au concile de Trente* (Gembloux: Éditions J. Duculot, 1971), 29–65.

8. Motolinía, *Historia de los indios,* treat. 2, chap. 6, 245. Mendieta reported a similar story involving an Indian woman, *Historia eclesiástica indiana,* bk. 4, chap. 26, 3: 115.

9. Similar expressions of humility among the friars were not unknown in Mexico. The Franciscan Pedro de Gante, who devoted most of his time in Mexico to the instruction of the Mexican Indians, never sought to be ordained, remaining a lay brother for the rest of his life, Mendieta, *Historia eclesiástica indiana,* bk. 4, chap. 44, 3: 212.

10. Torquemada, *Monarquía indiana,* bk. 16, chap. 21, 3: 189.

11. For a concise treatment of the controversy, Ricard, *La "conquête spirituelle,"* 148–52; for an overview of the different trends in the administration of the Eucharist in the American colonies, Constantino Bayle, "La comunión entre los indios americanos," *Missionalia hispánica* (Madrid) 1 (1944): 13–72. A transcription of the section on the Eucharist found in the *Directorio de Confesores,* an important source for the Third Mexican Church Council, can be found in Jose-Ignasi Saranyana, "La eucaristía en la teología sacramentaria americana del siglo XVI," in *Eucaristía y Nueva Evangelización. Actas del IV Simposio de la Iglesia en España y América: siglos XVI–XX,* ed. Paulino Castañeda and Carlos Martín de la Hoz (Córdoba: Caja Sur, 1994), 21–29.

12. As to the physical preparation to receive the sacrament, the church recommended that the sacrament be received without having ingested either food or liquids, except in the case of the infirm. Sexual activity immediately prior to accessing the sacrament was also discouraged.

13. "Diversos dizen cosas diversas hablando de la preparacion y aparejo que se requiere para rescebir el Sacramento del altar porque unos ponen aquesto con tanto temor: que apartan los hombres deste sacrificio del señor." Osuna, *Gracioso combite,* C2v. This type of "temor" contrasts with the fear experienced by the author as he set out to write about the sacrament: "porque contemplando yo la alteza deste sacramento esto tan atemorizado que pienso hazer me dios merced quando se me ofresce un tal examinador," A3r. In the opinions and discussions surrounding the Eucharist, fear is a notion often invoked; given the very nature of the sacrament this should not be cause for surprise. What seems to emerge under this label once again is a variety of experiences and responses to the sacred, the conceptual differences of which were worked out by scholastic thought.

14. Molina's advice, although slightly more severe, is in close agreement with the information provided by the Franciscans to Juan de Ovando in 1570 where we read that "el día antes de la Comunión se les hace plática de la limpieza que se requiere para recibir el Cuerpo del Señor, y aunque de antes están avisados, pero entonces de nuevo se les avisa que a lo menos aquella noche no duerman las mujeres con sus maridos, y si les pidieren el débito, que dejen la comunión para otro día; y que el día siguiente en que han de comulgar, no coman ni

beban cosa alguna, por poca que sea; y si acaso se descuidaren, dejen también la comunión para otro día, y que vengan lo más limpio que pudieren en sus vestiduras." García Icazbalceta, *Códice franciscano*, 91. On the shift from receiving the host in the hand to Communion in the mouth, Pierre-Marie Gy, "Quand et pourquoi la communion dans la bouche a-t-elle remplacé la communion dans la main dans l'Église latine?" in *La liturgie dans l'histoire*, 205–10.

    15. Mendieta, *Historia eclesiástica indiana*, bk. 3, chap. 45, 2: 145. According to Gil the discussions started in June 1946 probably without the presence of Bartolomé de Las Casas, and more likely continued until the end of October, *Primeras "Doctrinas" del Nuevo Mundo*, 250. For Parish and Weidman the final meetings took place in November, *Las Casas en México*, 105, n. 73. Because of the paucity of sources, it has been difficult until recently to reconstruct in detail what transpired in these meetings. Parish and Weidman uncovered hitherto unknown documents that have helped filling in some important gaps, *Las Casas en México*, 57–62.

    16. García Icazbalceta, *Don Fray Juan de Zumárraga*, 2: 175.

    17. Motolinía, *Historia de los indios*, treat. 2, chap. 6, 245.

    18. "Y también se maravillan que de lejos se vengan a bautizar, casar y confesar, y en las fiestas a oir misa; pero vistas estas cosas es muy de notar la fe de estos tan nuevos cristianos." Motolinía, *Historia de los indios*, treat. 7, chap. 19, 188.

    19. Motolinía, *Historia de los indios*, treat. 2, chap. 5, 239.

    20. Mendieta, *Historia eclesiástica indiana*, bk. 3, chap. 45, 2: 146.

    21. Motolinía provided a rich description of the celebration of Corpus Christi in Tlaxcala in 1538, *Historia de los indios*, treat. 1, chap. 15, 192–95. On the development of missionary theater, Fernando Horcasitas, *El teatro nahuatl: épocas novohispana y moderna* (Mexico City: Universidad Nacional Autónoma de México, 1974), especially 71–80; and most recently Burkhart, *Ash Wednesday*.

    22. *Historia de la nación mexicana*, ed. and trans. Charles E. Dibble (Madrid: José Porrúa Turanzas, 1963), 71 and 95 respectively.

    23. *Anales de Tecamachalco*, 41.

    24. Motolinía, *Historia de los indios*, treat. 2, chap. 10, 262.

    25. Motolinía, *Historia de los indios*, 265–66; Constantino Bayle, *El culto del Santísimo in Indias*. Madrid: Consejo Superior de Investigacions Científicas, Instituto Santo Toribio de Mogrovejo, 1951, 183–206.

    26. Motolinía, *Historia de los indios*, treat. 2, chap. 7, 247–48; guidelines to clarify the legitimate status of Indian marriages according to church law were systematically set down by Juan Focher in his *Enchyridion*, and by the Augustinian theologian Alonso de la Vera Cruz in his work *Speculum Coniugiorum* [1556]. On both authors the reader may consult Sergio Ortega Noriega, "Teología novohispana sobre el matrimonio y comportamiento sexuales, 1519–1570," in *De la santidad a la perversión*, ed. Sergio Ortega (Mexico City: Grijalbo, 1986), 19–46; on the *Speculum Coniugiorum*, John T. Noonan Jr., "Marriage in Michoacán," in *First Images of America*, ed. Fredi Chiappelli (Berkeley: University of California Press, 1976), 1: 351–62; on ecclesiastical policy regarding marriage in México, Ragon, *Les Indiens de la découverte*.

27. The minutes from the first ecclesiastical meeting from 1526 explained: "Acerca de la Comunión Sacramental, aunque a el principio se les negó por Neophito, y rudos, despues se les concedio a discrecion de los confesores." Lorenzana, *Concilios provinciales primero y segundo*, 4; also in Mendieta, *Historia eclesiástica indiana*, bk. 3, chap. 45, 2: 146.

28. "Porende, S.A.C. declaramos, que los Ministros puedan administrar este Sacramento a los Indios, y Negros, en quien conocieren, que tienen aparejo, y vieren señales de devocion, y creencia, y deseo de recebirlo, sobre lo qual les encargamos las conciencias, en que no comuniquen indiferentement tan alto Mysterio a todos los recien convertidos, sino hallaren." Lorenzana, *Concilios provinciales primero y segundo*, 138.

29. García Icazbalceta, *Códice franciscano*, 90.

30. García Icazbalceta, *Códice franciscano*, 90

31. "Lo mismo pudiera ser en cuanto a la administración del santísimo sacramento de la Eucaristía a los indios, que tomando el medio de la discreción pudiéramos convenir todos en un parecer, rigiéndonos por la regla de los juristas, que dice: 'Haz diferencia de los tiempos, y concordarás los derechos,' Pues para esto es la discreción, para discernir y considerar diferentemente las cosas, conforme a los tiempos y personas y negocios, y no subirnos a las nubes o arrojarnos a los abismos." Mendieta, *Historia eclesiástica indiana*, bk. 3, chap. 45, 2: 144–45.

32. Mendieta disqualified laymen and priests opposed to administering the Eucharist to the Indians by pointing out that they ignored the languages spoken by the Indians, *Historia eclesiástica indiana*, 145

33. Mendieta, *Historia eclesiástica indiana*, 146.

34. "[H]arto los llamamos, convidamos, y persuadimos, a lo menos a que todos le pidan para cumplir con su obligación, y que el Confesor, despues vea lo que a cada uno le conviene, mas son pocos los que se disponen." Torquemada, *Monarquía indiana*, bk. 16, chap. 21, 3: 187.

35. Torquemada, *Monarquía indiana*, 187.

36. Dávila Padilla, *Historia de la fundación*, 83.

37. Ley, xviiij, *Recopilación de leyes de los Reynos de las Indias*, vol. 1, bk. 1, tit. 1, 7.

38. "Lo que con más fervor predicaban y con más cuidado enseñaban estos grandes ministros del Evangelio era la sagrada Comunión: movidos a que de la misma manera que para vivir no basta nacer, sino que es menester comer: así no le bastará a los indios haber nacido por el bautismo a la vida de gracia, sino que habían menester comer este pan de vida," Grijalva, *Crónica de la orden de N. P. S. Agustín*, 108.

39. Grijalva, *Crónica de la orden de N. P. S. Agustín*, 109.

40. Grijalva, *Crónica de la orden de N. P. S. Agustín*, 109.

41. "Por esto digo que en mi religión aún el día del Bautismo los convidaban a estas bodas procurándoles abrir las ganas con un sermón, en que les proponía el misterio, la necesidad que había en la Comunión, sus efectos y su dulzura; y junto con esto les proponían la disposición necesaria con que se debe llegar," Grijalva, *Crónica de la orden de N. P. S. Agustín*, 110.

42. Grijalva, *Crónica de la orden de N. P. S. Agustín*, 453–54.

43. If sinners of this kind repented, the confessor could determine whether to admit them to Communion out of the public sight: "De tal manera, que despues de la secreta penitencia, podían ser admitidos a la Eucharistía en secreto, no en público, sino uviesse hecho pública penitencia, por el escándalo," Pedro de Agurto, *Tractado, de que se deven administrar los Sacramentos de la Sancta Eucharistia, y Extrema unción: a los indios de esta nueva España* (Mexico City: Antonio de Espinosa, 1573), 14v. Agurto's discussion of public sinners, which revolves around the notion of infamy, opens up an important set of questions regarding the use of European legal categories such as honor in a cross-cultural context.

44. An interesting example of Agurto's legal approach can be seen in his rejection of suspicion as a basis to deny the Eucharist to the Indians, an issue closely related to his discussion on the procedure to prove whether someone might be a serious sinner, Agurto, *Tractado*, 42v–44v.

45. "Pues querer dezir, que los Yndios son desta manera peccadores para los poder negar communion, seria manifiesto falso testimonio, que se les impondria," Agurto, *Tractado*, 15r.

46. Agurto, *Tractado*, 29r.

47. Agurto, *Tractado*, 22r.

48. Agurto, *Tractado*, 22v–23r.

49. "Quanto mas no que ya no se les puede convenir este titulo de nuevos en la fee, porque ya los mas dellos fueron baptizados en su infancia, como lo fuimos nosotros: y si ay algunos que adultos se baptizaron, ha mas de trynta o quarenta años," Agurto, *Tractado*, 44v–45r.

50. Agurto, *Tractado*, 45v–46r.

51. Agurto, *Tractado*, 58v.

52. "Item. Atento a que esta gente es nueva en la fé, y conforme al Apostol, a los nuevos en ella se les ha de dar leche espiritual y no mantenimiento de que usan los mayores: S.S. ap. Mandamos que por el presente, hasta que estén más instruidos y arraigados en la fé y conozcan mejore los misterios y sacramentos, solamente se les administren los sacramentos del baptismo, penitencia y matrimonio." Vargas Ugarte, *Concilios Limenses*, vol. 1, const. 14, 14.

53. *Concilios Limenses*, vol. 1, const. 58, 186.

54. *Concilios Limenses*, vol. 1, const. 59, 186–87.

55. For a recent appraisal of Acosta's overall influence in the council, Francesco Leonardo Lisi, *El Tercer Concilio Limense y la aculturación de los indígenas sudamericanos* (Salamanca: Universidad de Salamanca, 1990), 57–83. Back in Spain in 1587, Acosta worked on the edition of the Third Provincial Church Council, which was published in Salamanca in 1590.

56. Lisi, *El Tercer Concilio*, actio secunda, 138. This explanation, which faults the Indians for their lukewarm commitment to Christianity, contrasts with the reasons advanced to account for the refusal of the viaticum. In this case the council found that the priests were to blame, led by negligence or a misplaced zeal, p. 136.

57. Lisi, *El Tercer Concilio*, actio secunda, 136. On the concept of "miserable" in Spanish legislation, P. Castañeda Delgado, "La condición miserable del

indio y sus privilegios," *Anuario de Estudios Americanos* (Sevilla) 28 (1971): 245–335.

58. Acosta, *De procuranda,* bk. 6, chap. 8, 2: 390. Agurto touched on this issue only briefly, *Tractado,* 28r–28v.

59. Acosta, *De procuranda* bk. 6, chap. 7, 2: 384. Francisco de Osuna reminded his readers of the divine origin of receiving Communion in stark terms: "Sino paramientes que el derecho divino te dio Christo para rescebir su cuerpo quando te dispusiesses ni aun el papa te lo puede quitar," *Gracioso combite,* M2v.

60. Agurto, *Tractado,* 6r–12v.

61. Torquemada, *Monarquía indiana,* bk. 16, chap. 20, 3: 186–87.

62. "Si enim sacramenti cuiusque necessitas ex ipsius significatione intelligenda est." Acosta, *De procuranda,* bk. 6, chap. 7, 2: 386.

63. Acosta, *De procuranda,* 2: 386.

64. Those who receive the sacrament spiritually are "aquellos que recibiendo con el deseo este celeste pan, perciben con la viveza de su fe que obra por amor, su fruto y utilidades." *El Sacrosanto y Ecuménico Concilio de Trento,* session 13, 168–69. The church distinguished this group from the sinners who actually receive the sacrament and those who do it both sacramentally and spiritually. The so-called spiritual Communion posed to the theologians a new challenge when it came to determining whether its efficacy equaled or differed from the efficacy of sacramental Communion.

65. Acosta, *De procuranda,* bk. 6, chap. 9, 2: 400; see chap. 1.

66. Acosta, *De procuranda,* bk. 6, chap. 9, 2: 406.

67. Llaguno, *La personalidad jurídica,* 140–42.

68. "[Y] no se da por mérito sino por remedio y medicina de los que los resciben como deben; de la cual medicina e ayuda e socorro no menos nescecidad tienen los flacos y enfermos, que los sanos y perfectos." García Icazbalceta, *Don Fray Juan de Zumárraga,* 3: 175–76.

69. Acosta, *De procuranda,* bk. 6, chap. 10, 2: 416.

70. John W. O'Malley, *The First Jesuits* (Cambridge: Harvard University Press, 1993), 152–57.

71. For the congregations in Italy, see Michael W. Maher, "How the Jesuits Used Their Congregations to Promote Frequent Communion," in *Confraternities and Catholic Reform in Italy, France, and Spain,* ed. John Patrick Donnelly and Michael Maher (Kirksville, MO: Thomas Jefferson University Press, 1999), 75–95.

72. O'Malley, *The First Jesuits,* 152; Sara T. Nalle, "Literacy and Culture in Early Modern Castile," *Past and Present* 125 (November 1989), 85. Known in Spain under the title *Contemptus mundi,* this work was translated into Spanish by Fr. Luis de Granada in 1536, Bataillon, *Erasmo y España,* 48.

73. On Osuna and the literature on frequent Communion that appeared after the publication of his treatise, Fidel de Ros, *Le Père François D'Osuna* (Paris: Gabriel Beauchesne, 1936), 219–26.

74. Osuna, *Gracioso combite,* Mv, ss. Osuna recommended Communion every Sunday: "La conclusion deste punto esta en que todo devoto christiano aunque biva en el mundo: o en el palacio se deve disponer para comulgar cada domingo aunque sienta en si muy malas inclinaciones: y aunque peque mortal-

mente no dexe de luchar consigo mismo y levantarse del peccado: y disponerse creyendo que quando se llega a la sagrada comunion va a todo el remedio de nuestra salud donde si usa recebir al señor," M6v.

75. The *Gracioso combite* saw at least five editions between 1530 and 1554, Ros, *Le Père François D'Osuna*, 169.

76. Fernández del Castillo, *Libros y libreros*, 477.

77. "Porque aunque no haya precepto para que los adultos comulguen más de una vez al año, deben, por sergratos a tan gran beneficio y por otros fines, frecuentar más el uso de este sacramento, como lo hacen los hombres que tienen cuidado de sus almas y salvación." Carranza de Miranda, *Comentarios sobre el catecismo christiano*, 2: 225.

78. J. M. De Bujanda, "Los libros italianos en el Índice Español de 1559," *Bibliothèque D'Humanisme et Renaissance* (1972): 102–3.

79. "Grandes bienes se pierden por nuestra tibia vida; y grandes peccados se remediarian si se frequentassen las comuniones," Zumárraga, *Doctrina cristiana*, 244.

80. Zumárraga, *Doctrina cristiana*, 248.

81. On the term "alumbrado" see Asensio, "El erasmismo y las corrientes espirituales afines," 71–72. The bibliography of the alumbrados is vast and widely divergent in opinions as to the spiritual sources of the movement.

82. De Bujanda, *Index de L'Inquisition Espagnole, 1551, 1554, 1559,* 464.

83. "Pues siguiendo la doctrina de estos dos santos, Santo Tomás y S. Augustín, pareeceme gran temeridad juzgar ni condenar a los que comulgan muchas veces ni a los que dejan de comulgar; sino avisar a los unos y a los otros de los frutos de este sacramento," Carranza de Miranda, *Comentarios sobre el catecismo christiano*, 2: 228.

84. See for example, Ponze de la Fuente, *Suma*, 229–37; and his *Catezismo cristiano* in the same volume, pp. 347–50.

85. This concern was still voiced in the seventeenth century by, for example, the archbishop of Mexico Juan Palafox y Mendoza, who declared that there were up to sixteen different manuals for the administration of the sacraments in use in Mexico, *Manual de los Santos Sacramentos conforme al ritual de Paulo V* (Mexico City: Diego Fernández de León, 1691), 14v.

86. Motolinía, *Historia de los indios*, treat. 1, chap. 2, 127. The whole section of chap. 2 brings together the Mexican's practice of theophagy and anthropophagy and Christian Communion, tracing an arc that begins with the eating of hallucinogenic mushrooms (*tonacatlatl,* flesh of the god), which Motolinía compared disparagingly with the eating of sacrificial victims.

87. On the documentary sources referring to *tzoalli,* the dough made of amaranth seed used for the images of Huitzilopochtli, see Elizabeth H. Boone, *Incarnations of the Aztec Supernatural: The Image of Huitzilopochtli in Mexico and Europe,* Transactions of the Philosophical Society 79, pt. 2. (Philadelphia: American Philosophical Society, 1989), 34–40.

88. Sahagún, *Historia general*, bk. 3, chap. 1, 1: 205.

89. Durán, *Historia de las Indias,* 1: 17.

90. Durán, *Historia de las Indias,* 1: 119.

91. Durán, *Historia de la Indias,* 1: 165.

92. Two verbs given by Molina capture the idea of representation and replacement: *ixiptlayotia* ("sustituir a otro en su lugar") and *yxiptlati* ("asistir en lugar de otro, o representar persona en farsa"). On the ixiptlas as the key to understanding the ritual life of the Mexicas and their notions of the sacred, see Clendinnen's beautifully crafted speculation in *Aztecs*, 236–63.

93. According to Sahagún the lord was given the "heart" of Huitzilopochtli, while the rest was distributed. Sahagún also referred to the body of the god. Sahagún's Spanish version is not free of ambiguities: "Y el corazón de Huitzilopochtli tomaban para el señor o rey, y todo el cuerpo y pedazos que eran como huesos del dicho Huitzilopochtli en dos partes lo repartían entre los naturales de México y Tlatilulco," *Historia general*, bk. 3, chap. 1, 1: 204–5. Durán described how the youngsters offered tzoalli in the shape of bones to the image of Huitzilopochtli, adding: "A esta masa en figura de huesos llamaban "los huesos de Huitzilopochtli y la carne," *Historia de las Indias*, 1: 29. It is important to point out that a cloak of bones was among the visual attributes used to represent Huitzilopochtli, Boone, *Incarnations*, 8.

94. The drive to visualize the sacred—to investigate visually the economy of the sacred by reordering the natural and material world—was a feature of Nahua religion early noted by the Spaniards. Sahagún's version of the *Book of Wisdom* directly addressed this issue. Outside the religious domain, Spanish commentators similarly remarked that on the Nahuas' superb skills to reproduce objects.

95. Durán may be one of a few writers to have called attention to this particular sensorial dimension of the ritual experience of the Nahuas and to have concluded that pleasure derived from food—as well as the smelling of flowers—was part of that experience. This less dramatic aspect of Nahua religious life was left unexplored in Clendinnen's interpretation on the aesthetic experience as an organizing principle of Nahua rituals.

Conclusion

1. This proposition was elaborated and further developed by Jacques Derrida, first in a reading engaged with the work of Marcel Mauss and other anthropologists and later in direct conversation with theology, Derrida, *The Gift of Death*, trans. David Wills (Chicago: University of Chicago Press, 1992). The import of this problematic on the interpretation of cross-cultural interactions was explored by David Murray, *Indian Giving. Economies of Power in Indian-White Exchanges* (Amherst: University of Massachusetts Press, 2000). Natalie Z. Davis recently called attention to the gaps between the Catholic perspective on the sacrifice of the Mass and the notion of gift giving that prevailed in sixteenth-century French society, *The Gift in Sixteenth-Century France* (Madison: University of Wisconsin Press, 2000), 105–10.

2. A study of how medieval and early modern writers thought about these issues can be found in Cary J. Nederman, *Worlds of Difference: European Discourses on Toleration, c. 1100–c. 1550* (University Park: Pennsylvania State University Press, 2000).

Glossary

Alcaldía: mayoralty

Alguacil: staff bearer, constable

Audiencia: court and governing body under the jurisdiction of the viceroy

Cabecera: head town

Cabildo: municipal council

Cacique: local lord

Cartilla: primer

Cédula: a royal order

Custodio: *custos,* the administrative officer of a custody in a religious order

Encomendero: holder of an *encomienda*

Encomienda: Royal grant that allowed Spanish beneficiaries to receive tribute from Indians

Letrado: University graduate with degrees in canon or civil law

Macehual: commoner

Patronazgo or Patronato: Royal Patronage; authority granted by the papacy to the King of Spain to supervise ecclesiastical affairs throughout his territories

Procurador: proxy, legal representative

Sujeto: a subject town or community

Bibliography

Primary Sources

Acosta, Joseph de. *Historia natural y moral de las Indias* [1590]. Ed. Edmundo O'Gorman. Mexico City: Fondo de Cultura Económica, 1962.

———. *De procuranda indorum salute* [1588]. 2 vols. Madrid: Consejo Superior de Investigaciones Científicas, 1987.

Actas de cabildo de la ciudad de México. Ed. Ignacio Bejarano. Paleography by Manuel Orozco y Berra. 12 vols. Mexico City, 1889–1900.

Agurto, Pedro de. *Tractado, de que se deven administrar los Sacramentos de la Sancta Eucharistia, y Extrema unción: a los indios de esta nueva España.* Mexico City: Antonio de Espinosa, 1573.

Alcocer, Francisco de. *Confessionario breve y muy provechoso para los penitentes.* Salamanca: Juan de Canova, 1568.

Ambrose. *Omnia Opera.* 4 vols. Basilea, 1527.

"Anales de San Gregorio Acapulco, 1520–1606." *Tlalocan* 3 (1949–57): 103–41.

Anales de Tecamachalco, 1398–1590. Ed. Eustaquio Celestino Solís and Luis Reyes García. Mexico City: Fondo de Cultura Económica, 1992.

Anales de Tlatelolco y Códice de Tlatelolco. Ed. Heinrich Berlin, with commentary by Robert H. Barlow. Mexico City: Antigua Librería Robredo, 1948.

Anthonino de Florencia. *La summa de confession llamada defecerunt de fray Anthonino arçobispo de florencia del orden de los predicadores. En romance.* Salamanca: Hans Gieser, [1500?].

Anunciación, Juan de la. *Doctrina christiana muy cumplida donde se contiene la exposición de todo lo necesario para doctrinar a los yndios, y administralles los Sanctos Sacramentos.* Mexico City: Pedro Balli, 1575.

Arte para bien confesar. Zaragoza, [ca. 1500?].

Assadourian, Carlos Sempat. "*Memoriales* de Fray Gerónimo de Mendieta." *Historia Mexicana* 37, no.3 (1988): 357–422.

Azpilcueta, Martín de. *Enchiridion sive Manuale Confessariorum at Poenitentium.* Romae: Georgij Ferraij, 1584.

Ballesteros Gaibrois, Manuel, ed. *Papeles de Indias.* 2 vols. Madrid: Mestre, 1947–48.

Bautista, Juan. *Confessionario en lengua mexicana y castellana.* Mexico City: Melchior Ocharte, 1599.

————. *Advertencias para los confessores de los naturales.* Mexico City: Pedro Ocharte, 1600.

Bede. *De Tabernaculo, De Templo, In Ezram et Neeiam,* Corpus Christianorum, Series Latina, vol. 119A. Turnholt: Brepols, 1969.

Benavente, Toribio de (Motolinía). *Memoriales.* Ed. Edmundo O' Gorman. Mexico City: Universidad Nacional Autónoma de México, 1971.

————. *Historia de los indios de la Nueva España.* Ed. Georges Baudot. Madrid: Castalia, 1985.

Biblia Sacra Iuxta Vulgatam Versionem. Stuttgart: Deutsche Bibelgesellschaft, 1983.

Bonet, Juan Pablo, *Reducción de las letras y arte para enseñar a hablar a los mudos.* Madrid: Francisco Beltrán, 1930.

Boniface. *The Letters of Saint Boniface.* Trans. Ephraim Emerton. New York: Octagon Books, 1973.

Carranza de Miranda, Bartolomé. *Comentarios sobre el catecismo cristiano.* Ed. José I. Tellechea. 2 vols. Idígoras. Madrid: BAC, 1972.

Cartas de Indias. 2 vols. Madrid: Biblioteca de Autores Españoles, 1974.

Cartas de religiosos de Nueva España, 1539–1594. Ed. Joaquín García Icazbalceta. Mexico City: Salvador Chávez Hayhoe, 1941.

Cassian, John. *Conlationes XIIII.* Ed. Michael Petschenig. Corpus scriptorum ecclesiasticorum latinorum, vol. 13. Vindobonae: apud C. Geroldi filium, 1886.

Castañega, Fr. Martín de. *Tratado de las supersticiones y hechicerías* [1529]. Madrid: Sociedad de Bibliófilos Españoles, 1946.

Catecismo del Santo Concilio de Trento para los párrocos. Madrid: Imprenta Real, 1785.

Catherine of Siena. *The Dialogue.* Ed. Suzanne Noffke. New York: Paulist Press, 1980.

Ciruelo, Pedro. *Reprovación de las supersticiones y hechizerías.* Ed. Alva V. Ebersole. Valencia: Albatros Hispanofila, 1978.

Codex Aubin. Historia de la nación mexicana: reproducción del Códice de 1576 (Códice Aubin). Ed. and trans. Charles E. Dibble. Madrid: José Porrúa Turanzas, 1963.

Colección Canónica Hispana. Ed. Gonzalo Martínez Diez and Félix Rodríguez. 5 vols. Madrid: Consejo Superior de Investigaciones Científicas, 1966–92.

Colección de documentos inéditos, relativos al descubrimiento, conquista y organización de las antiguas posesiones españolas de América y Oceanía, sacados de los archivos del reino, y muy especialmente del de Indias. 42 vols. Madrid, 1864–84.

Colección de documentos inéditos relativos al descubrimiento, conquista y organización de las antiguas posesiones españolas de ultramar. Madrid: "Sucesores de Rivadeneyra," 25 vols. Madrid, 1885–1932.

Concilium Mexicanum Provinciale III. Mexico City: Josephi Antonii de Hortas, 1770.

Córdoba, Pedro de. *Doctrina cristiana para instrucción y información de los indios, por manera de historia* [1544]. Ciudad Trujillo: Universidad de Santo Domingo, 1945.

Córdova, Juan de. *Relación de la Fundación, Capítulos y Elecciones, que se han Tenido en esta Provincia de Santiago de ésta Nueva España, de la Orden de Predicadores de Santo Domingo. 1569*. Mexico City: Vargas Rea, 1944.

Covarrubias, Sebastián de. *Tesoro de la lengua castellana o española*. Ed. Martín de Riquer. Madrid, 1611; Barcelona: Horta, I.E., 1943.

Cruz y Moya, Juan José de la. *Historia de la Santa y Apostólica provincia de Santiago de Predicadores de México en la Nueva España*. Ed. Gabriel Saldívar. 2 vols. Mexico City: Librería de Manuel Porrúa, 1955.

Cuevas, Mariano, ed. *Documentos inéditos del siglo XVI para la historia de México*. 2nd ed. Mexico City: Porrúa, 1975.

Dávila Padilla, Fr. Agustín. *Historia de la fundación y discurso de la Provincia de Santiago de México, de la Orden de Predicadores* [1596]. Mexico City: Academia Literaria, 1955.

Da Vinci, Leonardo. *Treatise on Painting [Codex Urbinas latinus 1270]*. Trans. A. Philip McMahon. 2 vols. Princeton: Princeton University Press, 1956.

De Bujanda, J. M., ed. *Index de L'Inquisition Espagnole, 1551, 1554, 1559*. Centre d'Études de la Renaissance. Èditions de l'Université de Sherbrooke/Librairie Droz, 1984.

Doctrina cristiana en lengua española y mexicana por los Religiosos de la Orden de Santo Domingo. México: Juan Pablos, 1548. Madrid: Ediciones Cultura Hispánica, 1944.

Duns Scotus, Johannes. *Quaestiones in Librum Quartum Sententiarum*. In *Opera Omnia*, 22 vols. Parisiis: Apud Ludovicum Vivès, Bibliopolam Editorem, 1894.

Durán, Fr. Diego. *Historia de las Indias de Nueva España e Islas de la Tierra Firme*. Ed. Angel Ma. Garibay. Mexico City: Porrúa, 1967.

Erasmus. *Obras escogidas*. Madrid: Aguilar, 1964.

Escobar, Olmedo Armando, ed. *Proceso, tormento y muerte del Cazonci, último gran señor de los tarascos por Nuño de Guzmán, 1530*. Morelia: Michoacán, 1997.

Fernández del Castillo, Francisco, ed. *Libros y libreros en el siglo XVI* [1914]. Mexico City: Fondo de Cultura Económica, 1982.

Focher, Juan. *Itinerario del misionero en América* [1574]. Ed. Antonio Eguiluz. Madrid: Librería General Victoriano Suárez, 1960.

———. *Manual del bautismo de adultos y del matrimonio de los bautizandos (Enchiridion Baptismi Adultorum et Matrimonii Baptizandorum)*. Trans. José Pascual Guzmán de Alba. México: Frente de Afirmación Hispanista, A.C., 1997.

Friedberg, Emil, ed. *Decretum Magistri Gratiani, Corpus iuris canonici*. 1. Graz: Akademische Druck-u Verlagsanstalt, 1955.

Gante, Pedro de. *Cartas de Pedro de Gante*. Ed. Fidel J. Chauvet. México: Provincia del Santo Evangelio de México. 1951.

García Icazbalceta, Joaquín, ed. *Códice franciscano, siglo XVI*. Mexico City: Salvador Chávez Hayhoe, 1941.

———, ed. *Códice Mendieta* [1892]. 2 vols. Mexico City: Edmundo Aviña Levy, 1971.

García Pimentel, Luis, ed. *Descripción del Arzobispado de México hecha en 1570 y otros documentos.* Mexico City: José Joaquín Terrazas e Hijas, 1897.

Gerson, Jean. *Tripartito del Christianisimo y consolatorio doctor Juan Gerson de doctrina Christiana: a qualquiera muy provechosa* [1544]. Mexico City: Libros de México, 1949.

González de Cosío, Francisco, ed. *Un cedulario mexicano del siglo XVI.* Mexico City: Frente de Afirmación Hispanista, 1973.

Granada, Fr. Luis de. *Obras de Fr. Luis de Granada.* 3 vols. Madrid: Biblioteca de Autores Españoles, 1944.

Grijalva, Juan de. *Crónica de la orden de N. P. S. Agustín en las provincias de la Nueva España.* Mexico City: Porrúa, 1985.

Hernáez, Francisco J. *Colección de bulas, breves y otros documentos.* 2 vols. Bruselas: Imprenta de Alfredo Vromant, 1879; Vaduz, 1964.

Hernández, Francisco. *Nova plantarum, animalium et mineralium mexicanorum historia.* Romae: Vitali Mascardi, 1651.

Konetzke, Richard, comp. *Colección de documentos para la historia de la formación social de Hispanoamérica, 1493–1810.* 3 vols. Madrid: Consejo Superior de Investigaciones Científicas, 1953.

Las Casas, Bartolomé de. *Apologética historia sumaria.* Ed. Edmundo O'Gorman. 2 vols. Mexico City: Universidad Nacional Autónoma de México, 1967.

Ledesma, Bartolomé de. *De septem novae legis sacramentis summarium.* Mexico City: Antonio de Espinosa, 1566.

León, Martín de. *Manual breve y forma para administrar los santos Sacramentos a los Indios universalmente.* Mexico City: María de Espinosa, 1614.

Liber de vera et falsa poenitentia. Vol. 40 in *Patrologia cursus completus,* ed. J. P. Migne, Series latina, 1113–30. Paris, 1844–64.

López Medel, Tomás. *De los tres elementos. Tratado sobre la naturaleza y el hombre del Nuevo Mundo.* Ed. Berta Ares Queija. Madrid: Alianza, 1990.

Lorenzana y Buitrón, Francisco Antonio. *Concilios provinciales primero y segundo celebrados en la muy noble y leal ciudad de México.* Mexico City: Joseph Antonio de Hogal, 1769.

———. *Concilium Mexicanum Provinciale III.* Mexico City, 1770.

Luther, Martin. *Works.* Ed. Jaroslav Pelikan. American edition. 55 vols. Saint Louis: Concordia Pub. House/ Philadelphia: Fortress Press, 1955.

Madrigal, Alonso de (El Tostado). *Confessional del Tostado.* Logroño: Miguel de Eguia, 1529.

Manual de confessores, e penitentes em ho qual breve e particular, e muy verdadeyramente se decidem, e declaram quasi todas as duvidas, e casos, que nas confissoes soen occorrer acerca dos peccados, absoluiçoes, restituyçoes, e censuras: Composto por hum religioso da ordem de Sam Francisco da provincia da piedade. Coimbra, 1549.

Manual de los Santos Sacramentos conforme al ritual de Paulo V. México: Diego Fernández de León, 1691.

Medina, Bartolomé de. *Instrucción de como se ha de administrar el sacramento de la penitencia.* Alcalá: Iván Gracián, 1591.

Medina, Juan de. *De Penitentia, Restitutione & Contractibus.* Ingolstadii: Davidi Sartorii, 1581. Reprint, Hants: Gregg Press Limited, 1967.

Mendieta, Fr. Gerónimo de. *Historia eclesiástica indiana.* 4 vols. Mexico City: Salvador Chávez Hayhoe, 1945.

Molanus. *Traité des saintes images.* Ed. François Boespflug, Olivier Christin, and Benoît Tassel. 2 vols. Paris: Cerf, 1996.

Molina, Alonso de. *Vocabulario en lengua castellana y mexicana y mexicana y castellana* [1571]. Mexico City: Porrúa, 1977.

———. *Confesionario mayor en lengua mexicana y castellana.* Int. R. Moreno. México: Antonio de Espinosa, 1569; México: Universidad Nacional Autónoma de México, 1984.

Mota y Escobar, Alonso de la. "Memoriales del Obispo de Tlaxcala Fray Alonso de la Mota y Escobar." *Anales del Instituto Nacional de Antropología e Historia* 1 (1945): 196.

Muñoz Camargo, Diego. *Descripción de la ciudad y provincia de Tlaxcala.* Ed. René Acuña. Mexico City: Instituto de Investigaciones Filológicas, Universidad Autónoma de México, 1981.

———. *Historia de Tlaxcala* (Ms. 210 de la Biblioteca Nacional de París). Int. Luis Reyes García. Tlaxcala: Gobierno del Estado de Tlaxcala/Centro de Investigaciones y Estudios en Antropología Social, Universidad Autónoma de Tlaxcala, 1998.

Olmos, Andrés de. *Tratado de hechicerías y sortilegios.* Ed. Georges Baudot. Mexico City: Estudios Mesoamericanos, serie 2, 1979.

Onis, Carlos de, ed. *Las polémicas de Juan Bautista Muñoz.* Madrid: José Porrúa Turanzas, 1984.

Osuna, Francisco de. *Gracioso combite de las gracias del sancto sacramento del altar.* Sevilla, 1543.

———. *Tercer Abecedario Espiritual.* Vol. 2 of *Místicos franciscanos españoles.* 2 vols. Toledo, 1527; Madrid: Biblioteca de Autores Cristianos, 1998.

Palencia, Alfonso de. *Universal Vocabulario en Latín y en Romance.* 2 vols. Seville, 1490. Madrid: Comisión Permanente de la Asociación de Academias de la Lengua Española, 1967.

Peter Lombard. *Magistri Petri Lombardi Parisiensis episcopi Sententiae in IV libris distinctae.* 2 vols. Grottaferrata (Romae): Editiones Colegii S. Bonaventurae Ad Claras Aquas, 1971–81.

Ponze de la Fuente, C. *Suma de doctrina cristiana.* Barcelona: Librería de Diego Gómez Flores, 1983.

Puga, Vasco de. *Provisiones, cédulas, instrucciones para el gobierno de la Nueva España.* México: Pedro Ocharte, 1563; Madrid: Cultura Hispánica, 1945.

Recopilación de leyes de los Reynos de las Indias. 3 vols. Madrid: Viuda de Joaquín Ibarra [1791]. Reprint, Madrid: Centro de Estudios Políticos y Constitucionales y el Boletín Oficial del Estado, 1998.

Remesal, Fr. Antonio de. *Historia general de las Indias Occidentales, y particular de la gobernación de Chiapa y Guatemala.* Ed. Carmelo Sáenz de Santa María. 2 vols. Madrid: Biblioteca de Autores Españoles, 1964–66.

Ripa, Cesare. *Iconologia.* Venice: N. Pezzana, 1669.

Rocha, Diego Andrés de. *El origen de los indios* [1681]. Ed. J. Alcina Franch. Madrid: Historia 16, 1988.

Román y Zamora, Jerónimo. *República de Indias* [1575]. 2 vols. Madrid: Victoriano Suárez, 1897.

Ruiz de Alarcón, Hernando. *Tratado de las supersticiones y costumbres gentílicas que oy viven entre los indios naturales de esta Nueva España. 1629. Vol. 2. Tratado de las idolatrías, supersticiones, dioses, ritos, hechicerías y otras costumbres gentílicas de las razas aborígenes de México,* ed. Francisco del Paso y Troncoso, 2 vols. Mexico City: Fuente Cultural, 1953.

El Sacrosanto y Ecuménico Concilio de Trento traducido al idioma castellano por Don Ignacio López de Ayala. Madrid: Imprenta Real, 1785.

Sahagún, Bernardino de. *Florentine Codex: General History of the Things of New Spain.* Ed. and trans. Charles Dibble and Arthur J. O. Anderson. 12 vols. Santa Fe: School of American Research and the University of Utah, 1950–82.

———. *Psalmodia Christiana* [1583]. Trans. Arthur J. O. Anderson. Salt Lake City: University of Utah Press, 1983.

———. *Coloquios y doctrina cristiana.* Ed. Miguel León-Portilla. Mexico City: Universidad Nacional Autónoma de México, 1986.

———. *Historia general de las cosas de Nueva España,* 2 vols. Madrid: Alianza, 1988.

Sánchez, J. *Doctrina cristiana del P. Jerónimo de Ripalda e intento bibliográfico de la misma. Años 1591–1900.* Madrid: Imprenta Alemana, 1909.

Suárez de Peralta, Juan. *Tratado del descubrimiento de las Indias* [1589]. Mexico City: Consejo Nacional para la Cultura y las Artes, 1990.

Thomas Aquinas. *Opera Omnia.* 34 vols. Parisiis: Apud Ludovicum Vivès, Bibliopolam Editorem, 1871–80.

———. *Quaestiones disputatae.* 2 vols. Taurini: Marietti, 1953.

———. *Summa theologiae.* Ed. Petri Caramello. 3 vols. Taurini: Marietti, 1956.

———. *Summa theologiae.* 61 vols. Blackfriars, NY: McGraw Hill, 1964–81.

Tira de Tepechpan. Ed. Xavier Noguez. Mexico City: Biblioteca Enciclopédica del Estado de México, 1978.

Tommasso Di Vio (Cajetan). *Opuscula Omnia.* 3 vols. Lugduni: Officina Iuntarum/Hildesheim, 1587; Hildesheim: Georg Olms, 1995.

Torquemada, Juan de. *Monarquía indiana* [1615]. Int. Miguel León-Portilla. 3 vols. México: Porrúa, 1986.

Valadés, Diego. *Retórica cristiana* [1579]. Int. Esteban J. Palomera. Trans. Tarsicio Herrera Zapién. Mexico City: Fondo de Cultura Económica, 1989.

Van Haeften, Benedictus. *Schola cordis sive aversi a Deo ad eundem reductio et instructio.* Antwerp, 1629.

Vargas Ugarte, R., ed. *Concilios Limenses (1551–1772).* 3 vols. Lima: 1951–54.

Vitoria, Francisco de. *Comentarios a la Secunda secundae de Santo Tomás.* Ed. Vicente Beltrán de Heredia. 6 vols. Salamanca: Biblioteca de Teólogos Españoles, 1932.

———. *Relectio de Indiis o libertad de los indios.* Ed. L. Pereña and J. M. Pérez Prendes. Madrid: Consejo Superior de Investigaciones Científicas, 1967.

————. *Political Writings*. Ed. Anthony Pagden. Cambridge: Cambridge University Press, 1991.

Yebra, Melchior de. *Libro llamado Refugium infirmorum*. Sevilla, 1593.

Zumárraga, Juan de. *Doctrina breve muy provechosa de las cosas que pertenecen a la fe catholica y a nuestra cristiandad en estilo llano para comun inteligencia*. México: 1544; *The Doctrina Breve*, New York: United States Catholic Historical Society, 1928.

————. *Doctrina cristiana: mas cierta y verdadera para gente sin erudicion y letras: en que se contiene el catecismo o información para indios con todo lo principal y necessario que el cristiano debe saber y obrar*. México: 1546.

————. *Regla cristiana breve* [1547]. Ed. José Almoina. Mexico City: Editorial Jus, 1951.

Secondary Sources

Acker, Geertrui van. "El humanismo cristiano en México: los tres flamencos." In *Historia de la evangelización de América. Simposio Internacional, Ciudad del Vaticano, 11–14 de mayo de 1992*, coord. José Escudero Imbert, 795–819. Ciudad del Vaticano: Libreria Editrice Vaticana, 1992.

Akeley, T. C. *Christian Initiation in Spain*. London: Darton, Longman and Todd, 1967.

Anawalt, Patricia R. *Indian Clothing before Cortés*. Norman and London: University of Oklahoma Press, 1981.

Anciaux, Paul. *La Théologie du Sacrament de Pénitence au XIIe siècle*. Louvain: É. Nauwelaerts, 1949.

Andrés, Melquíades. *La teología española en el siglo XVI*. 2 vols. Madrid: Biblioteca de Autores Cristianos, 1976.

Artigas, Juan B. *Metztitlán, Hidalgo: arquitectura del siglo XVI*. Mexico City: Gobierno del Estado de Hidalgo/Universidad Nacional Autónoma de México, 1996.

Asad, Talal. *Genealogies of Religion. Discipline and Reasons of Power in Christianity and Islam*. Baltimore: Johns Hopkins University Press, 1993

Asensio, Eugenio. "El erasmismo y las corrientes espirituales afines. Conversos, franciscanos, italianizantes." *Revista de Filología Española* 36 (1952): 31–99.

Azoulai, Martine. *Las péchés du Noveau Monde*. París: Albin Michel, 1993.

Bainton, Roland H. "The Paraphrases of Erasmus." *Archiv für Reformationsgeschichte* 57 (1966): 67–76.

————. *Erasmus of Christendom*. New York: Charles Scribner's Sons, 1969.

Barasch, Moshe. *Gestures of Despair in Medieval and Early Renaissance Art*. New York: New York University Press, 1976.

————. "The Crying Face." In *Imago Hominis: Studies in the Language of Art*, 85–99. Vienna: IRSA, 1991.

Bataillon, Marcel. "El 'Enchiridion' y la 'Paraclesis' en México." In *El enquiridión o manual del caballero cristiano*, ed. Dámaso Alonso, 527–34. Madrid: S. Aguirre, 1932.

———. *Erasmo y España. Estudios sobre la historia espiritual del siglo XVI.* Trans. Antonio Alatorre. Mexico City: Fondo de Cultura Económica, 1966.

Baticle, Jeannine. *Zurbarán.* New York: Metropolitan Museum of Art, 1987.

Baudot, G. *Utopia e historia en México. Los primeros cronistas de la civilización mexicana (1520–1569).* Madrid: Espasa Calpe, 1983.

———. "La 'conspiración' franciscana contra la primera Audiencia de México." In *La pugna franciscana por México,* 37–58. Mexico City: Alianza Editorial Mexicana, 1990.

Bayle, Constantino. "La comunión entre los indios americanos."*Missionalia hispánica* (Madrid) 1 (1944): 13–72.

———. *El culto del santisimo Indias.* Madrid: Consejo Superior de Investigaciones Científicas, Instituto Santo Toribio de Mogrorejo, 1951.

Beltrán de Heredia, V. *Las corrientes de espiritualidad entre los dominicos de Castilla durante la primera mitad del siglo XVI.* Salamanca, 1941.

Berthe, Jean-Pierre. "Les franciscains de la province mexicaine du Saint Évangile en 1570: un catalogue de Fray Jerónimo de Mendieta." In *Enquêtes sur l'Amérique Moyenne. Mélanges offerts à Guy Stresser-Péan,* ed. Dominique Michelet, 213–34. México: Instituto Nacional de Antropología e Historia/Centre d'Études Mexicaines et Centraméricaines, 1989.

Bezler, Francis. *Les pénitentiels espagnols. Contribution a l'étude de la civilisation de l'Espagne chrétienne du haut moyen âge.* Münster: Aschendorff, 1994.

Boone, Elizabeth H. *Incarnations of the Aztec Supernatural: The Image of Huitzilopochtli in Mexico and Europe.* Transactions of the Philosophical Society 79, pt. 2. Philadelphia: American Philosophical Society, 1989.

Borah, Woodrow. *Justice by Insurance. The General Indian Court of Colonial Mexico and the Legal Aides of the Half-Real.* Berkeley: University of California Press, 1983.

Borobio, Dionisio. "Los teólogos salmantinos ante el problema bautismal en la evangelización de América (s. XVI)." *Salmanticensis* 33 (1986): 176–206.

Boronat y Barrachina, Pascual. *Los moriscos españoles y su expulsión.* 2 vols. Valencia: Imprenta de Francisco Vives y Mora, 1901.

Bossy, John. "The Social History of Confession in the Age of Reformation." *Transactions of the Royal Historical Society,* 5th ser., 25 (1975), 21–38.

Bouhot, Jean-Paul. "Explications du rituel baptismal a l'époque carolingienne." *Revue de études augustiniennes.* 24 (1978): 278–301.

Boularand, Ephrem. "Crainte." In *Dictionnaire de Spiritualité,* 2463–2511. París: Beauchesne, 1984.

Braeckmans, Louis. *Confession et communion au moyen âge et au concile de Trente.* Gembloux: Éditions J. Duculot, 1971.

Brown, D. Catherine. *Pastor and Laity in the Theology of Jean Gerson.* Cambridge: Cambridge University Press, 1987.

Brown, Peter. *The Rise of Western Christendom.* Oxford: Blackwell, 1997.

Brundage, James A. *Law, Sex, and Christian Society in Medieval Europe.* Chicago: University of Chicago Press, 1987.

Buc, Philippe. *The Dangers of Ritual: Between Early Medieval Texts and Social Scientific Theory.* Princeton: Princeton University Press, 2001.

Buchem, L. A. van. *L'homelie pseudo-eusebienne de Pentecote*. Nijmegen: Drukkerij Gebr, Janssen N. V., 1967.

Burkhart, Louise M. *The Slippery Earth: Nahua Christian Moral Dialogue in Sixteenth-Century Mexico*. Tucson: University of Arizona Press, 1989.

———. *Ash Wednesday: A Nahua Drama from Early Colonial Mexico*. Philadelphia: University of Pennsylvania Press, 1996.

Burrow, J. A. *The Ages of Man. A Study in Medieval Writing and Thought*. Oxford: Clarendon Press, 1986.

Burrus, Ernest J. "Key Decision of the 1541 Mexican Conference." *Neue Zeitschrift für Missionswissenschaft* 28 (1972): 253–63.

Bustamante García, Jesús. "Retórica, traducción y responsabilidad histórica: claves humanísticas en la obra de Bernardino de Sahagún." In *Humanismo y visión del otro en la España moderna: cuatro estudios*, ed. Berta Ares, Jesús Bustamante, et al, 245–375. Madrid: Consejo Superior de Investigaciones Científicas, 1992.

Camille, Michael. *The Gothic Idol: Ideology and Image-Making in Medieval Art*. Cambridge: Cambridge University Press, 1989.

Carrasco, Pedro. "La jerarquía cívico-religiosa de las comunidades mesoamericanas: antecedentes prehispánicos y desarrollo colonial." *Estudios de cultura nahuatl* 12 (1976): 165–84.

Castañeda Delgado, P. "La condición miserable del indio y sus privilegios." *Anuario de Estudios Americanos* (Sevilla) 28 (1971): 245–335.

———. "La Iglesia y la Corona ante la nueva realidad lingüística en Indias." In *I Simposio de Filología Iberoamericana (Sevilla: 23 al 30 de marzo de 1990)*, 29–41. Zaragoza: Libros Pórtico, 1990.

Ceccherelli, C. "El bautismo y los franciscanos en México (1524–1539)." *Missionalia hispánica* (Madrid) 12, no. 35 (1955): 209–89.

Cervantes, Fernando. *The Devil in the New World. The Impact of Diabolism in New Spain*. New Haven: Yale University Press, 1994.

Chauvet, Fidel. *Fray Juan de Zumárraga. O. F. M.* México: Beatriz de Silva, 1948.

———. "Catecismos franciscanos del siglo XVI en México." In *Catecismos y métodos evangelizadores en México del siglo XVI*, 113–40. Guadalajara, México: Imprenta Lumen, 1977.

Chauvet, Louis Marie. *Du symbolique au symbole: essai sur les sacrements*. Paris: Les Éditions du Cerf, 1979.

Christian Jr., William. "Provoked Religious Weeping in Early Modern Spain." In *Religious Organization and Religious Experience*, ed. J. Davis. A.S.A., Monograph 21, 97–114. London: Academic Press, 1982.

Clark, S. "The Scientific Status of Demonology." In *Occult and Scientific Mentalities in the Renaissance*, ed. Brian Vickers, 351–74. Cambridge: Cambridge University Press, 1984.

Clendinnen, Inga. "Franciscan Missionaries in Sixteenth-Century Mexico." In *Disciplines of Faith. Studies in Religion, Politics and Patriarchy*, ed. Jim Obelkevich, Lyndal Roper, and Raphael Samuel, 229–45. London: Routledge and Kegan Paul, 1987.

————. *Aztecs*. Cambridge: Cambridge University Press, 1991.

Cline, H. F. "The Relaciones Geográficas of the Spanish Indies, 1577–1648." In *Handbook of Middle American Indians,* ed. Howard F. Cline, vol. 12, 183–242. Austin: Texas University Press, 1972.

Cline, S. L. *The Book of Tributes. Early Sixteenth-Century Nahuatl Censuses from Morelos.* Los Angeles: UCLA Latin American Center Publications/University of California, 1993.

————. "The Spiritual Conquest Reexamined: Baptism and Christian Marriage in Early Sixteenth-Century Mexico." *Hispanic American Historical Review* 73, no. 3 (1993): 453–80.

Collish, Marcia. *Peter Lombard.* 2 vols. Leiden: E. J. Brill, 1994.

Congar, Yves M.-J. *Tradition and Traditions: An Historical and a Theological Essay.* New York: MacMillan Company, 1967.

Corcuera de Mancera, Sonia. *Del amor al temor. Borrachez, catequesis y control en la Nueva España (1555–1771).* Mexico City: Fondo de Cultura Económica, 1994.

Cramer, Peter. *Baptism and Change in the Early Middle Ages, c. 200–c. 1150.* Cambridge: Cambridge University Press, 1993.

Cuevas, Mariano. *Historia de la Iglesia de México.* 5 vols. Mexico City: Imprenta del Asilo "Patricio Sanz," 1921.

Daniel, E. Randolph. *The Franciscan Concept of Mission in the High Middle Ages.* Lexington: University of Kentucky Press, 1975.

Danvila y Collado, Manuel. *La germanía de Valencia.* Madrid: Tipografía de Manuel G. Hernández, 1884.

Davis, Natalie Z. "The Rites of Violence." In *Society and Culture in Sixteenth-Century France,* 152–87. Stanford: Stanford UP, 1965.

————. *The Gift in Sixteenth-Century France.* Madison: University of Wisconsin Press, 2000.

De Bujanda, J. M. "Los libros italianos en el Índice español de 1559." *Bibliothèque D'Humanisme et Renaissance* 34 (1972): 89–104.

Dedieu, Jean Pierre. " 'Christianization' in New Castile: Catechism, Communion, Mass, and Confirmation in the Toledo Archbishopric, 1540–1650." In *Culture and Control in Counter-Reformation Spain,* ed. Anne J. Cruz and Mary Elizabeth Perry, 1–24. Minneapolis: University of Minnesota Press, 1992.

Denzinger. *The Sources of Catholic Dogma.* Trans. Roy J. Deferrari. St. Louis, MO: B. Herder Book Co., 1957.

Derrida, Jacques. *The Gift of Death.* Trans. David Wills. Chicago: University of Chicago Press, 1992.

Dictionnaire de spiritualité ascétique et mystique, doctrine et histoire. 107 fasc. París: Beauchesne, 1932–95.

Domínguez Ortíz, A. and Bernard Vincent. *Historia de los moriscos.* Madrid: Alianza Universidad, 1989.

Dondaine, H. *L'attrition suffisante.* Paris: Librairie Philosophique J. Vrin, 1943.

Douglas, Mary. *Natural Symbols. Explorations in Cosmology.* London and New York: Routledge, 1996.

————. "Sacraments and Society: An Anthropologist Asks, What Women Could

Be Doing in the Church?" In *Anthropology and Theology: Gods, Icons, and God-Talk*, ed. Walter Randolph Adams and Frank Salamone, 391–406. Lanham, MD: University Press of America, 2000.

Durán, Juan Guillermo. *Monumenta Catechetica Hispanoamericana (Siglos XVI–XVIII)*. 2 vols. Buenos Aires: Facultad de Teología de la Pontificia Universidad Católica Argentina "Santa María de los Buenos Aires," 1984.

Elliott, John H. "The Discovery of America and the Discovery of Man." In *Spain and Its World, 1500–1700*, 42–67. New Haven: Yale University Press, 1989.

Estrada Quevedo, A. "Neyolmelahualiztli." *Estudios de cultura nahuatl* 2 (1960): 163–75.

Fernández del Castillo, Francisco, comp. *Libros y libreros en el siglo XVI* [1914]. Mexico City: Fondo de Cultura Económica, 1982.

Fischer, J. D. C. *Christian Initiation: Baptism in the Medieval West*. London: Alcuin Club/S.P.C.K., 1965.

———. *Confirmation. Then and Now*. London: Alcuin Club/S.P.C.K., 1978.

Flynn, Maureen. "The Spectacle of Suffering in Spanish Streets." In *City and Spectacle in Medieval Europe*, ed. Barbara A. Hanawalt and Kathryn L. Reyerson, 153–68. Minneapolis: University of Minnesota Press, 1994.

Foucault, Michel. *La volonté de savoir*. Vol. 1 of *Historie de la sexualité*. París: Gallimard, 1976.

Garcia Càrcel, Ricard. *Las Germanías de Valencia*. Barcelona: Península, 1975.

Garcia Càrcel, Ricard and Eduard Císcar Pallarés. *Moriscos i Agermanats*. Valencia, 1974.

García Icazbalceta, Joaquín. *Don Fray Juan de Zumárraga, primer obispo y arzobispo de México*. Ed. Rafael Aguayo Spencer and Antonio Castro Leal. 4 vols. Mexico City: Porrúa, 1947.

———. *Bibliografía mexicana del siglo XVI* [1886]. Ed. Agustín Millares Carlo. Mexico City: Fondo de Cultura Económica, 1954.

García Oro, José, *La reforma de los religiosos en tiempo de los Reyes Católicos*. Valladolid: Instituto "Isabel La Católica" de Historia Eclesiástica, 1969.

Garrido Aranda, Antonio. *Moriscos e Indios. Precedentes hispánicos de la evangelización en México*. Mexico City: Universidad Nacional Autónoma de México, 1980.

Gibson, Charles. "The Identity of Diego Muñoz Camargo." *Hispanic American Historical Review* 30, no. 2 (1950): 202–3.

———. *Tlaxclala in the Sixteenth Century*. Stanford: Stanford University Press, 1952.

———. "The Aztec Aristocracy in Colonial Mexico." *Comparative Studies in Society and History* 2 (1959–60): 169–96.

———. *The Aztecs under Spanish Rule*. Stanford: Stanford University Press, 1964.

Gieben, Servus. *Christian Sacrament and Devotion*. Leiden: E. J. Brill, 1980.

Gil, Fernando. "Las 'Juntas eclesiásticas' durante el episcopado de Fray Juan de Zumárraga (1528–1548). Algunas precisiones históricas." *Teología. Revista de la Facultad de Teología de la Pontificia Universidad Católica Argentina* 26 (1989): 3–20.

————. *Primeras "Doctrinas" del Nuevo Mundo. Estudio histórico-teológico de las obras de Juan de Zumárraga († 1548).* Buenos Aires: Facultad de Teología de la Pontificia Universidad Católica Argentina Santa María de los Buenos Aires, 1992.

Gliozzi, Giulianno. *Adamo e il Nuovo Mondo.* Firenze: La Nuova Italia Editrice, 1976.

Gómez Canedo, Lino. "Conventuales, observantes y reformados. (Política indigenista y filiación espiritual de los primeros franciscanos en Indias)." *Anuario de Estudios Americanos* 23 (1966): 611–22.

————. "Hombres o Bestias? (Nuevo examen crítico de un viejo tópico)." *Estudios de Historia Novohispana* 1 (1966): 29–51.

Grafton, Anthony. *New Worlds, Ancient Texts.* Cambridge, Mass.: Belknap Press of Harvard University Press, 1992.

Greene, Thomas M. "Ritual and Text in the Renaissance," *Canadian Review of Comparative Literature* (June–September 1991): 179–97.

Greenleaf, Richard E. *Zumárraga and the Spanish Inquisition, 1536–1543.* Washington, DC: Academy of American Franciscan History, 1961

Gruzinski, Serge. "Confesión, alianza y sexualidad entre los indios de Nueva España." In *El placer de pecar y el afán de normar,* ed. Sergio Ortega, 169–215. México: Joaquín Mortíz, 1988.

————. "Individualization and Acculturation: Confession among the Nahuas of Mexico from the Sixteenth to the Eighteenth Century." In *Sexuality and Marriage in Colonial Latin America,* ed. Asunción Lavrín, 96–117. Lincoln and London: University of Nebraska Press, 1989.

————. *Man-Gods in the Mexican Highlands: Indian Power and Colonial Society, 1520–1800.* Stanford: Stanford University Press, 1989.

Guerrero, José Ramón. *Catecismos españoles del siglo XVI. La obra catequética del Dr. Constantino Ponce de la Fuente.* Madrid: Instituto Superior de Pastoral, 1969.

Gy, Pierre Marie. *La liturgie dans l'histoire.* Paris: Cerf/Saint-Paul. 1990.

Handbook of Middle American Indians. General editor Robert Wauchope. 16 vols. Austin: University of Texas Press, 1964–76.

Harnack, Adolf. *Militia Christi.* Trans. David Mc Innes Gracie. Philadelphia: Fortress Press, 1981.

Harvey, H. R., "The Relaciones Geográficas, 1579–86: Native Tongues." In *Handbook of Middle American Indians,* ed. Howard F. Cline, vol. 12, 279–323. Austin: Texas University Press, 1972.

Haskins, Susan. *Mary Magdalen: Myth and Metaphor.* New York: Hartcourt Brace and Co., 1993.

Hassig, Ross. *Aztec Warfare: Imperial Expansion and Political Control.* Norman and London: University of Oklahoma Press, 1988.

Heath, S. B. *Telling Tongues. Language Policy in Mexico.* New York: Teachers College Press, 1972.

Heynck, Valens. "A Controversy at the Council of Trent Concerning the Doctrine of Duns Scotus." *Franciscan Studies* 9, no. 3 (1949): 181–258.

Hill, Jane H. "Weeping as a Meta-signal in a Mexicano Woman's Narrative." In *Native Latin American Cultures through Their Discourse,* ed. Ellen B. Basso, 29–49. Bloomington: Folklore Institute, Indiana University, 1990.

Horcasitas, Fernando. *El teatro nahuatl: épocas novohispana y moderna.* Mexico City: Universidad Nacional Autónoma de México, 1974.

Huerga, A'lvaro. "Sobre la catequesis en España durante los siglos XV–XVI." *Analecta Sacra Terraconensia* 61, no. 2 (July–December 1968): 299–345.

Jedin, Hubert. *A History of the Council of Trent.* Trans. Dom Ernest Graf. St. Louis, MO: B. Herder Book Co., 1957.

Jordan, W. "Catalogue." In *El Greco of Toledo,* ed. Jonathan Brown, W. B. Jordan, R. Kagan, and Alfonso E. Pérez Sánchez, 225–63. Boston: Little, Brown and Co., 1982.

Kafka, Franz. *Parables and Paradoxes.* New York, 1961.

Kagan, Richard. *Lawsuits and Litigants in Castile, 1500–1700.* Chapel Hill: University of North Carolina Press, 1981.

Karttunen, Frances. "Nahuatl Literacy." In *The Inca and Aztec States, 1400–1800,* ed. George A. Collier, Renato Rosaldo, and John Wirth, 395–417. New York: Academic Press, 1982.

Karttunen, Frances and James Lockhart. *Nahuatl in the Middle Years: Language Contact Phenomena in Texts of the Colonial Period.* Berkeley: University of California Press, 1976.

Kelly, Henry Angstar. *The Devil at Baptism.* Ithaca: Cornell University Press, 1985.

King, P. D. *Law and Society in the Visigothic Kingdom.* Cambridge: Cambridge University Press, 1972.

Klein, Cecelia F. "Fighting with Feminity: Gender and War in Aztec Mexico." In *Gender Rhetorics. Postures of Dominance and Submission in History,* ed. Richard Trexler, 107–46. Binghampton, NY: Medieval and Renaissance Texts and Studies, 1994.

Klor de Alva, J. Jorge. "Spiritual Conflict and Accomodation in New Spain: Toward a Typology of Aztec Responses to Christianity." In *The Inca and Aztec States, 1400–1800,* ed. George A. Collier, R. Rosaldo, and John Wirth, 345–66. New York: Academic Press, 1982.

———. "Contar vidas: la autobiografía confesional y la reconstrucción del ser nahua." *Arbor* 131, nos. 515–16 (1988): 49–78.

———. "Sahagún and the Birth of Modern Ethnography: Representing, Confessing, and Inscribing the Native Other." In *The Work of Bernardino de Sahagun. Pioneer Ethnographer of Sixteenth Century Aztec Mexico,* ed. J. Jorge Klor de Alva, H. B. Nicholson, and Eloise Quiñones Weber, 31–52. Albany: Institute for Mesoamerican Studies, SUNY, 1988.

———. "Sin and Confession among the Colonial Nahuas: The Confessional as a Tool for Domination." In *La Ciudad y el Campo en la Historia de México. Papers Presented at the VII Conference of Mexican and United States Historians. Oaxaca, 1985,* vol. 1, 91–101. Mexico City: Universidad Nacional Autónoma de México, 1992.

Knowlson, James R. "The Idea of Gesture as a Universal Language." *Journal of the History of Ideas* 26 (October–December 1965): 495–508.

Lamirande, Émilien. "Ages de l'homme et âges spirituels selon Saint Ambroise. Le Commentaire du psaume 36." *Science et Esprit* 35, no. 2 (1983): 211–22.

Lampe, G. W. H. *The Seal of the Spirit*. London: S.P.C.K., 1967.

Lea, Charles. *A History of Auricular Confession and Indulgences in the Latin Church*. 3 vols. Philadelphia: Lea Brothers and Co., 1896.

———. *The Moriscos of Spain: Their Conversion and Expulsion* [1901]. Westport, CT: Greenwood Press, 1968.

Le Goff, Jacques. "Metier et profession d'après les manuels de confesseurs au Moyen Age." *Miscellanea Medievalia* 3 (1964): 44–60.

Leigh Stone, Cynthia. "Rewriting Indigenous Traditions: The Burial Ceremony of the Cazonci." *Colonial Latin American Review* 3, nos. 1–2 (1994): 87–114.

Lisi, Francesco Leonardo. *El Tercer Concilio Limense y la aculturación de los indígenas sudamericanos*. Salamanca: Universidad de Salamanca, 1990.

Llaguno, José A. *La personalidad jurídica del indio y el III Concilio Provincial Mexicano (1585)*. Mexico City: Porrúa, 1963.

Lockhart, James. "The Social History of Colonial Spanish America: Evolution and Potential." *Latin American Research Review* 7, no. 1 (spring 1972): 6–45.

———. *Nahuas and Spaniards: Postconquest Central Mexican History and Philology*. Stanford: Stanford University Press/UCLA Latin American Center Publication, 1991.

———. *The Nahuas after the Conquest: A Social and Cultural History of the Indians of Central Mexico, Sixteenth through Eighteenth Centuries*. Stanford: Stanford University Press, 1992.

———. "Double Mistaken Identity: Some Nahua Concepts in Post Conquest Guise." *Of Things of the Indies. Essays Old and New in Early Latin American History*, 98–119. Stanford: Stanford UP, 1999.

López Austin, Alfredo. *The Human Body and Ideology. Concepts of the Ancient Nahuas*. Trans. Thelma Ortíz de Montellano and Bernard Ortíz de Montellano. 2 vols. Salt City: University of Utah, 1988.

López-Rey, José. "Spanish Baroque: A Baroque Vision of Repentance in El Greco's St. Peter." *Art in America* 35 (1947): 313–18.

Lyell, James P. R. *Early Book Illustration in Spain*. New York: Hacker Art Books, 1976.

Lynch, Joseph H. *Godparents and Kinship in Early Modern Europe*. Princeton: Princeton University Press, 1986.

MacCormack, Sabine. *Religion in the Andes. Vision and Imagination in Early Colonial Peru*. Princeton: Princeton University Press, 1991.

———. "Limits of Understanding. Perceptions of Greco-Roman and Amerindian Paganism in Early Modern Europe." In *America in European Consciousness, 1493–1750*, ed. Karen Ordhal Kupperman, 79–129, Institute of Early American History and Culture, Williamsburg, Virginia. Chapel Hill: University of North Carolina Press, 1994.

———. "The Incas and Rome." *Garcilaso de la Vega. An American Humanist*.

A Tribute to José Durand, ed. José Anadón, 8–31. Notre Dame: University of Notre Dame, 1998.

Mackin, Theodore. *The Marital Sacrament.* New York/Mahwah, NJ: Paulist Press, 1989.

Maher, Michael W. "How the Jesuits Used Their Congregations to Promote Frequent Communion." In *Confraternities and Catholic Reform in Italy, France, and Spain,* ed. John Patrick Donnelly and Michael Maher, 75–95. Kirksville, MO: Thomas Jefferson University Press, 1999.

Mâle, Emile. *L'art religieux du XVIIe. siècle.* Paris: Armand Colin, 1984.

———. *Religious Art in France. The Thirteenth Century.* Princeton: Princeton University Press, 1984.

Mansfield, Mary. *The Humiliation of Sinners. Public Penance in Thirteenth-Century France.* Ithaca: Cornell University Press, 1995.

Maravall, José A. "Los hombres de 'saber' o letrados y la formación de su conciencia estamental." In *Estudios de historia del pensamiento español. Edad Media. Serie primera,* 345–80. Madrid: Ediciones Cultura Hispánica, 1967.

———. *Poder, honor y élites en el siglo XVII.* Madrid: Siglo XXI, 1979.

Martín, José Luis and A. Linaje Conde. *Religión y sociedad medieval: el catecismo de Pedro de Cuéllar (1325).* Salamanca: Junta de Castilla y León, 1987.

Maza, Francisco de la. *Fray Diego Valadés, escritor y grabador franciscano del siglo XVI.* México: Instituto de Investigaciones Estéticas, 1945.

McAndrew, John. *The Open-Air Churches of Sixteenth-Century Mexico.* Cambridge: Harvard University Press, 1965.

McKeever Furst, Jill. *The Natural History of the Soul in Ancient Mexico.* New Haven: Yale University Press, 1995.

McKendrick, Geraldine and Angus MacKay. "Visionaries and Affective Spirituality during the First Half of the Sixteenth Century." In *Cultural Encounters: The Impact of the Inquisition in Spain and the New World,* ed. Mary Elizabeth Perry and Anne J. Cruz, 93–105. Berkeley: University of California Press, 1991.

McNeill, John T. and Helena M. Gamer. *Medieval Handbooks of Penance.* New York: Columbia University Press, 1938.

Mignolo, Walter. *The Dark Side of the Renaissance.* Ann Arbor: University of Michigan Press, 1998.

Miranda, José. *El erasmista mexicano Fray Alonso Cabello.* México: Universidad Nacional Autónoma de México, 1958.

———. "La fraternidad cristiana y la labor social de la primitiva iglesia mexicana." *Cuadernos Americanos* 141, no. 4 (1965): 148–58.

Monzó, S. "El Bautismo de los judíos en la España visigoda. En torno al canon 57 del Concilio IV de Toledo." *Cuadernos de Trabajos de Derecho* (Roma) 2 (1953): 111–55.

Morse, Richard. *New World Soundings: Culture and Ideology in the Americas.* Baltimore: Johns Hopkins University Press, 1989.

Mostaza Rodríguez, A. "La edad de los confirmandos." *Anthologica Annua* 4 (1956): 341–84.

Muir, Edward. *Ritual in Early Modern Europe*. Cambridge: Cambridge University Press, 1997.

Murphy, Ronald G. *The Saxon Savior: The Germanic Transformation of the Gospel in the Ninth-Century Heliand*. New York: Oxford University Press, 1989.

Murray, David. *Indian Giving. Economies of Power in Indian-White Exchanges*. Amherst: University of Massachusetts Press, 2000.

Nader, Helen. *The Mendoza Family in the Spanish Renaissance*. New Brunswick: Rutgers University Press, 1979.

Nalle, Sara T. "Literacy and Culture in Early Modern Castile." *Past and Present* 125 (November 1989): 65–96.

Nederman, Cary J. *Worlds of Difference: European Discourses on Toleration, c. 1100–c. 1550*. University Park: Pennsylvania State University Press, 2000.

Nicholson, H. B. "A 'Royal Headband' of the Tlaxcalteca." *Revista mexicana de estudios antropológicos* 21 (1967): 71–106.

———. "Religion in Pre-Hispanic Central Mexico." In *Handbook of Middle American Indians,* ed. Gordon F. Ekholm and Ignacio Bernal, vol. 10, 395–446. Austin: University of Texas Press, 1971.

Nieto, José C. *El Renacimiento y la otra España*. Geneva: Librairie Droz, 1997.

Nirenberg, David. *Communities of Violence*. Princeton: Princeton University Press, 1996.

Nock, A. D. *Conversion. The old and new in religion from Alexander the Great to Augustine of Hippo*. 1933; Lanham, MD: University Press of America, 1988.

Noonan Jr., John T. "Marriage in Michoacán." In *First Images of America,* ed. Fredi Chiappelli, vol. 1, 351–62. Berkeley: University of California Press, 1976.

Nutini, Hugo. *Ritual Kinship: Ideological and Structural Integration of the Compadrazgo System in Rural Tlaxcala*. 2 vols. Princeton: Princeton University Press, 1984.

Nutini, Hugo, Pedro Carrasco, and James Taggart, eds. *Essays on Mexican Kinship*. Pittsburgh: University of Pittsburgh Press, 1976.

Oberman, Heiko A. *The Harvest of Medieval Theology*. Durham: Labyrinth Press, 1983.

O'Malley, John W. *The First Jesuits*. Cambridge: Harvard University Press, 1993.

Ortega Noriega, Sergio. "Teología novohispana sobre el matrimonio y comportamiento sexuales, 1519–1570." In *De la santidad a la perversión,* ed. Sergio Ortega, 19–46. Mexico City: Grijalbo, 1986.

Parish, Helen-Rand and Harold E. Weidman. *Las Casas en México. Historia y obras desconocidas*. Mexico City: Fondo de Cultura Económica, 1992.

Patton, Hugh. *The Efficacy of Putative Attrition in the Doctrine of Theologians of the XVI and XVII Centuries*. Roma: Herder, 1966.

Payne, John B. *Erasmus: His Theology of the Sacraments*. N.p.: M. E. Bratcher, 1970.

Pelikan, J. *The Growth of Medieval Theology (600–1300)*. Chicago: University of Chicago Press, 1978.

———. *Reformation of Church and Dogma (1300–1700)*. Chicago: University of Chicago Press, 1984.

Pelorson, Jean-Marc. *Les Letrados juristes castillans sous Philippe III*. Poitiers: Université de Poitiers, 1980.

Pérez Sánchez, Alonso and Nicola Spinosa. *Jusepe de Ribera, 1591–1652*. New York: Metropolitan Museum of Art, 1992.

Périnelle, J. *L'Attrition d'après le Concile de Trente et d'après Saint Thomas D'Aquin*. Kain: Le Saulchoir, 1927.

Peterson, Jeanette Favrot. *The Paradise Garden Murals of Malinalco*. Austin: University of Texas Press, 1993.

Pettazzoni, Raffaelle. *La confessione dei peccati*. 3 vols. Bologna: Forni Editore, 1968.

Phelan, John Leddy. *The Millennial Kingdom of the Franciscans of the New World*. 2nd. ed. Berkeley: University of California Press, 1970.

Plann, Susan. *A Silent Minority. Deaf Education in Spain, 1550–1835*. Berkeley: University of California Press, 1997.

Poole, Stafford. "Church Law on the Ordination of the Indians and *Castas* in New Spain." *Hispanic American Historical Review* 61, no. 4 (1981): 637–50.

———. *Pedro Moya de Contreras. Catholic Reform and Royal Power in New Spain, 1571–1591*. Berkeley: University of California Press, 1987.

Poschmann, Bernhard. *Penance and the Anointing of the Sick*. New York: Herder and Herder, 1964.

Rafael, Vicente. *Contracting Colonialism. Translation and Christian Conversion in Tagalog Society under Early Spanish Rule*. Ithaca and London: Cornell University Press, 1988.

Ragon, Pierre. *Les Indiens de la découverte: evangelisation, mariage et sexualité. Mexique, XVIe siècle*. Paris: L'Harmattan, 1992.

Reeves, Marjorie, *Joachim of Fiore and the Prophetic Future. A Medieval Study in Historical Thinking*. Stroud: Sutton, 1999

Resines, Luis. *Catecismos americanos del siglo XVI*. 2 vols. Madrid: Junta de Castilla y León, Consejería de Cultura y Turismo, 1992.

Reyes García, Luis. "Introducción." In *Historia de Tlaxcala (Ms. 210 de la Biblioteca Nacional de París)*, by Diego Muñoz Camargo, ed. Luis Reyes García. Tlaxcala: Gobierno del Estado de Tlaxcala/Centro de Investigaciones y Estudios en Antropología Social, Universidad Autónoma de Tlaxcala, 1998.

Ricard, Robert. *Etudes et documents pour l'histoire missionaire de l'"Espagne et du Portugal*. Louvain, A.U.C.A.M./Paris: J. M. Peigues, 1931.

———. *La "conquête spirituelle" du Mexique*. Paris: Institut D'Ethnologie, 1933.

Rodríguez, Pedro. *El Catecismo Romano ante Felipe II y la Inquisición española*. Madrid: Rialp, 1998.

Rojas Garcidueñas, José and José Juan Arrom, *Tres piezas teatrales del virreinato*. México: Universidad Nacional Autónoma de México, 1976.

Ros, Fidel de. *Le Père François D'Osuna*. Paris: Gabriel Beauchesne, 1936.

Rubial García, Antonio. "Evangelismo y evangelización. Los primeros franciscanos en la Nueva España y el ideal del cristianismo primitivo." *Anuario de Historia* 10 (1979): 95–124.

————. *El Convento Agustino y la Sociedad Novohispana (1533–1630)*. Mexico City: Universidad Nacional Autónoma de México, 1989.

Ryan, Michael T. "Assimilating New Worlds in the Sixteenth and Seventeenth Centuries." *Comparative Studies in Society and History* 23, no. 4 (October 1981): 519–38

Sandstrom, Alan R. *Corn Is Our Blood: Culture and Ethnic Identity in a Contemporary Aztec Indian Village*. Norman and London: University of Oklahoma Press, 1991.

Saranyana, Jose-Ignasi. "Tres teólogos académicos mexicanos del siglo XVI: Vera Cruz, Ledesma y Pravia." *Hispania sacra* 44 (1982): 545–85.

————. "La eucaristía en la teología sacramentaria americana del siglo XVI." In *Eucaristía y Nueva Evangelización. Actas del IV Simposio de la Iglesia en España y América: siglos XVI–XX*, ed. Paulino Castañeda and Carlos Martín de la Hoz, 21–29. Córdoba: Caja Sur, 1994.

Schiller, Gertrud. *Ikonographie der christlichen Kunst: Die Kirche*. Gütersloh: Güterloher Verlagshaus Gerd Mohn, 1976.

Schmitt, Jean-Claude. *La raison des gestes dans l'Occident médiéval*. Paris: Gallimard, 1990.

Schwaller, John. F. *The Church and the Clergy in Sixteenth-Century Mexico*. Albuquerque: University of New Mexico Press, 1987.

Sears, Elizabeth. *The Ages of Man: Medieval Interpretations of the Life Cycle*. Princeton: Princeton University Press, 1986.

Sebastián López, Santiago. "El arte iberoamericano del siglo XVI." In *Summa Artis*, vol. 28, 9–311. Madrid: Espasa-Calpe, 1985.

Smet, A. de. "Érasme et la cartographie." In *Scrinium Erasmianum*, ed. J. Coppens, vol. 1, 277–91. Leiden: Brill, 1969.

Snyder, James. *Northern Renaissance Art*. New York: Harry N. Abrams, 1985.

Spykman, Gordon J. *Attrition and Contrition at the Council of Trent*. Kampen: J. H. Kok, 1955.

Stock, Brian. *The Implications of Literacy*. Princeton: Princeton University Press, 1983.

Stocking, Rachel L. *Bishops, Councils, and Consensus in the Visigothic Kingdom, 589–633*. Ann Arbor: University of Michigan Press, 2000.

Sullivan, Richard E. "The Carolingian Missionary and the Pagan." *Speculum* 28, no. 4 (October 1953): 705–40.

Tellechea Idígoras, José Ignacio. "Los prolegómenos jurídicos del proceso de Carranza." In *El arzobispo Carranza y su tiempo*, vol. 1, 105–243 Madrid: Ediciones Guadarrama, 1968.

Tentler, Thomas. "The Summa for Confessors as an Instrument of Social Control." In *The Pursuit of Holiness in Late Medieval and Renaissance Religion*, ed. Charles Trinkaus and Heiko Oberman, 101–26. Leiden: E. J. Brill, 1974.

————. *Sin and Confession on the Eve of the Reformation*. Princeton: Princeton University Press, 1977.

Terraciano, Kevin. "Native Expressions of Piety in Mixtec Testaments." In *Dead Giveaways: Indigenous Testaments of Colonial Mesoamerica and the Andes,* ed. Susan Kellogg and Matthew Restall, 115–40. Salt Lake City: University of Utah Press, 1998.

Thomas, Hugh. *Conquest: Moctezuma, Cortés and the Fall of Old Mexico.* New York: Simon and Shuster, 1993.

Thomas, Keith. *Religion and the Decline of Magic.* New York: Charles Scribner's Sons, 1971.

Torre Villar, Ernesto de la. "Los catecismos, instrumentos de evangelización y cultura." In *Catecismos y métodos evangelizadores en México del siglo XVI,* 141–89. Guadalajara, México: Imprenta Lumen, 1977.

Trexler, Richard. "Aztec Priests for Christian Altars: The Theory and Practice of Reverence in New Spain." In *Church and Community, 1200–1600: Studies in the History of Florence and New Spain,* 469–92. Roma: Edizioni di Storia e Letteratura, 1987.

———. *The Christian at Prayer: An Illustrated Prayer Manual Attributed to Peter the Chanter (d. 1197).* Binghampton: Medieval and Renaissance Texts and Studies, 1987.

Ulloa, Daniel. *Los predicadores divididos (Los Dominicos en Nueva España, siglo XVI).* Mexico City: El Colegio de México, 1977.

Uribe, Ángel. "Guevara, inquisidor del Santo Oficio." In *Estudios acerca de Fray Antonio de Guevara en el IV centenario de su muerte,* 186–281. Madrid: Archivo Ibero-Americano, Revista de Estudios Históricos, 1946.

Valton, Emilio. *Impresos mexicanos del siglo XVI.* México: Imprenta Universitaria, 1935.

———. *El primer libro de alfabetización en América.* Mexico City: Antigua Librería Robredo, 1947.

Victoria, José Guadalupe. *Arte y arquitectura en la Sierra Alta, siglo XVI.* Mexico City: Universidad Nacional Autónoma de México, 1985.

Wagner, Henry Raup. *The Life and Writings of Bartolomé de Las Casas.* Albuquerque: University of New Mexico Press, 1967.

Ward, Benedicta. *Harlots of the Desert: A Study on Repentance in Early Monastic Sources.* Kalamazoo: Cistercian Publications, 1987.

Warren, Benedict. *The Conquest of Michoacan.* Norman: University of Oklahoma Press, 1984.

Wethey, Harold E. *El Greco and His School.* 2 vols. Princeton: Princeton University Press, 1962.

———. *The Paintings of Titian: The Religious Paintings.* London: Phaidon, 1969.

Wood, Stephanie. *Transcending Conquest: Nahua Views of Spanish Colonial Mexico.* Norman: University of Oklahoma Press, 2003.

Worgul, George S. *From Magic to Metaphor.* Lanham, MD: University Press of America, 1985.

Index

Acosta, Joseph de, 102; on administering the Eucharist to the Indians, 145–51; on confessions through interpreters, 114; on frequent communion, 154

Agurto, Pedro de, 142–44

Alcocer, Francisco de, 126

Arte para bien confesar, 121

Attrition, 84, 87–88, 101. *See also* Contrition; Penance

Augustinians: on administering the Eucharist to the Indians, 141–42; and administration of baptism, 37; arrival in Mexico, 3. *See also* Agurto, Pedro de; Religious orders

Baptism: of adult Indians, 31; by aspersion, 41, 42; bull *Altitudo divini consilii,* 35–36, 47; controversy over, 20, 26–32, 33–38; essential and nonessential parts, 25, 26, 29; in relation to the Eucharist, 45; of the four lords of Tlaxcala, 22–24; and instruction, 44–45; of Moctezuma's son, 23–24; of Muslims in Spain, 39–40; uniformity in its administration, 36; validity of Franciscan baptisms, 38; and violence, 41

Bautista, Juan, 7, 66; on confession of sick Indians, 127–28; on penance, 102–3

Benavente, Toribio de, 2, 98; administration of the sacrament of penance, 90–92; and authority to administer confirmation, 58; baptismal controversy, 27–29, 37; on baptism of Moctezuma's son, 23–24; on calmecac, 75; Diego's story and the Eucharist, 131–32; on Juan de Tecto, 32; on *letrados,* 33–34; and mutes, 108; on Nahua confessions, 106–7; on ordination of Mexican Indians, 49–51; on Panquetzaliztli, 156. *See also* Franciscans; Religious orders

Bilingualism, among Mexican Indians, 112–14. *See also* Indigenous languages; Nahuatl

Cabello, Alonso de, 64

Cajetan (Tommasso Di Vio), 97

Carranza de Miranda, Bartolomé, 186n. 34; on confirmation, 56–57, 70; on frequent communion, 152, 153–54; his works in the *Index,* 153

Cassian, 122

Catherine of Siena, Saint, 122

Communion: Comuniotlacatl, 141; frequent, 151–55; and Nahua rituals, 156–57. *See also* Eucharist

Confession: and cross-cultural communication, 105; and ethnography, 80; among Indians, 124; indigenous responses, 115; obstacles, 125; and the sick, 126; of sins in preconquest times, 94–95; use of interpreters, 111, 114; written, 106. *See also* Attrition; Penance

PLATES

Fig. 1. Altarpiece of the Seven Sacraments. Rogier van der Weyden. (Courtesy of Koninklijk Museum voor Schone Kunsten, Antwerp.)

Fig. 2. *Redemption*. Vrancke van der Stockt. (Courtesy of Museo Nacional del Prado, Madrid.)

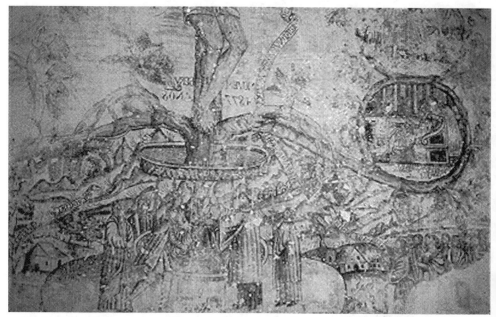

Fig. 3. Fresco of the sacraments. Convento de los Santos Reyes, Metztitlán, Hidalgo. (Photograph courtesy of Prof. Samuel Y. Edgerton.)

Fig. 4. Baptism in Tlaxcala. *Lienzo de Tlaxcala.* (Courtesy of the Biblioteca Nacional de Antropología e Historia, Mexico City.)

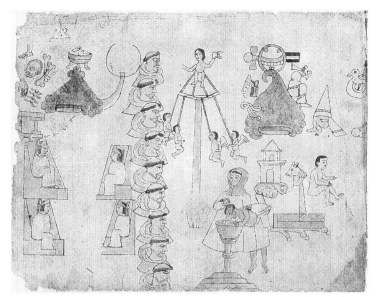

Fig. 5. Franciscans administering baptism. *Codex Azcatitlan.* (Courtesy of Bibliothèque Nationale de France.)

Fig. 6. Baptism, confirmation, and penance, left panel of the Altarpiece of the Seven Sacraments. Rogier van der Weyden. (Courtesy of Koninklijk Museum voor Schone Kunsten, Antwerp.)

Fig. 7. The Franciscans in New Spain. Diego Valadés, *Rhetorica christiana* (1579). (Courtesy of The John Carter Brown Library at Brown University.)

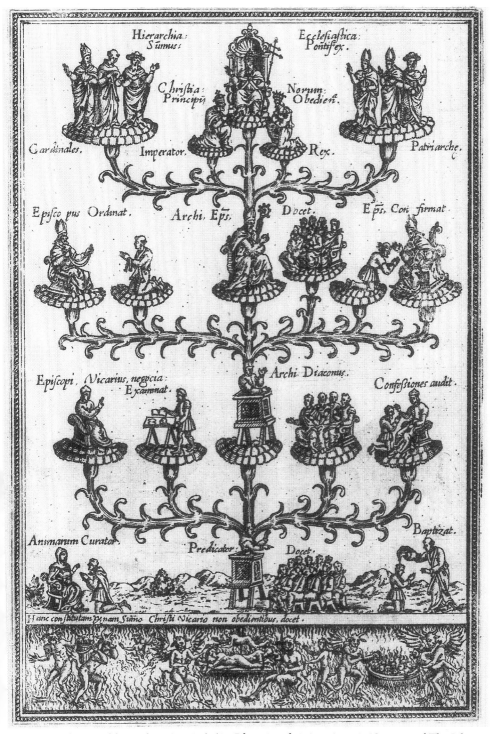

Fig. 8. Ecclesiastical hierarchy. Diego Valadés, *Rhetorica christiana* (1579). (Courtesy of The John Carter Brown Library at Brown University.)

Fig. 9. Indian receiving the sacrament of confirmation in 1548. *Tira de Tepechpan*. (Courtesy of Bibliothèque Nationale de France.)

Fig. 10. Hoitziloxitl.
Hernández, *Nova plantarum,
animalium et mineralium
mexicanorum historia.*
(Courtesy of Beinecke Rare
Book and Manuscript
Library, Yale University.)

A. CONFIRMATIO. B. *Materia* Chrisma, quod est oleum oliuarū cum. balsamo mixtum

C. *Forma* Præscripta Verba ad Episcopalē achonem

D. Miles Christianus. E. Scutum fidei

EFFECT' *confirm.is* Roborare militem Christianū ad certamen cōtra hostes animæ, Mundum, Carnem et Diabolum.

Fig. 11. The sacrament of confirmation. Gaspare Crispoldi after an engraving by Matthäus Greuter (ca. 1566–1638). (Courtesy of Museo Francescano, Rome.)

Fig. 12. Tlahuiztli. *Codex Mendoza.* Fols. 27ʳ. (Courtesy of The Bodleian Library, University of Oxford.)

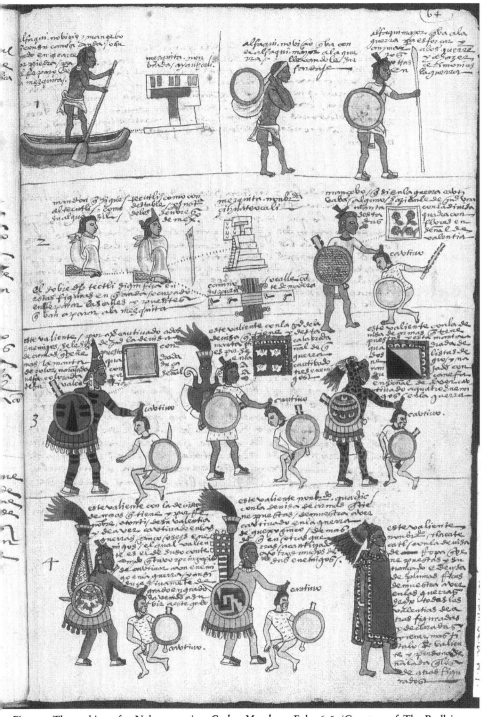

Fig. 13. The making of a Nahua warrior. *Codex Mendoza.* Fols. 64ʳ. (Courtesy of The Bodleian Library, University of Oxford.)

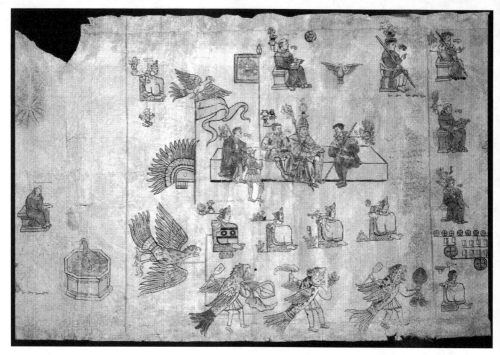

Fig. 14. Mexican Indians wearing warrior costumes dance at an official ceremony. *Códice de Tlatelolco.* (Courtesy of the Biblioteca Nacional de Antropología e Historia, Mexico City.)

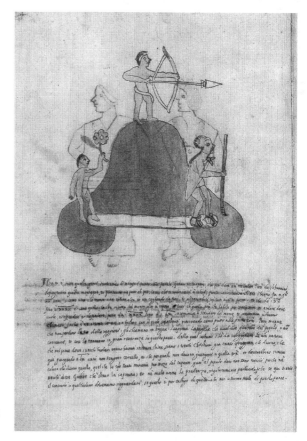

Fig. 15. The ages of man. *Codex Vaticanus 3738* (Courtesy of the Biblioteca Apostolica Vaticana.)

Fig. 16. Penance. Molina, *Confessionario mayor*. (Courtesy of The John Carter Brown Library at Brown University.)

Fig. 17. *St. Mary Magdalene*. Titian. (Courtesy of Galleria Palatina, Florence.)

Fig. 18. *The Repentant Magdalene.* El Greco. (Courtesy of Worcester Art Museum, Worcester, Massachusetts.)

Fig. 19. *The Penitent Magdalene.* El Greco. (Courtesy of The Nelson-Atkins Museum of Art, Kansas City, Missouri.)

Fig. 20. *The Tears of St. Peter.* El Greco. (Courtesy of The Bowes Museum, Barnard Castle, County Durham.)

Fig. 21. *The Repentance of St. Peter.* El Greco. (© National Gallery, Norway.)

CORDIS HVMILIATIO.

Deprime COR tuum et suftine. *Eccli.2.2.*

COR, nimis, heu, sese, gaudens sublimibus, effert;
Ni super impositum, deprimat illud, onus.
12.

Fig. 22. Humiliation of the heart. Van Haeften, *Schola cordis sive aversi a Deo ad eundem reductio et instructio.* (Courtesy of The Lilly Library, Indiana University, Bloomington, Indiana.)

CORDIS CONTRITIO.

COR contritum et humiliatum,
Deus non despicies. *Psal.* 50. 19.

In partes quam mille velim contundere COR hoc,
Quod fuit auctori sponte rebelle suo.
ii.

Fig. 23. Contrition. Van Haeften, *Schola cordis sive aversi a Deo ad eundem reductio et instructio.*
(Courtesy of The Lilly Library, Indiana University, Bloomington, Indiana.)

Comiença el A B C, ó Alphabeto del Seraphico Doctor S.Buenauentura.

AMa no ser conocido, y en nada ser tenido, porque te será mas proue-choso para entrar en el cielo, que ser alabado,y reputado de los hombres.

BEnebolo seras a todos, buenos, y malos, y a nadie seras pesado, ni enojoso.

Con

Fig. 24. Alphabet for the deaf. Yebra, *Libro llamado Refugium infirmorum* (1593).

COn cuydado, y diligencia, guarda tu coraçon de pensamientos va-gos, y tu boca de palabras ociosas, y los otros sentidos con rigurosa disci plina.

DEues amar mucho el silencio, y so-ledad, para tener quietud, y buena conciencia, porque donde ay ayunta-miento de muchos, siempre ay estruen do, ruydo, y destraymiento.

Escoge

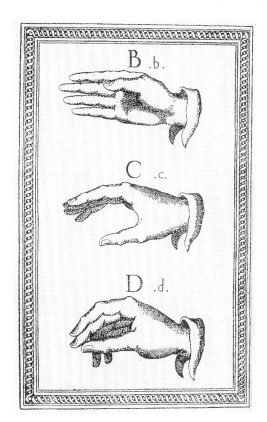

Fig. 25. Alphabet for the deaf.
Bonet, *Reducción de las letras*
(1620).

Fig. 26. Compunction. Ripa, *Iconologia*. (Courtesy of Beinecke Rare Book and Manuscript Library, Yale University.)